Invisible Loyalties

Invisible Loyalties

Reciprocity In Intergenerational Family Therapy

Ivan Boszormenyi-Nagy, M.D.

Professor and Chief of Family Therapy Section,
Department of Mental Health Sciences,
Hahnemann University, Philadelphia, Pennsylvania;
Director, Institute for Contextual Growth,
Ambler, Pennsylvania

Geraldine M. Spark, M.S.W.

Clinical Assistant Professor,
Hahnemann University, Philadelphia, Pennsylvania

 BRUNNER/MAZEL, *Publishers* • **New York**

Second Printing

Library of Congress Cataloging in Publication Data

Boszormenyi-Nagy, Ivan.
  Invisible loyalties.

  Reprint. Originally published: Hagerstown, Md : Medical
Dept., Harper & Row, 1973.
  Bibliography: p.
  Includes indexes.
  1. Family psychotherapy. I. Spark, Geraldine M.
II. Title. [DNLM: 1. Family therapy. WM 430.5.F2 B747i 1973]
RC488.5.B65 1984   616.89'156   83-26300
ISBN 0-87630-359-9

Copyright © 1984 by Ivan Boszormenyi-Nagy and Geraldine M. Spark

Published by
BRUNNER/MAZEL, INC.
19 Union Square
New York, New York 10003

MANUFACTURED IN THE UNITED STATES OF AMERICA

Contents

Preface

We live in an age of anxiety, fear of violence and questioning of fundamental values. Confidence in traditional values is being challenged. Waves of prejudice seem to endanger our trust in one another and our loyalty to society. Television and other communications media have perhaps too deeply affected the outlook of contemporary youth and young adults. There is much talk about a "generation gap," making one wonder if formative family experience has become obsolete and irrelevant.

The "strength" of family relations or their effect on individuals is extremely difficult to measure. The authors of this book believe that observable changes in the family do not necessarily alter the member-to-member impact of family relationships. The real forces of bondage or freedom are beyond observable power games or manipulative tactics. Invisible loyalty commitments to one's family follow paradoxical laws: The martyr who doesn't let other family members "work off" their guilt is a far more powerfully controlling force than the loud, demanding "bully." The manifestly rebellious or delinquent child may actually be the most loyal member of a family.

We have learned that family relationships cannot be understood from the laws that apply to social or incidental relationships such as those between fellow workers. The meaning of relationships depends on the subjective impact emerging between *You* and *I*. The so-called "closeness," feared by many people, develops as a result of loyalty commitments which become evident in a prolonged period of living and working together, whether the commitments are recognized or denied. We can terminate any relationship except the one based on parenting; in reality, we cannot select our parents or children.

The essence of therapy and of any human relationship is a capacity for commitment and trust. By coming to the therapist for help, the patient or client brings this precious commodity to the office. With growing conviction we have learned that whether the therapist involved with relationships sees one or all members of a family, he must develop a perceptivity to the manifestations of loyalty commitments and reciprocity of fairness; otherwise he will not be let into the loyalty system.

Any kind of therapeutic relationship represents a challenge both to the therapist's capacity for trusting and to his capacity for professional and personal commitment. Eventually, the psychotherapist must integrate his own family relationships with his professional experience. This becomes especially important with the family therapist because instead of dealing with patients' verbal productions, he deals with ongoing relationships.

This book was written in order to share our experience as family therapists not only with professionals but with families. We are convinced that the family approach has a very broad scope; it is not just another psychotherapy technique. We perceive our approach as the extension of and meeting point between dynamic psychology, existential phenomenology and systems theory in understanding human relationships.

Our therapeutic experience includes many years of almost exclusive work with families and couples in addition to previous therapeutic work with individuals. We have seen families with all types of problems, from those with a member with seemingly minor learning or behavior disturbances to those with several severely psychotic members. We have seen the families of prominent professionals, businessmen and community leaders as well as families of murderers and sexually deviant persons. We have worked with families of successful men, intellectuals, workers and also with deprived people in the ghettos. We have spent hundreds of hours in the homes of families and thousands of hours in our office. The professional settings of our work include a specialized clinic in family therapy with city-wide referral, a community mental health center, specialized projects in the treatment of schizophrenia and delinquent adolescents, and our private office.

We have tried to convey what we have learned in these many years with many families. We have, as a result, learned to recognize the superficiality and deceptiveness of many valued contemporary myths and slogans. The "technical" points presented in this book cannot be understood without a fundamental analysis of man's ethical priorities. We believe that while dealing with all parties to a conflict, the family therapist cannot avoid the ethical implications of the inevitable relational victimizations and exploitations. In contrast with individual therapy, the therapist of relationships is confronted with the moves and reactions of all participants.

In time, we became less and less satisfied with preexisting conceptual frameworks and felt pressed for a more relevant understanding of the motivations of family members. We have learned to look at family life as governed both by individual psychological and quasipolitical principles. An important aspect of our family therapy is a search for and an identification of unadmitted or even unconscious loyalty conflicts in which the seeming "traitor" is being destroyed through lack of autonomy. Often the treason consists of what is regarded by society as normal steps toward autonomy.

Family therapy, as all psychotherapy, is based on the values of openness and directness in close relationships, as opposed to denial and secretiveness. Openness is not synonymous, however, with a mere abreaction or ventilation of each individual's accumulated feelings; nor does it mean that a sense of individual boundary or a regard for privacy should be abolished. The ideal is a genuine dialogue among the family members regarding important issues of family life, done in a manner which recognizes differences and conflicts as valuable reconcilable ingredients, rather than obstacles to relating and growth.

As a result of these challenges we have experienced important growth. Having consciously chosen the path of empathic participation in the human process over a cool, technical, managerial attitude to interactions, we had to respond to the impact of the irrational upon our own common sense. In this we have been helped considerably by our own teamwork. The senior author started family therapy in 1956 and in 1963 was joined by the coauthor. Since then we have worked as cotherapists both with each other and with many other therapists. Often we had to struggle for our individual points of view as two persons, as man and woman, coming to new, higher syntheses of understanding. Our insights were arrived at both through our struggles for separation and through our integrity as a team.

Since many families are seen separately, too, we do not claim that good therapeutic results cannot be achieved by a single therapist. Neither does competent therapy necessarily involve work with every family for many years. The depth and duration of family therapy is ultimately determined by the subjective goals and capacities of the family members. Some of our families wanted only symptomatic relief; others were challenged by and endured the hardships and pains of a long therapy which would result in basic change and growth. We have not found valid the claim that the family's goals can be predicted from their cultural, social class or educational backgrounds.

The road to becoming a competent family therapist is far from easy. Awareness of one's own struggles in close relationships is just as necessary as a capacity for conceptualizing about one's work. Various critics may label us as adherents to one or another of the schools of professional thought because we use elements of psychoanalytic, existential, ethical, accounting and other conceptual frameworks. Actually, we assume that real growth in our field can only be based on a respect for all useful knowledge, whether it comes from preceding generations or from contemporary contributors.

To obtain an "operational" proof of result is difficult enough in individual psychotherapy and even more so in family psychotherapy. We make no claim for ultimate answers in this book, but we hope to give a reasonable account of our approach. This book starts with our main concepts, followed by a sequence of contract, therapy and termination, adding certain specific points of clinical and theoretical significance. It is meant to be a book based on a particular point of view, not on a mosaic of authorships. We believe that at this point the field will progress more from specific elaborations of convictions than from the continuation of broad-spectrum texts.

Although our book contains no autobiographic material, we know that our viewpoints and concepts as authors reflect our professional as well as private experiences and convictions. The senior author must have found a new balance of loyalties following his radical separation from his whole existential ground twenty-five years ago when he moved from his native Hungary to the United States. At the same time when there was nothing else to be committed to other than his new country with its new opportunities, internally he must have relied on invisible loyalties to people, especially his parents who gave him the foundations of interest and trust in the human phenomenon.

By contrast, Geraldine M. Spark constantly tried to integrate her family therapy experiences with her prior training as a psychiatric social worker and her two years of theoretical courses in the Philadelphia Psychoanalytic Association. She has continued to balance her role in her family of origin with her current nuclear family which now includes grandchildren. In addition, her more than twenty years of experience in child guidance clinics has provided a specialized skill in relating to and understanding children and has greatly facilitated her work with families.

In the development of our family therapeutic approach, an undeniable credit has to go to the opportunities offered by the original, broad-minded design of Eastern Pennsylvania Psychiatric Institute. In accordance with the initial state-wide mandate for this research and training institute, its Board, through the Research Departments, invited the senior author in 1957 to build up an innovative psychiatric program, subject to the Board's periodic review. Throughout the years, persistent fundamental administrative support has been provided to the Family Psychiatry Division by William A. Phillips, M.D., Medical Director and by Joseph Adlestein, M.D., and William Beach, M.D., as well as previous Commissioners of Mental Health in Pennsylvania.

Important input has come to our understanding from various other settings in which we have worked and taught. Several clinical research projects under the leadership of Alfred S. Friedman, Ph.D., of Philadelphia Psychiatric Center should be mentioned. There, as at E.P.P.I., our numerous colleagues and trainees have substantially contributed to our clinical experience and clarity of understanding. The senior author's four years of affiliation with the West Philadelphia Community Mental Health Consortium (under the Directorship of Robert L. Leopold, M.D., and Anthony F. Santore, A.C.S.W) and Geraldine M. Spark's two years with the Thomas Jefferson Medical School's Child Psychiatry outpatient and in-patient units housed at the Philadelphia General Hospital, as consultants, have also added to our perception of the family approach as indispensable, especially in the problems of ghetto families. The family approach is also the most powerful unifying basis of staffs of clinics struggling with differences between the middle class, professional and lower-class, nonprofessional backgrounds of workers.

The varieties of training experiences have helped considerably in clarifying our thinking. Our teaching experiences in the Family Institute of Philadelphia has been especially gratifying, as we have watched its program develop from our initial hopes and planning to a substantial and promising professional school of learning. Ivan Boszormenyi-Nagy's one month training experience in Holland in 1967, teaching a nationwide selection of professionals, started a long-term contact with people and developments of the family therapy field in that forward-looking country.

The conceptual framework expounded in this book is indebted to the writings of many thinkers, especially: Martin Buber (Also as interpreted by Maurice Friedman), Sigmund Freud, Mahatma Gandhi, G.W.F. Hegel, Ronald Fairbairn, Konrad Lorenz and Thomas S. Szasz. Deeply appreciated were the live stimulating exchanges with Helm Stierlin, M.D., to whom our special thanks are due for his thoughtful suggestions for revisions, Maurice Friedman, Ph.D., Robert Waelder, M.D., Abraham Freedman, M.D., Isadore Spark, M.D., and Elaine Brody, M.S.W.

Throughout the years the authors have continued to learn from their contacts with the early leaders in the field of family therapy—to mention a few: Nathan Ackerman, Murray Bowen, Don D. Jackson, Carl Whitaker, and Lyman Wynne; among members of the Family Psychiatry Division, James L. Framo, Leon R. Robinson, and Gerald H. Zuk.

We express our thanks to those who helped this volume to become a reality. Mrs. Mary Jane Kapustin helped with the initial phases of the manuscript. The almost limitless patience and devotion of Mrs. Doris Duncan was most essential to the preparation of the final manuscript. Mrs. Kathryn Kent has helped with many details of the later stages.

Our personal families not only deserve credit for the origins of our deepest notions of family relationships, but as an arena for sharper and often more painful personal battles, exactly because we are family therapists. We stress our indebtedness also to our families of origin which we revisited in our thoughts as a source for basic orientation and understanding.

Finally, we believe that the most significant contributions in the future will lie in the increased understanding of previous loyalty ties to one's family of origin and the continued need for balancing individual autonomy and the reciprocal justness of current relationships with the multigenerational account of family loyalties–into the third and fourth generation.

Foreword

This book represents the beginning of the construction of a synthesis of our years of clinical practice and efforts at conceptual clarification. As conviction grew about the clinical effectiveness of the family approach, the demand became that much higher for defining its theoretical framework.

It became clear to us that a new conceptual framework had to be devised for our understanding of new phenomena. At the same time we were not satisfied with a host of theoretical inclinations, coming from both psychodynamically oriented and systems oriented colleagues. They seemed to propose that family therapy is a field where one can disregard both depth of personal experience and life-long integrity of the whole of human life.

As we chose to try to retain both individual depth and multiperson system complexity of the family field of forces, we were greatly helped by a dialectical outlook on relationships. We were able simultaneously to consider the interaction of divergent or apparently contradictory trends and to understand how the individual's actions and motivations are determined on both psychological and relational system levels.

Loyalty has turned out to be one of the key concepts which refers to both systemic (social) and individual (psychological) levels of understanding. Loyalty is composed of the social unit which depends on and expects loyalty from its members and of the thinking, feelings and motivations of each member as a person.

As we learned to apply the concept of loyalty to our day-by-day clinical work, the need arose to include the entire panorama of the positions, actions and inner motivations of family members into one fundamental framework. At the same time we felt the need to cast this conceptual realm into a humanistic rather than intellectual-cognitive-scientistic language.

The concept of justice seemed to be the next step in our search for a more adequate and comprehensive framework. Justice and injustice, fairness and unfairness, reciprocal consideration and exploitation are everyday concerns of all human beings regarding their relationships. While justice as an ethically grounded issue may sound alien to most current psychological and psychodynamic investigations, it seems to us to offer the advantage of an intrinsic structure of familial expectations and obligations. Such structure then can be affected by the ongoing chain of interactions among members.

As we tried to return from the intrinsic bookkeeping to more concrete aspects of each individual's position vis-a-vis the ledger, we were confronted with a need for evaluative and normative considerations: what are health and pathology in terms of relationship systems? Obviously, multipersonal concepts were needed which transcended the individual-based concept of pathology, essentially a medical concept. The concepts of balance and imbalance seemed to fill part of this gap. As the individual is placed by his familial position and history at the vantage point of a particular balance of the justice ledger, his capacity for healthy function may be strained to the point that his feedback to the system begins to affect the latter. Individual psychopathology and system pathogenicity are in an ongoing dynamic interaction.

After discussion of the pervasively significant relational imbalance called parentification, we described the multiperson systemic loyalty implications of a phenomenon central to psychoanalytic theory and therapy–transference. As a transition, we review the convergence and divergence between certain concepts of psychoanalytic theory and their applicability to our theory of relationships.

Subsequently, we review a number of clinical problems in connection with the applications of our framework. We discuss a systemic view of the formation of therapeutic alliance between family and the team, clinical applications of a three-generational view of the inclusion of elderly family members in the therapy process, special clinical aspects of work with children, questions connected with the treatment of a family that battered a child.

A special chapter is devoted to a detailed account of the treatment of a family in which a variety of issues developed, affecting all members of three generations. Special attention was given to the practical and theoretical significance of the opportunity for balancing the intergenerational ledger of justice as trust and hope are reinvested into a mother's relationship with her dying mother.

A chapter devoted to a summary of therapeutic principles consonant with our theoretical framework is followed by implications for society and for further work with families.

In summary, we have intended to provide a cohesive theoretical foundation for understanding the deeper structuring forces of meaningful human relationships. Such understanding will lend itself for broad-based applications in family therapy and for integration with the reader's notions of individual psychodynamics and interactional technology.

Although the book was written jointly and each chapter was developed by cooperative effort, Ivan Boszormenyi-Nagy is mainly responsible for Chapters 1–7 and 13, and Geraldine M. Spark for Chapters 8–11. Chapter 12 represents the results of combined efforts. Parts of Chapter 7 are reprinted with a few minor changes from an article titled "Loyalty Implications of the Transference Model in Psychotherapy" which appeared in *Archives of General Psychiatry* (27: 374–380, 1972). Chapters 8–13 constitute a thematic unit, in that they serve the explication of therapeutic aspects following from the foregoing theoretical themes.

Invisible Loyalties

1

Concepts of the
Relational System

The structuring of relationships, especially within families, is an extremely complex and essentially unknown "mechanism." Empirically, such structuring can be inferred from the existence of lawful regularity and predictability of certain repetitious events in families. Through the years, much of our concerted effort has been directed clinically and conceptually to spelling out these multiperson system laws.

Certain families carry easily recognized multigenerational patterns of relationships. In one family we learned that for generations there were recurrent episodes of violent death of women caused by the men with whom they were sexually involved. In another family we saw a recurrent pattern of wives being allegedly martyred by their husbands through their obvious and constant involvements with mistresses. In another family three or four generations revealed the pattern of one daughter ending up as an outcast because of the "sin" of disloyally marrying outside the family's faith. We have seen families in which incest sequences occur for at least three or four generations.

The determinants of such recurrent relational organizations within families are only beginning to be discerned. Careful, long-term study of multigenerational systems of extended families under stress may reveal some of their crucial "pathogenic" determinants. But in order to construct a true multigenerational patterning of family relationships we have to rely on retrospective information, including the memories of the living about the dead. Without an interest in these formative, long-range, vertical family relational laws of function, the therapist will remain handicapped in dealing with pathogenicity and health in families. We distinguish here between ameliorating here and now interactions and thoroughly, i.e., preventively, intervening in the system.

1

We believe that health and pathology are jointly determined by: (1) the nature of the multiperson relational laws, (2) the psychological characteristics ("psychic structure") of individual members, and (3) the interlocking between these two realms of system organization. A degree of flexibility and balance regarding the individual's fit into the higher system level contributes to health, whereas inflexible adherence to system patterns may lead to pathology in individuals.

We want to avoid the pitfall of reductionism in describing the complex realm of relational structuring. A number of dimensions described in the literature are pertinent to the nature of deep relational patterns, but none are sufficient by themselves to describe the complex whole of their dynamic organization. Some of the main elements and forces that determine deep relational configurations of the system are interactional patterns of functional or power characteristics; drive tendencies which aim at one person as another's available drive object; consanguinity; patterns of pathology; collective aggregate of all unconscious superego tendencies of the members; encounter aspects of ontic dependency among members; and unwritten and unspoken accounts of obligation, repayment, and exploitation and their changing balance throughout the generations.

It is probable that one of the main contributions of the family therapy approach has been the multiperson or system concept of motivational theory. This concept conceives of the individual as a disparate biological and psychological entity whose reactions are nonetheless determined both by his own psychology and by the rules of the entire family unit's existence. Generally speaking, a system is a set of mutually interdependent units. In families, psychic functions of one member condition functions of other members. Many of the rules governing family relational systems are implicit, and family members are not conscious of them. The vicarious or implicitly exploitative role of a mother in a father–daughter incest, for instance, may not become apparent in early phases of family therapy.

Aspects of the basic motivational structuring of family systems may manifest themselves through certain patterns of tangible action organizations or rites, for example, sacrificial offerings, treason, incest, family honor, interfamily vendetta, scapegoating, grief, care of dying ones, anniversaries, family reliquiae, wills, etc. These rites fit into unconsciously structured relational gestalts, affecting all members of the system. Besides performing specific functions, each rite has its contribution to the balance between exploitative versus giving positions and attitudes. An unspoken family script or code guides the various individuals' contributions to the account. The code determines the equivalency scale of merits, advantages, obligations, and responsibilities. A cluster of interrelated rites characterizes the manifest relational system of a family at any given time. Rites are patterns of learned reactions, whereas the intrinsic script of the system is grounded in genetic and historic relatedness.

This distinction has practical significance for the family therapist. Ritualistic patterns interlock with the existential substrate of the family's multiperson system in unique ways which may puzzle the outside observer. The often described difficulty in dealing with apparently meaningless communications of a family in treatment is partly caused by the therapist's understandable need to find a "logic" in the way the relational rites causally interlock with one another. It takes time and special learning to assess the basic accounts of the historic, vertical, and depth dimensions of action systems. Without an understanding of the hierarchy of obligations, no logic will be apparent.

A major system aspect of families is based on the fact that consanguinity or genetic relatedness lasts for a lifetime. In families the bonds of genetic relatedness have precedence over psychosocial determination, insofar as the two realms can be conceptually separated.

My father will always remain my father, even though he is dead and his burial ground is thousands of miles away. He and I are two consecutive links in a genetic chain with a life span of millions of years. My existence is unthinkable without his. Secondarily or psychologically, his person imprinted an indelible mark on my personality during the critical stages of emotional growth. Even when I rebelled against all that he stood for, my emphatic "no" only further confirmed my emotional involvement with him. He was obligated to me, his son, and subsequently, I have become existentially indebted to him.

My father-in-law is not blood-related to me, yet I am reminded of kinship whenever I notice my son's physical resemblance to him. I keep wondering whether my son's mental characteristics will be like his just because some of my son's spontaneous mannerisms and facial characteristics remind me of him. The in-law relationships attain a further quasi-blood-related aspect through the birth of grandchildren. Furthermore, my father-in-law and I become connected through the emerging extended familial balance sheet for reciprocity of give and take.

Literature on systems theory in family relationships began with notions influenced by "sick" or "abnormal" function. Expressions like "symbiotic," "guilt-laden," "double-binding," "schizophrenogenic," etc., would suggest that the only language that exists for description of the phenomena of relationship patterning has to be tinged with notions of pathology. The needs of the family therapist pressed for more effective explanatory concepts as guideposts for his work.

In the family therapy movement, the concept "pseudomutuality" of Wynne *et al.* constitutes the first major systematic attempt to explain the fundamental determinants of family relationship patterns. They state: "The social organization in these families is shaped by a pervasive familial subculture of myths, legends, and ideology which stress the dire consequences of openly recognized divergence from a relatively limited number of fixed, engulfing family roles."[93, p. 220] In an obvious effort to integrate the sociological with the psychoanalytic point of view, Wynne *et al.* characterize the "internalized family role structure and associated family subculture which serve as a kind of primitive superego which tends to determine behavior directly, without negotiation with an actively perceiving and discriminating ego."[93, p. 216]

The implications of a subculture of familial expectations constitute a milestone on the road toward defining the structure of relationships as sets of obligations imposed on family members. When Wynne *et al.* compare familial secrecy and investigative mechanisms with anxious superego surveillance, they come very close to our early formulation of an important family pathogenic mechanism, the "counterautonomous superego."[11] It is easy also to recognize a kinship between the concepts of primitive family superego and long-range balance sheets of merit in families. The efforts of Wynne *et al.* formed an important bridge toward the truly multipersonal dynamic model. Their use of such individually based concepts as superego, ego, repression, dissociation, or role in a familial context reveals their struggle for transcending the boundaries of psychology when approaching the field of what we call dialectical relational theory. Their language is essentially psychological when they elaborate on "internalization of role structure," and "sense of reciprocal fulfillment of expectations." The main struggle in the pseudomutual family is described in cognitive terms as "efforts to exclude from open recognition any evidence of noncomplementarity."

From our point of view, the basic issue of family relationship theory is: What happens in the action context and how does it affect the family's propensity for keeping the system essentially unchanged? According to this framework, although loss by death, exploitation, and physical growth are inevitabilities of change, every move toward emotional maturation represents an implicit threat of disloyalty to the system. Unaltered survival of the system is then the contextual aim of the interlocking expectations, obligations, and loyalty. An unaltered balance of the system includes the law of mutual consideration for optimal avoidance of causing unnecessary pain to anyone e.g. through facing grief. The ancient tribal and biological basis of the family system was production and raising of offspring. In our view, the child-rearing function has remained the core existential mandate of contemporary families. Loyalties anchored in the requirements of biological survival and of integrity of human justice are subsequently being elaborated in accordance with the historic ledger of actions and commitments.

Viewed from the vantage point of these deeper dialectical connections, patterns which constitute pseudomutuality or other psychosocial arrangements represent merely secondary "psychological" elaborations of fundamental existential realities; they are examples of particular rites in the context of a relationship system. The core of family system dynamics is part of the basic human order which is only secondarily reflected in cognitions, strivings, and emotions of individuals. The basic human order relies on the historical consequences of inter-member events in the life of any social group. Each member's motivations are embedded in the contexts of his own and his group's history.

A clinical example illustrates the interweaving among the symptomatic individual, a dyad, and the total gestalt of multigenerational accounts in a relationship system. The family was referred for Diane's tense, irritable behavior, recently noted both at home and school. Diane, 10 years old, talented in art, was closely attached to her grandmother, Mrs. H, 58. When Diane was only 6 days old, her mother became psychotic and she has been in a mental hospital ever since. Mrs. H has raised Diane. As an apparent side comment, it was also mentioned that there are violent arguments with physical threats between grandmother and grandfather.

The first family therapy session was conducted in the home. It revealed a severe marital tension between the grandparents. Contrary to the expectations of the caseworker assigned to Diane, the grandmother actively sought the attention of the therapist almost from the beginning. Although initially she sounded incoherent and evasive, she became very clear and explicit when she started to point out her resentments toward her husband: "There are two things I wouldn't forgive him as long as I live," she said, explaining the reasons for her refusing him sexually.

As Mrs. H described her lack of sexual responsiveness toward her husband, she added: "When I needed and wanted him in my younger years, he was running around." Noticing the therapist's interest in her background, she proceeded to give a strikingly personal account. With little apparent hesitation she described that when she was 14, one night while her mother was on a trip, her stepfather had come into her bedroom and attempted to rape her. She tried to obtain her mother's moral support the next day, but her mother sided with her stepfather and she was shipped to her grandparents. All her life she could not tell anybody about this incident except for her mother and grandmother. As this very lonely, secluded woman began to talk more openly, it was easy to empathize with the outpouring of her genuine life-long pain and despair.

This initial session demonstrates very clearly the dialectical approach to exploring relationship systems. No single account or individual statement is taken to be absolute. The child's problems are explored from the beginning in the context of the family's vertical dimension of three generations. This has led into the exploration of the horizontal dimension of grandmother's marriage. From there it has been natural to shift again to the vertical dimension of Mrs. H's childhood conflicts with her parents. It is easy to see how an unsettled account between herself, her mother, and her stepfather will have to be "taken out" on her marriage. The resulting helplessly hostile and frightening atmosphere of the home must have been reflected then in the child's desperate call for attention at school.

The purpose of this illustration is not to claim that an initial session would uncover the ultimate roots of the system determinants of a child's symptomatic behavior. Despite the genuineness and great force of this lonely, hungry woman's communication, it would be unrealistic to regard Mrs. H's character development as fully explained by the simple relational metaphors of her condensed story. Nevertheless, the examination of her key childhood experience, exploitation by her stepfather and the seeming disloyalty of her mother's response, pointed at a fundamental injustice which may have contributed to Mrs. H's life-long pattern of distrust toward males and relationships in general. This session illustrates the interconnected dimensions of individual psychology, reciprocity in relationship systems, and justice of the human world, as they become invisible records throughout generations.

In conclusion, the violation of the justice of one person's basic human order can make that event a pivot around which the destinies of his own and his descendants' further relationships revolve. Just as it would be unwise while exploring individual motivations to consider a symptom to exist in isolation from the patient's total personality, it is necessary to explore the whole family system as it relates to the signal function of the designated patient member's "pathology." Interest in the justice aspect of human order tends to lead to discovery of one member who at first appears as if having acted unjustly. The question arises: Is the unjust one an actor and initiator of deeds or is he a link in a chain of processes? Once this member's own suffering through past injustices can be explored, the process of family therapy is well under way.

Martin Buber's dialogic philosophy and certain existential authors' writings point to a way of "using" others which forms another important dimension of relational dynamics. Yet, instead of stressing the exploitative aspects of the human relationship, Buber focuses on its mutually confirmative potential. In designating meaningful personal relationships as of the I–Thou type, he states that the basic pronouns are not I, Thou, and It but I–Thou and I–it. The existential phenomenological analysis of social existence presupposes a personal commitment dimension: I do not just happen to be around with the one whom I address with Buber's "Thou." The other thus addressed is not just an implement for my or his emotional expressiveness, but at least for the time, the "ground," the dialectical counterpart of my existence. But even as ground for the other, the person is a distinct I for himself.

The genuine I–Thou dialogue transcends the concept of the other's being a mere "object" or gratifier of my needs. The mutuality of care and concern is not only experienced by the participants, but it transcends their psychology through entering the realm of action or of commitment to action. The dialogue as defined by Buber becomes one characteristic of the system of family relationships. The experiential reciprocity between two humans, both of whom are confirmed by their meeting on an I–Thou basis, creates a mutually supportive base among family relationships. Perhaps this is connected with what Buber refers to as the zone of the "between."[26, p. 17]

While the concept of the mutually confirming dialogue unquestionably enriches our understanding of relationships, in general our position is that family relationships have their own specific existential, historic structuring. An accidentally met, yet profoundly responsive traveller on the train may qualify, for the moment at least, as partner to a genuine I–Thou dialogue. Psychologically, the aftereffect of such genuine dialogue might be a lasting confirmation of my person and identity, even if that particular relationship remains ephemeral. Thus, the Thou of the genuine dialogue can be found everywhere and replaced by another Thou. Certain dimensions of group therapy, marathon, and encounter group techniques, sensitivity training, etc., are based on the hopeful expectation that mutual confirmation will occur among persons not belonging to a consanquineal family system.

It is of great practical significance to recognize the specific nature of family relationships. After a life-long hostile relatedness, two brothers may make strenuous efforts to reconcile and rebuild their relationships so that positive friendliness may ensue. They may now discover and understand each other in a new way, almost as if each was meeting a new person. Nevertheless, whether seeming enemy or friend, they have always been members of the same consanguineal family system. If I help any suffering human being, I am likely to enter into a genuine I–Thou dialogue with him. If, however, he happens to be my son, he constitutes, in addition, a unique counterpart of my existential realm; he is irreplaceable with any other human being. No particular behavior, however perfect the imitation of him, could substitute his meaning for me. Furthermore, both he and I belong to a multigenerational relationship system. Commitment, devotion, and loyalty are the most important determinants of family relationships. They derive from the multigenerational structure of the justice of the human world as it is built up from the historical account of intermember actions and attitudes.

In summary, the most important dimension of close relationship systems evolves from the multigenerational balance sheet of merit and indebtedness. We believe that the system level, on which basic loyalties are formed is connected with other, more visible system levels of interactive behavior and communications.

We believe that the hierarchy of obligations is of crucial importance for all social groups and society as a whole. Like many previous ages, ours suffers from a gradual erosion of the quality of human relationships. Ever since the late 19th century the existential authors have tried to alert us to a danger threatening the quality of genuine relatedness between human beings. Urbanization, automation, mass transportation, and communication media, etc., contribute to this erosion. The family theorist now focuses attention on a specific existential dimension that is being avoided, denied, and eroded in our age: the accounts of the justice of the human world. Escaping from contacts with the extended family on the one hand, and desperately possessive clinging on the other, create a paradox of conflicting forces between old and new generations with little chance for resolution. The conservative older generation gets more and more entrenched in its rigid, defensive position, whereas by escapism and denial the rebellious youth may destroy the base from which they could utilize their freedom should they acquire the ability to face and balance the accounts of intergenerational justice. In their feeling of deprivation, the young often cannot see that destructive retaliation leads to further and deeper deprivation. In the end both generations are losers.

The current wide popularity of encounter, marathon, sensitivity, etc., meetings testifies to modern man's realization of the erosion of personal relationships. New rites are formed every day based on this realization combined with the myths of the ultimate value of just "expressing one's feelings" towards strangers. Buber's I–Thou dialogue, when partially understood, can be wishfully exploited as a magic formula applied to encounters of ritualized forms. The family therapist does not reject the validity of encounter as a meaningful and helpful "technique" of contemporary society; it is one dimension of his own work with families. On the other hand, if this dimension is elevated to magical omnipotence used for the denial of the hard realities of historical justice of one's life and generational position in the family merit ledger, it is capable of limited achievements only. Furthermore, through its false claim, it may be the source of great disappointments.

THE CLINICAL SIGNIFICANCE OF THE SYSTEM OUTLOOK

The distinction between multiperson, system-based and individual motivations has great practical significance for the therapist. His colleagues frequently question him about his attitude to such key therapeutic questions as: What are the criteria of indication for family therapy? What are the therapeutic goals? How does he assess the results of his therapeutic work, etc.? The answer to these questions is connected with the understanding of the interlocking between individual and multiperson system levels of motivation.

The conceptualization of the interlocking between individual and multiperson system levels requires not only a basic familiarity with general systems theory, but thinking in terms of a dialectical model. According to the latter, the "intrapsychic" realm becomes meaningless if it is taken out of the relational (I–you) context. Dynamically, every subjective experience implies an underlying self–other or symbolically interpersonal context. Through internalized patterns the individual injects into all current relationships the programming of his formative relational world. Naturally, the self is the experiential center of the individual's world, but the self is always a subjective I, unthinkable without some You.

The present authors subscribe to a comprehensive view of clinical theory in which individual (intrapsychic) and multiperson system levels of motivation should be considered in their mutually antithetical and complementary relationship. We find it ill advised and incorrect to ignore the multipersonal reciprocal motivational significance for the intrapsychic formulation of such experientially important events as separation, falling in love, growth, sexual maturation, fear of death, pain over loss of loved ones, etc. On the other hand, we realize that most of our current theory of psychopathology and psychotherapy is phased in individual terms which have to be broadened to encompass the context of the motivational dimensions of family systems.

For instance, in answer to questions about therapeutic indication, goals, and assessment of family work, the family therapist may be unable to communicate with his colleagues if the latter are exclusively individual oriented. He may be asked: Is family therapy indicated in a case of school phobia? His answer should be neither yes or no. He has to point out that in this form the question is intrinsically inappropriate and unanswerable. Since family therapy is concerned with helping every family member, the question should be rephrased: Is it helpful and feasible for the members of this family of a schoolphobic child to work together for mutual benefits? Strictly speaking, however, even the designation "family of a schoolphobic child" is individual-based. The experienced family therapist knows that within a few weeks the symptomatic "patient" role may shift from the schoolphobic to the depressed mother, the delinquent brother, or the psychosomatically ill father. Our challenge is how to designate a family in multiperson system terms rather than merely prefacing traditional individual diagnostic terms or phrases with "the family of a . . ."

The lack of a widely acceptable categorization of families according to multiperson system criteria has been a serious handicap to the family therapist's efforts to communicate his point of view. He has felt that even though he could not conceptually define the system entity of a family, it is not a fictitious image but a clinical reality to work with. In fact, in the course of one or two years' experience family therapists usually learn how to work with the group dynamics of a particular family system as one entity rather than with a summation of the various members' individual dynamics. Ultimately, he has to treat the conglomeration between individual pathologies and system configurations.

The family therapist's ultimate task is to define symptom, diagnosis, and nosological entity in system terms. The traditional medical concept of symptom originated from the dichotomy between noticeable signs and that which was inferred as underlying, causally definable disease process. Whereas suggestive, hypnotic, or behavioral therapeutic measures have for unknown centuries been clearly aimed at removing symptoms, the concern of Freudian psychoanalytic theory has been defined to go beyond the symptoms and focus on an underlying core mechanism in the patient's fundamental personality organization.

The family therapist has to learn to integrate individual, descriptive, and dynamic concepts with such relational system dimensions as: (1) functional interaction patterns, (2) drive-object relatedness, (3) consanguinity, (4) interpersonal pathology, (5) interlocking unconscious mechanisms of individuals, (6) encounter aspects of ontic dialogue, and (7) multigenerational accounts of justice.

A boy's delinquent actions, for example, may be viewed as motivated by several individual and familial factors. On an individual level he may be seen as striving to satisfy his needs for instinctual (sexual, aggressive) gratification (2), assert himself toward his father (2, 6), become equal to his peers (1), etc. On a multiperson level the delinquent boy may vicariously satisfy his parents' unconscious tendencies for delinquency (5), e.g., he may be expected in wishful fantasy to repay all of his parents' suffered losses through punishing society (7), he may loyally bind his parents together through making them into a collusive disciplinary team (1); he may unwittingly provide his family with an excuse for badly needed controlling intervention on the part of society through its authorities (1,2,7). On an even broader scale, he may test the parenting capacity of society as a whole and provide covert dependence and gratification to all members (3).

THE MORE IT CHANGES THE MORE IT IS THE SAME THING

All relationship systems are conservative. Their logic demands that the members' shared investment of care and concern should serve to balance out all injustices and exploitations. Through both the unchangeability of genetic relatedness and the continuity of obligation accounts, families constitute the most conservative systems of all relationships. Through identification with the future of our children, grandchildren, and all unborn generations, we can, at least in fantasy, justify every sacrifice and balance every frustration.

In a sense the existential structuring of familial consanguinity is unchangeable. Families which struggle with pending or actual separations of members will never be able to afford to "existentially" lose any member of the system. The divorced or deserting father will never be internally replaced as father in the minds of his children. Even in cases of earliest adoption, the existential significance of the natural parents usually keeps the minds of adopted children occupied for a lifetime. They may surprise their adoptive family with their vehement desire for more knowledge of and contact with at least the memory of the natural parents.

Another large area of loyalty conflict is connected with that type of injured human justice which is based on unbalanced emotional exploitation. The exploration of these issues is often beclouded by considerations of financial matters in the family. In other instances exploitative possession of a person is disguised as love, as if the gourmet's love for pork could ever mean love from the pig's vantage point. Extensive studies of certain exploitative techniques in relationships have been reported by authors of the Bateson school (for a comprehensive summary see Watzlawick[88]) and by Berne.[7] The family therapist has to caution, however, against any early conclusions about what constitutes exploitation in family relationships. Superficial interactions among family members, especially if a dyad is considered in isolation, may be gravely misleading. Genuine understanding of what constitutes exploitation hinges on the reciprocal balances of merit and recognition of merit.

Familial and larger societal processes interlock in a meaningful fashion. Contemporary Western civilization encourages escape through denial from hard confrontation with one's relationship system. Greatly increased physical mobility, overburdened capacity for communication through the media, glorification of superficial success in "adjustment," confusion of emotional freedom with physical separation, and a high valuation of a superficial and unfounded pseudofriendliness are among our society's "advantages" which support refuge from rather than facing of the accounts of relationships.

The history of Western civilization appears as a long struggle in which the individual has striven to free himself from the power of oppressive rulers. The myths of the Greeks and Hebrews provided early definitions of the individual as a hero who faces insuperable odds and ultimately, even though succumbing, inspires future generations to heroic assertions of their own. The passive acceptance of the power of the ruler makes one a member of the mob, not worthy of recognition or reminiscence. On the other hand, a simple physical separation and escape from the overpowering force does not really liberate the escapee. Much less can one solve the tyranny of one's own obligations by simply shunning the creditor to the obligations. A mass escape for fear of responsibility of filial obligations can infuse all human relations with unbearable chaos. The individual can become paralyzed by amorphous, undefinable, existential guilt.

CONSERVATIVE MODERNISM: ESCAPE FROM PRIVACY

Based on the manifest realities of their everyday experience, some family psychotherapists are inclined to construct their field as one of cold, manipulative games. They seem to lose connection with the layers of personal commitment, intrinsic in any relationship.

It appears that family-intervention therapy can appeal to the impersonally and mechanistically oriented professional as an arena for the manipulation of people. He may claim that a capacity for empathy, which is essential for most forms of individual psychotherapy, is dispensable in family therapy. Some therapists prefer to ignore the subjective growth process of family members, and they consider family therapy as simply aimed at the changing of patterns of visible interaction. The guidelines of their intervention could then be based on entirely technical principles, e.g., straightening out of communicational styles, teaching the principles of "good" fighting, pointing out and eliminating the double binds, etc. Some therapists insist on setting up an artificial agenda, they move people around in the room, make them sit and talk in a certain way, invent "operationally feasible" tasks, they themselves may leave the room, etc. In contrast, our own orientation to family relations in therapy is of a personalized nature. It is our conviction that growth in our personal life is not only inseparable from growth in our professional experience but that it is also our greatest technical tool.

The family therapist's attitude to the question of individual privacy and subjective experience determines his conceptualization of therapeutic goals. By elevating the patient's eventually accomplished, presumedly nonneurotic function as the ideal goal of therapy, individual psychodynamic theory tends to delimit its scientific and human concerns to the boundaries of the individual. While the theory admits that only the tip of the iceberg, i.e., the conscious aspects of motivations, can be seen, it nonetheless postulates that the invisible nine-tenths can be reconstructed with the knowledge of mental mechanisms within an individual's mind, e.g., repression, transference, resistance, defense, regression, etc.

In working with families in vivo, the therapist's concern moves on beyond that of reconstructing the essential core of individuals to the rebalancing of relationships in the multiperson system. In this sense family therapy lies at one pole of the spectrum of therapies with classical behavior therapy being at the opposite pole and psychodynamic (Freudian) therapy in the middle. It is important to recognize the fallacy of a commonly believed dichotomy: as if intensive therapy equaled individual exploration, while conjoint family therapy meant a more superficial, imprecise hit-or-miss work which could never reach the private, internal core of the participants; as if one-to-one, confidential patient–therapist discussions were the necessary requirement for intensity or depth of therapeutic "work." Whereas, no doubt, family exploration broadens the scope of the therapist's intervention, its distinctive characteristic is not mere horizontal amplification. Rather, the therapist's commitment to helping every family member intensifies the emotional impact of a new feedback process affecting every participant. However, the commitment to helping all family members can lead to a true intensification of the therapy process only if the therapist himself can keep pace with the rate of emotional escalation.

The reason for the family therapy situation presenting more of an emotional demand on the therapist than individual therapy is that the true measure of human *emotion* is not the intensity of its affective or physiological concomitants, but the relevance of its interpersonal context. This shows the difficulty inherent in trying to objectify or quantify relational events. Contextual relevance can be assessed by matching of content with context. Like casting with die, they either fit or they don't. Relevance is a nonlinear and nonquantifiable measure.

Conceptual development in the fields of family therapy and theory is still hampered by a long-standing confusion about the role of scientific thinking as applied to the human scene. Some of the best trained researchers still believe in the value of studying essentially nonmeaningful but technically well-definable phenonema. They may opt for looking at family life as motivated by power games and aim at producing excellently documented, convincing data about sharply conceived but marginally relevant behavioral issues. The most important, yet the most difficult, task of research is the creation of a conceptual framework capable of handling the complexities of the theory of relationship systems.

IS THERE ROOM FOR OBJECTIVE "REALITY" IN CLOSE RELATIONSHIPS?

It is deceptive to consider relational reality as less personally dynamic or less subjective than the internal reality of a person. The adjective "objective," as contrasted with "subjective," connotes a quality of freedom from false, incorrect information and from distortion of facts through emotional bias. Yet, the reality of the person in his close relationship is composed of his subjective, transferred, familial internal reality plus certain factual attributes of the partner. Naturally, from the partner's vantage point, his own internal reality is subjective, rather than actual.

There is no objective reality as a middle ground between the mutually confronting "need templates"[12, p. 46] of two relating members. If objectivity has any meaning here, it lies in the mutual awareness of each participant's simultaneous need configurations by the other, while both strive to make one another the object of their needs and wishes. Yet, we have to keep in mind that the individual's needs contain the condensations of the unsettled relational accounts of his family of origin, in addition to reenactment of his own early psychic processes.

When it comes to an analysis of close relationships, the therapist first has to be clear about the main determinants of the participants' motivations or relational attitudes. He has to learn about each member's position in the system: obligations, commitments, the history of merits, exploitations, etc. For example, aside from scapegoating attitudes, stifling and overpowering "love" can also victimize its object. The "object's" need for a genuine dialogue are equally overlooked.

Relational attitudes in their affective–programmatic structuring contain the blueprints of the person's future actions. The design of these blueprints is always composed both of the person's fundamental needs and his "imported" system obligations. What is most important in a scapegoating act, for instance, is not that it distorts reality, but that it expresses needs of the scapegoater—and of course, the expectations of all participants in the scapegoating system. The same could be said of a process of inverse scapegoating, e.g., falling in love. First and foremost the lover has a need for seeing (distorting) the love partner as a fitting object of his own need configuration (sexual, protective, dependent, taunting, etc.). *Amor coecus est*—love is blind. What we have to add here is that love is even more blind because of each individual's burden of the hidden obligations coming from outside the dyad. Through a husband and wife, two family systems, not just two individuals, find their match.

What balances the one-sided subjectivity of two partners' needs is whether the lover can make the loved one respond and, ultimately, whether the latter's own needs will in turn find him to be a satisfying object. A close relationship is a dynamic encounter between need templates. There is no objective middle ground or "undistorted reality" between partners in a relationship. Their realistic goal is not that their needs should be aligned with the "objective" characteristics of the other, but that they learn to discriminate one another's needs as valid and distinct from their own needs.

From the point of view of our relationship theory, a person's need template is a short-hand formula, comprising both his personal needs and the invisible expectations due to the disturbed balance of the justice of his and his family's past relationships. He owes reciprocity to those who gave him so much, regardless of whether they felt cheated or exploited by fate. He may assume that the prospective partner is aware of his built-in frustrations and obligations. Naturally, the other has to incorporate into his attitude the history of his own family's balance of merits.

WHAT IS THE OBJECTIVE REALITY OF THE PERSON?

The foregoing discussion depicted the individual as dovetailing with the context of his relationships. It also assumed that the person is a given and defined entity with an identifiable boundary: His needs and style of responding are uniquely his own. We assume that at least through his actions the individual is an integral unit.

A more inclusive theory of relationships, however, has to take the minute-by-minute fluctuation of the degree of individuation into account. The person is mainly definable through the range and extent of his needs, obligations, commitments, and responsible attitudes taken in the relational field. Even seemingly well-individuated, socially prominent, and responsible citizens may act like unreliable, irresponsible partners when seen in the context of a "symbiotic" family relationship. They may panic if they are expected to take a responsible look at their function within the family. They may hide behind a "we" instead of an "I" form of grammatical expression in trying to explain their own feelings and intentions. They may focus exclusively on the functions or symptoms of their children or unwittingly create an image of false individuation and health of their marital ties. For example, they can argue with deceptive freedom, overtly revealing great personal disagreements over issues, only to be revealed as unchangeable because of the family members' unconsciously merged personalities.

Our system view places individual psychic structures in the context of their relationships in working with families in treatment. The translation from here to a more fully understood individual structural analysis has not yet been made. We could equate symbiotically undifferentiated relational function or poorly resolved system indebtedness with a "weak ego" structure in individual terms, but the correspondence of these terms is only partial. The language of "ego weakness" ordinarily assumes a weak but discrete personal identity. Vicariously or collusively symbiotic functioning, on the other hand, can be observed only in the presence of two or more closely related individuals. Inference from individual therapeutic (transference) to family relationships is an incomplete one.

In short, the system point of view is of great practical, therapeutic significance. Our therapeutic contract is to be formed with the total membership of the family relationship system, instead of with the symptomatic member or with his adult guardians.

The contract means that the therapist has to offer and actually make available himself as willing to help all members, whether they come to therapy sessions or not. In turn, he has to extract commitment for participation from all members of the family. He wants all those present to expose their opinions, needs, and wishes for help, and he tries to make sure that the messages of even the smallest child are being heard and responded to. As part of the contract, he offers courage to face obligations and to face guilt over delinquent payment of emotional debts.

Although a major part of the therapist's initial efforts have to do with the establishment of the therapeutic contract with the family as a whole, the therapist is not the one who creates or imposes the family system point of view of dynamics and therapy upon the family members. There would be no family without an underlying foundation of solidarity and an intrinsic loyalty originating from before the time the children were born.

The implications of the conjoint, family or relational therapy are so revolutionary that they are bound to force either a break with our widespread societal ethics or a retreat into some form of denial and compromise out of weakness. The question of exploitation, rugged individualism, suppression by powerful elders or political bosses, kings, dictators, etc., are related to the forces that govern the family system. What would be ethically required of an automobile manufacturer when it is expected to turn out safe and lasting vehicles in the midst of competition and labor disputes is similar to the demand on a divorcing couple for consideration of their children's interests.

When we explore in other chapters the dimensions of loyalty, reciprocity, and justice, we are not likely as family therapists to be able to hide behind convenient individual, efficiency-oriented concepts. System concepts of impersonal effectiveness, e.g., good communication patterns, problem solving, adjustment, or even "mental health" fall short of the real essence of human relationships. A study of responses without a commitment to responsibility and accountability is socially self-defeating or at least meaningless.

Without a capacity for facing the accounts of integrity of family relationships, the family therapist himself will be overwhelmed and may be driven to the kind of despair which talks of the "death" of the family.[29] He can get caught in a dilemma similar to that of an advertising specialist who would shift his concern from the effectiveness of the design of commercials to their honesty and integrity. The individual therapist can, if he wishes to, remain a designer of fronts for individuals. The family therapist cannot in the long run close his eyes to relational integrity, including his own.

In summary, the system orientation comes out of the logic of empirical observations of family therapists. Independently, many early therapists came to the conclusion that there exists a lawful organization (homeostasis) regarding shifts of the sick role in families. While the field of family therapy would need a theoretical foundation based on further, more precise description of the empirical facts of systemic homeostasis, most therapists' interest has understandably been preoccupied with the question of what dynamic forces regulate such homeostasis. The goal-oriented mandate of the therapist challenges him to master the secrets of control and causal determinism of family relationships.

2

The Dialectic Theory of Relationships

We have indicated in the previous chapter that we consider the deepest human understructure of relationships to consist of a network (hierarchy) of obligations. While sociologists have compiled lists of manifest obligations, we are more interested in the covert ones. There is a constant give-and-take of expectations between each individual and the relationship system he belongs to. We oscillate constantly between posing and discharging obligations. A relationship system can be thought of as held together by a gyroscope which keeps up-to-date accounts of the total balance of obligations among members.

Each member's ethical relationship to his relationship system, e.g., his family, his work situation, or his community, makes up the crucial part of his existential world. The balance between obligations and fulfillment of obligations constitutes the justice of the human world. What are the measures by which to judge where the balance stands? On what basis is the balance sheet judged negative or positive?

We propose that the understanding of the structure of a relational world requires a dialectical rather than absolute or monothetical way of thinking. The essence of the dialectical approach is a liberation of the mind from absolute concepts which in themselves claim to explain phenonema as though the opposite point of view did not exist. According to dialectical thought, a positive concept is always viewed in contrast with its opposite, in the hope that their joint consideration will yield a resolution through a more thorough and productive understanding. The principles of relativity and indeterminacy in physics and the concept of homeostatic regulations of living things are examples of increasingly dialectical orientations in natural sciences.

Our position is dialectical in a number of ways, some different from everyday contemporary usage of the term. In a Hegelian sense, we use dialectic as a challenge to the one-dimensional limitations of the definition of any phenomenon. In this sense it can be predicted that life's basic unpredictability will introduce challenges to any equilibrium. The qualitatively new event will upset the whole principle of equilibrium instead of simply tilting its valence from one homeostatic phase to the next. By adding a necessary new component, today's imbalance leads to tomorrow's new balance. The false and the mundane turn out to be valuable as they help dispel stagnation. As injury and unfairness become balanced through restitution, the spontaneity of autonomous motions of individual members is bound to create new imbalance and new injustice which if recognized and faced, leads to a richer, safer definition of freedom and concern among members. The prevalence of movement over stagnation is the essence of the dialectic view of family relationships and the family therapist helps the process through his commitment to change, recognition of change, and synthesis of change with unchangeable sameness of being.

Psychology, psychotherapy, and psychopathology have also been in a gradual transition toward a more dialectic viewpoint. While the traditional individual point of view thought in terms of monothetical or absolute concepts: instinct, power, control, love, hatred, intelligence, communication, etc., the dialectical approach defines the individual as partner to a dialogue, i.e., in a dynamic exchange with his counterpart: the other or nonself. He and his counterpart constitute his relational world. An orange does not have to be defined in terms of a counterorange, whereas, for example, a person's individuation has to be viewed in the perspective of its dynamic balance with symbiotic, deindividuating forces. According to the dialectic law, movement in one direction causes pull and eventually movement in the opposite direction. The dialectical resolution is never a bland, gray compromise between black and white, it is living with live opposites. An important contribution to a dialectic formulation of basic dynamics was made by Stierlin.[84]

A frequently encountered situation in family therapy illustrates man's struggle for the resolution of the antithetical paradoxes of his living. Whether in the course of everyday life or during therapy, a person can become aware of his deep-seated resentment towards his parents over their real or alleged rejection or lack of love. In the absolute sense the person would need help through traditional psychotherapeutic practices which aim at individuation through insight and overt expression, leading to growing autonomy. Consequently, he should not be concerned whether his image of his parents will be a hateful one. He should feel free to face and express his resentment, at least in the course of therapy, and to invest other persons as suitable objects of his loving aspirations. Thus, in an absolute sense, one would logically expect a pure emotional gain from drawing the practical conclusions of what used to be a passively experienced, frustrating, and hurting situation. Yet, in our clinical experience, no one ends up a winner through a conclusion which predicates a hopelessly incorrigible resentment and contempt towards one's parent.

While conscious confrontation with one's hateful feelings amounts to progress, it does not represent a therapeutic endpoint. Unless the person can struggle with his negative feelings and resolve them by acts based on positive, helpful attitudes towards his parent, he cannot really free himself of the intrinsic loyalty problem and has to "live" the conflict, even after the parent's death, through pathological defensive patterns. A suspicious rejection of the spouse or perhaps of the entire world may be one defensive attempt at resolving this sort of conflict. It can be mentioned here that positive transference to the therapist can itself amount to intrinsic disloyalty to the rejected parent and, naturally, revert to negative transference. Frequently, the final outcome is the rejection of the therapist in order to escape from the annihilating effects of a "victory" over one's parents. The cost of such victory would be guilt, shame, and a paradoxically binding loyalty, disowned, denied yet paralyzingly adhered to at the same time.

A variety of everyday human and clinical situations can illustrate the relational dynamics based on the reasoning that we call dialectic. First we have to realize that *overt,* conscious attitudes may conflict with *covert* expectations. Much has been written about the paradox of the psychotherapeutic process in which the patient has to grow temporarily dependent on the therapist in order to gain independence and spontaneity of living. Everyday life experience shows amply how often an angry, chastising response from the person in authority can be preferred to a patient, tolerant, permissive one. The first response may prove an attitude of involvement and caring, whereas the second may simply convey indifference and lack of concern. The parentification of a child illustrates another paradox: how the object of protection may simultaneously become the source of both strength and dependent support. By the same logic, the parentified child who performs overly grownup for his age, can progress only if he is first given a chance to assume overly childish patterns. Real strength is gained, thus, through apparent weakness.

A very important, deep-seated paradox lies in the antithetical relationship between *individuation* and *family loyalty.* Whereas it appears on the surface that failure to develop and to mature makes a child disloyal toward his family's aspirations, a more basic truth is that every step leading toward the child's true emancipation, individuation, or separation tends to touch on the emotionally charged issue of every member's denied but wished-for everlasting symbiotic togetherness with the family of origin.

RELATIONAL BOUNDARIES

One of the most important aspects of the relational dialectic pertains to the concept of intergroup boundary between "us" and "them." Ontologically, "they" create "us" as a meaningful and purposeful entity. Through otherness the outgroup becomes a suitable target of prejudice. We may resent them but we need them. We may wish that they get lost, that they get out of our way, but without them we loose purpose and meaning. Almost every great event of the history of mankind can be identified as based on a strong division between an in-group and those on the outside. Without having the chance for a contrast or perhaps contest with the outsider, the in-group loses zest of functioning.

The internal identity of the in-group is inseparably connected with the boundary of otherness towards the out-group. The ancient Hebrews were God's chosen people. The early Christians felt convinced that only they shared a great secret which would conquer pagan religious beliefs. The ancient Greeks believed that they spread the light of a superior culture among Barbarians, and the Romans thought that they had a mission to conquer the world and give it peace and justice. Even movements which search for universal human goals can flourish only as long as they see themselves in opposition to ignorant, reluctant, or antagonistic outsiders.

Family life has to obtain mastery of subgroup antithesis rather than hope for absolute unity. In family life the differentiation, individuation, and ultimately the separation of children, adolescents, and young adults create the meaning of parenthood. Parents may often fantasize an ultimate peace and gratification in a later period at which the children are already separated. They may believe that it is the children who create all their conflicts. The actual fact, however, is that separation that leads to loss of relationship tends to weaken, or at least challenge, rather than reinforce the isolated parental marriage. Even the intrusive in-laws, who are often thought of as great obstacles to the smoothness of the marriage and to the peace of the nuclear family, are actually reinforcers of family solidarity and shared meaning. In summary, separation, separateness, otherness or difference, recognized in their anti-thetical, dialectical dynamic balance with closeness of relationship, constitute a vital force. On the other hand, taken in an absolute sense, they resemble the peaceful quiet ultimately offered by the cemetery.

Psychologically, one could conceive of the boundary that separates the in-group from the out-group as a cognitive one: knowing that we are different; an affective one: feeling that "we" belong together as separate from "them"; or being of the nature of action: counting what "we" do for "them" and what "they" have done for "us". Our concern with loyalty and with the justice of the human order naturally stresses the third, the factual, give-and-take aspect of boundary. We are interested in what parents give to children and what they receive from their children—the way in which the gap of generations is both maintained and bridged by actions and attitudes.

The balance of intergenerational attitudes constitutes an important criterion of family health. Ideally, the parents should be comfortable in accepting the dependence of their child. They should be comfortable and generally gratified in being the leaders and sources of support while accepting the child's need for nurturance, guidance, and correction. Naturally, it is inevitable that at times the parent feels like having given more than he is able to, having listened longer than he is capable of, without a chance to voice his own feelings of depletion, exhaustion, and exploitation. At such times the parent may unwittingly ask his child for trust, support, and reward, and usually the child is able and happy to repay the parent for the care and support received. In other words, temporary parentification of a child is a normal part of family life and a vehicle for the child's learning how to be responsible.

In families where there is *parentification* in a pathological sense, this *reversal of positions* becomes the rule rather than the exception. In extreme cases the child becomes so overburdened with demands for responsibility that he is never given the chance to be a child. Such children become specialists in dealing with infantile adults while they are getting developmentally depleted as children in their own right.

Adolescence exemplifies the dialectical contraposition of the generational differential. The adolescent is both childish and adultlike, yet he is neither a child nor an adult. He learns how to be childish with respect to the behavior of mature adults. As he is able to lean on adults, he can dispense with some of his needs for childishness. Yet, the mere avoidance of childishness does not lead to a grown-up status. Through the experience of being on the child side of the adult–child differential, the adolescent gradually learns how to be on the adult side of the boundary

toward someone in a position junior to him. The therapeutic significance of relational boundaries can be illustrated with certain aspects of
a three-generational family treatment case:

Mrs. G, a mother of two adolescent girls has been struggling with her mother's alleged overtly resentful and rejecting attitude most of her lifetime. She
even seemed to relish the fact that her marriage was born out of an atmosphere
of hostile rebellion against her mother. In her case hostility was immediately
manifest. This woman had no difficulty in describing the mutual resentments
and hurts suffered by her and her mother.

In the course of family treatment initiated because of the psychotic episode
of the younger daughter of 15, the 17-year-old "well sibling" sister started to
make definite moves toward separation. She entered college and began a chain
of rebellious, self-defeating actions. It seemed that, outside her awareness, Mrs.
G herself began to slip into the role of the disapproving, rejecting, and morally
condemnatory mother vis-à-vis her rebelliously separating daughter. Yet, when
the family therapist made a comparison between her "rebellious" marriage and
her daughter's adolescent rebellion, she angrily rejected the analogy. She could
not yet allow herself to recognize her dual position vis-à-vis the mother–child
boundary.

It wasn't until Mrs. G discovered that her mother had cancer that the possibility of a change became realistic. As she became capable of assuming the nurse's
role, i.e., a symbolic mothering towards her dying mother, she began to view
her daughter in the light of a desperately struggling young woman rather than
a morally objectionable delinquent. Interestingly, soon after she had become
able to move into a concerned, loving, and parentlike role with regard to her
mother, her daughter was able to shift from a self-endangering delinquent to
a constructive pattern of behavior, both in her private life and towards members of her family.

This family illustrates the usefulness of one member's striking out for
definite action, taking definite positions, and facing the consequences
of the action. Such behavior tends to upset the stale avoidance and
postponement patterns which prevent many families from becoming
"laboratories" for personal growth through facing conflicts and resolving them.

The system concept of family relationships requires an interdependent distribution of roles. In certain families the therapist will find the
existence of a rigid polarization around roles or positions which seems
to put members into genuinely opposite positions. Yet the very fixity of
their antithetical roles can make the two members vicariously dependent on one another's function in such a manner that neither faces his
own relational world as a whole person. An old shrewd fox of a business-

man can get trapped into a mutually exploitative pseudodialectic with his son, the "ethical businessman." At the same time when the two have overt contempt for the weaknesses of one another, they also need and mutually exploit the disapproved characteristics of each other. Instead of a genuinely antithetical dialogue, they have what we call a *polarized fusion* of roles. Their antithesis cannot lead to boundary formation and creative synthesis. A mutually exploitative vicarious "using the other" prevents them also from sharing and assessments of reciprocal contributions.

In similar manner overadequate family members can depend on the failure of underadequate members. The socially outstanding member can be dependent on the performance of the sick or delinquent member. Naturally, the wellness of the well member and the sickness of the designated patient member are codetermined by their broader social functions rather than just their own dyadic vicariousness. Ultimately, however, the fixity of their roles serves the requirements of the total family obligation network.

Fixity of frozen role obligations can be contrasted with the atmosphere of basic trust existing in a family. Basic trust, though coined as a psychological stage of individual psychosocial development,[34] is predicated upon a relationship structure in which each individual as a separate entity can draw from and has to be accountable to a just human order. A just order does not imply absence of injustices; it implies that genuine accountability should be a stronger role than any other fixed obligation. Vicariously fixed, compliant role performance among family members constitutes a family system which blocks and postpones rather than resolves old accounts. In such a system no one really has to face his own self as a free agent of accountability. In order to design an effective long-range strategy, the family therapist has to assess the balance of the human justice and the hierarchy of expectations within the family system through listening to each member's subjective construction of his accountability to the rest of the family and vice versa.

Straight-line causation type thinking looks at illness as determined by one cause or a chain of causes. A dialectic point of view, on the other hand, looks at the dual psychic reality of any relationship. Yet no dialogue should be considered as limited to two participants. In each dialogue one person and his human world meets the other and her human world. As each contributes his own position within a family hierarchy of obligations, a new balance or network of credits and debits is created. No matter how much we would wish to be independent of the weight of the past, the basic structure of our existence and of our children's existence remains at least partially determined by the unsettled accounts of past generations.

OBLIGATION HIERARCHY AND "INTERNALIZATION OF OBJECTS"

The extreme of the social system purist point of view in the family field would maintain that it is only the here-and-now or behavioral level of interpersonal relationships that the therapist has to be concerned about. The purist would tend to ignore the historic structuring of accounting of obligations and commitments and reduce the family relational field to just another small group with behavioral, observable, interacting reality. Since from our point of view the "accounting" of acts of loyalty is the key determinant of relationship structures and ultimately of individual behavior, we regard the internalization of object relationships as one of the indicators of the justice of one's human world. For instance, the deprived child who was rejected by his parents can internalize such a degree of bitter resentment that he might subsequently use the whole world for getting even through revenge. Furthermore, by scapegoating his wife as a miserable mother, he not only gets even with his internalized parents through re-projection of pent-up resentment upon another person, but also protects his parents by taking his revenge out on someone else. Unconsciously he avoids blaming their memory while sacrificing his loyalty to his wife.

It is not incidental that detailed records of the subjective justice of the human world are likely to be kept more closely and for a longer time in the invisible patterning of family relationships than in any other group, probably because families are concerned with the production of the offspring. This is a long-term goal, and an irreversible act with far greater ethical consequences than any other individual human function could be.

Extrafamilial life situations may or may not be unjust for a period of time. We may move around at great speed from job to job, from town to town. Loyalty to an old boss may not count in a new business relationship. Injustices caused while climbing up the social scale may be forgotten when the successful climber enters his new position. In the family, however, the consequences of action remain written into the deepest substrate of transgenerational accountability. The fate of the offspring can be held up as a mirror in front of the parents. The crucial regulatory force of family relations is the principle of accountability and trustability.

POWER VERSUS OBLIGATION AS ALTERNATE BASES FOR ACCOUNTING

Our theoretical position has to be differentiated from one which pictures family dynamics and therapy as taking place in a power-motivated arena. A power framework would emphasize the importance of freedom versus subordination in family relationships. It would view marriage and family mainly as arenas for control or for power over the other, for instance when it portrays the brutal father or the domineering mother as power-thirsty culprits in family pathogenesis.

Perhaps these views complemented the trend of what can be called the two antiauthoritarian decades: the period between the late 1940s through the late 1960s. Authoritarian and antiauthoritarian trends hold an oscillating balance in any society. The tradition of American society has made all leadership and manifest power roles especially vulnerable. As a result, commitment to overt responsible leadership is often seen as a less effective manipulative lever than, for instance, affluent background combined with persistent criticism of all leadership.

Blitsten gave a description of the American family of the same period in corresponding terms: "Emphasis on . . . deprecation of the assets of age and exaggeration of the assets of youth, curtailment of parental authority, and extreme notions about equality in family relationships—these factors in combination account for much that is unique in American family life."[9, p. 37]

The overemphasis of the importance of the social regulatory leverage of power, by necessity, underestimates the significance of control via obligations and inner commitments. Is an anomic disintegration of contemporary society caused by relaxation of control through power or by loss of internal commitment to obligations? Dicks implies a connection between the societal and intrafamilial aspects of disintegration: "If disintegration of the cells of the social organism is growing at this rate, what chain reactions will it bring in its train for our future community? Not only in the frustrations of the wish for stability, enduring love, and support of many of the partners themselves, but especially in the geometric progression of deprived children whose minds cannot trust or be trusted to make lasting and undivided emotional commitments in their marriages or in human relations generally. A society is only as good as the emotional state of its component individuals will allow it to be. A marked and rising proportion of broken or grossly disturbed marriages is bound to swell the numbers of conflict-torn, potentially destructive offspring to whom the world, its culture, and its institutions are the enemy."[31, p. 5]

In conclusion, monothetical power accounting represents a much more superficial aspect of social structuring than the accounting of obligations. An irresponsible loosening up of the hierarchy of loyalties is more detrimental to the survival of societies than is seemingly excess authority.

Man's vulnerability through his commitments is different from but connected with his "ontic dependence."[12, p. 37] It is more difficult to describe how we can get hurt through existential interdependence than through power exploitations. As Lujpen phrases it: "Precisely because man is essentially in the world it is impossible for him, despite the fact that he lives for love, not *also* somehow to destroy the other's subjectivity."[63, p. 293] The self and the other, while mutually constructive in the relational dialectic, are also capable of extinguishing each other through active or passive exploitation.

The following letter given to the therapist by the 16-year-old daughter illustrates the survival struggle of family members in connection with the desperate separation moves made by an 18-year-old daughter. They all suffer from their existential interdependence which is inseparable from their loyalty commitments to the family and to one another:

What you have just seen (my giving Lucille a cigarette) was a demonstration of how Lucille used other people as tools for her revenge against our parents. I did not want to give it to her, but it's a sort of "damned if you do and damned if you don't thing—if I give her a cigarette, it hurts my mother to see her smoking, but if I don't it would hurt my mother to hear her verbal abuse of her sister, or to see her get up and walk out. I forget what the game she's playing is called, but it's in Eric Berne's "Games People Play."

She is constantly using other people to advance her own aims (i.e., to be completely irresponsible for herself or anyone else). My father wants to kick her out with nothing, so he "subtly" provokes her until she leaves, or threatens to, or tries to get out of the situation by becoming hysterical. One of these days she may find guts enough to kill herself, but I doubt it—she couldn't enjoy my parents' (mainly my mother's) remorse if she were dead. So she comes close to destruction, but never reaches it. This is only another paradox in her life. To quote her, "What's wrong with having lots of paradoxical thoughts?" My answer, "Everything!"

From her sister's letter it would seem as if Lucille were playing a power game of winning, but something appears to be a paradox to her. From our viewpoint one paradox lies in the antithetical relationship between success based on power and guilt over such success. The fear of destroying the other is balanced by the risk of destroying the self.

SURFACE–DEPTH ANTITHESIS

The relationship between power, on the one hand, and guilt over power, on the other, highlights the dialectic that connects these two dimensions. Movement in one direction on the manifest, behavioral level (more power) tends to produce an antithetical, functionally inhibiting movement on the implicit, feeling level (guilt over power). By contrast, in a monothetical, nondialectical thought framework, power is expected to be checked by another, superior, opposing force. The principle of dynamic internal control of one's aggression or exploitative success is inherently dialectical.

This inherent dialectic regulatory principle of life events is to be distinguished from a mere pattern of communications which is characterized by contradictory messages on two levels of meaning, the "double bind."[4] The dialectical orientation stresses the dual motivational structuring of all relational ("psychological") events: overt, behavioral and covert, obligational. Correspondingly, relationships should be viewed as inherently connected with two accounting systems: those of overt, power-determined motivations and those of the hierarchy of obligations.

This type of dual determination and accounting can be observed in individuals, interacting nuclear families, multigenerational chains of extended family relationships, and entire societies. Unsettled loyalty accounts influence the life of subsequent generations. The exploited child often turns into a symbiotically possessive parent. Longitudinal family studies might substantiate the biblical statement that seven generations can be afflicted by the sins of a father. As the ledgers become progressively overencumbered with guilt over exploitation, more and more damage is inflicted upon the future generations. The skillful exploiters become the ultimate losers, eventually. As in greater society, the slave ultimately becomes victorious over the slaveholder.

The shifting between powerful and guilt-laden roles in a scapegoating "system" can illustrate this antithetical relationship between power and guilt over power. Without the assumption of such a dialectic, one could only see a rule by power in absolute terms: the winner would be on top and the underdog hopelessly under. Family life would approximate the economic and political scene where, at least temporarily, wealth and power usually lead to more wealth and power. In family life, however, people are too close to an inescapable accounting of justice to bypass guilt over abuse of power.

As the therapist views the unfair victimization of the scapegoated member, he is bound to react to the power dimension of relational dynamic in the system. He may try to side with the victim and defend him against the obviously unfair scapegoaters. The therapist may follow the principle—correct in theory—of reversing a one-sided, overloaded situation. He may sense correctly where the projection-laden distortion lies. Usually it becomes all too obvious in the process of making someone a scapegoat, especially when done by several others in collusion. Finally, the therapist may follow his own inclination to restore the human order of justice which has been upset by an undue exploitation of relational power.

In practice, however, the therapist's effort to restore justice and remedy the injury caused to the scapegoat is seldom rewarded by the outcome of his intervention. Frequently he himself gets caught in the collusive system forces which help perpetuate the scapegoating process as a needed, repeatedly recurring situation. Often, to his surprise, the inexperienced therapist will feel rejected even by the scapegoat, who turns out to be just as addicted to the game as his persecutors. The therapist may then opt to construe him as a masochist who likes to be hurt. Soon the victim doesn't even seem to be hurt at all; in fact, he seems to be cherished rather than despised by the other family members. Understandably, their respect for this decreasingly relevant therapeutic intervention dwindles.

If the therapist would have included in his strategy the dimension of guilt over success, he would have understood the scapegoating game. Since successful scapegoating inevitably induces guilt in the perpetrators, the victim is likely to obtain the key leverage in the guilt induction hierarchy. The loser may turn into winner; a simple restitution of his rights would amount to a monothetical unidirectional goal. Therefore, in view of the dialectical implications of his role, the scapegoat ought to be recognized and congratulated as a major contributor and leader. Conversely, the scapegoaters should be regarded as prospective underdogs due to their liability to increasing guilt over their unfair act. Unless the therapist succeeds in breaking the cycle of the latters' emerging guilt, he can expect a cyclic continuation of the process. Furthermore, as a martyr the scapegoated member will be left without both internal superego checks and external control. He will subsequently be inclined to act out in a fashion which will provoke external control through renewed projective blaming on the part of the other members as they recover from their guilt. The process then repeats itself over and over.

As a general rule, without an intimate knowledge of the merit accounting system of a particular family, it is impossible to tell the real extent of any seeming relational gain or injury. What appears a brutal fight between members, for instance, can actually produce an increase of reliance and loyalty out of the mutuality of their misery and suffering; it all amounts to one form of "closeness."

The nature and extent of personal indebtedness determine what in each relationship may constitute exploitation. One wife can feel exploited and betrayed after 30 years of marriage upon finding out that her husband has been regarded as a dashing man by the women in his office, while another wife may obtain a sense of pride and confirmation from such a discovery. Periodic "walking out" can weaken one marriage, while it can strengthen another.

Similar to guilt and power, *shame* and *dignity* tend to take antithetical positions between manifest and deeper levels of relational patterning. Conjoint family therapy sessions may resemble a tribunal at which shameful and guilt-laden acts are to be confessed. The intrusion of the therapist as an outsider markedly increases this implication of the setting. Yet, the dignity of open confrontation with truth may far outweigh the manifest shamefulness of revelations, e.g., those made by a parent in front of both his children and the professional "intruders":

Family dynamic exploration was introduced into the individual treatment of a young woman who had a number of delusional preoccupations. Individual psychotherapy proved to be rather unproductive in this case; it led only to sterile ruminations. The worker attempted to get some clues from a few joint sessions with some of the family members and decided to ask for a family dynamic evaluation.

At the first conjoint session, which included the patient, her mother, and six of her siblings, an important breakthrough occurred.

The consulting family therapist kept encouraging the family members to try to be as open as possible. All of a sudden, the mother announced: "there has been incest in this family." After an initial uneasy silence, the oldest brother added an account of his incestuous experiences. This was followed by revelations of numerous intermember incestuous experiences on the part of several other members. It seemed as if mother would have given the permission to open up this shameful secret. What initially amounted to mother's opening up and exposing her own and the family's shame has turned into a most dignified effort at helping the entire family obtain professional help. The value of search for truth and justice replaced the value of loyalty through secretiveness.

In summary, the surface–depth dialectic of both individual and relational dynamics determines how movement in one direction on one level may produce countermovement on another level. This is one reason why it is almost impossible for an outsider to determine where overt hurting ends and genuine relational damage begins.

RETRIBUTIVE DYNAMIC BASIS OF LEARNING

The relational basis of learning and its disabilities is one of the most important clues for understanding why it is that in certain neighborhoods children grow up to school age with a social incapacity for learning. If teaching is assumed to be analogous to parental giving, then learning, in turn, amounts to receiving. Therefore, the latter ought to diminish frustration through restoring the balance of justice of one's human world. Yet, at least in cases where early developmental frustration in the justice of the human world is excessive, our assumption is that learning amounts to giving to rather than receiving from the teacher.

Learning requires tolerance for the input of new, ego-alien knowledge. It takes just as much of a giving attitude, a willingness to bend, stop, listen, respect, take in, retain, digest, integrate with self, etc., as does the correction of reality distortions and of narcissistic investments in the course of psychotherapy. Insofar as learning requires a giving, trusting attitude, the child's capacity for taking in new knowledge depends on the balance of retributive credit–debit accounting. Early developmental frustration overloads the child's scale toward intolerance for injustice. From his vantage point the world will appear as essentially frustrating, not giving and thus unilaterally in debt to him. Consequently, he is not going to be in an emotional disposition to "give" by accepting, i.e., to learn, to take in. Therapeutically, it follows then that the child should first be permitted to have his justice recognized and possibly repaired so that he can afford himself the option of learning rather than turning into a self-destructive and learning-incapacitated person. It is not easy to avert the development which leads to an unconsciously retributive, revengeful resistance to learning and to all intellectual development. Considering the strength of every child's invisible loyalty, his justice should be recognized by the therapist in such a way that his parents should not be scapegoated in the same process. It may be learned, for instance, that the deserting parent was himself growing up in a frustrating, unfairly depriving system. If at the same time the families of origin can be saved from blame, the increment in the positive merit of the whole system should be rewarded by progress toward more receptiveness for learning.

INDIVIDUATION OR SEPARATION?

Autonomy is a typically dialectical concept, and misuse of this concept as therapeutic goal can be blamed for many failures in therapy. Although few therapists would adopt such an unsophisticated view as to simply equate autonomy with physical separation, much of therapeutic practice stresses separate living as an important goal and proof of psychic emancipation. Separation is usually encouraged from the culturally supported point of view that if the offspring and parent can sustain physical separation, they will develop coping mechanisms which eventually will make them emotionally less mutually interdependent. However, on a depth relational level, physical separation may promote an internally offsetting, counterautonomous shift in the balance of merit accounting in the family loyalty system. Separation in this sense may induce guilt feelings in the perpetrator, and guilt is the greatest obstacle to the success of genuinely autonomous emancipation. If one's entire mental equilibrium ultimately hinges on the handling of guilt-laden obligations to be available to one's parent (or child), the chance of any increase in guilt is too high a price to pay in exchange for the acquisition of independent functional patterns.

Perhaps paradoxically, we maintain that more individuation can be achieved through the family's joint exploration of mutually interdependent, guilt-laden obligations than through abrupt separation. Staying while openly examining the possible resolutions of one's obligations leads to more independence than premature running away to avoid the "accounts."

DOVETAILING BETWEEN SYSTEMS OF MERIT ACCOUNTING

If, indeed, marriage represents an encounter between two family systems, it is important to explore how they will mutually affect one another's chances for balancing their members' accounts of merit. One family system may have been entrenched in the positive feedback process of continuously decompensating exploitative and scapegoating patterns, alienation, incest, or sacrificial self-paralysis; therefore its chances for a growth-promoting reequilibration of its accounts may have become progressively remote. New hope may emerge after one member marries into another system.

At the same time, on an individual level, one can assume that the spouse's choice may be unconsciously determined by one of the following: (1) wish to obtain a just "order of the human world" through access to the spouse and his hopefully more giving family; (2) a hope to find a more receptive group where one can act more justly toward others and expiate past debts; (3) a projective use of the other and the other's family for the purpose of rehabilitating one's family of origin. Naturally, the risks and existential complexities of such relational ventures are considerable. Many people burdened with unresolvable guilt accounts rather choose alternate paths of working for humanity, missionary efforts, or other self sacrificing contributions, while remaining single and bypassing family life as an opportunity for ethically meaningful rebalancing of past accounts.

A young couple came to therapy with a chronically vindictive and deteriorating marital problem. There were mutual accusations of sexual incompetency as well as morally condemnatory attitudes. Both being Catholics, each tried to implicate the other in responsibility over practicing birth control.

The wife's family was reported overtly failing in that her father was a drunkard, incessantly chastised by his wife. The husband's parents were described as rigidly puritanical and emotionally nongiving. In one session in which the wife's mother participated, important clues were revealed regarding the mutual impact of the two family systems. The maternal grandmother stated amid profuse tears that 5 years earlier the paternal grandmother had warned her never to return to the young couple's home because of her alleged bad moral influence on them. After all, her daughter was dating men at 12 or 13. The maternal grandmother claimed then that this insinuation was her reason for not having visited her daughter's home ever since. She had not been able to discuss the matter with her daughter either.

The husband was visibly embarrassed upon hearing this and he sided first with his mother-in-law, denouncing his own mother as a troublemaker with all daughters-in-law. In the next week's session the couple behaved as a cooperative team as they reported their seeming agreement over the main points of this incident and discussed the shortcomings of their mothers. In the subsequent session, however, the wife started to accuse the husband of incestuous inclinations, e.g., his habit of lying down for half an hour in bed with the 7-year-old daughter (as well as with the 8- and 12-year-old sons) before going to sleep. The husband was beside himself with anger and retaliated by abruptly telling his daughter that she should never come into the parents bed anymore, nor will he go to her either. In the ensuing weeks both spouses developed overtly and passionately critical stances toward the other's family of origin.

It seems that in like cases the spouses carry the burden of overcharged multipersonal system accounts for their entire families of origin. They could restore marital harmony only by rebalancing the networks of their respective intrafamilial dynamics at the same time. The inexperienced therapist could miss these complex multipersonal system dynamic determinants and use all his therapeutic leverage on the overtly observable and symptomatically relevant issues of sexual and religious conflict.

GENERAL IMPLICATIONS

The dialectical model of conceptualization has enabled us to think about relationships from a consistently multilateral point of view. While our approach can be looked upon as a generalized relativity theory of human relationships, we propose it for its heuristic and epistemological value. What the model proposes is not merely paradoxes of function but a description of the essentially dialectical nature of life phenomena in general and of human relations in particular. By contrast, communication models, while descriptive of the connecting links of interpersonal existence, are monothetical and fail to explain the complexity of relationship systems.

Dialectical relationship theory retains the individual as a center of his universe but views him in an ontologically dependent interaction with his constitutive others. We propose that the main dynamic dimension of such reciprocity is anchored in the accounts of justice. Beyond the subjective antithesis between I and You, each close relationship has a bookkeeping of merits as a synthetic, quasiquantitative, and quasiobjective system characteristic. The bookkeeping includes both short-term and long-term implications of both overt and implicit relational events.

We have referred to merit as determined by personal, relational, rather than outside, value criteria. We use the term merit to describe the balance between intrinsically exploitative versus mutually enhancing aspects of any relationship. Overt exploitation is difficult enough to judge; implicit exploitation, structurally inherent in close relationships, is even more difficult to define. Dynamic psychological theory has neglected to account for the vicissitudes of justice and injustice in the human world of close relationships.

In taking this attitude, dialectical relationships theory aims at a synthesis of psychodynamic and existential phenomenological concepts of man's struggle for a good and sane life. Psychodynamic emphasis has been on rational, reality-oriented mastery of man's basic nature, while existential authors have stressed their concern about the dehumanizing effects of the material progress of our industrial age. Our relationship theory strives to define that authentic human realm in which the intrinsic balances between hidden loyalty ties and exploitations rather than functional efficiency criteria constitute "reality."

False filial respect can mask the taboos and injunctions against genuine exploration of the true relationship between one's self and one's parents. Yet learning about the authentic struggles of the older generation could lead to a more genuine respect for them. The developing dialogue of open and courageous question and answer between child and parent makes the latter more of a parent.

It is exactly the great likelihood of exploitation that makes the parent–child relationship so vulnerable to exploration. Yet the question of who is exploiting whom becomes extremely relative when it comes to close relationships. Axiomatically, no constructive resolution can be expected from intensified inculpation of the other party. That would perpetuate exploitation. What breaks the chain is exculpation of the self through exculpation of the other. The dialectic of relational dynamic prescribes that progress can at times be arrived at from an antithetically opposite direction.

The bilateral ethical and existential indebtedness inherent in the parent–child relationship makes family relations classical illustrations of the relational dialectic. The undefinable boundaries between need and obligation on either party's side make it impossible for a third party to judge the justness and fairness of any particular action on their part. The outsider does not even begin to see most of what can be counted as false respect, deceit, martyrlike guilt making, pathological parentification, etc.

Where is the boundary between an ambivalent, guilt-laden obligation and a desperate dependent hunger for a failure to receive in a relationship? A young professional describes how his mother piles chaos upon chaos with her children as he weeps over the prospect that his mother may even prefer not to die in the presence of her children. It appears that she may prefer to rely upon her younger sister for comfort after having extracted the maximum of frustrated concern from her children. From joint sessions one can observe how in both parent and child dependence interlocks with a simultaneous frustrated wish to give.

Although it would be easier to disregard the inherent retributive ethics of relationships and instead base concepts of strength, health, and normality on monothetical criteria of power, efficiency, adjustment, symptomatic improvement, and sexual competence, such traditional attitude would impoverish our grasp of relationships and of people. For example, no absolute criteria can ever describe the dialectics of interpersonal boundary as it derives from the inevitable otherness between individuals and as it leads to accompanying prejudicial projections.

Without a certain amount of projective identification we cannot maintain the boundary of our own identity.

No concept of health and pathology can ignore the hierarchy of expectations in any relationship system. The bookkeeping of the fluctuations of such hierarchy, on the other hand, has to interlock with each member's own personal definition of a quasiquantitative scale of merits and of give-and-take between the self and the other. Real strength is consistent with openness to the investigation of the obligation hierarchy of one's human world. Freedom from considering the basic merit bookkeeping of systems is deceptive and self-defeating. Physical leaving or separation without facing of the balance is at best a postponement of growth.

Finally, without a dialectically flexible openness we cannot fully explore the immense untapped potential of human relationships for prevention of suffering and for an urgently needed revision of law, education, administration, news interpretation, city-planning—to name only a few.

3
Loyalty

The concept of loyalty is an important one for the understanding of family relationships. It can have many meanings, ranging from an individual, psychological sense of loyalty to national and societal codes of civic allegiance. The concept must be defined according to the requirements of our relationship theory.

THE INVISIBLE FABRIC OF LOYALTY

The concept of loyalty can be defined in moral, philosophical, political, and psychological terms. Conventionally, it has ben described as a reliable, positive attitude of individuals toward what has been called the "object" of loyalty. The concept of a multipersonal loyalty fabric, on the other hand, implies the existence of structured group expectations to which all members are committed. In this sense loyalty pertains to what Buber called "the order of the human world."[25] Its frame of reference is trust, merit, commitment, and action, rather than the "psychological" functions of "feeling" and "knowing."

Our interest in loyalty as both a group characteristic and a personal attitude surpasses the simple behavioral notion of law-abiding behavior. We assume that in order to be a loyal member of a group, one has to internalize the spirit of its expectations and to have a set of specifiable attitudes to comply with the internalized injunctions. Ultimately, the individual can thus be subjected to the injunctions of both external expectations and internalized obligations. It is interesting and pertinent in this regard that Freud conceived of the dynamic basis of groups as related to superego function.[40]

The ethical obligation component in loyalty is first tied to the arousal in the loyalty-bound members of the sense of duty, fairness, and justice. Failure to comply with obligations leads to guilt feelings which then constitute secondary regulatory system forces. The homeostasis of the obligation or loyalty system depends thus on a regulatory input of guilt. Naturally, various members have varying degrees of guilt thresholds, and a purely guilt-regulated system is too painful to be maintained for long. Whereas the loyalty structuring is determined by the history of the group, the justice of its human order, and its myths, each individual's extent of obligation and style of complying is codetermined by the particular member's emotional set and by his merit position in the multiperson system.

The issue of loyalty fabrics in families is closely connected with those of alignments, splits, alliances, and subgroup formations, often discussed in the literature of family therapy and related studies (see Wynne,[92] in particular), Wynne has defined alignment along functional lines: "the perception or experience of two or more persons that they are joined together in a common endeavor, interest, attitude, or set of values, and that in this sector of their experience they have positive feelings toward one another."[92, p. 96] Alignments on such functional or emotional–experiential levels are significant in the changing scene of family life, but more significant relational dimensions of family alignment are based on guilt-laden loyalty issues as they are affected by the balance of reciprocal obligations and merits.

NEEDS OF THE INDIVIDUAL VERSUS NEEDS OF THE MULTIPERSON SYSTEM

Aside from the strictly heterosexual attraction, deeply rooted personal needs for positive responses from the other have traditionally been described in the psychodynamic literature in dependent, oral terms. The malfunctioning individual is seen as hungry for acceptance, attention, love, and recognition rather than actualizing his capacity for a more mature, independent goal orientation in life. Consequently, dependent motivations in an adult are usually adjudged as infantile and regressive.

Certain affiliative needs of a higher developmental nature are attributed to guilt-laden feelings of obligation, service, and self-denying sacrificial altruism. In the latter case the seeking of recognition is traditionally perceived as partly transacted between the person and his internalized, censoring parent (superego), and, secondarily, between the obligated self and the other. A more mature affiliative attitude is defined by Erikson[34] under the term "generativity." Generativity also encompasses the parenting of one's dependence on his own role via his desire for establishing and concern for guiding the next generation.

While the evolving organization of the individual's needs into a personality structure can be viewed as passing through developmental stages, the concept of the multiperson system presupposes continuous accounting of events within a reciprocal, quasiethical, or obligation-hierarchy framework. We do not imply that the family therapist has to be concerned with the prevailing religioethical value orientations of the various individuals or of the family as a whole. Instead, we are interested in the ethics of personal fairness, exploitation, and reciprocity. Although it seems to be in keeping with current sophisticated parlance to ignore it, any social group must rely on an ethical network or else face that aspect of disintegration which Durkheim described under "anomie."[32]

The concept of loyalty is fundamental to the understanding of the ethics, i.e., the deeper relational structuring of families and other social groups. The special meaning of the term loyalty must be defined for the purpose of this chapter. Dynamically, loyalty can be defined according to its sustaining principles. Members of a group may behave loyally out of external coercion, conscious recognition of interest in membership, consciously recognized feelings of obligation, and unconsciously binding obligation to belong. Whereas external coercion can be visible to outside observers and consciously felt interest or obligation can be reported by members, unconscious commitments to a group can only be inferred from complex, indirect clues, often only after prolonged acquaintance with the person and the group concerned. Ultimately, loyalty in a family will depend on each individual's position within the justice of his human world, which in turn constitutes a part of the intergenerational family account of merits. Once alerted to the significance of loyalty commitments, the family therapist is in an advantageous position for studying both the individual and the system manifestations of relational forces and structural determinants.

Loyalty commitments are like invisible but strong fibers which hold together complex pieces of relationship "behavior" in families as well as in larger society. To understand the functions of a group of people, nothing is more crucial than to know who are bound together in loyalty and what loyalty means for them. Each person maintains a bookkeeping of his perception of the balances of past, present, and future give-and-take. What has been "invested" into the system through availability and what has been withdrawn in the form of support received or one's exploitative use of the others remains written into the invisible accounts of obligations.

Perhaps no age has mass produced children who grow up without responsible parenting on as large a scale as ours. Our society might ultimately be burdened by profoundly resentful and justifiably disloyal citizens, as long as children are being mass produced by parents who do not intend or are emotionally unable to care for them. All authorities, all loyal members of society or the whole world may then be justifiable targets for the frustrated revenge of those who were essentially betrayed in the cradle. They will become easy prey to prejudice-mongering demagogues. Naturally, children can be exploited in many subtly covert ways. Manifest abandonment can only be a partial reason. All aspects of relationships which tend to keep a child captive in a relational imbalance tend to become exploitative without personal intent for unfair gain on anyone's part.

When we talk of a "bond of loyalty," we imply more than reliable (accountable) commitments for mutual availability among several individuals. In addition, they owe a shared loyalty to the principles and symbolic definitions of the group. The biological existential basis of family loyalty consists of bonds of consanguinity and marriage. Nations, religious groups, families, professional groups, etc., have their own myths and legends to which each member is expected to be loyal. National loyalty is based on cultural identity definition, common territory, and shared history. Religious groups share certain faiths, convictions, and norms. History, by keeping accounts of past persecutions and other injustices, reinforces intragroup loyalty.

In families, as well as in other groups, the most fundamental loyalty commitment pertains to maintenance of the group itself. We have to go beyond conscious behavioral manifestations and specific issues if we want to understand the meaning of basic loyalty commitments. What seems to be shockingly destructive and irritating behavior on the part of one member towards another, may not be experienced as such by the participants, if the behavior conforms to a basic family loyalty. For instance, two siblings may owe it to their parents to maximalize their jealous rivalry so that the parents' marital failure can be masked.

The novice therapist usually lacks an explicit and operationally useful orientation to the issue of family loyalty. He may want to help, for example, the feuding parents of an 18-year-old daughter by trying to clarify their overtly very garbled and desperately hostile communications. He may not realize that the parents' confusing interaction may at the same time serve a highly invested purpose in terms of family loyalty: It delays the emotional separation and eventual outside (heterosexual) involvement of the adolescent daughter. Though it may delay individuation and separation, it may also balance excessive guilt over ingratitude in the emancipating adolescent. The parents' implicit dependent demand on the daughter may also neutralize their feelings of having been exploited through their devotion to the parenting role. The degree of their actual exploitation is, of course, codetermined by the extent of their unsettled accounts within their respective families of origin. The unconsciously parentified child may be used for a delayed rebalancing of the parents' accounts with their parents.

It is not easy to assess the adolescent's or young adult's true readiness for outside commitments. He may appear ready for physical separation and heterosexual involvement, but at his core he may be very reluctant to enter into a loyalty bond with anyone outside the family. It is difficult to define in any family which acts of seeming rejection serve, paradoxically, to avert the adolescent's premature individuation—a threat to family loyalty. Aggressive attacks, insulting neglect, physical departure, withdrawal of respect, etc., can all hurt the parents and yet not touch the basic question of loyalty. Overt roles and verbal attitudes rarely explain the status of underlying deep commitment. A "sick" or "bad" member may effectively complement the role of an outstanding, socially creative other member. Loyalty ethics often conflict with the ethic of self-control. A mother who says to her teenage daughter: "You can go out and have a good time as long as you tell me all about it," may be prepared to retain her daughter's loyalty commitment, at the price of sexual permissiveness, perhaps forever.

Loyalty systems can be based on both latent, cognitively unformulated, preconscious collaboration among members and on formulated "myths" of families. Their power can be disguised most of the time, but their effects can emerge and become tangible under the threat of disengagement by a member or when the impact of the therapy process begins to disturb the homeostatic balance of the system. By definition, growth or maturation on any member's part implies a degree of personal loss and relational imbalance.

Loyalty bonds may be considered as operationally implemented via relationship techniques, yet they themselves are of the nature of *aims* rather than *means* of relational existence. They are the substance of group survival. Reliable ways of measuring the extent of loyalty commitments do not exist, as a result of our lack of understanding even of their main dimensions.

Existential involvement in quantification of loyalty can be illustrated by the common joke about the pig and the chicken. When these two found out that they are brought together only for the production of ham and eggs, the pig keenly felt the disparity of involvement: "You are being asked only for a contribution whereas they expect total commitment from me." (Further attempts at quantification of commitments will be found in Chapter 4.)

Insight into the particular meaning of its loyalty is fundamental to the understanding of the deep structure or dynamics of any social group. The loyal member will strive to align his own interest with that of the group. Not only does he participate in the pursuits of his group and share their point of view, but he will subscribe to or at least carefully consider their ethical code of behavior. The relational criteria of loyalty should be construed from the member's behavior, conscious thought, and unconscious attitudes. From the outsider's point of view, the member's loyalty may appear overt or covert. The overt codes, myths, and rituals always have their more important covert counterparts in unconsciously collusive or exploitative patterns of group function.

Origins of loyalty go back to various sources. Familial loyalty is characteristically based on biological, hereditary kinship. In-law relationships usually have weaker loyalty impact than ties of consanguinity. External coercion may control, though not necessarily determine, loyalty to many social groups. Sometimes, it is the recognition of shared interests which leads to voluntary identification with the group. On the other hand, familial loyalty or loyalty to one's school or place of work can be reinforced by gratitude for or guilt over unrequited meritorious performance of those elders who gave self-denying attention and generous gifts of love to the young. Gratitude towards and recognition of the value of one's elders tends to lead to internalization of obligations by adopting their value system, consciously and unconsciously.

The etymology of the word loyalty points to the French root *loi* or law, and thus it implies law-abiding attitudes. Families have their own laws in the form of unwritten shared expectations. Each family member is constantly subject to varying patterns of expectations to which he does or does not comply. Young children's compliance is enforced by outside disciplinary measures. Older children and adults may comply out of internalized loyalty commitments.

Loyalty as an *individual's* attitude thus encompasses identification with the group, genuine object relatedness with other members, trust, reliability, responsibility, dutiful commitment, faithfulness, and staunch devotion. The expectation hierarchy of the *group*, on the other hand, connotes an unwritten code of social regulation and social sanctions. Internalization of expectations and injunctions in the loyal individual provide structural psychological forces which can coerce the individual just as much as external enforcement within the group. Without having a claim for their deeper loyalty commitment, no group can exert a high level of motivational pressure on its membership.

As we suggest that understanding of loyalty commitments provides the clue to important, covert system determinants of human motivation, we also realize that we depart from the concept of deeper motivations as traditionally restricted to the psychology of the individual. Consequently, any satisfactory relationship theory must succeed in connecting individual motivational with multipersonal or relational system concepts.

Phenomenological and existential studies have emphasized the ontic rather than functional dependence of man on his relationships. The writings of Martin Buber, Gabriel Marcel, and Jean Paul Sartre are examples of this school of thinking. Man, suspended in ontological anxiety, experiences a groundless void if he cannot establish a meaningful personal dialogue with someone or something. Ontically meaningful relationships must be motivated by mutually interlocking patterns of past and present concern and caring, on the one hand, and of possible exploitation, on the other. From this ontic dependence of all members on their relationship with one another arises a main component of the superordinate, multiperson level of relationship systems. The sum of all ontologically dependent mutual dyads within a family constitutes a main source of group loyalty. The family therapist must be able to conceive of a social group whose members all relate to one another according to Buber's I–Thou dialogue. If the therapist disregards such an understanding, he will fail to differentiate between family and accidental group relationships, perhaps even in his own family.

Dependency is usually defined by the needs of the individuals involved. After Freud we think about human motivations in terms of needs, drives, desires, wishful fantasies, and instinct—all of them individually based concepts. The family therapist will have to keep in mind, however, that the bridge between closely related persons is built more by actions and intentions than by thought and feelings. The framework that holds a relationship together relies on an ethical fabric that pervades the members' intentions and actions:

Have you proven to me that you can hear me, consider me, and care for me? If your actions prove that you do, it is natural for me to feel and act loyal to you, i.e., to consider you and your needs. You oblige me through your openness. Even though we may appear to an outsider like two fighting enemies, only we can judge whether, when, and how one of us might have broken and betrayed our mutual loyalty bond. Our seeming fight may be our way of rebalancing the accounts of reciprocity.

The implications of the above vignette for family therapy are obvious. Psychoanalysts or psychotherapists tend to assume that intensity, depth, and relevance of treatment reach their utmost in the confidential privacy of the individual therapeutic relationship, and that any decrease in one-to-one privacy is bound to lead to a more superficial (supportive, educational, behavior modification) therapeutic involvement. Yet experience has shown that the main effect of the relational or family treatment approach consists not only in *amplification* but in *escalation* of therapeutic involvement. Working with all partners in a relationship network makes "depth" issues and connections unavoidable, provided the therapist can empathize with people and is sufficiently aware of the subjective meaning of reciprocal binds of indebtedness made invisible through denial.

The family therapist must learn to distinguish between the elementary fabric of loyalty commitment systems and their secondary manifestations and elaborations. For example, a symbiotic overcommitment between a married woman and her mother has to be recognized and therapeutically explored even though it may consciously manifest itself as a hostile, rejecting pattern. The overt quality of the relationship (e.g., avoidance, scapegoating, passionate warfare) is less significant in determining therapeutic outcome than the extent of investment and the degree of unresolved and denied obligations within each partner.

The individual's dynamic interrelatedness with his human environment is a personal one, and it cannot be pertinently characterized by concepts like "general cultural pattern," "average expectable environment," or "interpersonal techniques." In Chapters 4 and 5 we suggest that man's relationship to his context is governed by a balance of fairness or justice. The fact that societies and families keep a bookkeeping account of merit is underestimated in social science literature. Our age is accustomed to renouncing issues of ethical consequence as dynamic factors. Having been raised with a positivistic and pragmatistic overvaluation of science, we are inclined to doubt whether there are any valid ethical issues left between hypocrisy on the one hand and neurotic guilt feelings on the other.

Among psychoanalytic authors Erikson has emphasized the genetically social character of the human individual: "The phenomenon and the concept of *social organization,* and its bearing on the individual ego was, thus, for the longest time, shunted off by patronizing tributes to the existence of 'social factors.' "[34, p. 19] Writing about the origins of basic trust he says: "Mothers create a sense of trust in their children by that kind of administration which in its quality combines sensitive care of the baby's individual needs and a firm sense of personal trustworthiness within the trusted framework of their community's life style."[34, p. 63]

Trustworthiness thus implies the concept of proven merit. Furthermore, the phrase "trusted framework of their community" points at a source of trust which is located in the social background outside mother and child. As the parenting environment "earns" trustworthiness in the eyes of the child, the child becomes a debtor to his mother and to all those who have given him trust by the worthiness of their intentions and actions. The system itself begins to place structured ethical demands and expectations on the child long before this sort of obligation has a chance of becoming conscious. Furthermore, as long as the child lives, he will never be really free of the existential indebtedness to his parents and family. The more one's environment was worthy of trust, the more one gets indebted; the less one has been able to repay the benefits received, the higher will be the accumulating debt.

The reader may wish to interpret this point in a psychological rather than existential–relational framework, but we are not referring to a "pathology" of neurotic guilt feelings. We simply refer to the fact of existential indebtedness which results from having been taken care of by the parenting others in a trustworthy manner. Erikson's expression, "the trusted framework of their community," just like Buber's term, "justice of the human world," imply that many personal relationships, spanning several generations, may be required to build up an atmosphere of balance between trust and mistrust.

In the course of marital therapy a young husband describes his lasting unresolvable indebtedness to his parents. The reason for this is not only that they tried to give him the best educational, etc., opportunities, but that he was a recurrent troublemaker and that his father used to bail him out of many tight situations with courts, police, schools, etc. In response, his wife exclaims: "Do you think that our children will also owe us that much?" It should be noted that the problem of this couple revealed the kind of loyalty conflict which other couples uncover only gradually: The husband was torn between his obligations to his parents and to his wife. In this family there was also an overt and actual friction between the two families of origin. The wife's loyalty conflict took more complex expressions. She seemed to be eager to wage a war with her in-laws, and she also admitted a feeling of frustration about lack of closeness in her own family of origin.

In most families it is possible to discover the ways in which members have been victimized by unbalanced loyalty expectations and by being drawn into mutually vindictive, displaced balancing efforts. It is up to the family therapist to begin, at least in his own mind, to map out the confusing and destructive exchanges within their appropriate multigenerational perspective. Gradually, as family members learn that an apparent victimizer was once himself a victim, a more balanced view of merit reciprocity among members may develop. The bookkeeping of merit and loyalty obligations helps to elucidate the interlocking between system expectations and each individual's "need templates."

The system concept does not invalidate the motivational significance of each member's internalized patterns, i.e., his repetitious wishes for the replication of certain early relational experiences. Many of the various individuals' actions and attitudes can be derived from knowledge of their respective internalized relational orientations. Yet the bookkeeping of merit within the total system has its own factual reality and corresponding motivational structuring throughout the generations. At each marriage it is not just bride and groom who are to be joined but also two family systems of merit. Without an ability to intuitively perceive the prospective mate as a nodal point in a loyalty fabric, one gets married to the wishfully improved recreation of one's own family of origin. Each mate may then struggle to unwittingly coerce the other to be accountable for his or her felt injustices and accrued merits from the family of origin.

Viewed from the perspective of invisible loyalties, family relationships tend to obtain a more relevant, coherent meaning in the eyes of the therapist. Family myths gradually reveal their understructure as an indigenous merit bookkeeping which is overtly or covertly shared by the members. The guilt feelings of individuals are seen to correspond to the contours of the merit configuration. Patterns of visible "pathological" or "normal" behavior constitute the next system level. For example, scapegoating of individuals is often determined by shared loyalty to the merit system as defined and described by the family myth. Eventually, it begins to make sense to the family therapist why individuals let themselves be willingly sacrificed in order to honor the multigenerational chains of obligation and existential indebtedness.

TRANSGENERATIONAL ACCOUNTING OF OBLIGATIONS AND MERIT

The origins of loyalty commitments are typically dialectical in nature. Their internalized pattern originates from something owed to a parent or to an internalized image of a parent representation (superego). In a three generational system repayment for the instilling of norms and for care and concern given to us by our parents may go to our children, unrelated others, or to the internalized parents. Loyalty commitments are restricted ordinarily to certain areas of function, usually connected with the raising or training of children. As the adult is eager to impart his own normative value orientation to his child, he now becomes the "creditor" in a dialogue of commitments, in which his child becomes the "debtor." The debtor will eventually have to settle his debt in the intergenerational feedback system by internalizing the expected commitments, by living up to the expectations, and eventually by transmitting them to his offspring. Each act of repayment of reciprocal obligation will raise the level of loyalty and trust within the relationship.

The criteria of the "health" of the family obligation system can be defined as capacity for propagation of offspring, and compatibility with the eventual emotional individuation of the members. Individuation should be viewed as being balanced against the loyalty obligations of the maturing child toward the nuclear family. Its definition and measure can be better expressed in terms of capacity for balancing old and new loyalty commitments rather than in functional or accomplishment terms. The potential or freedom for new involvements (e.g., engagement, marriage, parenthood) has to be weighed against old obligations which pull toward lasting symbiotic togetherness.

The measure of symbiotic committedness to one's family of origin is difficult to assess if the commitments have become internalized and structuralized while what appears on the surface is a neglect of family relationships. We see persons who are rigidly attached to self-destructive patterns continue on in an unresolved or seemingly unresolvable loyalty impasse with their family of origin:

A 16-year-old boy was referred by the court because of what the worker described as "chaotic living, truanting, and multiple drug use to the point of personality disintegration."

In the first family interview also attended by the boy's separated parents and two married sisters, a largely different picture emerged. The entire family was suffering from a variety of personal and marital problems which they tried to present in alleged isolation from each other. They all seemed to be worried, at least on the covert level, about the ultimate outcome of the parents' marital alienation. Who was responsible for the fact that 10 years ago the then 20-year-old marriage led to separation? The family members kept leaving almost in regular intervals: father first, then the older daughter got married, then the younger daughter, then the older son moved to another town. The 16-year-old boy was left as the last one to stay with the depressed, anxious, and obese mother.

While on the overt level this boy was conducting an irresponsible, pleasure-determined life, on the family loyalty level he performed a valuable sacrifice for the entire family. "I know I don't live responsibly," he said, "it is no fun to be responsible. When I have to be responsible, I will." In effect, the self-destructive pattern of his living served as an assurance that as the last member he is not capable of leaving mother.

The therapeutic effect of both making the loyalty aspects of this boy's behavior visible and exploring the direct personal implications of the parents' relationship led to a striking behavioral change within weeks: The boy acquired a job which he then kept for months. Simultaneously, though temporarily, the mother in turn lost her job and thus, for a while, more overtly depended on her son. Eventually, she was able to obtain a much more gratifying job about which she had always dreamt but never dared to undertake.

A commitment to nonindividuation was even less visibly loyalty bound in the lives of the two daughters. The younger daughter was at first more able to concede that she needed help with her own life. She stated that she was married to an alcoholic like her father and that her marriage was frighteningly similar to her parents' marriage. The older daughter first hesitated to acknowledge her need for help. Yet in the course of the next few months of treatment she became the most actively participating member of the family therapy sessions. She revealed her deeply disturbing marital impasse and was even able to invite her husband to participate in the sessions. As it turned out, she felt that her mother was living vicariously through her life and that an atmosphere of constant anxious tension prevailed between herself and her mother. She never felt enough moral courage to risk hurting her mother's feelings and discuss her dissatisfactions with her. Ultimately, she reported great gains after being able to openly discuss their triangular, amorphous emotional entanglement.

The more rigidly the maturing child is tied to his parents with invisible loyalty commitments, the more difficult it will be for him to replace the original loyalty with a new relational commitment. As the new commitment leads to marriage and parenthood, it is far easier to develop a deeply loyal devotion to one's child than to one's spouse. The inherent right and merit of a helpless infant to be cared for is probably the strongest factor to counterbalance his parent's guilt over loosening his own life-long filial obligations. Thus, the rewards of parenthood include, aside from the obvious possessive gain, the exoneration from guilt of disloyalty through fulfillment of an obligation. Parenthood is a unique chance to pay reparation for internally sensed guilt over imputed disloyalty.

GUILT AND ETHICAL IMPLICATIONS

The loyalty system point of view thus implies that commitment to one's spouse may be secondary to an implicit indebtedness to the not-yet-born offspring. In all traditional societies young married couples must have been far less vulnerable to the guilt of disloyalty than their modern counterparts in urban, industrialized communities. The fact that parents used to arrange for the marital choice of their children helped the young couple to escape guilt. They were able to feel free to even project responsibility for their marital frictions upon the choice initiated by their parents.

As an interesting extension of these arguments, we can examine their implications for the origins of sexual guilt and social taboos for heterosexuality. In addition to the moral trespass implications of any pleasure and the ethical significance of responsibility for a potential new human life, one of the deepest roots of *sexual guilt* and *inhibition* must be based on fear of disloyalty to the family of origin. As heterosexual involvement leads to the prospect of production of offspring, it should effectively disrupt the adolescent's or the young adult's filial loyalty. The structure of this guilt is different from Oedipal guilt which is based on the concept of a triangular, heterosexual jealousy between child and parents.

It is common to see a breakdown of symbiotically loyal, young individuals at the point of their first heterosexual infatuation. One young girl connected her psychotic breakdown with sexual guilt over having to shut her parents' bedroom door while "necking" with her boyfriend during the late hours. Ordinarily, it was a family rule that no bedroom doors were to be shut at night. Symbolically the channeling of loyalties seemed to be hinged where the doors were. Many married persons discover their inability to form loyalty ties with their spouses only after the initial glow of sexual attraction has worn off. It may take family treatment to fully face the extent of the invisible commitments that they have retained towards their families of origin. They feel that an undischarged obligation to repay their parents, no matter how undeserving, deprives them of the right to enjoyment.

Most of these people have no difficulty with recognizing and accepting their loyalty to their children. The ethical demands of parenthood are so strong that they are seldom violated even if a tremendous amount of personal sacrifice is required. It is rare (as in child abuse) that a child is sacrificed to counterbalance the parent's filial disloyalty. It is more common to observe the scapegoat role assigned to the mate or to the in-laws.

In the so-called ghetto or slum families the situation seems to differ somewhat from middle-class patterns of family loyalties. Middle-class morality expects responsible parenthood to be based on a "respectable" marital relationship. A sizable proportion of poverty families, aided by the welfare system, are inclined to bypass the marriage requirement with the help of strong reliance on the maternal family of origin and on the exploitation of the somewhat older children. In these amorphous, large, matrilineal systems there is no requirement for a clearcut shift from filial to parental loyalty commitment—the infant is born to the family, as it were. In some cases grandmother is more of an actual parent than mother. The conflict here may center on whether the young mother can afford to become sufficiently committed to motherhood or whether she owes it to bestow her infant on her mother as a proof of her unchanging loyalty.

The struggles about loyalty commitments often remain invisible, and only secondary rationalizations are accessible, even to the participants. In one family we were beginning to believe that the father was indeed a complete failure until we discovered that all six of the mother's siblings had marriages in which the spouse was regarded worthless. At the same time the mutual reliance of the seven siblings was foremost, and little effort was given to hiding their mutual preference for each other over their respective spouses.

Marriages, love affairs, paramours, and homosexual "spouses" can all be (often unconsciously) used for the purpose of reinforcing, rather than replacing, filial loyalty commitment. Flaunting these attachments in front of one's parents may amount to a reinforcement of the old devotion by testing it through a new challenge, by making the parents jealous. When the loud battle seems to indicate imminent emotional separation between the young adult and his family of origin, the outside observer can underestimate the extent of underlying, never-changing loyalty.

From the viewpoint of multiperson systems, we are interested in the role of deeply ingrained loyalties which are seemingly directed at extrafamilial objects. Religion is a typical area for deep devotion and fundamental loyalty ties. We have seen the importance of this issue magnified in families of mixed religious background. When both spouses reject their loyalty to their religious backgrounds, an implicit alliance of loyalty is formed between them at the expense of religion and, symbolically, of the family of origin. The spouses, by cutting relationships with their respective in-groups, form a new loyalty structure by default, so to speak. Yet the family therapist must tend to wonder whether the displacement of the separation issue to the religious area means that these parents have not resolved their separation from their own parents and that their children will be put into a bind of an even more intricate, invisible loyalty.

INTERGENERATIONAL STRUCTURING OF LOYALTY CONFLICTS

As generation follows generation, vertical loyalty commitments keep conflicting with horizontal ones. Vertical loyalty commitments are owed to either a previous or a subsequent generation; horizontal loyalty commitments are owed to one's mate, siblings, or peers in general. The establishment of new relationships, especially through marriage and the birth of children, raises the necessity of new loyalty commitments. The more rigid the original loyalty system, the more severe the challenge for the individual: Whom do you choose, me, him, or her?

As the developmental phases of the nuclear family evolve, all members face new demands for adjustment. Adjustment does not mean a final resolution, a closing of a previous phase but a continuing tension to rebalance old but surviving expectations with new ones. Birth, growth, sibling struggles, individuation, separation, preparation for parenthood, aging of grandparents and finally mourning over the lost ones are examples of situations which demand rebalancing of loyalty obligations.

Instances of developmentally required transitions of loyalty are connected with the following expectations:

1. Young parents have to shift their loyalty from their families of origin towards each other; they now owe each other sexual fidelity and nurturance. They have also become a team to produce the offspring.

2. They owe a redefined loyalty to their families of origin—their national, cultural, and religious backgrounds and their values.

3. They owe loyalty to children born out of their relationship.

4. Children owe a redefined loyalty to their parents and to the older generation.

5. Siblings owe loyalty to each other.

6. Blood-related family members owe avoidance of sexual relations among themselves, yet they owe an affectionate relating to one another.

7. Fathers owe support to their nuclear families while they continue owing support to their aging or incapacitated parents and relatives too.

8. Mothers owe homemaking and child rearing care to their nuclear families, but they are expected to be available to their family of origin as well.

9. Family members owe a solidarity in how they behave towards friends or strangers, but they also owe good citizenship to society.

10. All members owe loyalty to maintaining the entire family system, but they should be prepared to accommodate the new relationships and the resulting changes of the system.

A classical example of unresolved loyalty conflict between marriage and families of origin is the story of Romeo and Juliet. Shakespeare's prologue summarizes the familial meaning of the tragic death of the two lovers: "The fearful passage of their death marked love, And the continuance of their parents' rage, Which, but their children's end, naught could remove, Is now the two hours' traffic of our stage."

Loyalty, a key concept of this book has been described as a motivational determinant which has self–other dialectical, multipersonal, rather than individual roots. Though etymologically loyalty is a derivative of the French word for law, its real nature lies in the invisible fabric of group expectations instead of manifest law. The invisible fibers of loyalty consist of consanguinity, maintenance of biological life and family lineage on the one hand and earned merit among members on the other. It is in this sense related to a familial atmosphere of trust, built on reliable availability and proven deserts of the other members. The next level of conceptualization requires the description of justice as a systemic realm for coding or at least describing the balance of loyalty expectations.

4
Justice and
Social Dynamics

Perhaps the reader may feel that our terminology is unfamiliar or alien to his own professional conceptual framework. We could have used, for instance, the language of behavioral-interactionalism or psychodynamic-individual psychology. We could have stressed the inevitable "power game" elements implicit in the victimization of the mate, the grandparent, or the therapist as they may occur in succession during family treatment. However, we have felt that it is more important to explore the motivational layer in which hope resides for repairing the hurt human justice.

The reason for introducing justice as a major dynamic concept in family theory issues from the significance of loyalty patterns in the organization and regulation of close relationships. In order to conceptualize loyalty as a system force rather than merely as a disposition of individuals, we have had to consider the existence of an invisible ledger which keeps an account of past and present obligations among family members. The nature of the ledger interlocks with the phenomena of psychology; it has a multiperson, systemic factuality. Reciprocal gratification as a goal transcends the individual's needs by definition. The individual family member's "slate," so to speak, is already loaded before he begins to act. Depending on whether his parents were overly devoted or neglectful, he is born into a field of greater or lesser obligations. The fact that his parents and their ancestors were all caught in similar expectations and had to balance filial with parental obligations makes it necessary to think of the ledger as a multigenerational structure. The structure of expectations makes up the fabric of loyalties and, together with the accounts of actions, the ledger of justice.

The invisible familial ledger of justice is a relational context, it is the dynamically most significant component of the individual's world, although it is not external to him. The essence of his realm is related to the ethics of relationships and it cannot be mastered by intelligence or shrewdness alone. Some of the least trusting and least just people may master their human environment mainly through rational calculations which fail to do justice to their own ultimate needs as whole human beings.

Furthermore, justice is an existential given. The child's indebtedness to the parent is determined by the parent's being, quantity and quality of his availability and active ministrations. Similarly, exploitation does not necessarily require intentional unfairness of others, it may result from structural properties of close relationships. The subjective injustice of any member's position in the family relationship system may determine much of what will be diagnosed as paranoid personality formation.

Thus, though motivationally we must consider other factors in loyalty —ties of blood, love, ambivalence, common interest, external threats, etc.—we have been interested in the structure of reciprocal obligations itself. We postulate that deeper, long-range motivations have their own familial, systemic homeostasis, even if its criteria are less visible than, e.g., those of problem solving or manifest symptomatic role shifts, etc. The family therapist can be greatly helped in his work by the knowledge of the deeper relational determinants of visible behavior.

We believe that the concept of justice of the human order is a common denominator for individual, familial, and societal dynamics. Individuals who have not learned a sense of justice within their family relationships are likely to have a distorted judgment of social justice. The family therapist can learn to sharpen his perception of that order of justice, fairness, or reciprocity which determines the degree of trust and loyalty in family relationships. Justice can be regarded as a web of invisible fibers running through the length and width of the history of family relationships, holding the system in social equilibrium throughout phases of physical togetherness and separation. Perhaps nothing is as significant in determining the relationship between parent and child as the degree of fairness of expected filial gratitude.

At this point the reader might ask whether he is faced with concepts extraneous to the traditions of psychotherapy and psychological theory, even if considered in a broader sense. Is justice a concept which should belong to law or religion rather than to a study of human motivations? After having eliminated concepts which imply individual, psychological, or merely superficially interactional connotations as unsatisfactory, we could have chosen "reciprocity imbalance" to avoid the value connotations of the word justice. We purposely chose the word justice because we feel that it connotes human commitment and value in all their rich motivating power and meaning.

The idea of justice as a relational dynamic originates from the system implications and existential connotations of guilt and obligation. In individual psychodynamic theory, guilt is assumed to result from infringements of taboos that the individual has internalized from his elders. The concept of justice, on the other hand, views the individual in a multidirectional ethical and existential balance with others. He "inherits" transgenerational commitments. He is obligated to those who raised him and is in a field of reciprocal exchanges of give-and-take with his contemporaries. He also faces his essentially unilateral obligations towards his dependent, young children.

Justice has a particular relevance for family life. Reciprocal equity, the traditional framework for assessing justice among adults, fails as a guideline when it comes to the balance of the parent–child relationship. Every parent finds himself in an asymmetrically obliged position toward his newborn. The child has a source of unearned rights. Society does not expect him to repay the parent in equivalent benefits.

Society itself as a whole can be charged with unearned guilt as far as each emerging generation is concerned. Whereas few contemporary white Americans would accept guilt for the enslaving of hundreds of thousands of Africans several generations ago, the impact of slavery has affected the justice of black children for a number of generations. It is reasonable to assume that the white person who wants to deny or ignore the current and continuous implications of past slavery for the justice of black citizens is guilty of what Martin Luther King called "covering misdeeds with a cloak of forgetfulness."[71, p. 409] However, justice as a social determinant could still be conceptualized in unidirectional and monothetical concepts of good and bad. A relational concept of sensitive concern with the fairness of obligations should not be confused with abstract notions of economic power distribution based on assumed equality.

The fact that the individual must balance unearned and stored accounts of justice and injustice necessitates the assumption of an implicit quantification of equity exchanges—an invisible ledger, a transgenerational bookkeeping of merits. Merit connotes a subjectively weighed property which cannot be objectively quantified as material benefits can be. Webster's Third International Dictionary defines merit as, "spiritual credit or stored moral surplusage regarded as earned by performance or righteous acts and as ensuring future benefits."[89] Every loyal relationship is based on earned or unearned merit and justice is concerned with the distribution of merit in a whole relationship system.

FAIRNESS AND RECIPROCITY

The crucial significance of justice for cohesion of social structures has been recognized by sociologists. Gouldner[47] analyses the meaning of "reciprocity" of transactions. Reciprocity is defined as mutuality of benefits or gratifications, and Gouldner states: "The *norm* of reciprocity is a concrete and special mechanism involved in the maintenance of any stable social system."[47, p. 174] Although we agree with the sociological view that a "generalized norm of reciprocity" becomes internalized in the members of social systems, as family therapists we want to focus on a multiperson or systemic ledger of justice which resides in the interpersonal fabric of human order or "realm of the between."[26] The ledger comprises all those cumulative disparities of reciprocity which are inherent in the group's past history of interactions. It is the basis for the equivalency of returns. The weight of past, unrequited merit transactions modifies the equivalency of the mutually contingent exchange of benefits in ongoing interpersonal relationships. Nonreceiving parents affect the ledger and therefore the personality development of their children differently than nongiving parents.

In examining the dynamic significance of justice, obligation, loyalty, and the ethical fiber of groups, one of the most important issues is the one of *exploitation*. Ordinarily, exploitation is connected with the concepts of power, wealth, and domination. A much broader and more relevant conceptual framework is required for an understanding of the true dialectic of relational exploitation in families. We propose that the concept of exploitation be discussed as a basis for a quasiquantitative treatment of merit accounting. Exploitation is a relative concept which encompasses an implicit quantification. Shifts in power positions are unreliable measures of exploitation; there are ways in which a parent, boss, or leader can be exploited by those in lesser power positions.

The concept of exploitation is frequently implied during spontaneous arguments between family members. Parents tend to compare the "amount" of concern and affection they are expected to give their children with what they have allegedly received from their parents. They seem to be searching for an intrinsic balance. Grown-ups may be able to articulate retrospectively how they were "robbed" of their childhood by having to play judge to their constantly arguing parents. Sexual relations are often viewed as selfish and exploitative by wives who complain that they are not experiencing enough satisfaction or by husbands who feel that they are manipulated through sexual favors. Traditionally, incest is viewed as exploitation of the child by one parent. However, a closer look at the underlying family dynamics of incest reveals at minimum a three-person interactional system which includes the failing marital relationship of the parents as an added component.

It is especially important to understand the implications of the child's role as the unwitting potential exploiter of a parent, since the child "deserves" to receive in exchange for nothing. Many parents feel that they are not permitted to complain about their sense of being exploited, and they unconsciously cover their feelings with overprotectiveness, overpermissiveness, martyrlike devotion, or other defensive attitudes. Combined with a sense of being exploited by their family of origin, these feelings can tip the balance of motivation towards serious child abuse. Furthermore, if parents persistently make it difficult for their children to repay their obligations, they undermine another dimension in the system of balanced reciprocity in the family. A full dialogue requires a mutuality of both giving and acceptance of giving.

Important considerations of exploitation can arise in unequally committed heterosexual relationships. For example, the traditional restrictive and overprotective attitudes toward female sexual behavior have tended to view a rejected girl as the exploited one, especially if her romantic infatuation was not matched by a corresponding sentiment on her lover's part. Yet many discarded lovers contend that despite the acute pain of loss, it is better to be courted and jilted than not to have been courted by the object of their passion. The balance between receiving and being used is an intrinsic property of every relationship which can be understood only in its relationship to all other balances of justice.

PERSONAL VERSUS STRUCTURAL EXPLOITATION

The concept of reciprocity as a relational system dynamic can imply two major kinds of exploitation: First, one family member can be exploited, overtly or subtly, by another through nongiving or nonreciprocal taking. This person-to-person exploitativeness must be distinguished from the second kind, structural exploitation. The latter originates from system characteristics which victimize both participants at the same time.

The meaning of the word retribution includes either reward or punishment given or exacted in recompense. A relationship can develop between two people in such manner that it denies both participants the chance for all or certain aspects of balanced retribution. Undischarged revengeful feelings are just one aspect of such fixed relational imbalance. A parent may be suffering from hunger for recognition and gratitude while his child is choked with an unexpressed and unrecognized wish for showing filial gratitude. Similarly, a child may be hungry for a corrective, angrily chastizing response from a parent which the parent is unable or unwilling to put forth. Undischarged love and revenge are fundamental strategic considerations of a relationship; issues of whether the parents should agree in front of the children or how good a "team" they are in disciplining the children are of secondary, tactical significance.

We must stress how important it is, particularly in family relationships, to define the specific issues of reciprocity—especially those beyond the material realm. Power here is definable in different terms than in society at large. What appears to be weak, chaotic, or fragmented family relationships may present the strongest bind for the members because of inherent guilt and excessive devotion. The accumulated merit accounts of both present and previous generations affect the baseline for the accounts of what may appear as a balance of current functional reciprocity. Gouldner[47] mentions disparities of reciprocity which are introduced by the different power positions of the members of any social group. For instance, the powerful partner can maintain an asymmetrical relationship despite giving less to the weak one than he receives in return. Other compensatory mechanisms for maintaining disparity of reciprocity include attitudes of "turning the other cheek," *noblesse oblige,* and clemency.[47, p. 164]

We know that in families unsettled obligations do survive from the past and that they may compensate for present imbalances of gratitude, guilt over nondelivered obligations, anger over exploitation, etc. An imbalance concerning the equity of merit or exchange of benefits between two or more partners in relationships registers subjectively as an exploitation by the other.

QUANTITATIVE ASPECTS

Gouldner implies that reciprocity has an intrinsic quantitative measure, determined by the extent of equity in exchanges. On one extreme there is the full equity of exchanged benefits and, on the other, the situation in which one party gives nothing in return for benefits received. Between these two limiting cases lie a variety of seeming or real exploitations.

The question of how to define equivalence of mutually exchanged benefits is a key issue in parent–child relationships. The youngest infant requires the most care and concern from the mother, yet, paradoxically, most women experience more gratification in caring for infants than for older children. Then how does the baby give to the adult and how can we measure the degree of equivalence in the mutual give-and-take of their day-to-day relationships? In the language of sociology one can speak of *heteromorphic* "tit for tat" and *homeomorphic* "tat for tat" reciprocity.[47, p. 172] As Gouldner suggests, homeomorphic reciprocity must have been important in early societies as their talionic measure of punishment and reparation for crimes. Gouldner adds, "We should also expect to find mechanisms which induce people to *remain* socially indebted to each other and which *inhibit* their complete repayment." He quotes a Seneca Indian statement to illustrate this point: "A person who wants to repay a gift too quickly with a gift in return is an unwilling debtor and an ungrateful person."[47, p. 175]. How many forms of parental refusal to accept repayment on the part of the child fit this model?

SYSTEM LEVELS OF BOOKKEEPING

Ultimately, the considerations of justice and reciprocity bring us back to the issue of levels of depth of inquiry. Equivalence of exchanged benefits is easiest to assess when the exchanges are superficial or material. However, the more important layers of motivation are connected with a private, imponderable range of interactions. In order to be able to grow, one must recognize and deal with the invisible bonds originating from one's formative period of growth. Otherwise one is apt to live them out as repetitive patterns in all future relationships. A therapeutic rationale based merely on the observable behavior of families will by necessity collude with an element of escapism and denial. Nonetheless, it is true that behavior can, at least temporarily, be changed without affecting its motivational components. The intrinsic therapeutic "contract" will determine the extent of change in the system. Both the therapist and the family have many options to make the change in superficial rather than essential dimensions of family relations.

SYSTEMIC AND INDIVIDUAL CONSIDERATIONS OF SOCIAL ETHICS

To differentiate between multiperson systemic and individual levels of obligations in families, we assume that justice as a generalized moral norm is a fundamental social mechanism and that as such it transcends both the actions of any particular individual's motivations and internalization processes. Transgression committed by the member of one family against a member of another family apparently is an individual act, but it can produce a systemic response when it leads to a vendetta between the families. Individually, each family member may internalize the reciprocity implications of the vendetta, but the whole is more than the sum total of all internalizations. Justice is composed of the synthesis of the reciprocity balance of all current individual interactions plus the ledger of past and present reciprocity accounts of the entire family.

The concept of balanced justice ledgers epitomizes the difference between individual and relational, e.g., family dynamic, theoretical models. As long as change is aimed at the individual's personality through the analysis of his experiences and character development, the therapist can ignore change in a relational system. Only through a consideration of the hierarchies of obligations in the total system and of motivations of all individuals can we begin to understand and affect the total context of persons in relationship.

Individually based psychodynamic or motivational theories are inadequate to handle the socioethical reality of the consequences of human action. One person's assertiveness, achievement, or sexual prowess, while centrally relevant to the individual's self-seeking goals, do not encompass the vicissitudes of how they will affect the needs of others. While classical Freudian theory appropriately emphasizes the importance of individual responsibility as a valid therapeutic goal, its disregard for the ethics of social reality calls for urgent reconsideration. However valuable its contribution to the understanding of man as a closed system, any psychodynamic theory which confines its motivational orbit to the individual can potentially be socially destructive. Such a theory lags behind our age, with its increasing ethical demands for being aware of and responding to the needs of others.

One might conclude that the dialectical relationship theory is hostile to individual psychodynamic or existential notions and that it gives its full support to those "system purists" who propose to do away with all considerations of the psychology of the individual except in the context of group goals. Nothing would be further from our position. We believe that through exploration and integration of his respective needs and obligations each individual obtains a better defined dignity and meaning, while providing the social group with both stability and initiative for change. A dialectical relationship theory can be simultaneously individual and social system based.

What we need is a theory for the integration of the interlocking values of individual motives and group ethics. The dialectic of social life revolves around a constant ebb and flow of conflict and resolution of give-and-take, loyalty and disloyalty, love and hatred, etc. Social systems as higher levels of organization have their own survival and stability requirements which depend on the resolution of all constituent members' needs.

How can the theory of justice be applied to the work of the family therapist? As he tunes into the most emotionally invested attitudes of family members, he should train himself to recognize the ethical issues with their underlying justice implications. He should form in his mind a ledger of justice along with the construction of the family tree membership. How was the overtly offensive member himself injured? By whom? How to avoid simply falling into a crusade against the apparent wrongdoer? What factors determine the wrongdoer's attitude toward the apparent victim? How do the other members fit into the whole?

In our search for the dynamic dimensions of the moral fabric of any social group, value does not connote for us an objectively definable norm or a consensually validated canon of behavior. The values of each individual can be determined only from the perspective of the subjective world in which he is living. Justice represents for us a personal principle of equity of mutual give-and-take which guides the individual member of a social group in facing the ultimate consequences of his relationship with others. The sum total of the subjective evaluations of the justness of each member's relational experience makes up the climate of trust that characterizes a social group. Such a climate is, in the long run, more significant in determining the quality of relationships within the group than any particular set of interactions.

The ultimate ethical consequences of human action may for a long time remain invisible. Certain individuals may be constructed in such a way that they will never face or even recognize guilt over disregarding the injustice inflicted upon others, except through the penalty their children and grandchildren may have to pay. However, a systematic thinking through of the causal connections of family relationships within and through generations raises the question of the significance of retributory justice as a key family dynamic principle.

A cynical avoidance of concern for each individual's need for justice in the name of a scientifically "valueless" stance is just as destructive as a rigid authoritarian definition of order and enforcement of a dogmatic point of view. The cynicism of corruption, on the one hand, and tyranny, on the other, are alternate symptoms of social decay, both stemming from a widespread fear and avoidance of confrontation with every human being's natural concern with the balance of right and wrong. We believe, for instance, that the shortest way to the correction and prevention of prejudices would be through exploration of every affected person's subjective ethical judgments and a selective and courageous confrontation with basic issues, rather than through denial, avoidance, and lukewarm compromise.

The tabulation on p. 63 indicates the semantic components of the structure of merit and the quantitative, normative dimensions of the justice of the human world in a multiperson relational system. Toward the top in each column the reader finds conditions which are saturated with merit and justification, while toward the bottom of each column conditions of lower merit and higher obligations prevail.

The first column describes the *balance of obligations* ranging from moral (right versus duty) through quantitatively accounting to religioethical (curse versus blessing) conceptual dimensions. In the second column, *merit accounting* reflects the extent of regard accorded to or accumulated by any member of a relationship system. Vertically, the midposition is neutral around which positive and negative merit are polarized as endpoints.

The third and fourth columns describe dimensions which are mainly psychological. The *personal identity* of the highly regarded member is good, righteous, proud or like that of a lienholder who has a right to demand rather than pay. On the opposite end of the merit scale is the position that carries bad, worthless, or shameful identity as though belonging to a lienee who owes rather than demands. *Feeling attitudes* cluster around the condition of the member's conscience. A low state of merit corresponds to guilt feelings, while its counterpart characterizes the angrily indignant person. Bad conscience and indebtedness coincide with fear of retaliation or captively owed gratitude, while good conscience is consistent with freedom of action, even of vindictiveness and an awareness of deserved claims aimed at the partner.

The inverse relationship between high regard or merit and power or possession is further illustrated in the fifth column by the distribution of *role* examples. The infant or the underdog, while in a vulnerable power position, command the support and sympathy of most others. We tend to feel concerned about the underdog's rights, whereas we tend to watch the boss, the winner, or the parents to see whether they live up to their obligations to their inferiors.

The downward direction of the dimensions points toward progressive encumbrance with guilt, and the upward direction leads to progressive defrayment. If parents in several successive generations have acted toward their children with suspicion that the children are "getting

Semantic Components of Merit Structuring
Figure 1
Quantitative dimensions of the justice of the human world

	Balance of Obligations	Merit Accounting	Personal Identity	Feeling Attitude	Role Example
Obliged to	Right	Positive +	Anger	Good	Infant
	Credit, Asset	Highly Regarded	Vindictiveness	Righteous	Underdog,
	Merit		Demanding-ness	Proud	Victim
	Exoneration			Lienholder	Martyr
	Blessing			Asking	
		Neutral	Good Conscience		
Expected of			Bad Conscience		
	Curse	Infamous	Gratitude (owed)	Owing	Beneficiary
	Indebtedness	Negative −	Fear of Retali-ation	Lienee	Boss, Winner
	Obligation			Ashamed	Parent
	Debit		Guilt feeling	Worthless	(despite giving)
	Duty			Bad	

away with murder," the result will be progressive intergenerational encumbrance with guilt. If they have acted on the premise that their children didn't ask to be born and that they deserve care and guidance, their investment of faith and trust will lead to intergenerational defrayment of guilt-laden obligations. The diagram illustrates the principle that in relational dynamics power is inversely related to merit.

The measure of the "condignity" (appropriateness of reward and punishment) of every human exchange is anchored in two or more persons' mutually interlocking subjective evaluation of the merit ledger. On an individual psychological level Franz Alexander's concept of "bribing the superego"[3, p. 62, 63] represents an intrapersonal negotiation about what constitutes condign superego retribution from within. Puritanical protestant ethics offered to balance guilt over acquisitive gratification with self-deprivation concerning everyday hedonism.

Our concept of dimensions of merit or condignity resembles in form but differs in essence from Lederer and Jackson's interactional *quid pro quo.*[60, p. 182] We do not propose the study of mere action–interaction patterns. Instead of restricting the "tit for tat," e.g., of a marital situation, to the behavioral range, we include in the merit equivalency all past, present, and future interactions. A wife's nagging or a husband's attempts at forcing her to change are dynamically connected with unfinished, past retributive efforts which the spouses carry over from their families of origin. For instance, a wife's unsettled emotional account with her deceased father may survive in her attitude toward her husband.

DOUBLE STANDARDS OF IN-GROUP LOYALTY

The definition of any social unit—family, nation, religion, or race— is inseparable from an intrinsically preferential, prejudicious definition of the in-group as superior to the out-group. Even in cases where the definition is sophisticated enough not to claim superiority for the in-group, the ethical standard is set in such a way that the member owes more loyalty to the in-group and is comparatively less condemnable for despising or exploiting the out-group.

The typical family raises its children to be able to absorb the injustices of the world in what appears to be "good spirit" but also to "get away" with as much as possible as long as their actions advance their own or the family's benefits. Traditionally, males are expected to be loyal to their spouse and children, while waging a dog-eat-dog war against outside competitors. The family teaches the child to have a double measure for justice. Invariably, though usually invisibly, he will be inbued with a sense of guilt-laden obligation toward his parents, while he may be taught to feel less accountable to his peers. This parental attitude may in part be responsible for the type of adolescent rebelliousness which reverses the loyalty situation and for a while makes it appear as though loyalty to one's peers would entirely replace one's loyalty to the family of origin. Whereas the roots of a child's obligation to the family that raised him may not always be easy to trace, there can be no doubt about an underlying obligation framework which binds a family together.

THE JUSTICE OF THE HUMAN WORLD AND THE REVOLVING SLATE

Buber's concept of justice of the human order implies the possibility of a conceptual quantification of exploitation, considering that he whose action impinges on existential guilt toward the other "injures an order of the human world whose foundation he knows and recognizes as those of his own existence and of all common human existence."[25, p. 117] Thus, according to Buber, the criteria of violating the order of the human world reside in what the individual feels he is committed to as the innerly recognized foundations of all common human existence, including his own. In order to objectify these criteria, we must define and, ideally, quantify the give-and-take of human relationships. We need not seek "objective" measurability from the vantage point of outside observation, but rather from that of intersubjective, consensual validation. A synthesis of each partner's comparative gratification as a function of his needs and expectations with the other's obligations and "giving" in turn will determine the dialectic of the justice of the human world.

Stress on the question of justice as a motive is not new. Dickens observed: "In the little world in which children have their existence, whosoever brings them up, there is nothing so finely perceived and so finely felt as injustice."[30, p. 59] Piaget stated: "Reciprocity stands so high in the eyes of the child that he will apply it even where to us it seems to border on crude vengeance."[70, p. 216] An excerpt from a family therapy session provides further insight:

We have heard a woman tell her husband "you have taken advantage of me all my life—all my married life." The slip of the tongue is significant: This woman's feeling of injured sense of justice has become overwhelming and unjustly accusatory in turn. We also learn in the course of family therapy that her mother has always regarded her as ungrateful and made her feel guilty over anything she has ever done. Since, as she agrees with the therapist, this matter is unnegotiable between her mother and herself, she probably has sought a balancing of her "account" through her husband. She seems to act as if her husband were accountable for her lifelong relationship with her mother. Her husband states: "when I begin to point out that she is messy, neglects housekeeping, etc., she retorts that I don't have a clean slate either."

We can call this phenomenon the "revolving slate," in that the unsettled account that stands between a person and the original "culprit" can revolve and get between him and any third person. An innocent third person may be used (scapegoated) as a means for balancing the account. Thus, justice is a historically formed ledger, recording the balance of the mutuality of give-and-take. It should be considered as a dynamic principle which explains the seeming irrationality of projections and prejudices. According to his own existential accounting formula, each person is programmed to seek a fair balance of give-and-take between himself and the world. His human world originally included his past relationship with parents, but it has successively involved other emotionally significant relationships. The extent of his sensed imbalance of justice determines the degree to which he will exploit all later relationships:

A father who himself had a painfully deprived childhood addressed his mildly rebellious daughter, upon her being discharged from the hospital where she had been treated for schizophrenia: "First you must repent and then do good acts!" Like other "symptomatic" members of so many other families, this girl was considered both "mad" and "bad."

A wife, after seemingly having accepted the revolving slate in her marriage, discovers her own sense of suffered injustice and expresses it in a most dramatic statement: "Mrs. S: You said something very, very important—*which* had been in my mind ever since I married you. You have always felt that I had a wonderful childhood: I had parents, which I didn't from 13 years up. He didn't. He had a hard life. So now that we are married together, I am supposed to give everything to him because he never had nothing. I am supposed to shower everything on him, which I do; I am trying to make him happy. I try to give him a lot of affection, show him that I care for him. But, where is *my* thirst coming in? (cries) *I am thirsty too.*"[13, p. 121]

Retributory projection on all parentlike persons may be an important component of the hostility that exists between youth and the older generation in any culture. The issue is not so much a gap of information or understanding as a claim for wished-for justice. In older cultures this tension may have been handled by practices that emphasized unconditional respect toward elders and by channeling revengeful manifestations into wars or into migrating towards new geographic frontiers. The energy of these conflicts can also be channeled into prejudices which may escalate to formal subjugation of others, as demonstrated amply by dictatorships throughout history. As industrialization, crowding, and sophistication of society removes some of these outlets, the energy of youth may turn against the "establishment" of society which is to be punished *in loco parentis*. The tendency toward vandalism, for example, seems to be on the increase in both democratic and oppressive political systems.

LEDGERS OF JUSTICE AND PSYCHOLOGICAL THEORY

The revolving slate establishes a *chain of displaced retributions* in families and becomes the source of repetitious, cyclic feedback, a dynamic system force to be considered in its own right. Is the cause for resentful accusations imaginary or real? Or, rather, by what criteria is it relevant or irrelevant? Freud was interested in the "distortion" only insofar as distortion was injected into another relationship through "projection" or negative transference, i.e., through pathological function on the part of the individual himself. This followed from Freud's lack of interest in the reciprocity of relational justice unless it was internalized in an individual. His concept of the superego represented an internalized agency for preserving a historically outdated merit accounting between the individual and his formative environment.

Ricoeur in his classic essay on Freud comments about various aspects of guilt: "The fear of being unjust, the remorse for having been unjust, are no longer taboo fears; damage to the interpersonal relationship, wrongs done to the person of another, treated as a means not an end, mean more than a feeling of a threat of castration. Thus, the consciousness of injustice marks a creation of meaning by comparison with the fear of vengeance, the fear of being punished."[74, p. 546]

Justice thus transcends the psychology of the individual and of his partners in relationships. We regard justice as a multipersonal homeostatic principle with equitable reciprocity as its ideal goal. Yet the pendulum swings perpetually between multiple iniquities. The individual can be "caught" in existential guilt through the actions of others as one inherits a place in the multigenerational network of obligations and becomes accountable to the chain of past obligations, traditions, etc. One may not readily be aware of the long-range *quid pro quo* moves, only of short-term obligations and repayments. The less he is aware of the invisible obligations accumulated in the past, for instance, by his parents, the more he will be at the mercy of these invisible forces. In families the system unit of accounting tends to include generations. According to the Scriptures, seven generations may balance out one major sin of an ancestor.

The family therapist must learn how to reconstruct a minimally three-generational balancing of accounts of justice. Children can be blamed for their solidarity with their parents by the grandparents who consider the parents disloyal to themselves and their family (e.g., in matters of religious or other tradition). The child, then, unconsciously may fit into a strategy for the exoneration of the parents or perpetuate the guilt encumbrance through the following generation. Further examples could be given of daughters who were raised by "respectable" relatives because of their mother's "life of shame" and who decide to seek out and join their mothers; of sons who suffer while hiding the secret of their mother's suspected murder by father's girlfriend, etc. Ultimately, the greatest relief these children can find lies in the vindication in their own eyes of their parents, through understanding the unfairness of the circumstances which led their parents to their condemnable actions.

To the extent that groups are held together by values, the supreme cohesive value is justice. If need for equitable balancing of benefits is a major regulatory and motivational force of any social group, it is our task to understand what are the social arrangements which monitor justice. What social mechanisms evaluate and regulate, for instance, such matters as: What is every man's due in his family? What does a child deserve? What do his parents owe him? How do parent and child evaluate the justness of their *quid pro quo?* How much gratitude will any child owe his parents?

Using the concept of justice we can define a social system on a more fundamental motivational level than using an interactional framework. The human order is a concept based on a subjective, normative sense of justice or equity. It should be contrasted with functional and descriptive definitions, e.g., "A social system is a system of the actions of individuals, the principal units of which are roles and constellations of roles."[67, p. 197] Obviously, the fact that I have betrayed my friend or his confidence is a structural aspect of relatedness on a different plane from role definitions.

Christian Bay cites Aberle's list of the functional prerequisites of a society: "Provision for adequate relationship to the environment and for sexual recruitment; role differentiation and role assignments; communication; shared cognitive orientations; shared articulated set of goals; the normative regulation of means; the regulation of affective expressions; socialization; and the effective control of disruptive forms of behavior."[5, p. 267] We regard a generalized climate of trust and the justice of the human order as a more fundamental structural characteristic of society than the institutionalization of the regulation of specific functions.

Holmberg describes the Siriono of Eastern Bolivia as a collection of the "most primitive, seminomadic" bands whose energies are consumed in the search of food, and who therefore have no social solidarity among them beyond the immediate family. After having made such an overly simplified statement, the author nevertheless reveals the underlying social structure which pervades that primitive society: "Generally speaking, it would seem that the maintenance of law and order rests largely on the principle of basic reciprocity (however enforced), the fear of supernatural sanction and retaliation, and a desire for public approval."[55, p. 60, 61]

In our opinion, technical or institutionalized systems of societal justice in so-called advanced civilizations may have lost their anchoring in reciprocity and equity. In our pseudosophisticated efforts to avoid any value bias, we tend to deny and ignore those great issues which make up the ethical understructure of contemporary society.

FROM TALIONIC TO DIVINE JUSTICE

A short and far-from-complete review of the place of retributive justice in human history may help to place familial justice in the context of its universal social dynamics. No doubt, cruel retribution must have been the judicial procedure of early societies. As civilizations became more sophisticated, the management of retributive justice became more rational but not necessarily more equitable and relevant. Modern man's illusion of replacing rather than mitigating retributive justice with humanity might constitute one of the greatest hypocrisies, and a threat to the dynamic fiber of society itself.

Early in man's struggle for a sane social order there appeared the law of a talionic reciprocal justice. Its development must have been connected with that of religion and divine justice. According to Kelsen, "Only a religion whose deity is supposed to be just can play a role in social life."[57, p. 25] With the development of higher religion in any tribe the simple rule of "a tooth for a tooth, an eye for an eye" yielded to a much more complex merit-accounting system. Divine justice as an invisible law of the universe was believed to extend into life after death. Immediate revenge to the wrongdoer became less urgent for the devout religious man. In the hands of the deity the primitive talionic law of absolute retribution obtained a buffer which obviated the necessity of an immediate settling of accounts by human hands.

Kelsen states that in early Greek mythology and philosophy the logic of causality appeared simultaneously with man's juridical view of both society and the world. Accordingly, the origin of the search for a causal law of natural events can be traced back to the principle that man should return good for good and evil for evil. Kelsen quotes Anaximander, the pre-Socratic philosopher: "Into that from which things take their rise they pass away once more, according to necessity. For they make reparation and satisfaction to one another for their injustice according to the order of time."[58, p. 301] Thus, the earliest statement of causality coincides with a statement on retributive justice—the wrong is the cause and the punishment is the effect. Kelsen adds that the Greek word for causal necessity can be deduced etymologically from the meanings of merit and merited allotment.

The anthropomorphic world image of Greek mythology pictured the Sun as maintaining its course under the supervision of the goddesses of revenge who would punish him whenever he would wish to trespass from his prescribed course in the heavens. No one in the entire universe seemed to be free of the talionic principle. The word *talio* comes from the Latin word *talis,* meaning *such,* implying that the punishment should fit the crime. The simple tit-for-tat became with the sophistication of Roman law: *suum cuique;* everyone his due.*

The idea of a quantitatively fitting (condign) amount of punishment or reward is essential for the development of any group's concept of justice. From prehistorical times transgressions were paid for in ransom and the amount was set to fit the seriousness of the offense. Ethics and justice converge toward the principle of reciprocal equity. Ethical conduct requires that one should not trespass; equity requires that others should not get away with one-sided gratification either. Any lasting damage to the principle of equity carries with it the connotation of explicit or implicit exploitation of certain members of a social group.

Ordinarily, ethics is defined in terms of the individual and his obligations, his relationship to what is good or bad. As it pertains to restraint of pleasure and moral duty, the individual relates to his conscience or

---

*A grandiose outgrowth of this principle was the view of the inflated mandate of the Roman Empire as the keeper of justice among nations: *"Parcere subiectis et debellare superbos"* (clemency for the subjected ones and breaking down the proud ones). The traditional early Roman concern for law and equity for all citizens was turned into a screen behind which to build up exploitative, imperialistic strategies for world domination.

God. If his trespasses do not violate anyone else's rights and interests, he is not directly contributing to the ledger of retributive justice. Selfish pleasure orientation which does not harm anyone else would violate only the abstract code of equality of distribution of happiness among all humans; a concept devoid of relational meaning.

Contrary to distributive justice, retributive justice of personal exchanges is of prime importance for relationship theory. Virtues and vices exchanged among closely related people create the deepest meaning of their existence. Retributive justice involves at least two interacting people between whom merited rewards and punishments can be fairly or unfairly adjusted. Ethics regulate an individual's principles of function, justice those of an entire social group.

As a dynamic context of social groups, justice is an even more comprehensive and fundamental framework than ethics. This is especially true if ethics is defined mainly in terms of the individual's control of his drives. According to Freud, "Conscience is the internal perception of the rejection of a particular wish operating within us."[43, p. 68] Yet we have seen that justice pertains to actions within the order of the human world. The "illegimately pregnant" daughter who gave her infant away for adoption and did not even look at his face was not primarily burdened by guilt over her "wish" to destroy her child. In relational reality, her transgression was in having actually shirked parental responsibility and in not taking care of her child. Even though her act could have been condoned by her parents, on some level she must sense that she committed the fundamental crime of refused existential responsibility owed to another helplessly dependent human life.

It appears that with the development of the great religions and the belief in just deities the expression of man's need for a sense of ultimately prevailing justice has obtained a sharper formulation, as belief in an omnipotent and just god has helped to defer punishment. The invisible accounts of God are thought to be inescapable. "Vengeance is mine" is the attributed statement of the just god. Ultimately, He will settle all deferred accounts in Heaven and in Hell. The divine bookkeeping of merits is described in countless metaphors throughout the writings of all major religions: "He who performs one precept has gotten to himself one advocate and he who commits one transgression has gotten to himself one accuser" says the *Pirque Abboth*.[52, p. 562] God has become the symbol of an invisible bookkeeping of justice, and he also becomes involved as an injured party in every transgression that occurs between any two people.

Christianity began with the infusion of new concepts of retribution, reparation, and satisfaction expected of the trespasser. The concept of the Saviour dying for everybody's sins became a major balancing factor. Loving and forgiving attitudes were stressed. Religious procedures (repentance, confession, satisfaction, indulgences) gradually took the place of person-to-person justice. Around the tenth century, public confession for secret sins became almost extinct. By that time, private penance became the universal avenue for settling the sinner's account with God and, therefore, at least in cases of secret sins, with the victim as well. The victim did not have to be paid reparation unless it was made part of confessional penitence.

It is a historical fact, however, that the buffering function of a belief in divine justice could not eliminate for long the tendency towards tangible retributive action and for extirpating evil. Extremely cruel retribution prevailed, as shown, for instance, by religiously sanctioned witch trials. On the other hand, the historic evolution of court procedure also helped to extricate religion from the role of a guardian of actual reparations to be paid by the guilty to his victim. Secular penal procedure has assumed a considerable part of retributive justice.

No doubt the law of strict and absolute retribution is distasteful and frightening to contemporary Western man. Throughout history injustices have been committed more frequently through false justification of an absolute power and the rule of terror than through relaxation of retribution. Nonetheless, the principle of justice can suffer on the side of naive permissive liberalism as a substitute for thorough examination of what the issues of fairness and equity are. Implied divine justice began to vanish as the traditional foundation of society during the Age of Enlightenment; a vacuum was created, and modern man has not been able to fill that vacuum.

To the extent that strict religious regulation of conduct diminishes in society, the question arises: What takes the place of belief in divine justice? It seems inevitable that society needs a serious examination of the dynamic character of loyalty and its underlying principle, justice. Rational, postreligious, and liberal attitudes have often focused critically on the scapegoating aspects of retaliative criminal justice. It would be insane to condone self-justified mob violence, which in its extreme is lynching of victims whose main crime is being on the wrong side of a prejudicious discrimination. Even the punishment of verified criminals through legal court procedures could be considered undesirable since it might satisfy some people's sadistic needs. However, we have to examine the possible effects of a complete elimination of the principles of retaliatory justice and reparation. Whereas not holding the individual to absolute accountability and letting him have a "second chance" represents great and realistic progress in human history, the consequent scientistic dilution of the importance of the issue of justice could be retrogressive. What is needed is a constant attention to improvement of judicial principles and procedures. Attempts to replace the criteria of justice with scientific ones are nonscientific.

SOCIETAL IMPLICATIONS OF THE DYNAMIC VIEW OF JUSTICE

Adopting a pseudosophisticated scientific view, today's social science student may be inclined to regard the justice framework of motivational theory as moralizing. Inasmuch as moralizing is tantamount to having a prejudicial, blindly self-congratulatory judgmental attitude, we would be the first to agree that moralizing is inappropriate and nonproductive in both scientific and humanistic endeavors. We would like to stress, on the other hand, that without clarifying the ethical principles of what constitutes just or unjust acts in a given relationship, there cannot be an adequate motivational theory of group behavior.

The twentieth century has seen the relativization of the concept of absolute causal law even in natural science (e.g., Einstein, Heisenberg). The development of social sciences has made many of our time-honored values questionable. At the same time, there is no indication that the dynamic of our social organization could eliminate retributive justice as its basis. An important instance of the displaced retributional dynamic manifests itself in social prejudices. Loyalty to one's group and prejudicial rejection of outsiders has remained the most deeply ingrained motive of societies. Convinced of the justice of their nation or group, people may risk their lives in the battlefield and immolate themselves in protest against the powerful out-group. The conqueror believes that he merely repays the injustices of the past. By doing so he sets up the justification of his own downfall. Who can cut the revolving cycles of retribution? Yet without having a forum for at least studying the criteria of justice can there be any hope for stopping the chains of mutual vengeance?

A classical example of retributional dynamics applies to America's racial problem. It seems probable that all economic, political, and sociological approaches are bound to remain essentially sterile, unless white, middle-class dominated American society is willing to include the Blacks, Indians, and other racial minorities into its pragmatic concerns for fairness and equality. A large part of today's political dynamics pertains to a delayed search for equity which includes, for instance, the historical context of slavery and other, more inherent types of exploitation.

It is important to distinguish here between *personal responsibilities of individuals* and *collective responsibility* for a multigenerationally accumulated, systemic debt. The latter leads to even larger, societal ledgers of obligation and indebtedness. Today's white citizen would justly deny any personal responsibility for the importation of slaves from Africa many generations ago. On the other hand, he has to share awareness of an obligation for society to collectively repair the afteraffects of slavery that have continued to hamper and hurt many descendants of the slaves.

Similarly, one could easily recognize that despite its compelling rationale, the United Nations Organization falls short of its goals because of its inability to provide equity of justice in its dealings with large and small powers. It is obvious that the United Nations has not halted imperialistic conquest by brutal military means. Furthermore, the apparent equity-mindedness of industrially advanced Western democracies is to a great extent a cover for a contemptuous, patronizing attitude of convenience towards nations of lesser industrial development. Even pacifistic attitudes can at times become patronizing concern over cruelties of war rather than honest interest in the human quest for freedom and just society on the part of poor, strange people in underdeveloped countries.

The greatest cultural task of our age might be the investigation of the role of relational, not merely economic, justice in contemporary society; the greatest gap in our social science pertains to the denial of the dynamic significance of retribution. Szasz,[85] among others, has pointed to the tendency of our courts to escape from their retributive function by relegating it to mental health experts. A pseudoenlightened denial of the importance of the principle of equity and fairness tends to confuse and undermine the role of the courts—the courts may be unwilling to restrain even recurrent acts of injustice. Our age may go down in history as practicing the greatest apparent consideration, even toward coldly calculating murderers. Society's unwillingness to define criteria of reciprocity is masked by our "scientific" curiosity about the psychological motivations of criminals. Legitimate search for the understanding of psychology of criminals should not be used for beclouding the even greater social issue, safeguarding of the principle of a just society.

Traditionally, it has been the function of the parents and other elders to keep accounts of the family's just human order. Chieftains, kings, and emperors did the same, actually or symbolically, for the larger social units. Since the gods were believed to guard both natural law and ultimate human justice, kings referred to the deity as the source of their authority. In contemporary democratic society, justice is supposed to be maintained by codified law and by elected officials. However, the more there is real or suspected tendency towards injustice in society, the more the danger of chaos, alienation, distrust of elected leaders, and desperate political action. The ancient scriptures of any culture postulate that great injustices committed by a nation were punished by divine retribution. Today, modern technology has enabled one group to enslave or extinquish another group without human effort.

What has taken the role of divine retribution in the minds of modern man? Is there interest in the criteria of justice, and, if so, where are its ledgers kept? An implicit bookkeeping of merit represents a self-regulatory principle, often outside codified law or even the awareness of the actors. Mounting debits of injustice and accumulating guilt ultimately tend to eliminate the seeming gains accrued by successful exploiters. Exploitative parents may produce exploiting children and the chain reaction of generations may lead to more and more frustrated and less and less giving future parents, resulting in the destruction of the creative potential of family life.

Obligation or merit can accumulate on one side of a relationship, and be periodically balanced through word and symbolic or real action. However, nongiving or nonaccepting attitudes on the part of individual members can make rebalancing impossible.

A young man had an interesting decision to make on how to balance his obligations versus his merits accumulated in his relationship with his father. The son owned a sizeable company which was the product of both his father's invested money and his own hard work and disciplined thinking. In the course of family therapy it was often revealed how this man's apparently unconditional loyalty towards his father caused concern to his wife. She asked: "Are our children going to owe us that much too?"

At the point, however, when he was facing legal formalization of his business relationship with his father, the young man became aware of his ambivalence. He admitted that he considered it as a just solution if his father would share 50% of the business with him. But he could not decide whether he would gain more from obtaining factual, material equity from his father while continuing to feel obligated towards him, or from being cut short financially and therefore feeling free of all personal obligations towards a provenly unjust father. The two options obviously represented two possibilities for rebalancing the reciprocal equity of the father–son relationship.

Rituals are behavioral patterns which have traditionally dealt with contractual obligations among people and between God and man. Many ancient rituals were meant to balance unsettled accounts through sacrifice and through thanksgiving offerings. Wedding rituals formalized the rights of those who gave away the bride and the one who took the bride. Burial ceremonies and tombstones were meant to deal with the fears of unsettled accounts between the dead and the living. The haunting spirits had to be appeased and valuables taken to the grave. The bereaved ones had to face and accept their loss. The benefit of being blessed with a son also had to be requited through the offering of sacrifices. The ceremoniousness of courts reminds us of the traditional ritualistic significance of their societal function in that they legalize taking or giving of condign reparation and reward. Even such an atheistic, overtly power-motivated ruler as Hitler found it necessary to —inconsistently—refer to Providence as the traditional keeper of ultimate justice.

The marked tendency in today's youth for creating new rituals may be related to their reaction to the decline of traditional rituals as a result of scientific enlightenment. What has been conceptualized in terms of "identity diffusion"[34] or role confusion of modern youth can also be looked upon as a search about how retributive justice works in society today. Identity is essentially a cognitive proposition, whereas justice is inseparable from an action-experimentation context. If from a youth's vantage point the world appears hopelessly corrupt and disinterested, he will try to elicit a value-based response from society through provocative, challenging action. For certain young people this will take the form of self-destructive or "delinquent" acts.

In designing approaches to help alienated youth, we have to be aware of the influence of debilitating nonreceiving as well as exploitatively nongiving parental stances. Inability on the part of the elders to receive can lead to hostile guilt-laden alienation on the part of the younger generation. Conversely, guilt over inability to give to the parent may suddenly be activated in the child upon the parent's death. Guilt over undelivered acts of repayment to the parent can have conscious and unconscious components. Inasmuch as his parent's death means the ultimate autonomy, the already-mentioned "counterautonomous superego" function is certain to be unleashed upon the child, regardless of his unconscious death wishes, etc., towards the parent.

Man's relationship with other animals and with nature as a whole has been based on power and exploitation. Not only does man devour animals and plants to feed on, like other animals do, but through his technological power he damages the order of balanced growth and elimination of waste. There have been certain minimal efforts to rebalance man's relationship with nature on the part of individuals or groups. Some people have been vegetarians out of the principle of fairness to animals which have become a too easy prey to man. In certain societies animals are chosen to be sacred and inviolable. In other societies groups are formed to protect animals against human cruelty. The ethics underlying contemporary ecological drives tends to devalue man's power to change nature in favor of survival of others and preservation of a balanced feedback of all life processes. An ecological countertechnology is being built up to curb the power excesses of an exploitative, overly successful mastery of man over nature. On an emotional level the trend discharges man's gratitude to the natural world and diminishes his unadmitted guilt over needless butchery.

INDIVIDUAL VERSUS COLLECTIVE ACCOUNTABILITY

Throughout this chapter we have stressed that justice can be considered one of the most crucial regulatory forces and motivational determinants of partners in close relationships. While we have drawn a strong conceptual boundary between individual psychology and interpersonal patterning of action, in reality the two system levels of human phenomena are closely interwoven.

These two levels of system function can be represented as two kinds of accounting of obligations. Psychology is concerned with a person's reactions to his basic drives, his conscience, and his "outside world." His individual accounting of merits colors his experiences, feelings, thoughts, and wishes as they arise in his mind; they are retained in his memory and symbolically elaborated in his conscious and unconscious thought processes. A negative outcome of the individual's private accounting of his experiences is the emergence of guilt feelings, a positive outcome results in a sense of trust.

Conversely, the interpersonal accounting of a relationship system is based upon the various members' actions as they are elaborated through mutual individual responses of the other members and upon the ongoing long-term system properties of the group. The consequences of a person's actions are imprinted in the social system of which he is a part. For example, existential guilt which arises out of a deeply injured human order will remain consequential for the life of the group. In any social group, if a significant number can "get away with murder," the overall social climate will bear the consequences. A generalized loss of equity of justice can jeopardize the creativity or even the survival of the group, and its members' chances for achieving basic trust will diminish to a dangerous point.

Psychoanalytic and academic psychology have shared the viewpoint that the individual's human (relational) environment may be construed as essentially a constant, a locus of average normal expectations to which the individual may or may not adjust successfully. Our dialectical point of view not only postulates that the individual is embedded in a dynamically balanced, fluctuating, merit context, but that the latter is an indispensable component for the understanding of individual dynamics and motivation. Consequently, whereas an individual's *guilt feelings* can be understood without a consideration of the other members' feelings and reactions, the underlying *existential guilt* cannot.

Our postenlightenment scientistic heritage has fostered a conceptual one-upmanship, based on the denial of the ethical significance of interpersonal obligations. We have learned to indulge in the "game" of establishing elegant psychological formulae, e.g., for symbolic transformations and developmental timetables which have their merit in understanding individual dynamics. At the same time, however, we have become oblivious of the chain of actions and reactions which permeate the social system and determine its balance of justice. Even the meaning of the word "reaction" has shifted away from the sphere of action to that of psychological experience or reflection.

There is an apparent historical parallel between the process of softened retribution for crime and the progressive focusing on individual dimensions of accountability. Ancient societies through their talionic justice not only held the individual immediately accountable, but they often made the entire family responsible for its member's transgressions. Few would question the value of mankind's enormous advance toward the ideal of individual judicial accountability. No sane person would want to return to the days of sanctioned vendetta; the horrible possibility of collective retribution in the form of slaughter or enslaving of an entire race still haunts our age. Collective legal responsibility is the dangerous gate leading to the retrogressive steps of prejudice, scapegoating, and genocide.

Paradoxically, it falls upon the family theorist to point out factors of motivation in the family which could raise the question of familial judicial responsibility. It is entirely possible that, carried to its ultimate consequences, the concept of individual responsibility can amount to an inverse scapegoating. In not holding the innocent child accountable for the father's sins or the parents for their child's transgressions, we may overlook actual but hidden forces of complicity which reside in the family system. The dynamic significance of familial merit ledgers connects interlocking motivations with covertly shared ethical responsibility. In a sense, the parent should be legally accountable as an accomplice in violence when, even unintentionally, he manipulates his child's unconscious impulses which the child then acts out delinquently. Yet, who would open the dangerous door of punishing unconscious motivations and intentions? Furthermore, if the parents themselves have been victims of the unconscious motivations of their parents, etc., where should the ultimate focus of accountability lie? Where does the legal accountability of young children lead then? How can our legal system deal with implicit evidence of covert complicity?

What legal and judicial measures can the family therapist suggest as appropriate if current clinical observations about unconsciously vicarious participation of adults in juvenile delinquency are to be taken seriously? As one important step, a *shared family commitment to therapeutic or remedial programs* should be expected and be made legally justifiable in appropriate cases. Let us take an actual family treatment case as an illustration. A father was observed to act in a most objectionable, hostile way, unquestionably scapegoating his daughter. We could point out the sadomasochistic, dependent, and complexly defensive characteristics of the intergenerational struggle. We could register the hurt feelings of the victim and the guilt of the perpetrator. But the concept of the injured order of justice has more comprehensive, farther-reaching system implications for therapeutic practice. The family therapist will learn that certain past relational accounts which cannot be settled through self-reflecting analysis, transference resolution, and insight can actually be resolved through interpersonal initiative and corrective action, often in a three generational context.

When the justice of human order suffers, the psychology of guilt may be an essentially irrelevant issue, especially if the perpetrator has felt that the action was inevitable. An illustration of the extreme of this situation is the case of the murderer who upon committing the act feels no guilt, just a great relief of tension. He may claim that the act of murder has settled a prolonged conflict in his mind between having felt exploited and being incapable to feel any indebtedness to others. Through his alleged unfair exploitation in the past, the murderer was made virtually immune to guilt, fear of punishment, and even to the death sentence. In his own conscience he held the world in debt to himself and he felt acquitted in advance. However, his psychological state or even the motivational contribution of his subjective, existential justice are irrelevant to society's obligation for protecting the justice of the murder victim and of the common human order.

The case of the subjectively guiltless murderer highlights the importance of a balanced integration of individual and multiperson concepts for the therapist. The perpetrator of new injustices is likely to be the carrier of past system imbalances. In his "distortion" of present accountability he is influenced by past circumstances which made him a helpless victim of relational exploitation. Usually the therapist can enlist the perpetrator's responsible self-reflection on his acts only if the therapist can first reflect on the transgressions suffered by the transgressor.

Following the same pattern, the transgressor will not be able to resolve his ambivalent feelings toward his allegedly (consciously or unconsciously) exploitative parents until he can decide if—based on his parents' acts and attitudes—his resentment is justified. His inability to separate these elements may be shrouded in a fog, maintained both by acts of mystification and genuine lack of awareness. After having separated the two realms, the individual can begin to face his authentic guilt and learn about his relational defenses against guilt.

INDIVIDUAL AND MULTIGENERATIONAL ACCOUNTABILITY

In a brilliant summary of classical psychoanalytic theories, Fenichel gives a list of defenses against guilt. He states: "Reassurances against guilt feelings may be gathered from many sources. Certain characters use other persons only for this purpose; . . . they may be unkind and thus provoke punishment to 'have it over with' quickly or, if the pardon is not forthcoming, at least to attain the feeling that a terrible injustice has been done."[36, p. 500] Although the foregoing strategy is frequently practiced among family members, we must emphasize the important guilt-reducing mechanisms based on preexisting injustice. Actually suffered past injustices can themselves balance the ledger against guilt-laden responsibility for one's hostile feelings. Naturally, if one uses another person for defense against preexisting guilt, that relationship will have little chance for being balanced, and it leads to new exploitation and scapegoating.

Out of our growing recognition of the significance of multigenerational merit accounts, we suggest the inclusion of aged parents in the process of family therapy. By opening up the door to rebalancing of merits through action, the process of therapy may reverse the accumulation and perpetuation of loaded, unsettled accounts which could otherwise prejudice the chances of future generations.

HOW OBJECTIVE CAN MERIT ACCOUNTING BE?

From the individual's point of view, as Waelder[87] emphasized, a wish for an entirely just world can be regarded as a subjective, wishful need configuration. In the individual-based framework of psychoanalysis such a desire can be explored as a derivative of other fundamental strivings. Since every individual tends to distort the evaluation of his relationships according to his subjective wishes, it could be postulated that the notion of justice is entirely illusory in nature. According to a corresponding ethical subjectivism, the strongest member could justify that he is entitled to disregard the rights of all others.

Considering society as a whole, however, it could be argued that there exists an invisible dynamic balance between all competing individual notions of justice. Such intrinsic consensus about the principles of subjective justice, i.e., how everyone's equity of benefits is to be measured, constitutes the basis of the "objective" judicial bookkeeping of the group. An imaginary extrapolation of the sum total of all guilt-bound (superego-determined) regulative motivations of individuals is only part of such an intrinsic system. A social group's justice ledger takes its entire interactional history, in addition to its shared ethical principles, into account.

The intrinsic justice of any group is made up of two processes: the hierarchy or ledger of obligations and the totality of all retributive motivations. As each member is motivated to act out any significant revengeful (or grateful) impulse, an ongoing seesaw process of retaliative justice can be counted on. However, as we have seen, the individual is not always capable of discriminating sources of injury. The phenomenon of a "revolving slate" makes him act revengefully upon an inappropriate target, unaware of the displacement of the retribution. The accuracy of retributive justice moves is only statistical. What is true of the group process as a whole is not necessarily valid of the specifics of the individual's "niche."

Morris,[87] in his reply to Waelder, describes the inherent process of justice which gradually emerges in human civilization and leads from manifest inequality and exploitation towards slowly increasing equality of chance for an increasingly larger segment of humanity. The debate between the psychoanalyist and the professor of law highlights the dichotomy between an individual-based, clinical, although scientifically sophisticated, view and a broader, societal vantage point. Whereas the ideal goal of judicial systems consists in an approximation of a just society, based on essentially shared principles of equity, the justice of everyday human interactions is continually being assessed in the minds and hearts of the persons involved. Exploitation of a material kind can be quantified, but personal exploitation is measurable only on a subjective scale which has been built into the person's sense of the meaning of his entire existence. The specifics of a given mix between subjective and interpersonal realities of accounts can be gleaned from the ensuing imaginary vignette:

The fact that you have not called me for a whole week may not constitute unfairness, and I might not experience it as an injury to the justice of my human world. However, since it happened right after I had extended myself for you when you needed my attention, sympathy, or consolation, your lack of interest registers in my heart as a painful act of injustice. As a result, I feel that my ledger is out of balance, that I have given more than I received, and if I believe that you treated me like this knowingly, then I'm being exploited.

Even if this injustice can be established from my subjective experience only, the importance of the event may have registered in your mind in some form nevertheless. You may consciously have experienced guilt feelings or at least some dim awareness of having been unfair to me, or at least that you have stepped on my toes. Thus, even though you may not be aware of having violated any mutually shared ethical principle, our parallel subjective reactions have consensually validated the relative objectivity of my suffered injustice.

The importance of the argument illustrated by this vignette lies in its emphasis on the mutuality of an action dialogue which is more than the sum total of two persons' subjective experiences. Thus, while the concept of reality testing in psychology is a comparatively monothetical notion (one is either reality-bound or subject to distortion), the concept of the just order of the human world is a dialectical one. A man's betrayal of his friend involves more than the vicissitudes of his repressed childhood wishes, depressions, etc. To decide on the extent of distortion would depend on his friend's vantage point too.

As a practical outcome of this thesis, we caution the family therapist against disclaiming his intrinsic role in the personal, ethical, and justice issues, as well as against restricting his vision to the intrapsychic and psychological realms. However, being drawn into a debate, for instance, of someone's right for either blaming or not blaming his parents, would lead to a nondialectical pitfall. A dialectical therapeutic stance would strive to establish the area at which the authentic subjective justice accounting of each participant lies. By open discussion of these accounts, an avenue toward balancing them through an action orientation might be opened.

In cases of overt, apparently malicious scapegoating, the family therapist may be placed in a difficult position from the beginning. The rest of the family may indicate that unless the therapist goes along with the notion of the scapegoat's badness, they will not accept his help. The very crudeness and cruelty of the accusations, on the other hand, would call for a reciprocal counterblaming of the scapegoaters. The therapist's strongest move in such a case is to indicate his awareness of both possibilities: of his taking sides and also of his capacity to explore the reverse of both positions. For example, can the scapegoaters be looked upon as needing help, and can the scapegoat be looked upon as a potential helper?

THE SPECIAL POSITION OF THE FAMILY

Traditionally, family relationships seem to have a special exemption from strict retributive principles of justice. In many areas family members share a common boundary which separates them from the outside world. Statements like "blood is thicker than water" illustrate this basic human circumstance.

As a rule one can expect to be accepted by his family members simply on the basis of loyalty of consanguinity, regardless of one's merit. Even the failing, the weak, the sick or feeble-minded can expect care from most families. The welfare concept extends this principle to society as a whole, in sharp contrast with the ideal of "rugged" economic individualism which adhered to a competitive, "hard" accounting model of earned merit. The welfare ideal can thus be regarded as national nepotism.

Familial justice has undergone an evolution corresponding to its societal history. In antiquity and for some time during the Middle Ages, parents had absolute power over their children. Roman law permitted children to be sold into slavery or given capital punishment on the authority of the parents. Christianity and subsequently rational liberalism have contributed to a more forgiving treatment of the trespasses of children. Our age faces the opposite extreme, and concern has arisen about the abdication of parental responsibility in the form of overpermissiveness. Parental emotional depletion and lethargy tend to drive an increasing number of modern parents to the parentification of their children through permissiveness. Technical progress tends to further magnify the effects of a no-constraints attitude. The vast freedom of mobility and communication made possible through the automobile and television are not balanced by an increased competence of human authorities. The abandonment and subsequent alienation of youth is expected to continue to rise in most sections of society.

Overpermissiveness as a form of parental abandonment of children, aside from bordering on neglect, is probably one of the most widespread forms of exploitative parentification. It constitutes a true double bind,[4] since it appears to be giving something (freedom of actions) when its essence is in the nature of unilateral taking (nongiving of concern or limits, and expectations of spontaneous self-propulsion from the child). Frequently, the myths of permissiveness and family togetherness coexist and mutually reinforce each other. (See also Wynne *et al.*[93] (the concept of "pseudomutuality".)

The value system of an entire family can be characterized by certain myths that members have shared throughout generations. Some of these value myths may be anchored in religious or national concepts. Due to the dialectic nature of the boundary of the self's identity, families may be likely to depict outsiders as prejudicially as possible. The members of the out-group who do not share the in-group's values are, by definition, inferior. Loyalty to the family's value system constitutes an invisible, yet very important, dynamic regarding the accounting of merit in any individual member. Loyal adherence may balance the scale for many transgressions.

The family as a whole tends to incorporate into its ongoing bookkeeping of merit the prejudicial definition of their values at the expense of the scapegoated outsiders. However, a particularly strong reinforcement of familial value myths can occur through the scapegoating of one member of the in-group. Through the shared condemnation of the disloyal member, the rest of the in-group can reinforce their commitment to the shared value system. In ancient society, and still in some areas of the Near East, the head of the clan has the obligation to safeguard the honor of the family by killing the sister or daughter who gave away her virginity to a stranger.

It is fascinating to observe the multigenerational patterns of scapegoating in families undergoing family therapy. In some cases the pattern consists of a repetitive recurrence of the same type of scapegoating in several generations. In one family we have observed a voluntary assumption of the rebellious scapegoat role by three female members, each in a successive generation. In another family daughters in three successive generations were conditioned to fight the "badness" of their male partners. This led to heterosexually framed murder in two generations and attempted murder in the third.

Another pattern of scapegoating may consist in a gradual escalation of disloyal roles through several generations. We have seen the second generation in an orthodoxly religious family turn into rebellious atheists. After marrying a girl from a similarly traditional background, one man raised two daughters in an excessively liberal, permissive atmosphere with the avowed ideal of the unbeliever. The unresolved conflict between the first and second generation remained untouched until both girls made known their intentions to marry young men of another faith and of vastly different value orientations. Through the enormous injustice of the ensuing scapegoating of the two daughters by the entire extended family, their parents finally assumed a responsible stance to face and possibly settle the issue of disloyalty between themselves and the older generation. The scapegoating of the young generation was instrumental in the retroactive expiation of the guilt of the intermediate generation.

PARENT–CHILD LEDGERS

Although the merit ledger constitutes only one aspect of the structure of the parent–child relationship, we consider it as dynamically the most fundamental one. In this section we would like to spell out some of the major dimensions of the interpersonal accounting of justice, a principle with applications in all aspects of family life, marriage, and human relationships.

While much sociological investigation has been focused on the complementary roles, behavioral patterns, and psychological motivations of parenting, the fundamental issue of reciprocal equity of benefits exchanged between parent and child has remained relatively untouched. What are the criteria according to which parental devotion can become overburdening and detrimental to either the parent or to the child? How much filial devotion can repay parental availability? How far is parentification of a child "normal" and inevitable? Where do the parent's needs reach the point of exploitation of the child, and when does it constitute child abuse? What constitutes the symmetry of give-and-take between parent and child? What determines the choice of timing for repayment of obligations or selection of a substitute recipient for repayment? How does a family system as a whole balance the intrinsically asymmetrical parent–child accounts within its overall bookkeeping of merit?

The human order of ancient society expected the parent to give his child physical life, material support, and protection during the vulnerable stages of development. In return, the parent of antiquity was entitled to exploit most of the life reserves of the child and to punish him to an extreme for disobedience. The child owed perpetual obedience and respect to the parent. In turn, he could extract similar devotion and submission from his children. Parent–child relationships in our age are imbedded in a mixture of scientific knowledge and anachronistic, often hypocritical, and pseudoethical value formulations regarding the rights of parents and the rights of children. Progress toward an improved justice of parent–child relationships will depend on the clarity with which we define the relevant ethical issues as they are affected by the shift in roles of today's parents and children.

Since the reciprocity of parent-child justice is based on a minimally 3-generational context, what remained unbalanced in one generation, is expected to be balanced in the next. From the vantage point of the parent it appears that his child is entitled to more rights if he, the parent, was himself raised with the proper amount of love and consideration—and so the chain continues. Each generation is given in proportion to what the previous generation has received and the expectation posed on each generation is balanced with what is given in terms of care and concern.

A generation "gap" in the continuity of the interlocking chains of either parental ministrations or parental expectations of gratitude can upset the balance of justice between parent and child. In order to examine the balance of such complicated ledgers, we would have to know more about the essential dimensions of intergenerational justice.

Parents of today can still be more articulate in expressing their needs than their children are, although there is less social support of the parent's position than there was traditionally. Society has granted to the parents sexual possession of their spouse, expectation of a degree of loyalty from their children, and a legal sanctuary from certain aspects of individual accountability in the competitive power struggle of daily life. Yet what often remains overtly ignored and denied is the parents' deeply felt conviction about their right to expect from their child gratitude and at least a limited repayment of their ministrations.

Children's rights are more intrinsic, and young children are even less able to articulate them. They are entitled to be physically raised and guided toward life patterns which will help their development and ultimately liberate them from excessive obligation to their families. Society, which on the one hand prevents extreme cruelty to children by certain restrictions on parents, can also confuse the parents regarding the primacy of ethical values. The primary ethical obligation of raising one's child to maturity is commonly emphasized less than such secondary values as control of women's freedom to have abortions, shame of sexual functions, shame of premarital sexuality and pregnancy, etc. Even increasing the freedom of parents to obtain divorces is a questionable goal unless it is balanced by obligatory exploration of the extent to which parental strife will lead to exploitation of the children.

Any tendency toward emphasizing secondary ethical values tends to becloud rather than support the most important human obligation: to give to a helpless infant without expecting return of benefits, at least for some time. This is the point at which parents whose own background was not conducive to the establishment of trust in the justice of the world would need the most support from society. The paradox of giving to a child more than what one received himself as a child cannot be expected to be overcome by every parent.

As a birthright, children deserve to be reared responsibly; rearing is not a reward for their earned merit. Paradoxically, however, the child's privileged position, if carried to an extreme, may lead to his exploitation through his becoming permanently, symbiotically dependent on the parents. The secured possession of an obligated partner, especially if the latter is an overavailable parent, may lead to an insuperable wish never to relinquish the relationship. In addition, a guilt-laden obligation to the overdevoted parent might make every consideration of change and growth difficult. Excess indulgence thus can lead to as much exploitation as overt child abuse.

A multiplicity of factors may complicate parent–child accounting. Remarriages which bring children of varied parentage together are one example. Another confusing factor is inherent in cases of adoption. Further complications can be introduced by well-to-do parents who can afford to hire substitute caretakers to raise their children.

Due to the fact that small children are unconditionally under the authority of their parents, they may be completely unaware of the injustice of certain parental actions and omissions. Children are not able to directly retaliate even when their sense of justice suffers, whether it occurs instantaneously or cumulatively throughout their growth. Frequently, it is not until the child grows up and becomes a parent himself that he discovers his strong resentments about the earlier suffered abandonment, injustice, or exploitation. Many parents have reported that upon the discovery of their own long-swallowed childhood injustices they swore not to inflict the same on their children. Yet how many of them have discovered years later that, despite their conscious resolution, they had exposed their children to similar injustices?

It will always defy quantification just how much a parent remains in arrears with regard to what would ordinarily be their child's due. Children vary; some may be born physically weak or sick and need more reassurance in order to feel secure. Parental attention can also vary greatly. Some parents can give to their children within comparatively limited time. They make up for time through the quality of their attitudes. In our experience the quality of parenting always depends on the extent and integrity of the parenting the parent himself had once received as a child. The multigenerational accounting determines the balance of the new relationship.

Weiss and Weiss[90] published a father–son dialogue in which they explored the role of the son's filial obligation toward the parents for the financial sacrifice of putting him through college. According to the son, if a child has not been told about the existence of such implicit parent–child agreement and about his consecutive indebtedness, it is the parent's fault and the child is not bound by gratitude. His father responds: "No, if he's raised badly, he probably contributed to it. Don't forget that in a family everybody contributes to the final outcome. The child educates the parents; the parents educate the child; the children educate one another."[90, p. 84, 85] At another place, the son says: "You implied earlier that you don't owe loyalty to those who injure you in the family group. I find that very interesting in the light of our discussion of the problem of when a young person may judge what the other people are doing. I see a contradiction here. The implication was, a person not yet an adult cannot judge entirely what is or is not of value to him."[90, p. 50, 51] To this the father answers: "Certainly, no child is really in a position to judge whether full justice is being done to him in a family. Nevertheless, there are very ostensible cruelties which anyone can judge . . . But usually, normally, the kind of training and discipline to which a child is subjected is good for it."[90, p. 51] Our own concern in this chapter transcends the issues of right to discipline and of power, and places a much heavier emphasis upon the invisible aspects of obligations.

CHILDREN'S INHERENT RIGHTS

The rights of children in families are an extremely important area of concern since parents are not guided by the same kind of merit reciprocity ethics which governs relationships among peers. The dangers of implicit and unintended exploitation of children are therefore easily overlooked. Naturally, even the knowledge of this circumstance cannot always affect the unconsciously retaliative motivation of parents who experienced a higher amount of deprivation and exploitation in their childhood than they can absorb into a balanced outlook of fairness existing in the world.

The following are some of the practical consequences of these considerations:

1. No one should produce a human life without a commitment to raising the child to maturity. Abortion of the unwanted fetus can be a much kinder fate than being born unwanted.

2. The child has a right to be brought up in an atmosphere in which he will be imprinted with the value of parental responsibility as a value

of high priority. Consequently, he has the right not to be instilled with distorted ethical priorities, such as an undue emphasis on the absolute value of the suppression or denial of sexual urges, or of loyalty in a sexual partnership—especially if these values are divorced from the much more fundamental obligation to the life interests of one's children.

3. The child is entitled to be parented in a way which does not constitute overprotection, overpermissiveness, and overparentification. As a sign of subtle decay in any human group, psychological exploitation of children can be masked by permissive, protective, or martyr-like pseudogiving attitudes, which can amount to an abandonment of the child. Covert parentification of the child may take the appearance of an overdose of caring. In other words, it is the child's right and need not to be overindulged.

4. It is the child's right to be raised by adults who assert themselves in their own rights and who know what they should demand of the child, thus providing him with a structured outlook on society.

5. The child has the right not to be exploited through overt cruelty or scapegoated in displaced retributive revenge on the parent's family of origin. This type of exploitation is rarely intended consciously by the parents, except in cases of gross child abuse.

6. The child should be able to count on being loved and accepted by the family regardless of his earned merit. Yet at the same time, a capacity for meaningful contribution should be expected of every child.

7. It is the right of the child to be taught to deal with his siblings justly, to learn to respect the incest taboo, and to be available as a continuing resource to other members in their struggle for survival.

Growing up itself places a heavy demand on the justice of the human order. That which a child receives from responsible parenting in his formative years can never be repaid "in kind." To deal with this implicit obligation or "original sin" of growth, the individual has a number of options:

(a) He can repay his debt to his own children in as unilateral a way as he has been given to. This option is supported by the myth of the nuclear family and is the cause of much unrecognized stress. As the parents feel obligated to implicitly repay their parents through their children, at the same time they are encouraged to renounce all support that they could obtain from their extended families.

(b) The child may remain permanently indebted to his parents and repay them through pathological forms of loyalty, e.g., failure to ever grow emotionally or to separate. In this context any psychopathology and failure of maturation amounts to payment for owed gratitude and loyalty.

(c) We have found that in a number of families the goal of therapy consisted in balancing the asymmetry of conflicting obligations. Seeming total nongiving to one's parents was often attempted to be offset by excessive giving to the children. Therapy was aimed then at a balanced give-and-take in relationship to one's children along with a certain amount of "paying back" to one's parents. In many cases the terminal illness of the old parent offers the opportunity for repayment of obligations and subsequent emotional "liberation" of all three generations from guilt.

The predicament of a parent's experiencing imbalance between receiving as a child and giving to her children is strikingly illustrated in the following excerpt from family treatment:

Wife: "My father never told me I was pretty and my mother never loved me (cries) . . . I was tired of deciding how many kisses to give Tommy and Terry last night . . . You know what I did . . . I screamed at them to cut it out (cries harder) . . . I'm giving them more than I ever got . . . I'm trying something that I never received . . . Charles (her husband), you don't play ball any more often with Tommy than your father did with you . . . You can't compare your life with mine (screams). I never had anything damn it! The only thing I do that my mother ever did is to keep house. When I fix you a nice warm supper which isn't what my mother did for my father . . . Did your mother kiss you when you went to bed?"

Husband: "Yes, up to age 30."

Wife: "My mother never did it . . . I starved!" (Pattern of nongiving parenting)

Husband: "And I drowned!" (Pattern of nonreceiving parenting)

This woman had great difficulty in her marriage in the areas of both obtaining sexual fulfillment for herself and being able to emotionally give to her essentially timid and inhibited husband. Prior to undertaking family therapy she seemed to be entrenched in such amounts of hopeless resentment towards her chronically sick, hospitalized mother that she seriously considered suicide. In the course of family therapy she renewed a closeness with her lonely, divorced father and with her sister who lived 400 miles away. She also began making visits to her mother in a mental hospital a long distance away. In being able to improve the care of her debilitated mother, she seemed to be gaining immensely more than she could have by merely gaining insight into and elaborating her resentment toward her mother.

NOTES ON PARANOIA

Earlier in this chapter we emphasized that a suspicious, paranoid personality development can be based on the actual imbalance of a person's familial merit ledger. From his subjective vantage point of reciprocity, such a person may have been irreversibly emotionally exploited as a child. It is in the nature of the justice of the human world that if the parents remain in arrears in performing their parental obligations to a child, the child will tend to feel like a creditor in all his future relationships. He will regard the whole world and treat all people as debtors. The actual unsettled merit balance begets the basic formula for mistrust. "Since I had not reason to learn to trust the world, the world has to prove itself trustable." The paranoid person keeps the whole world "in arrears," so to speak.

It is an important therapeutic consideration to assess the paranoid person's "ego strength." Traditionally, it has been derived that an individual who has grown up with deficient basic trust turns out to be less capable of taking a responsible stance ("reality testing"). Therefore, in individual therapy with these people, the avenues of insight and working through insight do not constitute a repository of reliable personality resources. According to the precepts of traditional dynamic theory, they are poor analytical candidates and they respond better to supportive than to reconstructive psychotherapy.

The issue of *real* and *actual* exploitation is a major structural determinant in family relationships and consequently an avenue for therapeutic rearrangement. A person may distort or project, but the fact that he or she *did* suffer a real injustice transcends his psychology or pathology. If a human being has been too deeply hurt and exploited to be able to absorb his wounds, he is entitled to a therapeutic recognition of the reality of his wounds and to a serious examination of the others' willingness to repair the damage. Only through such a "concession by the world" will he be prepared to reflect on the possible injustice of his own actions to others. The reader may wonder whether this "technique" can justifiably replace the customary therapeutic expectations of critical self-examination. Yet, the badly hurt paranoid person should be given an extra chance, at least to the extent that the unfair balance of his justice is recognized. Whereas the reality of each member's early exploitation is anchored in the family's multigenerational ledger, each individual family member's sense of suffered injustice becomes his life-long programming for "emotional distortions,"; a psychological reality.

We once treated a man who could be labeled as "pathologically dependent" on his wife. He kept tormenting and accusing his wife for what he alleged was her "bad mothering" relationship with their two children. His behavior was so extreme that diagnostically it could only be labeled as a psychotically paranoid symptomatology. Nevertheless, there was apparently an internal logic to his madness. We learned that as a child he had been rejected and abandoned by his parents. Upon being sent back to the family a few years later, he found a younger sibling, warmly accepted by his parents. Shortly thereafter his parents perished in the holocaust of war and genocide. How could he possibly blame his parents without feeling guilty at the same time? Who would listen to his "little" tragedy compared to the major tragedies of others? He was left alone with his "unsettled account" of justice. In turn, he was driven—and at the same time exonerated—by his subjective sense of injustice to unjustly victimize another person (his wife). Yet he was completely unable to face the objective reality of what he was currently doing and sincerely expected the therapists to side with him.

THERAPEUTIC IMPLICATIONS

Our reasoning about justice should highlight the most significant leverage available to the family therapist through his work in the context of relationships. The relational context of a justice ledger is a more comprehensive and essential dimension than that of power negotiations or that of openness of communications. Whereas some therapists would mainly try to explore, for example, the emotional roots and inhibitions of the angry feelings among family members, our rationale would require that we first know what constitutes the criteria of fairness and exploitation in a three-generational existential context. We suggest active negotiations about the needs, hurt feelings, and rights of the partners. We have often encouraged spouses to prepare lists of negotiating points in the manner of labor–management negotiations. However, we have also tried to fit these struggles into the much larger structure of underlying obligations which tends to include the absent extended relationships.

To some readers our explorations may sound too heavily hierarchy-oriented. We agree that we do not want to be oblivious to the family's hierarchy of obligations. However, the statement that families are not democratic systems is not synonymous with endorsing autocratic submission to authority. The true alternative to antiauthoritarianism is to encourage parents and children to mutually assert themselves as leaders or negotiators in discovering what justice and fairness mean to this particular family.

Our emphasis on working within the context of relationships and on encouraging a constructively assertive action response requires a concrete delineation of our therapeutic rationale:

1. We do not believe that work, even if it is appropriately active and action-oriented, can be truly productive unless conducted in the context of balanced reciprocity. Talking about family relationships in individual, group, or encounter-type therapeutic settings, for instance, appears to us as lacking the pressure of relevance which gives family relational therapy its greatest leverage. Discovering my hidden shameful feelings towards my parent or my child to a third person in complete privacy is not nearly as shameful as having my relative present as well. Even those family therapists who pursue the technique of bombarding the family with instrumental tasks of the therapist's own design may in our opinion bypass the greatest leverage:—acting within the context of deep intrinsic existential indebtedness, obligations, etc. We prefer to expect from family members actions which are not framed in terms of task accomplishment but as efforts in the direction of maximal relational leverage. Even if such an effort leads to no visible effects, its ultimate yield is inevitable in terms of confrontation with rather than denial of the balance of reciprocal obligations.

2. Our emphasis on the action framework, furthermore, differentiates our rationale from that of seeking chiefly an *understanding* of patterns of expression of feelings or of style of communications, etc.—even when the latter is done in the context of family relationships. We do not subscribe to the magic therapeutic value of increased knowledge or conscious awareness if they are not channeled into new patterns of courageous action. Cognitive gains, even if accomplished in parallel by several members, do not lead to the correction of relational imbalances unless carried over into action.

Expression of concern for the other and accepting recognition of the other's concern lead to changes in the action dialogue rather than merely to improved individual insight. Opening up the issues of justified concern and gratitude are among the most difficult but crucial therapeutic tasks. A simple denial of the existence of an obligation hierarchy may appear as if the person lacked all tact and sensitivity to the feelings of others. Fears of hurting others and of getting hurt characterize many families which have given up search for reciprocal fairness.

A mother brings her seven children for a family therapy evaluation. As it turns out, the children have three different fathers, none of whom is maintaining any significant contact with the family. It is implicit in the situation that

either the mother is going to be blamed for inflicting all that pain and deprivation upon her children or, through sparing her sensitivity, the meaning of all
explorations will be practically nil. The therapist must be ready to risk the
mother's exposure sooner or later or he is not going to be regarded as courageous and competent.

The children react with embarrassed, hurt, and guilty feelings as the mother
agrees that her "fault" can be explored. It can be most reassuring to the mother
at that point to learn from the children that they are aware and protective of
her feelings of guilt and shame. However, without the mother's permission the
children may not be able to express any concern about their chronic state of
deprivation and loss.

As they obtain the mother's permission to talk, the children should be encouraged to express their consideration of their mother's feelings. At that point the
mother should be helped to tell the children about her awareness of the children's considerations, etc. It depends on the skill and experience of the therapist how courageously and securely he can move into sensitive areas of potential
shame, hurt, and guilt.

We used to remind family members not to regard our office as a
courtroom and that our function was not to tell who was right or who
was wrong. More recently, we have come to a different understanding
of the role of the family therapist. We now believe that it is essential
to our work to get a picture of each family member's sense of the justice
of the family's human order, even beyond the boundaries of the nuclear
family. Furthermore it is possible that the therapist will gain access to
the deep-lying multigenerational chains of merit accounting of the
family only if he also explores himself vis-à-vis his own family.

Transgenerational retributive accounts may constitute the most important structural forces to work with in treating a family. By comparison with these long-term involvements, other, e.g., work-related or
social, relationships are characterized by short-lived membership.
Membership in more superficially linked groups is replaceable, and
their interpersonal manipulations usually reach only the sphere of
power realities. An employee can be treated unjustly, fired, and replaced, yet the unfair boss may himself leave too, and the system will
not carry the consequences of unjust human action. The life process
does not permit such easy escapes from the familial consequences of
existential guilt. The study of families indicates that damage done and
suffered will always be kept in a personal quantitive account sheet of
the invisible ledger of justice. Furthermore, the account will affect the
"slate" which the next generation carries. It is for these reasons that any
theoretical (e.g., communicational, interactional, need-motivational,
etc.) framework which disregards the merit ledger will be insufficient

to explain motivations of even a single individual, not to mention multi-generational patterns.

The therapeutic exploration of multigenerational merit accounts is greatly facilitated by the actual inclusion of three generations in the sessions. Strong resistances may block the introduction of such explorations on the part of all members. In cases where this resistance can be overcome, the therapist's offer to help with the bankrupt, ambivalent, or emotionally nonavailable parent–grandparent relationship may turn into a powerful motivating factor. The frozen, hopelessly avoided relationship stalemate frustrates all three generations' wishes for love, sympathy, and repair of damages.

In encouraging an active confrontation among generations, the therapist has to be prepared for the risk of an emergence of unexpected disrupting feeling reactions in all participants. A sudden reopening of the yearning for love of and loyalty towards his parents can turn a husband temporarily against his wife. An impulsive wish for infidelity, separation, or divorce may emerge. In other cases the intensity of resentment toward the aged parents seems to be so great that painful accusatory statements unavoidably lead to mutually reinforced, guilt-laden withdrawal. The therapeutic relationship may be endangered by a suddenly emerging temptation: The family members might resolve their painful dilemma by assigning the scapegoat role to the therapist. Suddenly, placing all the blame on the therapist appears to them as an escape hatch through which to avoid the burden of guilt and accusation within the family.

Despite the discouraging aspects of such outcomes, it is our experience that it is worthwhile to try to induce the family members to take these difficult steps, provided the family therapist is experienced in the three-generational approach. One of the great opportunities of the three-generational approach lies in the possibility of rehabilitating the member's painful and shameful image of his parents. We have not seen anyone benefit from a therapeutic outcome in which a person only faces, realizes, and expresses his contempt and disaffection towards his parents. In our experience this is a losing game for everyone concerned.

The multigenerational approach invites each member to explore his parent's developmental past. In many cases this leads to a retroactive exculpation of the parent through learning about the overwhelming handicaps with which he had to grow up and become a parent. One can learn that one's parent was not "bad" for badness' sake. We believe that the major avenue toward interrupting the multigenerational chain of injustices is to *repair* relationships, not to magnify or deny injury done to particular members.

In a number of cases impending death of an aged parent opened up the possibility for reexamination and rebalancing of the account between parent and child. As the mature adult was able to do something for his dying parent, he became able to restructure his image of the parent. In other cases the impending death of one surviving parent helped pierce the wall of resentful withdrawal and open up the long-masked, unfinished mourning over the death of the other parent. The reawakening awareness of closeness was then channeled into action patterns. The task of the resolution of mourning was placed in the context of doing something for one's parent before it was too late. Death itself can mean a beginning of opportunity for therapeutic rearrangement.

FURTHER IMPLICATIONS

In summary, we have learned that the multigenerational balance of justice and injustice constitutes a dynamic motivational dimension of relationships, as well as of individuals. Since motivation theory is not a true causal theory, need and behavior can never be put in a simple, classical cause–effect model. The notion of a constantly recorded, although invisible, account of reciprocal obligations and responsibility adds an important dimension to the individual-based, developmental concept of an inherent need for love and for love objects. The concept of equity presumes the individual to be in a constant action dialogue, responsibly dealing with the important others around him. It stresses the ubiquitous but implicitly quantitative subjective scale which all of us are constantly—if unconsciously—using to determine where we stand in our family's multigenerational obligation hierarchy.

It would be interesting to pursue the reasons why the dimension of justice has been so greatly avoided and denied in traditional dynamic theory. Part of the reason for this denial may lie in the commonplace fear of the confusion of principles of equity of justice with impulsive, vindictive righteousness, on the one hand, and with hypocritical pseudoprinciples, on the other. We are aware of the limitations and pitfalls of the concept of justice as objectifiable reality. We know that people distort the picture of their relationships according to their own subjective needs, interests, biases, etc. We also understand that some people will use the concept of justice in cynical hyprocisy to exploit others. Nonetheless, without a consideration of justice as a dynamic societal process, our understanding of relationships would be greatly diminished.

In this chapter we have reviewed some of the reasons for our turning to justice as a suitable conceptual framework for the examination of crucial, guilt-laden obligations and loyalty binds. A discussion of justice may seem extraneous to a dynamic clinical theory of relationships. Yet, like "basic trust," justice characterizes the emotional climate of a relationship system. Both concepts lie beyond the realm of individual psychology, although both represent systemic points of convergence for fundamental individual dynamic dimensions. They are relevant for the reexamination of the theories of projection, reality testing, fixation, displacement, transference, change, ego strength, and autonomy, to name only a few.

Autonomy of an individual is not to be viewed solely within the confines of a person's ego strength and intrapsychic resourcefulness. The achievement of autonomy is dynamically antithetical to loyalty to the family of origin. Loyalty commitments of individual members are indicators of the familial ledger of justice: They constitute an invisible, intrinsic determinant of chains of action–reaction among family members through the generations.

People who are described from the viewpoint of individual, instinct–defense theory as having a pathological course of character development can in our view be regarded as "fixated" on a crusade to attain their alleged justice. Their formula of justice may be vague, hidden even to themselves, or explicitly and sharply formulated. Individually they may be labeled delinquent, psychotic, paranoid, sadomasochistic, etc. They may end up in prison cells or mental hospitals. Their vindictive course may lead them to murder or suicide.

Other individuals fail to achieve autonomy under the weight of implicit familial expectations. The invisible ledger of merit forces them to plunge into failure. Some could reexamine their life situation in individual therapy, but others resent the therapist's expectations that they be responsible for changing their course. These patients may feel that individual-based, uncovering therapy will increase their feeling of indebtedness even further. They do not have the ego strength for introspective analysis.

Our growing conviction of the importance of loyalty and justice networks in families has coincided with our belief that the minimal context of therapy should be the three-generational family unit. Working exclusively with the nuclear family could ultimately amount to implicit, technical scapegoating of the parents as originators of a detrimental, unjust treatment of their children. We have learned that all noxious relationship patterns have a multigenerational structuring.

Much can be learned from the insights of great playwrights. Classical

Greek drama, for instance, is usually a multigenerational family tragedy, culminating in catastrophic results for individuals.

> "Now I can say once more that the high gods look
> down,
> On mortal issues to vindicate the right at last,
> Now that I see this man—sweet sight—before me here,
> Sprawled in the tangling nets of fury, to atone
> The calculated evil of his father's hand."

Thus says Aegisthus in Aeschylus' *Agamemnon* about his lover's husband who is to be killed by the wife, Clytaemnestra.[2, p. 95]

We hold the opinion that any theoretical framework should ultimately have a programmatic and prescriptive contribution to the art of living. What can the therapist offer as his model for growth and health to families? Most psychopathological theories suffer from lack of prescriptive and guiding value systems. Many health models have derived from the efforts of second-generation authors to reverse the concepts of pathology in order to obtain ideal normality. Yet today it would be entirely too naive to construct the health model, for instance, of Freudian psychology, from a simple reversal of sexual inhibitions or of guilt-laden overconcern for the consequences of one's action.

We cannot claim to have offered a comprehensive formula for family health. Yet we believe that the significance of our theoretical framework transcends the scope of psychotherapy. A multigenerationally executed exploration of the hidden forces of family loyalty and ledgers of justice is a necessary part of reconstructive efforts which could free the younger generations from invisible mandates for excessive vindication. Making these connections explicit by facing them is the least a family can do toward rebalancing imbalances and investing in the emotional health of future generations. Then each individual's struggle for autonomy will become progressively less encumbered with obscure binding forces. In this perspective, we do not suggest that all investigations of instinctual, drive-determined, and unconsciously defensive intrapsychic mechanisms of individuals are herewith invalid. We do not even know the criteria of whether a given individual, in his moment-by-moment psychic survival and in the grip of invisible relational forces, is aided by his instinctual determinants ("Id") or hampered by them as by sly enemies attacking from the rear.

We would like to conclude with a statement about the personal demands of this work on us as therapists. We have found it equally difficult to face a genuine confrontation with two factors: The hierarchy of invisible familial obligations and the spectrum of intrapsychic forces and counterforces. While helping a family to face their own "skeletons," a parallel confrontation is taking place in the therapist's own psychic life as well as within his own family.

5

Balance and Imbalance in Relationships

RELATIONAL MALFUNCTION AND PATHOGENICITY

This chapter attempts to formulate a multiperson systemic counterpart to what psychopathology is in individual terms. The concepts of balance and imbalance in relationships imply a minimally two-person system as their unit. Relational pathogenicity is hypothesized to lie in the constantly changing balance of the long-range ethical ledger of obligations. It follows from the considerations of loyalty and justice.

In stressing the relational systemic aspects of pathogenicity we do not disclaim the validity of either individual psychopathology or normative interactional considerations. These two conventional realms of knowledge offer complementary contributions to the depth-relational system view of health and malfunction. Neither do we propose another set of games that people play (see Berne[7]). We believe that ethical ledgers lie on a deeper level of existential determinants than games, although the option of playing games is an important aspect of what we consider the "ontic dependence"[12, p. 37] between closely related people.

The theoretical considerations of this chapter are as important as their ultimate practical, therapeutic usefulness. Transformation of the individual model into multiperson system concepts requires more than semantic manipulation: The concept of relational balance does not replace but interlocks with the concept of individual depth psychology, in both its experiential and developmental aspects. A balanced relationship promotes healthy individual growth. The criteria of such balance are specific to each relationship. They do not exclude conflict and disappointment or, for that matter, a modicum of those conditions which may unbalance a relationship.

The individual also contributes to the balance of his relationships through his availability, actions, and personality.

Balance and imbalance imply a changing state of the justice and fairness of relationships. The ledger includes the consequences of imbalance and the participants' efforts at restoring balance. A parent's implicit burden of caring for the unhappy marriage of his parents, his bitterness about his own consequent early deprivations, his envy of his spouse's comparatively happier childhood, his rage over his role of having to be the rational and peaceful member in his family, etc. are all parts of the bookkeeping which has to be at least partly balanced through his current relationships.

The fact that the total end result of the ledger may be unbalanced at any given time is not the crucial determinant of health versus pathogenicity of a relationship. In that it requires a new effort at rebalancing, transitory imbalance contributes to growth in relationships. Only fixed, unchangeable imbalance with its consequent loss of trust and hope should be considered pathogenic.

Since our concept of dynamic balancing pertains to justice ledgers in families, its main dimensions include merit, obligation and other ethically meaningful aspects of relationships. Therefore, although it is relevant for the health of individual members, balance can never be ascertained from the extent of psychic stress or satisfaction of one member, without regard to the justice of the other(s) from his (their) viewpoint. Relational pathology of individuals has to be translated thus into system terms of pathogenicity.

While we stress the merit ledger of justice as the most fundamental relational pattern that requires balancing, we are aware of many individual needs and aspirations which all have to be balanced within such ledgers. Self-assertive, instinctual and security needs of individuals are examples of additional factors which affect the actual current balance of relational ledgers.

Less than individual health or normality still can permit balanced relationships. For instance, a mentally retarded individual can fit into relationships which are balanced for both his and the other persons' requirements. Since balance implies reciprocity, the healthy person's exchanges with the retarded one will require asymmetric accounting in order to remain balanced. The underlying principle of fairness can guide the parties to build up a satisfactory equity of exchanges. The same is true of relationships between any two or more partners of unequal power, provided there exists a tie of openness and integrity of accounting.

Lastingly unbalanced relationships imply individual psychopathology of at least one of the key participants. Imbalance in the reciprocity of a relationship is never static or stagnant and unless it can be rebalanced, it leads progressively to more explosive tension.

Although it is difficult to separate the detrimental implications of imbalance from those of exploitation, the essence of imbalance is always a chain of social processes rather than an individual's initiative or acts. Imbalance transcends one's conscious doing or fault. For example, a relationship system based on denial of reciprocity may be maintained in good faith on a power or economic basis. Parents may fight a battle with the shadows of their own past exploitation, unwittingly "using" the lives of their children for balancing any alleged unfairness of their childhood.

Pathology is an individual, medical concept. Its counterpart on a multiperson system level must be defined as a pathogenic relational configuration. We presently have no language to describe familial pathogenicity. It has been traditionally designated only through the resulting individual psychopathologies of family members. However, as family therapists we must define an appropriate structural, causal, and descriptive gestalt instead of relying on a mere aggregate of individual pathologies. The enterprise will require the use of the concepts of loyalty, justice, and order of the human world as building blocks.

The disarrangement of the system gestalt of merit accounting is no less real than individual pathology, psychology or physiology. As we explained in earlier chapters, the individual is a member of a relationship system through his loyalty commitments. He is committed to the family through both manifest and invisible obligations which in turn are regulated and continuously balanced by the members' interactions. It is a universal human tendency to expect fair returns for one's contributions and to owe fair return for benefits received from the others. Yet there are factors which overburden the members of any relationship system and cause them to avoid keeping a fair ledger of justice. This chapter describes the ways families deny and circumvent this responsibility and thereby induce pathogenic relational patterns between their members. We maintain that knowledge of the properties of the ledger is more fundamental than knowledge of the manifest patterns.

THE BURDEN OF KEEPING THE ACCOUNTS OF ADVANTAGES

People may find it natural to live up to simple obligations in the current manifest give-and-take of their social interactions. However, the long-term responsibility for the "bookkeeping" of accrued obligations begins to burden the individual with demands for both an ordered memory and a capacity for postponed balancing of ledgers. It is an even greater demand to consider the entire family's accrued obligations. The larger the extended family, the wider the range of possible emotional benefits for the members, but also the larger the scope of the hierarchy of obligations. The roots of obligations may go back several generations and lie beyond the knowledge of those living.

It follows from this that one of the requirements for a healthy or growth-promoting family relationship system is to have relatively comprehensible rules and criteria of obligations and of permissible individual autonomy. Clarity of the rules for keeping the ledger contributes to an atmosphere of basic trust in any social group. In the absence of such clarity, manipulativeness, suspicion, and a collapse of justice ensue. Chaos or rigid authority, as defense against chaos, are then bound to arise.

PATTERNS OF LOYALTY CONFLICT IN MARRIAGE

Loyalty conflict is intrinsic to any family life. All individual assertiveness is a challenge to the shared family loyalty. More conflicting loyalties are added when the young adult is ready for new, responsible peer engagements. Marriage often provokes confrontations between the two original family loyalty systems, in addition to its demands on both spouses to balance their marital loyalty against their loyalties to their families of origin.

We postulate that the deepest relational determinants of marriage are based on a conflict between each spouse's unresolved loyalty to the family of origin and his loyalty to the nuclear family. We call the unresolved obligation to the family of origin the "original loyalty." Original loyalty is not necessarily proportionate to the actual loving ministrations from the parental unit. Such loyalty can be focused on a grandmother or aunt, on nurturing siblings, a house, a city, a cultural subgroup, a country, or even on a helplessly sick, allegedly, nonparental, mother.

When a man and woman contemplate marriage, their loyalty to the anticipated nuclear family unit must grow to such pervasive importance that they can overcome their original loyalties. Other components of their motivation and capacity for balancing their new commitment originate from the reproductive instinct, consisting both of heterosexual attraction and mediated loyalty to children to be born out of the relationship. Affection, a capacity to love and to be loved, is another factor in the commitment. Another is the wishful fantasy of creating a better family unit than one's family of origin. In certain cases this is extended to a conscious feeling of rescuing the other or being rescued by the other from an undesirable, detrimental, shameful, or painful family situation. Additional balancing factors are: conforming to society's expectations, joining the peer values of other young married people, sharing in the dignity of parenthood and family rights, a sense of security, satisfaction in caring for and being cared for, and mutual friendship.

All of these factors must predominate to enable the mates to counterbalance their original loyalty bond. Yet given even an optimal mutual reinforcement among these factors, the original loyalty commitments can only partially and temporarily be ignored. Without some form of reconciliation or "working through," these original, mostly unconscious loyalty commitments tend to undermine the new commitments. Sensing the stress of such conflict causes many people to (a) shy away from marital commitment, (b) turn acutely disturbed at the point of formalizing the commitment, (c) resort to self-sacrificial (neurotic) defensive measures in an effort to "ethically" balance this conflict, or (d) dissolve their marriage.

A young female, the winner of several beauty contests, placed her conservative parents under great stress when she moved into a separate apartment and implied that she was having numerous love affairs. Following several months of "rebellious" existence, she became engaged to a young man. However, on the eve of her wedding she decided to renounce the engagement, stating that she "does not deserve" to get married. Based upon her behavior, she was diagnosed psychotic and was hospitalized.

After several months of family therapy the young woman was discharged from the hospital, whereupon her mother became the primary patient with a depression of long duration. The daughter then recognized her capacity for useful occupation and social life, but she kept choosing male companions whom she always had a good excuse for not marrying, while she remained completely available to her parents.

In another traditionally minded family none of the three active, unusually successful brothers married before the age of thirty. Each decided to wed only after being advised to do so by their parents. It is interesting to note that their father served warm milk in bed to the three brothers, long into their twenties.

In another family with four children in their thirties, only one son married. This man became psychotically depressed a few years after his wedding. Subsequently, he lost his job and, despite his intelligence and a college degree, returned to work at the family store as a shipping clerk and truck driver. His father paid him a low salary, and he was never made a partner in the business. His wife unsuccessfully championed his fight for independence and fair treatment within his own family. When he later developed a malignancy, the man rejected his wife's devoted ministrations and to his very last day professed exclusive loyalty to members of his family of origin.

The marital system may serve in many ways as a transitional depository of loyalty or trust. In historic times the marriage contract was founded on arrangements between the two families of origin; according to the myths of our times, it should be based on sexual attraction and affection between mates. The marital union, while not founded on "blood" relatedness, is nevertheless aimed at such loyalty through producing offspring. Ideally, the parents also form a solid loyalty team to support each other in responsibility emancipating themselves from their families of origin. However, probably due to the ethical implications of dependence, the vertical (transgenerational) loyalty alliances, though often denied or minimized, are more deeply founded and stronger than the horizontal alliances.

THERAPEUTIC POTENTIAL OF THE DIALECTICAL BALANCE OF LOYALTY OBLIGATIONS

Each loyalty system can be characterized as an uninterrupted book-keeping of obligations with alternatingly positive and negative balances. Showing of concern and caring add to the positive balance, and any form of exploitation depletes it. The balance between the parents and their families of origin is traditionally assumed to be a fixed one. It is part of our myths that parenthood is a one-way street for giving, and childhood for unilateral dependence. The parent is expected to acquiesce in the status quo regarding his frustrations of the past. On the other hand, whatever he is able to repay emotionally, he is expected to give to his children.

Our concept of relational autonomy pictures the individual as retaining a modified yet fully responsible and sensitively concerned dialogue with the original family members. In this sense the individual can be liberated to engage in full, wholly personal relationships only to the extent that he has become capable of responding to parental devotion with concern on his part and with the realization that receiving is intrinsically connected with owing in return. Loyalty thus is not synonymous with love or with positive emotions, although emotional "warmth" is inseparable from a sensivity to the fairness of human situations. In family therapy we assume and actively explore how *every* parent has a chance for an improved, more reciprocal loyalty exchange with his family of origin. A more giving attitude can yield beneficial returns for the parent himself, even if his own dependence on the family of origin can never be gratified. To liberate himself from his original debt and the guilt of unconcern, the parent can learn to obtain gratification from his remaining, increasingly giving relationship to the aging or ailing grandparent as if the latter were his child.

The nature of obligation balances is intrinsically dialectical, in that more giving may be the way to receive more in a given relationship. This perpetual motion characteristic of relational dynamic is partly based on the antithetical relationship between power and obligation. What is apparently given up in terms of self-assertive power positions while fulfilling an obligation to another, will at the same time result in a consequent improvement of one's position in terms of guilt accounts.

It follows from the dialectic nature of parent–child relationships that the more a parent shows true concern for the growth of his child, the more likely is the parent to reap emotional satisfaction. Parental neglect or exploitation of children are spurious shortcuts of energy investment. Inevitably they backfire in narcissistic injury and guilt to the parent and losses to all concerned. Although the parent–child system of loyalty and trust should be positively self-reinforcing, it needs priming from the parent's mastery in reconciling his loyalty obligations to his family of origin. The parent can use the child's innate capacity for affection for "refueling" his own supplies of basic trust—a phenomenon described by Harlow[50] in maternally deprived monkey mothers and their infants.

THE CHILD'S AUTONOMY REDEFINED (DEVELOPMENTAL DIMENSIONS)

The child's growing autonomy presents a conflict within the vertical loyalty system. Autonomy is a misleading concept, unless understood in relationship terms: It should encompass the capacity for rebalancing between vertical and horizontal commitments, rather than abandonment of the former. The child does not become loyal to himself in a vacuum. Autonomous development requires that the child disengage from an exclusive loyalty to the family of origin and devote himself to peer and marital relationships. While rebalancing these old and new loyalties, adolescents seem to be able to relate to society as a whole, ideas of progress, science, art, etc., as substitutes for human relationships. Erikson's[34] concept of a developmental moratorium is pertinent: A moratorium consists of postponed resolution rather than desertion of the original loyalties. Such a moratorium may be overly prolonged: As the individual remains in a state of relational stagnation, symptoms of individual pathology appear, with unresolvable and unchangeable, though denounced vertical loyalty commitments beneath.

In certain family systems any move toward autonomy on the part of a child constitutes an unforgivable disloyalty. Conversely, failure to develop autonomy is overtly deplored but covertly valued as proof of a loyal commitment to the family of origin. In order to sustain a viable relational system in any family, the growing independence of children must be constantly rebalanced with more mature forms of repayment of gratitude to their parents.

Autonomy in our sense should not be conceptualized in functional, executive, or effectiveness terms: An absolute executive autonomy would mean the antithesis of loyalty, concern, committedness, or even relatedness; it places the individual in a position of self-centered isolation.

Emancipation from the overdependence of childhood hinges on the success of the adolescent's attempts at rebalancing loyalty obligations. This must be emphasized because of the undue stress by individual therapists on the importance of unilaterally cutting off the manifestations of dependence during individuation of adolescents. It is true that throughout maturation the adolescent must learn to discount rigidly binding obligations for repayment of the parents' availability and services. Without a "liberation" from such obligation the adolescent is not able to free himself and use his potential, e.g., in the process of evaluating and committing himself to peers and prospective mates. However, to achieve a new balance, a prolonged process of *negotiation of compromises* must take place between the adolescent and his parents. This process is often bypassed through acts which are expected to magically resolve the conflicts of emancipation. Sudden physical separation or the offering of exoneration through the adolescent's self-destructive behavior may have this meaning. Such precipitate acts becloud the issues, making the struggle for autonomy go underground and reappear later, when it is even more difficult to evaluate and balance obligations.

While loyalty conflicts are important in adolescent maturation and separation, there are many other significant psychological issues. (See Stierlin's dialectical model for a broad spectrum of issues.[84]) The most respectable and intrinsically logical pattern for release from obligations to one's parents is parenthood. In becoming a parent, the young adult gains an excuse for discharging obligations to the child instead of the parent. Yet this form of resolution is far from being as successful as it appears in our fictions of parenthood. The assumption that the young parent can repay his parents (entirely) through ministrations to the subsequent generation is incorrect, based on partial denial, and therefore bound to lead to further conflicts.

THE REAL TRAITOR: A TRAGIC ITEM OF THE DAY

The rigidly unchangeable persistence of patterns of imbalance in the family's merit ledger can remain outside all members' awareness. Postponement of resolution or rebalancing can further be masked through involvement of one member in an outsider. An unbalanced overinvestment by the offspring of a spouse and children can result in unexpected explosion of retributive measures. It is well known that murder occurs most frequently among people tied to each other through kinship or affection. Seemingly inexplicable eruptions of violence can find their explanation in the multigenerational merit ledger.

Mrs. S, a young woman of 23, was fatally stabbed by her father as she prepared to leave her parents' house after trying to reconcile their argument. It was also mentioned that Mrs. S, a mother of two, was about to make plans for her third wedding anniversary.

The story seems paradoxical in that a young woman was killed at the point when her role was that of a devoted daughter. Was the father's attack intended on the mother? Was there an error involved and the daughter killed accidentally? Since the murder was committed with a knife, it is hardly possible that the daughter was mistaken for her mother. But if the argument was between the parents, why was the daughter punished?

Considering the dynamic meaning of parentification, the story does not seem that paradoxical. The daughter's preparation for her third anniversary might have meant to these parents an undeserved triumphant display of desertion. Any parent would, of course, be happy over the successful adjustment of a child. However, if the child personified to the parents their own parent on whom they felt dependent and by whom they felt abandoned, unconsciously they could blame their daughter as the culprit. The parents' continued arguing might then be multiply determined. One determinant could be a desire to retrieve the lost source of dependence. Their constant arguing would assure the child's continued caretaking involvement.

If the daughter was repeatedly recruited to solve the parents' endless conflict, reminding the parents of her own successful marital involvement would hit their dependent core, making the parentified daughter the implicit culprit. In this light the father's stabbing his daughter would follow from both parents' desperate hunger for parentification reinforced by a deeply felt right to restore hurt justice. The parents' argument could have been externalized from their own parent images upon their child and secondarily displaced upon each other. In the heat of their argument the secondary displacement may have collapsed for the father. Implicit sharing of the two parents' "justice" may have extinquished the father's guilt over murder.

FILIAL REGARD, LOYALTY, AND EGO STRENGTH

What is the place in relationship theory of what, in the individual framework, is described as ego strength? Does assertion of individuality conflict with consideration of loyalty obligations, or can the two mutually enhance each other? Dysfunctional relationships, especially detrimental loyalty configurations, exploit rather than support the individual. Exploitation in a relational sense means manipulation of losses. Depending on timing and total relationship configuration, qualitative deficiency in a parent–child relationship might be as damaging as early loss of parents.

It has been generally accepted that death and other forms of early deprivation diminish children's resources for self-esteem and functional competence in their later years. Naturally, there is room for reparation of losses either through the child's innate reserves or through compensatory influences in his other formative relationships. Fortunate circumstances can help the individual fill the gap in trust and dependence and undo the effects of what could become a crippling, pathological grief (e.g., the child's blaming himself for the parent's death).

The child who develops a genuinely low regard for his parent is probably worse off than one who loses a loved and respected parent. The exploitative, unfairly manipulative, relationally bankrupt parent places an implicit burden on his child to restore the parent's image before the child can achieve fairness in reciprocal dealings. Perhaps the heaviest encumbrance on one's merit balance sheet is contempt for one's parents. In having to be loyal in the face of a low regard for a parent, the individual experiences constant depletion of his reserves of trust. In many tragic instances, children protest disparagement of their parents without being appreciated or even noticed. The child's loyalty seems to be wasted and disconfirmed.

Loyalty conflicts are thus more vital and deeply rooted handicaps for the individual than communicational conflicts. Caught in a one-sided loyalty situation, one tends to escape through denial, rebellious acts of disloyalty, or scapegoating of another relationship, e.g., his marriage. By such indirect solutions, the person implicates himself in more profound inauthenticity which can undermine even his integrity. In a projectively accusatory marriage, one is crushed between an increasing guilt over destruction and a decreasing hope for relevant resolution of the original conflict.

LOYALTY IMPLICATIONS OF THE DEATH OF AN ADULT'S PARENT

The death of a parent terminates the possibility of further balancing obligations. In the sense that there is no more possibility—hence obligation—for rebalancing through direct action, death may seem to bring relief. However, death also can aggravate one's suffering, by closing all hope for acquitting guilt–laden obligations toward the dead parent.

In two cases where women had stated that they had low regard for their mothers as rejecting, exploitative, negative personalities, the death of their mothers produced entirely different results:

In the only session which involved her parents, Mrs. A, a mother of three, attacked her mother with vindictive anger and accusations. She pointed out how deeply hurt she had been when her mother had not invited her and her children on a religious holiday while her husband had been out of town. In the outpouring of emotions Mrs. A was hardly able to listen to her mother's arguments in self-defense.

Her mother died unexpectedly a few months later. Ten days prior to the death, however, Mrs. A and her mother had what she described as the only good conversation the two had ever had. Following the death she connected her anger and frustration with the fact that fate had not allowed her to improve her relationship with her mother. She seriously considered suing her mother's physician for negligence.

The bereavement caused Mrs. A to redirect her contempuous resentment. Instead of blaming her mother, she now attacked others: her father, brother, husband, children, and the therapists. Looking for the only available consolation, she planned to visit her mother's only surviving relative, a 78-year-old man. Through this she hoped to find circumstances which could explain and exonerate her mother's alleged shortcomings. To the extent the blame could be pushed further back to preexisting circumstances, Mrs. A could absolve her mother from part of the blame and shame. She also continually played with the possibility of scapegoating the female therapist.

Mrs. B had somewhat similar feelings toward her mother, and she was deeply pessimistic about the prospect of ever improving their relationship. In the course of family therapy she discovered that her mother was fatally ill. While this circumstance limited the time span for any successful improvement of the relationship, the pending loss acted as a stimulus for rethinking the still-remaining opportunities. As her mother became physically more dependent on her, Mrs. B was able to transform her attitude toward her mother from one of contempt and resentment to one of love, reversal of dependence, and respect. Death came as an acceptable relief which enabled Mrs. B to state: "I have lost my mother but I have gained a mother."

FLIGHT FROM FACING THE LEDGER

A major method for shunning the burdens of balancing relationships manifests itself in the establishment of a climate or "rules of the game"

under which personal obligations become obscured, mystified and ultimately, inscrutable.

REPUDIATION

We hold the opinion that the crisis of the contemporary family and
of society as a whole is related to a trend toward collusive denial of
invisible loyalties, intrinsic responsibilities, and their underlying ethical
meaning. Whereas denial on an individual level is definable in psychological terms, collusive denial does not postulate a simultaneous parallel
alignment of individual denials in all members. Our interest in ethical
issues is not concerned with the individual's religioethical values and
attitudes but rather with the social justice of relationships. Justice, as the
structure of collective normative expectations, forms the context of
relationships. Kelsen states: "It is important to distinguish as clearly as
possible between obligation in this normative sense of the term and the
fact that an individual has the idea of a norm as obligation; that this idea
has a certain motivating influence on him, and finally, leads to a behavior in conformity with the norm."[57, p. 191] Restated, the individual is
embedded in a social context of obligations whether he chooses to
recognize it or not. The normative expectations of one's human world
form the crucial element in one's normal or pathological functioning.

The concept of the objective justice of an individual's relational world
can be extrapolated to society as an ethical system. Reductionistic ideals
of our Western democracy may equate a free society with the sum total
of all competing and assertive motivations of all of its members; however, it is obviously inadequate to assume that the dynamics of, for
instance, American society consist of the randomly competitive, aggressive, and assertive power inclinations of its citizens and groups. Such a
view amounts to a denial of the basic patterning of relationships.

Every nation is measured and measures itself by the justice and fairness of its strivings. The exploited nation, although financially and politi-
cally the loser, may become stronger through the existenial reality of
its justice. Many successfully exploiting great powers in history suc-
cumbed not to external enemies but to internal challenges to their
justice, purpose, and action.

Many great religions and revolutionary movements began with ideals
of aiding the exploited and the underdog. Gradually these movements
turned into successful, powerful, and wealthy organizations. Concurrently, they produced anomie i.e. normlessness; individual members'
loyalty and commitment to action became increasingly confused by

hierarchical rather than ethical obligations and, subsequently, a vacuum of values.

Family systems, even more than entire cultures or societies, have their own intergenerational accounting of merit. The intergenerational chain may lead either to progressive accumulation of guilt and indebtedness or to progressive exoneration. The multigenerational histories of families show periodic oscillation between increase and gradual decline of vitality. The individual who is born into a guilt-laden phase may find himself at a disadvantage. The burden of intrinsic expectations to rebalance transgenerational indebtedness may induce him to escape by denying his human context—to live a life of "exile" from the family. What are the mechanisms of progressive encumbrance of the balance sheet for an entire family?

Since the problems of fairness, justice, and loyalty can never be fully resolved, all of us must resort at times to defensive avoidance and denial of reciprocity. In some families, however, these defensive mechanisms become almost exclusive ways of coping with loyalty conflicts. Growth and individuation become nearly impossible in the context of such binding relationships. (Some pathogenic adaptational patterns are enumerated in the early literature on family explorations in schizophrenia.[19, p. 44] Family members may mutually cultivate chaotic meaninglessness and mystification in order to perpetuate their symbiotic bond, as if they were obligated never to accomplish any task or to close any significant issue. Families may be collusively committed to avoiding the resolution of any grief and thereby jointly resist any change or emotional growth in any member.[14] They may dwell on material issues, success, school achievement, etc., in repetitious, nonproductive fashion, in an effort to avoid the resolution of loyalty obligations.

Adopted children face an almost inevitable mystification in growing up. The act of giving a child for adoption, the secretive way in which most adoptive agencies handle information about the biological parents, and the protective necessities of the adoptive family all have inherent denial characteristics. Partly because of this veil of denial, it is almost impossible for many adoptive children to resolve their conflict of loyalties regarding which set of parents is more genuinely giving and therefore deserves their devotion. If they side with either set of parents, they have to be disloyal to the other set, often without knowing the criteria and measure of their comparative indebtedness.

While it is rational to assume that an early adoption can create a situation psychologically equal to natural parenting, a closer study of adoptive families proves the situation to be more complex. As the children discover the fact of their adoption, they tend to grow curious about the reasons that caused their natural parents to give them up. How can they trust any adoptive parent if they cannot trust their natural parents? Furthermore, biological parenthood cannot be dissociated from a deep, even if conflicted, devotion. Depending on the child's fantasies about the mysteries of pregnancy, childbirth, and other early biological ministrations by the natural parents, the adoptive parents may appear as usurping undeservedly exclusive rights and credit.

The adoptive child tends to develop a myth about the real parents who appear "bad" in the light of how they abandoned their young child: He may believe that they were forced to do so against their loving inclinations. In his wishful myth the natural parents become intrinsically good people with whom the child can have unique and mysterious loyalty ties. Ties of blood thus may be the stronger even if the child has never met the real parents. The adoptive or foster child may have to spend a lifetime learning to balance his myth of the superiority of blood ties with the reality of dutiful obligations towards the adoptive or foster parents.

The adoptive parents, on the other hand, have to resolve the ambiguity between their initial certainty of their right and commitment to parenthood, on the one hand, and the fact of not having provided such biological ministrations. Moreover, if there are also natural children in the family, everyone eventually feels the difference that blood ties make. Despite their best intentions, the adoptive parents will have to base their parental devotion on at least partial denial of facts.

FORMS OF RELATIONAL STAGNATION

The concept of relational stagnation connotes pathogenicity through a pattern of lifeless living. It is determined by criteria both inside and outside the psychology of the participant individuals. It is thus to be differentiated from, e.g., withdrawal of an individual from the reality of relationship due to his own pathology. Relational exchanges continue to be a dynamically programmed ledger, but their options become rigidly limited to a stagnant pattern.

Family therapists are interested in the practical significance of relational stagnation: How is it detected and what can be done about it? As with other phenomena described in this chapter, relational stagnation first must be defined on a multiperson system level and then translated into its individual manifestations.

Family systems do not have the same developmental dimensions that individuals do. The individual has a finite life span from birth to death with a progression through identifiable phases. The family system, if defined as broader than the nuclear family, has an infinite existence. Nuclear families do disintegrate, and new generations add family names and roots to the family tree. Nevertheless, the emotional system of my brother's family dovetails with the system of my own nuclear family, even if, for instance, we have not seen one another for almost two decades and our children have never met. Insofar as we represent two poles of a relational position, someone in his family is likely to resemble my position and vice versa. Furthermore, both my brother's and my own nuclear family system meaningfully connect with our family of origin. That system, on the other hand, derives from both our parents' families of origin, etc.

Thus, the continuity of the merit ledgers of multiperson systems is timeless. The major purpose of families is their child-rearing function; a family system can be considered alive, healthy, and growing to the extent it fulfills that aim, and developmentally stagnant if it fails in this most important function. Arrest of the relational growth process in a family can range from the overt triumph of symbiotic possession, e.g., of a schizophrenic child, to various forms of pseudoindividuation. One extreme of pathogenic loyalty is graphically described by Bowen's term "undifferentiated family ego mass."[21, p. 219] On another level, vicariously acting out one's parent's impulses[56] can be considered as arrest of individuation due to unconsciously loyal filial obligations.

It is customary to describe one of the predicaments of contemporary man as alienation. We live in an era in which extreme importance is placed on the need for being "involved," "open," or learning how to be "turned on." Yet anomie, if anything, has increased in our civilization since Durkheim's time.[32] Decline of transcendental religion and other cultural values, as well as of the traditional extended family, have led to a weakening of the ethical support for the individual. The "information explosion" pouring out of the media has at the same time increased the demand for digesting and integrating the data upon which decision making is based. We have come a long way from the era of the "inner-directed man."[75]

The rapid growth of encounter and sensitivity group activities stems in part from the hope that, provided their members are "open" enough, incidentally meeting groups might create a sense of meaningful relatedness, even when the individual has lost his sense of existential belonging in the world of his origins and of his nuclear family. However, these methods may not be able to bring the individual out of his relational stagnation.

Marcuse emphasizes that the individual is overwhelmed by the "mass culture" with its "technological rationality." He voices the need for solitude, "the very condition which sustained the individual against and beyond his society."[64, p. 71] In our opinion, without facing and working at the resolution of his relational obligations, modern man will have no chance to improve his existential predicament and is at best doomed to stagnation. The fact remains that despite our great advances in scientific rationality and behavioral pragmatism, our new values cannot replace injustice and merit imbalance as the most significant social structuring and motivational forces in life.

Overt Failure (Disloyalty to Self?)

A child may fail in all outside social involvements and do so, paradoxically, in order to safeguard his loyal adherence to his family. The entire spectrum of individual psychiatric nosology provides the range of possible categories for such failure: psychosis, school phobia, learning failure, delinquency, etc. In exchange for his deep-seated family loyalty, the perpetually devoted symbiotic schizophrenic offspring is in return often permitted to be disrespectful and abusive towards his parents.

The person who marries a physically, socially, or intellectually inferior partner may unwittingly make an intricate compromise between personal failure and sacrificial accomplishment. At first, imputed disloyalty in leaving the nuclear family is counterbalanced by self-inflicted burdens and sacrificial giving to the handicapped mate. However, we have worked with women who defiantly married psychotic or physically crippled men only to discover the force of their unresolved loyalty commitments to their family of origin many years later. Their moral self-justification, stemming from martyrlike self-sacrifice, yields then to a frustrated ambivalence. As more self-assertive motivations begin to intrude into their marriage, their sacrifice may lose its impact; the inner balance of merits swings in the direction of guilt over disloyalty to their families of origin. Previously, the disloyalty was masked by sacrificial devotion; now it might be rebalanced through shattering hostility to and cruel rejection of their spouse.

Real or alleged delinquent acts by the offspring may serve to bring feuding parents together and thus divert the attention from their mutual destructiveness. Often the key to family treatment with overtly rebellious young people consists in bringing into the open the ways in which they have remained devoted to their parents. The interlocking of superficially rebellious and yet deeply loyal relationship patterns always has a complex, multigenerational structuring.

A three-generational system of exoneration was apparent in a family in which the father's adolescent rebellion and abandonment of the religious background of the family was magnified by the behavior and marriage plans of his two daughters to men of different religious and ethnic backgrounds. It was through the daughters' "disloyalty" that the father began to face his own unresolved loyalty conflicts with his parents.

Sexual Failure As Covert, Unresolved Loyalty Conflict

Uninterrupted, endless fighting between husband and wife, aside from resulting from each mate's personal motivations, is usually determined by the loyalty-based rules of the "homeostatic" feedback system of the marital dyad. By mutually rejecting one another and the marriage, the fighting mates unwittingly prove their unaffected loyalty to their families of origin. Impotence, frigidity, and premature ejaculation may all amount to covert attitudes of disloyalty to the mate to underline the invisible loyalty to one's family of origin.

Manifest problems in heterosexual relationships can often be shown to hinge on hidden loyalties to one's parents. In the following cases, unresolved guilt over disloyalty to one's parents is the substrate of unconsciously determined self-defeating choice of a partner or of failure in sexual functioning.

Miss C, a young black woman, came in to see her individual therapist on an emergency basis. She had cut both her wrists, though not too deeply, because of a pending separation from a young white man who was planning to leave town to enter medical school. She claimed she was all alone since her only relationship had been with Joe, whom she had hoped to marry. However, Miss C indicated that she had been in similar situations with a number of young men, including the one who was the father of her 3-year-old daughter.

When the family consultant asked her if it would be possible for her to include her mother in order to explore that relationship, she refused. She claimed she had no relationship with her mother. All her mother would say was that she was sorry about "her daughter's life getting messed up again." However, she dropped another clue: Her mother had been jealous of her relationships with all other boyfriends.

The family therapist suggested that Miss C might be more involved with her mother than she admitted. Perhaps she was waging a cold war against her mother, aiming to hurt her through her boyfriends. At that point, in a surprisingly spontaneous tone of voice, Miss C recalled a recent dream in which she felt very angry at her mother for paying more attention to a lady friend of hers than to Miss C. She added that she felt exactly the same anger toward her mother in the dream as toward Joe when he first mentioned his new girlfriend.

This woman's self-defeating romantic career can easily be connected with repetitious jealous-making maneuvers, aimed at relinquishing her deep loyalty toward her mother. While she succeeded in making her mother jealous through the boyfriends, the self-destructive choice of friends helped to counterbalance her guilt-laden loyalty obligations. The friendships carried their punishment within them.

Mrs. D came to a family therapy evaluation session because of a serious marital problem. She had been sexually uninterested for a number of years, and she had thought of leaving her husband, although she claimed she had no other male relationship. Previously, she was referred for psychiatric treatment for "low abdominal soreness." She almost seemed amused when she remembered that she used to hide her pregnancy and even the fact of her marriage from her parents. She added that since the beginning of their marriage whenever her mother was in the home she could not have sex with her husband. Sexual frigidity was this woman's first defense against her guilt over disloyalty to her parents, and her intended separation was the second.

Mrs. E, a woman of 38, was recovering from a recent hysterectomy. In the presence of her 20-year-old daughter she told the therapist that she had not been worried about losing her sexual functioning. She described a recent sexual dream in detail as evidence that nothing was wrong with her. The daughter eagerly added that she had similar experiences both in dreams and with other males, yet she had been consistently frigid with her husband. She added that she had to be grateful to her mother for providing her with "good equipment." Throughout the examination of their relationship, this daughter seemed to be heavily dependent on her mother. The negative aspect of their mutual ambivalence was counterbalanced through a shared devaluation of men and through the daughter's sacrifice of her allegedly hopeless marriage. Her inability to commit herself to marriage was an unconsciously willing act of devotion to her mother.

The child of constantly battling parents may feel hurt, rejected, overstimulated, or depressed. On a relational commitment level, however, the child will tend to feel obligated to save the parents and their marriage from the threat of destruction:

The daughter of a continually bickering couple attended family sessions only on vacations since she was attending college out of town. When asked about her rather inconsistently active social life at college, the girl explained that she was unable to involve herself in friendships or to date because she kept thinking about her parents constantly. Since she was no longer available to help or protect her parents, she was worried about the possibility of the occurrence of divorce or of a serious health hazard.

Freezing of the Inner Self

Another form of relational stagnation is an unconscious freezing of the inner self and an *incapacity for commitment* to anyone in a close relationship. Although this form of stagnation refers to an individual self, its determinants are located in a 3-generational ledger of justice. What happened in one generation, is balanced through events in the next two or more generations. Loyalty to the internalized family of origin precludes any deeper personal commitment. However, a pattern of productive functional performance may create an appearance of commitment and responsiveness:

A father of three in an overtly detached but symbiotically entrenched family lost both of his parents in an auto accident at 16. Being an only child, he thus lost his entire nuclear family. He responded to the loss with outward compliance to a maternal aunt who took him into her home. He could never free himself of irrational guilt feelings; due to a kind of amnesia, he often wondered whether—since he was in the car too—he was in some way responsible for the accident. Was this really a "psychological" guilt or was it an expression of a factual negative balance of his obligations? He would never again be able to repay his indebtedness to his parents, and he was doubly guilty for surviving. He was so frozen within that despite being a responsibly providing husband and father, he could not emotionally commit himself to his wife and children without a sense of betrayal and disloyalty to his dead parents. Ironically, his wife recalled that she had married this man for his capacity for "dogged devotion." Inner frozenness and relational stagnation may appear to some people as stability and reliability.

Many frigid women seem to be captives of ambivalent obligations towards their aging mother, as illustrated in a family referred for the two school-phobic adolescents:

The mother, Mrs. A, a professionally active woman, had a marginal involvement with her rational, nonaggressive husband. She refused his requests in many areas of household responsibility: messy housekeeping, indifferent food preparation, etc. She reported an essentially complete frigidity throughout the marriage. At the same time she felt obliged to invite her mother to her home almost every evening. Paradoxically, Mrs. A claimed she had become indifferent to her mother's demands, since she had worked out her obligations in years of individual psychotherapy. However, when asked to describe her current relationship with her mother, she would burst into tears.

In the second year of family therapy, Mrs. A finally consented to invite both her mother and married sister to a special session which her husband and children did not attend. We learned that the grandmother had come to this country at seventeen, married her first cousin, and lived a life which she thought was one of continuous sacrificial devotion. She and her husband ran a small store and raised two daughters. After losing her husband, she took turns living with each of her daughters, but those arrangements did not work out. In the past years she had been living in an apartment by herself and had worked in a full-time job.

Family therapy had revealed Mrs. A's gnawing, insoluble dilemma about how to please her lonely, friendless, frustrated, and self-sacrificing mother. She knew that for help she could unconditionally rely on her mother, who would be glad to come whenever her services were needed. On the other hand, Mrs. A could never rid herself of a sense of guilt-laden obligation towards her mother. She felt that she should be able to give more of herself to her husband and two children, yet whenever she made plans to spend some time with them, she began to feel guilty over her mother being left out.

As Mrs. A was able to overcome her reluctance and feelings of hopelessness, she invited her mother and sister to a special session; now she was ready to stand a triadic confrontation with her family's loyalty system.

The following are excerpts of representative statements made by the three women in this special session:

Sister: I wanted to come down from New York, but I was upset about mother being here. I didn't want her to be hurt by my sister . . . I was afraid I might accuse my sister badly. It is a thorn in our relationship how you (Mrs. A) treat our mother.

Mother: Our relationship's gone. It doesn't bother me anymore. Melitta (Mrs. A) has no time for me though I can also feel out of place with my other daughter. I am glad I work full-time even though I am 70. (cries)

Sister: Mother, I always have a place for you.

Mother: Melitta, in 1952 I was very sick and in the hospital, but you had more important things to do. Yet, I always did everything for your children.

Mrs. A: But mother, I went to the hospital twice every day.

Mother: Maybe you did, but when I really needed you, when I had to start walking again, you didn't come to help.

Mrs. A: But how should I have known about it? You didn't tell me.

Mother: I didn't have to be told when my children needed me. I was there; when I needed them they weren't there. To me, to die makes no difference.

Sister: I think Melitta's children don't treat mother nice; her daughter reflects her attitude. Melitta, you can be nice with a stranger and shrug your sister off. I am very angry; you are not grateful to mother.

Mother: Melitta, I don't feel you ever do anything for me. Forget about love, just at least consideration!

Mrs. A: Oh, mother, don't you think I love you? I feel I do as much for you as you do for me. Do you realize how often we change our family plans on weekends so that we can include you? Am I at fault not to know when you need me if you never tell me?

Mother: I was there all the time. You weren't there when I needed you. When I ask you to come with me to buy a coat, you have no time, but when you want me to go with you, I am 99% there.

After this session, perhaps because of the openness of confrontation with so many painful, deeper issues, Mrs. A must have felt reassured. Three days later, entirely on her own, she appeared with her mother for another separate session. This session began with Mrs. A telling about her satisfaction over her mother's direct expression of hurt and angry feelings. Again her mother insisted that it was better for Mrs. A to "drift away" because she had killed her mother's love. The mother added also that she was ashamed to say how badly she had felt after the previous session, how she had lost sleep and felt miserable for two days. Somehow, it seemed as though the cycle of guilt was gradually broken.

The cotherapists were able to help the angry and despairingly lonely grandmother to talk about her own background. She seemed to show a silent gratitude to the therapists for their sympathetic understanding of how much effort she had invested into her family, with how little success and gratification in return. "When anybody gives me something, I feel like I will owe them a lot," she told the therapists. She admitted to having difficulty in accepting anything from anyone. She described herself as a short-range doer, with little capacity for postponed repayment and trust.

It became clear that this woman had functioned most of her life according to a certain set pattern. As an individual, she could be described as a compulsive worker and a martyr. In terms of balancing of relational systems, she displaced her introjected relationship attitudes from her family of origin onto her daughter. In so doing, she became the child herself and demanded appreciation for her work from her parentified daughter, as if the daughter were the mother she had actually left in Europe at 13.

We can speculate about the foundations of this internalized, frozen relational imbalance: What was the relationship pattern of the grandmother's family of origin? Why did Mrs. A's mother respond with so much hypersensitivity and guilt when offered any considerations? Why was she blind to the transparent, crude scapegoating efforts she directed at her daughter? Why did she have to induce in her children a guilt-laden loyalty to herself? What enabled her to select a collusive husband with whom she could maintain the system? On the surface she had only words of praise for her deceased mother, yet she also told that when her husband, at 29, offered her a chance to visit her family, she turned it down. By that time her internalized multigenerational loyalty pattern must have been sufficiently formed to maintain an "internal dialogue,"[16, p. 66] without any awareness of the possibility of actually repaying her debts. The original bookkeeping system was then partially reprojected upon her nuclear family, and it would take great effort to redirect her internalized "gyroscope."

It is interesting to connect the picture obtained from these two sessions with the one that evolved from more than a year of family therapy for Mr. and Mrs. A and their children.

Originally, Mrs. A was unquestionably the outspoken, demanding parent and somewhat exploitative wife who seemed unbending in asserting her needs and expectations. The only expectation her husband was able to express was his constant dissatisfaction with her careless housekeeping. As treatment progressed and Mrs. A. began to reveal her involvement with her mother, she emerged as an overdevoted, parentified child, captively available for her mother.

Mrs. A had shown a tendency for crying profusely during sessions, especially when her mother was mentioned. Her view of her mother was also full of paradoxes: a disorderly housekeeper, yet eager to do housework in Mrs. A's home. Her mother expected loyalty, yet she was remembered as undependable and a person who didn't always keep her promises. "My mother is not really a person, she has no opinions, she is what you want her to be. Sometimes it is almost like I am her mother. She lives through us, she has no life of her own. I feel awful when I go to the swim club on Sunday and my mother sits home alone. Sometimes I feel I will be relieved when she is gone."

Mrs. A saw her 12-year-old daughter as a replica of her mother in that the daughter made her angry and guilty almost constantly. The daughter also felt that Mrs. A controlled her through continual guilt-provoking "nagging." Mrs. A reported that with her son she replicated her relationship with her father: a stimulating, impulsive, challenging man.

As a result of 2 years of therapy, Mrs. A, became capable of giving herself as a woman and a more understanding and receptive mother, almost in direct proportion to her willingness to face and actively approach her indebtedness to her mother.

Whether more giving marital relationships are possible depends on how rigidly frozen the patterns of transgenerational loyalty are. How can a spouse break into a tight loyalty system among three generations and alter it instead of being exploited and blamed for failure?

In systems governed by captive devotion, the successful martyr has the controlling influence. For the system discussed above, it is likely that in each generation a daughter is caught in the guilt of undischarged filial obligations. The obligations are not discharged because of the nonreceiving, though giving, attitude of each mother towards her daughter. The pain of the resulting blame makes the daughter helpless, with subsequent loss of capacity for relating in other situations. The model of freezing the self is perpetuated.

Marital Loyalty Obtained at the Expense of Vertical Disloyalty

Mixed religious marriages may at their beginning promise unusually stable loyalty commitments, as though both parties by becoming outcasts from their in-groups could form a new in-group. However, the spouses' mutually supported break in loyalty to their backgrounds may mask their unresolved individuation from the families of origin.

Resistance to facing and disclosing each spouse's invisible loyalty to his or her family of origin is important in the early phase of every family psychotherapy. One expression such resistance may take is collusively shared denial of the importance of the ties with the two families of origin. Another is shown in a couple's great willingness to discuss marital and sexual difficulties as their problem, totally excluding consideration of their families of origin. Experienced therapists may see a subtle negotiation by the family in continually exposing shameful aspects of individual and marital issues in order not to have to include a grandparent in the sessions. Scapegoating of a child and the child's willingness to accept the scapegoat role may also be utilized for resistance to multigenerational exploration.

Family members can be defined *traitorous* in terms of deeply invested *suprafamilial cultural* (e.g., religious) *values.* We have observed repetitious, multigenerational patterns of rebellion against religious loyalty. The more the rest of the family responds with passionate rejection of the member designated as traitorous, the more it is likely that he will remain tied to the loyalty system, albeit in the form of negative loyalty. The disloyal member may hold the rest of the family together at his expense.

Parents are seldom placed in the overtly condemned disloyal role by their children. However, from the viewpoint of basic human justice and parental obligations, parents who abandon their children qualify for that designation, whatever their individual explanation or excuse. Long-suppressed and subjectively justified anger about being given up for adoption or abandoned in other ways may erupt through displacement upon adoptive parents or a mate.

Two "disloyal" rebels may band together in mutual loyalty and simultaneous rejection of their respective in-groups, as in marriages which are racially or religiously mixed. Both partners become outcasts of their respective in-groups, while they form a small, new reference group which will regard both original ingroups as out-groups. However, such couples may substitute a "common cause" in place of personal commitment to each other. They reveal their latently surviving commitment to their original in-groups through their passionate crusading against their prejudices. Even two "deserters" of the same in-group may form a small out-group. Careful investigation of such marriages often reveals an informal "adoption" process whereby one party marries the other in the hope of acquiring a more strongly loyal family network at the expense of their mutually abandoned original commitments.

In the final analysis, such collusively disloyal marriages are exaggerated models of the "genuine" peer-level involvements of adolescents. A part of every infatuation consists of excitement about trading of loyalty from the in-group of the original family to a future nuclear family. Other sources of excitement are sexual attraction, the complexities of an encounter with another person, the prospect of creating a new human life, etc. However, it is probable that a significant proportion of such marital decisions are directly linked to parental disapproval.

Children may appear rather soon in such marriages, and can represent the "cause" with which the new loyalty system may claim justification of the imputed disloyalty to the families of origin. This use of children places them in an ambivalent position and makes them convenient targets for the parents' hidden parentification needs. Ultimately, when the children grow up and are ready to leave the parents' orbit, the prospect of separation threatens to deprive the parents of their cause.

On a manifest level the loss of the parents' involvement in the life of their children can lead to depression and emotional depletion. On a deeper level the threat of separation might lead to the emergence of latent, unresolved feelings of guilt towards the parents' families of origin. One way aging parents of separating children can symbolically revive their loyalty to their families of origin is through intensified marital fighting, as if their mutual destructiveness is a sacrifice offered to their deserted parents. In addition, such fighting may also serve the purpose of holding on to the departing children by maintaining in them a guilt-laden commitment to care for their unhappy parents.

Achievement as Relational Stagnation; Money As a System Dimension

Overt personal achievement in one family member can be used as a means of avoiding growth in all family relationships. The successful person may contribute money, political influence, fame, connections, and cultural prominence as substitutes for working on the quality of family relationships. Not infrequently, we have observed the coexistence of prominent and scapegoated, psychiatrically ill, or delinquent members in the same family. Regardless of their divergent external manifestations, they represent two components of the same homeostatic system of stagnation.

Financial interests are traditionally used as a reference point for family organization, but they can be used to avoid facing family relationships. Money can be used on many levels as a pretext or substitute for personal responses:

The teenage son of a wealthy and influential businessman became involved in progressively embarrassing conflicts with the law. In treatment it became clear that the boy needed—and covertly wished for—correction from his father. This man, who was absent much of the time either physically or emotionally, was able to give only detached and vague general responses. However, he was ready to use his wealth for bribing the court or police officials in order to keep those "dumb monkeys" from interfering. The most confirmed and supported family role of this father was that of the successful, powerful, and influential manipulator. On the other hand, in offering to bribe officials he deprived his son from getting the response he needed: to be held accountable for his behavior.

In the family of another financially successful businessman a psychotic son was hospitalized for many years at the "best and most expensive" private institutions. The parents' attitude towards the son's condition was one of extreme self-sacrificing helpfulness, as evidenced by the half-million dollars spent on his treatment. Even after considerable recovery, the father excused his 26-year-old son from every effort to change his completely bland, nonproductive existence, stating: "I had to struggle to put my wealth together, you can afford to choose to be merely a conservationist." Thus, the power and importance of monetary wealth can be the myth by which relational change or development is prevented.

We have found that in some families the only reference to personal relationships is made through issues connected with money. The members can talk about mutual reliability only in counting on one another for financial support in case of emergency:

An elderly businessman's fatherly relationship was expressed through wanting his two sons to enjoy his wealth while he was still living. Therefore, he extended large loans to his sons' business and stockmarket ventures in order to get love and appreciation from them and retain control over them.

The "well sibling" of the family is often viewed as one who has successfully escaped the pathogenic system and is unaffected by the paralyzing bind which has made one or several other members overtly symptomatic. In that sense the well sibling could be regarded as disloyal to the system, as one who defies it by maintaining a sense of reason and individuation. Yet on a deeper, loyalty-oriented level it has often been found that the well sibling is equally caught in a guilt-laden paralyzed commitment to overavailability. His role may be the hardest in that he is commissioned to take care of the entire family's needs for manifest reason and organization, thus allowing the other members to enjoy their regressive gratifications in safety.

Consideration of the various forms of relational stagnation, i.e., pathogenicity, raises fundamental questions about the meaning of life in terms of relationships. What degree of freedom does the individual have after all vis-à-vis the constricting programming power of myths and convictions? Just how realistic is it to expect that entire systems of relationships can ever change? How often indeed is it possible for members of a family to jointly rebalance the configuration of their loyalty expectations and mutual commitments? Does the individual really have a chance to be free, and what is the meaning of that freedom?

Autonomous growth and the overcoming of fixations to early relationship patterns can be inhibited by defensive characterological forces within each individual member's own emotional system, i.e., psychic structure in the classical Freudian sense. A significant dynamic determinant of fixated or distorted development is an unconsciously shared loyalty commitment to all other members' needs for stagnation, stability, or unchanging sameness of the family's relationship system. Even if one member were capable of overcoming the resistance to, e.g., resolution of grief, he would still remain duty-bound to "freeze" his capacity for growth in order not to cause feelings of hurt and loss in the other members. His unconscious personal commitments to maintaining the system will correspond to the actual expectations placed upon him by the other members.

SUBSTITUTE FORMS OF INDIRECT MASTERY

Certain patterns of family relationships present seemingly unbalanced interaction between the members. Such patterns may, however, indirectly balance invisible loyalties.

Negative Loyalty

Loyalty based on seemingly negative acts is important in understanding the underlying connections in relationship systems. The traitor and the scapegoat, for example, are not really outsiders to the system from which they are excluded; they are important connecting links in a chain of complementary relational positions.

Superficially traitorous but essentially loyal family relationships can be described by the paradox, "loyal traitor." Historically, the witch has been the carrier of negative loyalty system roles for society. There are numerous accounts of witches who willingly, though perhaps unconsciously, impersonated the roles that led to their cruel end. Negatively loyal marital attitudes can jeopardize the spouses' underlying attachment, unless help is available.

A resentful and vindictively angry wife stated in the first therapy session with her family: "The only thing I can depend on, as far as my husband is concerned, is his independability." She refused to be affectionate or sexually intimate with her husband and told him to go wherever he pleased. Yet he kept coming back to her; at times he was not let into the house, and he slept in a car parked outside the home.

The husband, a masculine, handsome factory worker, reported that he indeed was involved with another woman, but that he did so mainly to get even with his wife, who some 15 years ago, while he had been away in the Merchant Marine, had associated with another man. Although this could have been utilized in his defense in the therapy session, he refrained from doing so. The wife did not deny that this had happened and added that she would not mind if her husband slept with another woman as long as he did not bother her for another 5 or 6 months until she could cool off. There were also indications that she had been a neglectful mother.

The layers of disloyalty and loyalty between these two people were further complicated when it was revealed that the woman had been at constant war with her mother since early childhood. In a family session attended by her mother and grandmother it became clear that she had felt accepted by her grandmother but rejected by her narcissistically cold and superficial mother, to whom she was never able to express her love. Her deepest resentment was connected with the thought that her mother had never taken the trouble to try to straighten her out as a child. She described how she was struggling with her rebellious child rather than abandoning him as her mother had done to her. With the help of direct confrontations between her, her mother, and grandmother, this woman could have become much more acceptable, feminine, and accepting toward her husband. Once the origins of one's ledgers of justice are traced back to the family of origin, the need for relating to a spouse through negative loyalty usually disappears.

Deeper relational dynamics may make each family member wage a continuous struggle to balance his needs for individual autonomy and secure identity against subservience to guilt-reducing loyalty to the family system. The individual may be assigned a certain segment of the multipersonal network of meaning and is expected to fit in. It is his obligation to participate and not to upset the gestalt of interlocking personal meanings. In some families, scapegoating of one person provides the only semblance of meaningful interaction among the other members. Any "healthy" growth on anyone's part would upset the relational balance.

The martyr always plays the strongest role in a guilt-motivated system, since he is the least burdened by guilt feelings. His devoted suffering mitigates any guilt over past, present, or future disloyalties. This advantage is shared by the scapegoat, although his path differs from the martyr's. Ostensibly, anyone who is scapegoated is placed in that position through blame and condemnation. However, being collectively rejected and persecuted placed the scapegoat in a martyr role, i.e., having the strongest monitoring position as the controller of the others' guilt feelings.

This point is even more evident if we consider the vicissitudes of the dovetailing needs of the scapegoaters and blamers. By blaming and rejecting one person, the rest of the family members strengthen their mutual alliance, and each member can repair his own loyalty to the family. In a homeostatic relational system, without impairing my relationship with A, my relationship with B cannot improve.

Through his negative role, the scapegoat can diminish his own guilt-burdened debit account. Rotating the scapegoat or martyr roles among family members allows a serial balancing of all accounts. The members may not be able to accomplish this through positive acts of giving. Moreover, the kinds of benefits offered as repayment by one member may not be acceptable to others. As a result, a sense of unpaid obligations accrues, increasing guilt in one member and a sense of being exploited in the others. Through the acts of scapegoating and willing victimization, the victim is partially relieved of his guilt over nonpayment and the victimizers experience a temporary decrease of their frustration over having been exploited. From our viewpoint it is important not only to point out the relational meaning of an individual family member's attempts to atone for guilt through becoming a scapegoat, perhaps utilizing his masochistic inclinations, but to demonstrate a relationship system which functions in a phasic, multidirectionally scapegoating fashion.

In one family we saw scapegoating occur in an almost identical manner through three generations. In each generation there was one sister who defied family values, was considered a "black sheep," and was expelled or exiled from the family. In two generations the traitorous daughters entered into marriages with mates who belonged to different religions, and in the third generation a daughter was constantly threatening her outraged parents with such a marriage. The fact that the rest of the family members were rigidly conforming with their religion made this an unforgivable sin. The family reacted to these women with ostracism; they, in turn, conducted their lives in ostensibly self-chosen exile.

It is interesting to contrast the extreme rejection of the scapegoat with the uniformly "close" and nonindividuated relationships of the other members of this family. They lived in a uniquely unindividuated fashion regarding even major personal decisions. The slightest deviation from any unanimous position, e.g., planning for a minor vacation, would imply unacceptable disloyalty. We can assume that such excessive loyalty can be maintained only if it is balanced by an extreme distancing of the scapegoat.

Both the positive and negative relationship patterns were components of a total relationship system, rather than distinct human relationships in their own right. In the youngest generation a *bad* (rebellious, disloyal, inconsiderate) yet emotionally *well* (independent, brilliant) role for the daughter was balanced with the only son's role of moral *goodness* (loyal, reliably available, concerned, devoted) and emotional *sickness* (chronically psychotic, unproductive, dependent). It seems that in the absence of other members with which to share the burden, this boy had to carry the consequences of overdevotion to his parents, in never-ending symbiotic closeness. While the daughter was ostensibly disloyal and a nuisance, she too was devoted, in that she predictably performed the negative loyalty role and thus offered herself to the family as a complement to their positive loyalty.

A persistent commitment to a sacrificially negative role can be assumed to underlie many cases of delinquency in children and adolescents. The scapegoat role is reinforced in this case by further disapproval on the part of agencies of society. Erikson[34] stressed the psychic gain of "negative identity" of a delinquent youth as contrasted with the frightening alternative of "identity diffusion."

It can be assumed that a negative familial loyalty obligation may play a role in the phenomenon described by Freud[39] as "negative therapeutic reaction," where the analytic patient shows symptomatic impairment following appreciation of his therapeutic progress by the analyst. Freud linked the phenomenon with the patient's unconscious sense of guilt and need for punishment, i.e. masochism. From our viewpoint a negative therapeutic reaction can be co-determined by the patient's loyalty to the symbiotic family system. In this sense the reaction itself is indeed "psychologically incorrect," since the phenomenon is anchored in the multiperson system of obligations rather than the psychology of the individual.

In searching for a comprehensive, system-based motivational theory of delinquency, we must transcend (though not discard) the realm of individual determinants. Johnson and Szurek[56] described a lack of internalized impulse control ("superego lacunae") in the parents of delin-quents as a determinant of delinquency. In fact, the child's actions, by evoking society's subsequent punitive reactions (measures by police, court, school, etc.), constitute an external reinforcement of intrafamilial superego function, also to the benefit of the parents themselves.

A "socially redeeming" familial definition of delinquency would pic-ture the child's overtly objectionable behavior as being implicitly sanc-tioned. Accordingly, the delinquent child not only benefits from gain-ing what Erikson[34] called "negative identity," but also fulfills a *negative loyalty commitment* to his family of origin. Discharge of such loyalty obligations may explain the adolescent's striking lack of remorse over delinquency. Furthermore, the delinquent act may itself gratify the parents' parentifying, dependent needs, even without any controlling intervention by society. Family togetherness and feelings of security are reinforced in the "good" family members as a result of the child's allegedly "traitorous" behavior.

Therapists should be alert to the behavioral evidences of such hidden family relationship patterns. A child may be guided into covertly desir-able negative behavior by repetitious inverse injunctions—by learning what not to do. As the parents make a great issue out of forbidding marginally delinquent behavior, they unwittingly give approval through offering negative identity confirmation as the major relational option for their child. The parent–child dialogue becomes pathological not simply because of the existence of a negative confirmation, but because it is selectively overemphasized and because the parent–child dialogue narrows into essentially one dimension.

Sacrificed Social Development As Act Of Latent Devotion

Certain relationship systems are maintained for the purpose of escap-ing from the implications of invisible loyalties or, in a broader sense, from having to face and balance multigenerational accounts of merit and obligation. Entire families can become overencumbered with guilt over exploitation of members. Since the essentials of their justice ledg-ers remain forever unexamined, these families are less resilient rela-tionship systems than ones in which members are expected to face the balance of justice and to be concerned about the reciprocity of obliga-tions. A young member of an overencumbered family may intuitively seek to "borrow strength" by marrying into a "stronger" family with less avoidance of a sensitive, responsible accounting of relational justice. This capacity for courage and sensitivity must be distinguished from open expression of personal feelings by the individuals. The latter by itself does not prove the family's openness to exploration of the accounts of justice and merit. Divorced from its meaning within the context of relationships, mere expressiveness of feelings is of little value.

When we refer to comparative strengths of families, we must emphasize that *power* in an ordinary sense is an insufficient criterion of such strength. One dimension of strength is the degree of individuation that members can obtain in the family. Their differentiation of selfhood should enable them to live "authentically" under the aegis of an intrinsic principle of the self. Such a person can strive to integrate his moment-by-moment emotional needs with the long-term consequences of his actions. He is neither a mere self-sacrificing victim or martyr nor a careless, selfish denier of the needs and rights of others.

Bowen has mentioned a "differentiation of self" scale.[22] He conceives of an intuitively quantifiable scale of 0 to 100, in which 0 would categorize what he calls "undifferentiated ego mass' and 100 an ideal state of differentiation of self. Without elaborating on Bowen's theoretical system, we feel that more emphasis should be placed on characteristics of relationship systems as wholes, rather than on the primacy of thinking versus feeling in individuals. No authentic selfhood can be sustained without a capacity for facing the ledger of reciprocal responsibilities.

A scapegoating arrangement in families may serve to avoid unresolved family loyalties. However, scapegoating is multiply determined, and accomplishes a number of purposes within the nuclear family. The parents' painful marital discord can be masked through assignment of the culprit role. The scapegoated child can also serve as an object of parentification against whom the parents can act out their stored hostility and covert dependence. Furthermore, as is true of any behavioral imbalance, the object-retaining or possessive purpose of the scapegoating maneuver is an important motivational determinant. On an even deeper level, the scapegoating arrangement can interlock meaningfully with the loyalty obligation system of the parent's family of origin. A parent may not be aware of how he utilizes the interactions with his child for escaping from facing his own unresolved conflicts of separation and maturation. The parent's conscious notions of detachment from his parents may simply mask his latent feelings of obligation and guilt about disloyalty. Finally, the willing scapegoat may receive the covert advantage of being the loyal, good family member.

The case of a school-phobic girl of 12 can illustrate some of the complexities of interlocking hidden motivations. At the time of the family's referral to the Family Psychiatry Division, Alice had been out of school for over a year because of her propensity for uncontrollable fears and subsequent nausea. The parents placed great pressure on the therapist to hospitalize their daughter, whom they described as being in an uncontrollably agitated state as she threatened to tear her clothes to shreds, bang on the neighbor's walls, etc.

One of the most obvious early clues about the dynamics of this family system was the mother's hysterical aggressiveness toward both the meek and subdued husband and the therapist. Following the first evaluation session, the father called the therapist and complained that he did not know how to convince his wife to accept the idea of family therapy as a substitute for hospitalizing Alice. The therapist encouraged him to examine ways in which he could be more forcefully assertive and thereby helpful to his family.

The following day we received a message that the wife herself had been admitted to a psychiatric hospital. We also learned that during this period Alice was behaving "simply perfect." According to the father's reports she cooked and kept the home better than her mother. The mother was discharged from the hospital in two days, and in another week we were able to persuade the parents to force Alice's return to school. We advised that the mother perform volunteer work at the school for several weeks to help keep Alice in school, as well as to help herself cope with her anxious loneliness during the process of separation. Almost immediately, Alice resumed her previous level of good academic performance. Also, as she felt reassured by her mother's increasing involvement in the therapy process, she allowed herself to make new peer-level friendships—a new development for Alice.

As we started to learn more about the private fantasies of the mother, we found that she believed that her daughter had stayed home from school for fear that the mother alone might not be able to do a competent housekeeping job. In the same context she recollected early memories of her own mother having been absent from the home most of the time.

For several months during therapy the mother produced almost exclusively negative recollections of her family of origin. Then, gradually, an almost complete reversal occurred. She began showing concern about what image her relatives might have of her. She began to wonder whether she herself had been fair to her mother and sisters. This shift in the mother's loyalty to her family of origin coincided with the father's growing awareness concerning his obligations to his mother. We learned that he had grown up in an atmosphere of constant reproach, in which his mother had bitterly chastised his father for his drinking habit. However, he remembered his father as a steady worker and a good provider. He recalled that soon after his father had died one of his brothers abandoned his wife and children, lost his responsible job, and moved back to his mother where he then began drinking heavily and himself became the object of his mother's continuous, bitter chastisement. Somewhere at this point in therapy it also was learned that a secret correspondence had developed between the father and his mother. A key development came when one therapy session produced an open confrontation between paternal grandmother and wife, and the grandmother asserted her right to protect her son against the unreasonable wife.

We can postulate a rather insidiously conflicted superego development in the scapegoated child in this type of family. By the time the school-phobic symptom developed, Alice had to choose between two contradictory options for fulfilling filial obligations: to perform responsibly at school, or to remain loyally available to her mother and, in a broader sense, to the family. Such a "counterautonomous" superego development was postulated earlier.[11] This concept is related to Freud's definition[42] of certain character types, "those wrecked by success," whose conscience compels them to fail. From our vantage point, however, such individual characteristics make up only part of actual relational balance. For Alice, greater guilt was connected with separating from her mother and family than with "bad" behavior. We were more impressed by this child's excessive concern for her parents than by her own fears and dependency. Generally, as soon as school-phobic children and their families are confronted with their invisible loyalty bonds, the children can return to school and perform at least on an average level. It is important to stress that maintenance of a pathogenic family pattern is shared not only between parents and scapegoated child, but also with the "well sibling."

Splitting Of Loyalty

Split loyalty, in the sense of simultaneous rejection of one person and devotion to another, can be the source of great psychic pain and a frequent cause of intense jealousy. It is likely that paranoid symptoms of jealousy are mainly based on an internalized relational triangle which exploited one person's loyalty to obtain another's devotion. A young lover offers his best relational presentations to the one he is courting. At the same time, his family of origin can see him as nasty, inconsiderate, and neglectful. A mother may hurt her child by showing devotion toward strangers in the child's presence. A doctor's wife often feels that her husband gives his best devotion to his patients. A dog owner can exploit his pet unwittingly by eliciting its devotion and at the same time refusing to consider the needs of the eager animal. Since the keeping of ledgers is based on a quantitative merit accounting, it follows that *comparison of extent of devotion received* is a more important relational dynamic than the absolute amount of devotion enjoyed. Jealousy is the most sensitive indicator of someone's hunger for trust and loyalty.

Other split loyalty commitments were observed as crucial factors in the family lives of men of clergy; ministers and rabbis. These professions originate from magic, all-encompassing, ancient priestly roles. In a strict sense then, God should never have to take second place behind any loyalty to humans. However, the wife and the children tend to test the clergyman's comparative loyalties as a husband and father.

Therapeutic transference, a displacement onto the therapist of internalized relational attitudes among the family members, also has its important loyalty-splitting implications. Therapists should view transference phenomena not only as opportunities for resolving conflictual internalized psychic configurations, but also as manifestations of multiperson systems of loyalty commitments. One of the most important implications of loyalty systems for individual psychotherapy is that positive therapeutic transference is implicit disloyalty to one's family of origin. This is especially important in designing a therapeutic strategy for children and adolescents. When the therapist represents a competitor to the parents for the patient's loyalty, the emerging negative transference is welcome because it may improve the sense of loyalty to the real or internalized parents.

Important therapeutic leverages are also connected with the family's attempts to split loyalty to a treatment team, as part of their deep transference attitudes. Similarly, many parents test the family therapist's devotion to their mate and to their children, as if they were real competitors for the therapist's favors.

Family therapists often observe that a spouse, as he develops increasing guilt over disloyalty to his parents, may reject his mate. This may seem to him a suitable balancing move to appease the real or internalized parents. From the individual's vantage point, some of the split loyalty phenomena also can be characterized as efforts at displaced retribution. A near-murderous assault on the mate can relieve one's guilt over resenting one's parents. The heavier the guilt over disloyalty towards the resented parents, the more vicious the assault on the target of displacement.

Manipulation Of Displaced Retribution

The principle of debit–credit accounting in loyalty systems balances dynamically that which the parents owe their own parents against the extent they are devoted to parenting their own children. The parent may be caught in simultaneous dual obligations in such a way that when, for instance, obligation to his parents is denied or repressed, his parenting function becomes overburdened with guilt, neglect, or vindictive possessiveness towards his child. The child can also temporarily become the beneficiary of the parent's revengeful attitudes turned against his parents.

Attempts to analyze the displacements, projections, and other inappropriate, from our viewpoint retributory attitudes of parents toward the children will always remain incomplete without considering the anchoring of these relationships in preceding generations. The reason for an "irrational" displacement lies only partly in the parent's "psychological" inability to emotionally discriminate between two intergenerational boundaries of unconscious obligation when both simultaneously impinge on his sense of injustice or impaired guilt tolerance. According to the laws of actual injured justice, repayment in one direction cannot permanently rebalance nonpayment towards the other generation.

To some degree all marriages are burdened with the spouses' unsettled accounts of loyalty to their families of origin. The more such loyalties are hopelessly denied or wishfully given up, the more they will overburden the hidden accounts of the nuclear family's marital and parenting roles. Usually, it is not imagined but actual, time-proven hopelessness about restoring balance in the parent's original relationships that motivates his displacement of the overloaded accounts onto future relationships. Consequently, the most effective therapeutic relief for all family members concerned should follow from exploring the parent–grandparent relationship. Understandably, however, the same reasons which have created the need to deny the intergenerational accounts of obligations will produce resistance to facing them in therapy.

In contrast with individual psychotherapy, family or relationship-based therapy proceeds step by step to remove deeper and deeper layers of *inauthentic loyalty definitions.* Parents may begin therapy with complaints about a hostile child or about their marital relationship. The problem may be presented as one mate's resentment for being exploited sexually or emotionally by the other. Usually, all references to the grandparental generation are either barred or claimed to be irrelevant to the problems.

At other times the intergenerational origin of the parents' problems is only thinly disguised and ready to erupt. The wife may appear to side with her husband in criticizing her mother-in-law's behavior during their latest visit. The husband may agree and write a critical letter blaming his mother for being cold to the grandchildren, buying unnecessary or useless gifts, leaving too early, etc. The next day a violent debate may erupt, and the husband may impulsively side with his parents against his wife and decide to leave her. In other cases we hear about impotence, precocious or retarded ejaculation, frigidity, fear of murderous impulses, etc. In many instances these "symptoms" which resisted individual therapy for years can improve rapidly when three-generational exploration becomes productive.

One form of repetitious captive loyalty involvements is exemplified by a multigenerational pattern of *martyrlike mothering.* A mother can build up binding obligations in the offspring through excessive giving of herself and by never accepting or demanding returns from the child. Thus, martyrlike parents reinforce the child's guilt-laden obligations to the self-sacrificing and self-denying providers. The children's resulting ledger of obligations shows a hopeless amount of loyalty indebtedness which can never be significantly diminished.

Martyrlike parents can produce in their child an enduring longing, combined with bitter resentment, guilt-laden obligations, and a highly developed capacity for manipulating others' guilt. Since the parents substituted their child as means for rebalancing their unsettled accounts with their own parents, they have lost the relevant context for accomplishing their task. They can untangle the knot only by approaching again their own parents, in the hope that before it is too late they can induce a more giving pattern in their relationships. In other cases one or several persons are treated in a prejudicial manner within the family.

A particular form of the loyalty bind is one in which a child has to balance the parent's irreconcilable obligation to a grandparent, e.g., if the parent has had to remain available after the grandparent was widowed or abandoned:

The son of an aggressive and ruggedly selfish businessman relinquished his idea of becoming an engineer following the early death of his mother and entered his father's business. During the next 25 years this man seemed to have turned into a combination of an imitator of his father, on the one hand, and a reluctantly applauding audience to his father's success, on the other. The older man had accomplished an almost epic feat by succeeding financially from a very modest immigrant background. Allegedly, the son assumed more stringently ethical ways of doing business. The father kept comparing his son's ineffectiveness with his own sharp, "back-alley" ways of dealing in business. By becoming virtuous and law-abiding, the son was caught in the bind of simultaneously having to rebel against his father's ways while remaining loyal to the latter's basic, acquisitive value system. Whenever the father tried to enlist his adolescent son as an admiring audience of his value system, his son turned him down as if from his grandfather's value position. The grandson, a challenging, actively rebellious, adventurous person, became a critic of his father's passive, essentially losing position.

The issues of giving and receiving must be clarified before defining the criteria of relational exploitation. Contrary to popular concepts, demanding and expecting responsibility from the child amount to the most crucial forms of giving on the part of parents; permissive or "liberal" child rearing amounts to exploitation through evasion of obligations and through a covert expectation that the child take on a prematurely adultlike role, i.e., be parentified.

In system terms an overgiving, indulgent parenting amounts to *tyranny of permissiveness*. The child who has not received sufficient guidance to values from his parents tends to grow up resentful of all authorities which to him symbolically represent the despised, nondemanding, subtly exploitative parents. The child will feel that "they" did not care enough to guide and direct, and therefore have deprived him of internalized values: "They didn't teach me what is right or wrong." Unconsciously, the child of such parents tends to displace his furor upon alleged tyrants as if the latter were responsible for making his world so frightening and chaotic. Some of the most violent accusers of any political "establishment" come from the permissively raised children of liberal upper-middle-class parents.

Incestuous Attempts At Resolution Of Obligations

Another substitutive attempt at flight from relational stagnation consists of inbreeding, i.e., engaging in sexual relations within the family of origin. A variety of vertical (multigenerational) and horizontal incest patterns must be explained on this basis. The family's symbiotic, counterautonomous morality may approve of such loyalty even at the expense of breaking an important social taboo. Perhaps this is the point of the joke: "Incest is all right as long as it is kept within the family." The individual feels exonerated through his adherence to family loyalty.

The same basic familial "ethic" may account for situations in which any extrafamilial peer-level involvement of the offspring, especially with a chance of marriage, is treated as though it were actual betrayal:

A complex form of collusive avoidance of facing guilt over the disloyalty of individuation was observed in a family with multiple generations of incestuous behavior. The initial referral was for a daughter's near-psychotic withdrawal and depression aggravated with suicidal thoughts. Since the case was referred to an agency at which one of the authors served as a consultant in family therapy, following several months of unproductive attempts at individual treatment, a family explorative interview was suggested. Previously, the individual therapist had seen the patient once with one of her brothers. All attempts to explore sexual matters were blocked. The worker noticed that the brother's concern for his sister seemed to be tinged with heterosexual tenderness.

The patient was preoccupied with the memory of allegedly having been bitten by a dog on her "vagina" when she was three. She added that ever since then she had been searching for the right kind of food to undo the effect of this event. She had been labeled diagnostically as having a "schizophrenic reaction."

The mother and seven of the ten siblings, including the patient, appeared for the family evaluation session. At first a lively discussion developed about the way in which members of the family considered themselves as superior human beings, despite the fact that years ago the father had abandoned the family and returned to live with his mother. The feeling of superiority was apparently induced, as none of the siblings were permitted to play with other children, to avoid contact with what was considered a bad neighborhood. Most of the siblings were capable workers in the fields of art or business, defying the handicaps of their minority background.

The interview revealed that there had been incest between the father and several daughters. After a lively discussion the session ended with several members stressing that despite their knowledge of paternal incest, they opted to regard the good aspects of this family and of their parents.

In a subsequent meeting only the one brother who was living with the "patient" appeared. He proceeded to discuss how his sister had tried to seduce him several times, claiming that another brother had also had sexual relations with her. The family therapist encouraged the brother to take up this issue with his sister and other brother together. In subsequent meetings it was revealed that the patient had her first sexual experience with her mother's brother, a married minister. Furthermore, it was discovered that as a young boy one of the brothers had sexual intercourse with the uncle's wife.

As explorations uncovered one facet of the relationship after another, the entire picture of the members' interlocking loyalty system, adherence to the myth of superiority, and incestuous sexuality began to emerge in rich detail. What initially was a search into loyalty and covering up for father's "sin" turned into a large-scale exploration of an incestuous background within the maternal family of origin. It was easy to see that the intensity of involvement in this family's relationships was difficult to compare with that of their peers. They were severely handicapped in their struggle for genuine individual identity by guilt over incestuous, secret patterns which prevented the resolution of the symbiotic myth of family superiority.

Guilt Against Guilt

Another important relational system is based on the mutual escalation of guilt-inducing moves by both parent and child. While the parent may succeed in keeping the child in guilt-bound symbiotic loyalty, the child may fight back by knowing the leverages which cause guilt in the captivating parents. As the two incriminating moves cancel each other, the child may obtain bits of autonomy by installments.

The S family was seen for a family evaluation session in the hospital where the only daughter was a patient. She was a depressed, unfeminine-looking young woman of 27 who seemed hesitant to commit herself to any statements, especially about her family. She had stopped functioning in her usual monotonous way, both at home and in her clerical job, and was described by her mother as behaving agitated and restless at home. Miss S expressed occasional suicidal ideas. Mr. S, a severely emphysematic, illiterate man of foreign origin, was able to hold a job as a first-class welder mainly through his wife's high expectations of him. Mrs. S was described as a talkative, large, aggressively engulfing woman.

From the viewpoint of individual therapy, this young woman had to be regarded as a depressed, borderline psychotic, inhibited, sullen, and somewhat evasive to questioning. On a relational system level it was possible to observe an ongoing power struggle over engulfment versus autonomy. The mother's symbiotic hold on the daughter was dramatic and overt, probably reinforced by the threatened loss of her husband through physical illness. The staff hoped that the daughter had some capacity for autonomy, as indicated by the marginal relationships she could sustain with men. She had two boyfriends. One she had thought of marrying about 8 years ago but lost for some reason. The other man, 15 years her senior, had been in the picture for 8 years without much prospect for a marriage. This man was an extremely dependent person, not earning an income and living on his 82-year-old mother's social security check and Miss S' earnings.

According to a power-struggle model, the therapeutic strategy should be designed to counteract the mother's symbiotic intrusiveness and reinforce any autonomous trend in the daughter. However, if the system is formulated according to a guilt-laden loyalty commitment model, therapy should be designed to rebalance the members' denied, detrimental, fixed obligations.

Looking at this kind of family, the therapist gets the impression that the members are fatefully attached to each other, as if in a secret alliance against society. The mother would "protect" the daughter against any serious involvement in life, while the daughter would never break her primary allegiance to the mother. Their deepest cohesive force seems to be anchored in guilt. Guilt over disloyalty or treason may exist in any group; it can be exaggerated in systems with overencumbered intergenerational ledgers. Specifically, the developing child and the adolescent face a number of critical periods at which growth and separation are connected with guilt over abandoning the parent.

In certain families like the S family, however, the guilt of disloyalty was magnified by horror of secret miseries and sins. Struggle for individual survival seemed to rely on the pattern of using guilt against guilt. For instance, when the daughter faced the choice between moving out of the home or continuing her self-destroying, self-denying existence, excessive loyalty to the family began to impinge on her threshold of guilt, and she would begin to punish herself by becoming psychiatrically ill. At the same time, she could use the illness as a weapon to make her mother feel guilty. In response, the mother would lower the pressure of her guilt-inducing maneuvers, express worry about her daughter's illness, and cry helplessly. At that point the daughter would say very angrily: "Mother, don't cry."

In interviewing the family the therapist sensed a tight, defensive collusive arrangement. The system seemed to open up only for a moment when the therapist confronted them with their battle of "guilt against guilt." The daughter made a comment: "Well, maybe we should all just go home and forgive and forget." When the therapist urged her to define what there was to forgive and forget, an interesting piece of history came to the surface. The mother used to have fights with a drunken uncle who at times threatened her life. Miss S remembered times when she would ask her mother to call the police for protection and her mother would respond: "Leave me alone, it is my business how I handle my brother." Miss S would then be left frustrated and guilty: did she do the wrong thing?

Further clues about this fatefully interlocked system were obtained when the mother was asked about her own childhood. She answered that many horrible things had occurred. From earliest childhood she was forced to play music as a member of a family of carnival entertainers. Without further details, the mother implied that she was loyalty-bound not to reveal the shameful secrets that she had to share as a child growing up with show people who traveled from town to town. Her implied shameful past brought out the mother's life-long struggle to create a style of conventional middle-class living from a family pattern of social outlaws.

This family came for one evaluation session only, and therefore it is difficult to predict how they would have progressed in therapy. On the one hand, it was a favorable sign that this much of the mother's painful obligations to hide and deny could be revealed in a first evaluation. The daughter was caught in her own familial obligations, connected with both the prospect of her mother's lonely widowhood and her parents' multigenerational indebtedness.

The mechanism of "guilt against guilt" resembles the scapegoating system in that it too is governed by the most powerful motivational dimension—guilt. However, whereas in the scapegoating interaction guilt accumulates in the scapegoater, the mutual martyrdom in a guilt-against-guilt interaction lacks a cause–effect relationship between victimization of the other and subsequent guilt in the perpetuator. The struggle is deadly between a mother who, because of her own victimized childhood role, feels justified in parentifying her daughter, and the daughter whose life wilts away in self-perpetuated paralysis. This system is tighter and more subtly hostile than the scapegoating arrangement. Fighting guilt with guilt cannot lead the daughter far toward emancipation. She would have to discover new, factual ways of helping her parents in order to rebalance her "inherited" negative account of obligation to her parents.

On Repaying The Therapist In Transference

An often-encountered source of frustration for family therapists has both technical and theoretical implications. Therapy may begin in a usual way: A family appears for an evaluation session, and following a seemingly meaningful initial exploration another appointment is made. However, a few days later a telephone message is received: The parents have decided that while they recognize the need for family therapy, they must cancel the appointment, at least for the time being. In fact, they have already been helped, so they claim.

This paradoxical behavior usually annoys and disappoints the therapist. He may attempt to deal with it in a number of ways. Quite logically, he might be inclined to suggest to the family that they return for one more session and explore their decision in more detail and depth. This is often interpreted by the family as serving the therapist's personal need, which they turn down with noticeable satisfaction. Often, however the family sets up the telephone conversation to exclude even discussing the possibility of a further meeting. They may ask for a referral to individual therapy for the designated patient member— quite inconsistently, considering their apparent clear insight into family dynamics.

A fascinating aspect of this behavior is the suddenness with which the engagement of the family is terminated. It does not logically follow from the apparent meaningfulness of their responses to the therapist's suggestions and from the family's seeming perceptivity and responsiveness just a few days previous. Therefore, there must be another logic behind the family members' motivation to discontinue. By what process can the family members halt an interaction which seemed to have just begun? How can they see closure in a situation in which the therapist doesn't see any? How can they decide that they will disregard all those convincing clues that they themselves recently brought out?

The most likely explanation of this phenomenon is that certain families come to the evaluation session with a preexisting set of expectations in which to fit the therapist, regardless of what happens or what is said in the first evaluation hour. Possibly, the therapist is being covertly enlisted—through transference—to help rebalance the parents' early childhood frustrations. Conceivably, they experience a sudden decrease of guilt over the unpaid obligation to their parents; the relief offsets their guilt over the present exploitation of the therapist. They accomplish the dual feat of revenge on someone else and whitewashing their parents. The psychic economy of such a relational strategy for the family is obvious, although its impact may not be felt by the family members for several days. This scapegoating spares the actual blood relatives from the revengeful blow, and the family members' emotional satisfaction frequently lasts for some time after the rejection of the therapist. Long-stored-up painful feelings of resentment have been finally put into action with relatively little guilt ensuing. Their mutual loyalty to each other thus creates a kind of closure which is unknown in individual therapy.

Naturally, this use of the family therapy situation is not only non-therapeutic but antitherapeutic. It can lead to a prolonged pattern of avoidance and denial. The evasive mechanisms of displacement, scape-goating, and inappropriate acting-out are emotionally reinforced. In a dynamic sense the family is worse off afterwards. The well-known phe-nomenon of perpetual comparison shopping among individual therapy agencies is reinforced here by the collective force of the family process.

The question then remains how to handle this type of behavior both effectively and therapeutically for the family members. One measure for dealing with this challenge consists in the therapist's showing im-mediate curiosity about the extended family relationships, specifically regarding the two parents' families of origin. By refocusing attention on these original sources of deep, denied, or repressed feelings, the ex-perienced family therapist obtains leverage in the role of a courageous guide in murky waters. However, at any moment he is likely to become assigned the role of a symbolic substitute for the archaic personages. Preferably, he should become a forum for exploration and a potential ally against the accusing and punishing introjects. At the same time, he should try not to reinforce a blaming attitude towards the families of origin.

By looking for any minor clue in the way the past family relationships are either described or elusively denied and displaced upon a child—or even at this early stage upon himself—the therapist may gain valua-ble information about how to design his strategy along the major rela-tional configurations of the family. The therapist should be able to seize upon clues and to mobilize instantaneous courage and effort to examine their implications for how he may be used and exploited for the family members' needs. The family members might resist discussing their early relationships and, even more, their reactions to the therapist, and instead limit their discussion to the scapegoated patient member. Often it appears that the degree of fixation in scapegoating is inversely proportionate to the parents' readiness to discuss their families of origin. An important operational principle of family therapy should be remembered here: to secure alliance with healthy resources rather than with pathology in the families.

The following note illustrates one variety of politely revealing double messages about the intended use of the family therapist as a convenient buffer between the unresolved, internalized, past relationships and their externalization in marriage:

Dear Doctor: Since it is so hard to reach you by phone, I'm writing this note to explain why I will no longer be coming to you.

After I left you, that Saturday afternoon, I had an argument with my husband and he agreed to see you the following Saturday, but on Wednesday another small incident occurred, which by itself was meaningless, and I got an involuntary seizure of panic and terror which caused my husband to stay home from work and to call in our family physician who hospitalized me for 3 days. He kept me tranquilized until I could pull myself together, and of course I had to tell him my troubles.

Since then he has been attending me, and has not yet decided if I need analysis or not—but in the meantime my husband has given up his recorder group entirely and I am feeling much better. I hope my husband will resume his hobby as soon as I get my equilibrium back. I suspect I really do need psychoanalysis but naturally hesitate to start with it.

I doubt if we shall meet again. Thank you anyhow.

Sincerely

Liberation Of Siblings Through Suicide

Jeff was a 22-year-old male college dropout, the second oldest in a sibship of four, who while hospitalized killed himself by jumping from the fourth floor to the pavement. His head was completely deformed and his face became unrecognizable even to the family.

He previously had been hospitalized several times for short periods and was considered essentially psychotic since age 15. His parents never had any semblance of a good marital relationship. In Jeff's memory they continually debated the hopelessness of their marriage and the merits of a possible divorce.

The boy, a shy, inhibited, soft-spoken individual, was continually preoccupied with his unhappiness. He blamed himself for his parents' unhappiness, and he tried to escape from his guilt into chronic self-destruction. At this time he exhibited bizarre symptoms, e.g., a fixed gaze upwards to the right, coupled with an inability to look at the interviewer.

Unfortunately, while the family was involved in family treatment under the guidance of an individual-oriented preceptor, the therapist adopted an individually focused behavior-reinforcement therapy approach. Consequently, the patient was simultaneously pulled in two different directions of management.

When the therapist was about to move on to another training assignment, due to the patient's diminished symptoms, Jeff was judged to have sufficiently improved to be discharged from the hospital. No information was as yet given to him about how a new therapist was to be assigned. As in the past, his parents again refused to take him back home, so he planned to move to a halfway house. Then, after an evaluation interview, the halfway house also turned him down, stating that he was not sufficiently well for their criteria of admission.

As the family therapist consultant learned about these rapid developments, he urged full openness of information. During what turned out to be the last family session, Jeff expressed his disappointment over his therapist's transfer and added that he was considering leaving the hospital only because he didn't want to be assigned to another doctor. At this point, the mother voiced her suspicion whether the therapist wasn't leaving for some other purpose of his own besides the requirements of his training. It seems too that at this point the parents as well as the patient's therapist must have been rapidly losing Jeff's trust.

A week after the suicide the family requested one more family therapy meeting, ostensibly for the purpose of further therapeutic planning. Jeff's parents, his older brother, a maternal aunt, and her husband came to this meeting. The mother seemed to be extremely depressed and guilty, and the father talked in a slightly irrelevant manner, with the brother trying to make points in the most poignant and relevant fashion.

The session began with the maternal uncle's suggestion that Jeff's death be a legacy for the family, i.e., the parents, to "pull together." Apparently, this uncle and his wife had been continually used as parent surrogates by these helplessly infantile parents, just as were their children. The uncle's well-meaning, kindly, constructive comment also must have had a deeply accusatory implication for the parents.

The brother stated that he was somewhat puzzled by the extent of guilt shown by his mother. This comment also had implicit accusatory meaning, especially in the light of the brother's admitted perception of all four children of this family being chronically overburdened by the hopelessness and hostile unrelatedness between the parents. The brother explained that the children's burden was caused not so much by their individual relationships with the parents as by their concern about the parents' lack of a marital relationship. He added that as the children were growing up they became less available and exploitable, and thus a new vacuum was being created between them and the parents. This vacuum was then increasingly filled in by Jeff's sickness, who for the last 6 years demanded so much attention that at times the feuding parents even forgot their own conflicts.

Jeff's brother talked then about this being the time for positive rather than negative action. He described his own complex problems: He had just obtained a divorce. He also had often thought of suicide himself. In his judgment, his sisters also had many problems which they themselves would have to face now. He added that he had been completely surprised by his parents' request that he visit them after the funeral.

Toward the end of the session the brother added a very significant bit of information. He stated that two days prior to his brother's suicide, the two of them had a conversation in which Jeff mentioned his intention of killing himself. The brother admitted that after having heard about this so many times, he had replied that if Jeff indeed felt that way, he should be entitled to act on it.

This very powerful "postmortem" family session highlighted the issue of Jeff's legacy through suicide. He liberated his siblings, perhaps for the rest of their lives, from an obligation to feel responsible for the parents' marital predicament. The brother symbolically pointed an accusing finger, referring to Jeff's example: Is that what is expected of us? Jeff's suicide made the parents' extreme dependent demands on their children absurd and patently indefensible. When asked what impressed him the most as a personal message from Jeff's suicide, the brother answered that the most striking aspect of his death was its violent manner. He added that in this way there would be no question about the intentionality of the act. Thus, as in the case of the self-immolating students of a subdued nation, the violent manner of self-sacrifice became the most important factor in shaking an overpowering exploitative family system.

LIMITS OF CHANGE IN SYSTEMS

We have described the pervasive motivational contribution of the justice accounting framework to a variety of multiply determined familial patterns of "pathological behaviors." Pseudodistancing in family relationships, collusive rejection of all in-law relations, drug addiction, and bizarre sexual and destructive communal ventures can all be used to evade confrontation with the reciprocity of relational obligations.

Several months of family therapy with a nuclear family gradually reveals the initially disclaimed importance of occasional visits at the old family home, visits by the in-laws, telephone calls, and exchanges of letters. What appears as a hopelessly fixated or stagnant avoidance of contact with the extended family can often be infused with new hope. For example, a distant, mutually blaming parent–grandparent relationship can be brought to an adult-to-adult confrontation. A son who is also a husband and father may rediscover jointly with his aging parents that on some level he can also remain a son. Gradually, the acquired pseudoobjectivity and pseudodistancing wanes, and as a result aspects of childhood loyalties come to the surface. For a while both spouses may side loyally with their respective families of origin, explicitly rejecting the family of the other. Later, they may be helped to form an alliance and support each other as a team to jointly investigate and struggle with unresolved and denied issues with in both of their families of origin.

A clinical example of a complete failure in reconciling a conflict between marital and original family loyalty was observed in a family referred because of the schizophrenic condition of both children. It soon turned out that the parents' marriage was a never-ending series of mutual recriminations and separations. During most of the 24 years of their marriage the husband was either formally separated or had a job out of town. He stayed with the family on certain weekends only. However, this man remained a reliable financial provider.

A closer examination of this nuclear and extended family system revealed that the wife had remained extremely close to her five brothers and two sisters. The five brothers owned a family business, and at one time or another both brothers-in-law were employed by the company. The brothers and sisters consulted with each other daily on the telephone on all important problems. They met on all religious holidays as they had while their parents were alive. The eight siblings showed a striking unanimity in excluding their mates and sharing a condemnatory and contemptuous view of all spouses. One by one they were described as stupid, weak of character, physically inadequate, irresponsible, or a bad choice for some other reason.

Interestingly, in this case family therapy consisted of a series of sessions with the mother, her two psychotic children, and two or three of her siblings at a time. Her husband soon moved to another town and discontinued his appearances. However, meetings with the mother's siblings continued for over a year. In the process of this work we discovered that in almost all of the eight siblings' families there was at least one child who was psychotic or severely neurotic.

Escape into a "drug career" may bring with it a sense of "cure" for feeling alienated. Lennard *et al.*[62] comment that such apparent cure is a tragic self-deception because the pharmacologically "turned on" individual is even less likely to develop meaningful interpersonal relatedness. The drug decreases the pressure for alternative options and increases a sense of frustration and alienation. We must add, however, that in a number of cases the seemingly hopeless and irresponsible life pattern of the drug addict may mask an underlying responsible and loyal commitment to a concerned, helpful family role, e.g., being available as the last remaining child to an anxious mother. Accordingly, the drug addict is not only an escapee from the more visible pain of alienation but also a hidden resource for the family's overburdening relational expectations.

Our age challenges man's reproductive function as the most significant basis for genuine commitment to heterosexual relationship. Exhibitionistic sexual material in advertising media, liberated sexual morality, etc., may all be indications rather than causes of increasing alienation in an interpersonal sense. This is an era of unprecedented sexual exploration, based on the advance of contraceptive techniques and on a large-scale questioning of traditional values in society, as shown in certain new communes and other aspects of the "youth culture."

In our experience most young people seek life in communes with the avowed purpose of escaping traditional family life. It is unrealistic to question the validity of their need for peer involvement; a closer look, however, may reveal that they also remain unintentionally tuned in to the signals of helpless anguish of their permissively liberal parents. Behind the careless facade of the hippie culture there is an attitude of "passive aggressive" overinvolvement with critical societal authorities which are proven to be as concerned with these youths as their parents have been.

SOCIETAL MYTHS AND LOYALTIES

In view of man's age-old struggle against the oppressive responsibilities of accounting of obligations, individual autonomous needs naturally tend to form collusive alliances with certain political–economic trends. Certain culturally supported myths and values are antagonistic to the notions of family solidarity and obligations. Apparently, a person can fall back upon the family against the power excesses of ruthless political or economic forces and vice versa. At times an inability to face the responsibilities of reciprocal obligations in one's family may turn a person into a socially concerned idealist or, on the other hand, into a suspicious crusader against all or part of mankind.

One of the most pervasive myths of Western civilization is that of the individual's discreet independence as ideally an absolute, "monothetical" entity. Without questioning the value of the ideal of individual responsibility and moral accountability, family therapists must caution against regarding the individual as dynamically independent of or disconnected from his relational system. From earliest times, great playrights and novelists have always pictured man as part of a relational motivation system. Autonomy purchased through outwardly complete separation and denial of relatedness tends to be offset inwardly by the accumulation of guilt and responsibility.

Another set of cultural myths pertains to overvaluation of overt behavioral manifestations as criteria in judging the essence of relationships. Our scientific–industrial culture apparently must value every human endeavor by degrees of material progress, describable or measureable change, or capacity for "adjustment" to material progress. Commitment to an ever-improving material future and unlimited progress can mask our lack of courage for relational confrontations and our wish to elude the hard work of resolving conflicted obligations.

Myths of the separateness of the nuclear family as an ideally self-contained unit are used to cover up hidden, unresolved loyalty commitments to the extended family. Physical separation from the older generation is often encouraged—even by professional therapists—for its own sake, regardless of the extent of emotional maturation achieved or of the potential merits of continued living together.

The welfare system allegedly proves society's altruistic readiness to share responsibility for supporting children born under adverse familial conditions. Yet, on the other hand, we seem to lack the courage to explore the ethical implications of children being born without regard for their rights for a protected maturation. A hypocritical orientation to morality presents control of sexual pleasure and taboos against contraception and abortion as more important values than the obligation of parents to raise their offspring and children's right to a concerned, parenting environment.

Another frequently met familial hypocrisy can be a great obstacle to the resolution of conflictual obligations during family treatment. Many parents adhere to the belief that as long as they do not include their children in the discussion of their own conflicted relationship, their children will not be burdened with the consequences of such negative relationships. Naturally, genuinely private issues between the parents should not be discussed with the children present. However, it is our experience that children are far more burdened by being excluded from overt, honest discussions of differences. Their witnessing the parents' struggle to work their way out of chaos and unrelatedness is one of the greatest gifts that they can receive from their elders. Parents can make a great contribution to their children's growth by sharing with them the deeper human aspects of even these conflicts.

Finally, autocratic political systems may encourage detachment from the family in order to extract loyalty to the government or dominant party. Youth in a democratic and free society, on the other hand, may use anarchistic, counterauthoritarian emotionalism as escape from confrontation with relational obligations.

CONCLUSIONS

In summary, we would like to extend consideration of the underlying social structure of reciprocity of merits and justice to all areas of "pathology" manifested in humans in relationships. We believe that the "interhuman"[26] realm of justice of the human world is the foundation of the prospects of trust among people. At the same time, the keeping of accounts of reciprocity of justice tends to be an overwhelming demand on all members of any relational system, specifically of families. Attempts at denying or escaping such accounting constitute a major dynamic of every relationship system. While such escape may be necessary temporarily for the person's autonomous explorations, it must be uncovered and faced if the social system is to remain productive of healthy growth. When large areas of family relationships are based on denial of the criteria of just reciprocity, pathogenicity is imminent.

The system point of view of pathogenicity has important practical, therapeutic implications. Whereas individual psychotherapy aims at strengthening the responsible attitudes of the patient, at times with no regard for familial reciprocity and fairness, family or relationship-system-based therapy inevitably must consider every member's justifiable point of view. As one individual is made responsible in consideration of the total relationship, the therapist must broaden this base of concern and strive to "altruistically" include others.

Therapeutic conclusions can be developed only gradually from the system principles described in this chapter. A personal emotional growth process is an inevitable part of every psychotherapy. Whether the reader has practiced family or individual therapy or both, he must develop a personal formula for coping with the demands of confrontations with hidden accounts in close relationships. The implications of the therapist's work will inevitably affect his own capacity for openness in facing the balance of his personal relationships. As he admires the courageously assertive individual family member, he will inevitably discover in his patients replicas of himself, his parent, his spouse, and his child.

The therapist cannot help but witness human dramas of great intensity. He will observe a parent's options of either sacrificing the warmth of holding on to a growing child or giving in to possessive impulses and ignoring the next generation's mandate in the child's eyes. He will notice the adolescent's hesitation to begin living his own life before his parents can find comfort in their new-found loneliness.

Until the Post-Victorian age the issues of family loyalty were largely unformulated because they were taken for granted. Our age, on the other hand, denies these issues with the help of myths of individual material success and endless struggle against the threat of authority. Our pervasive social fragmentation may make it appear as if loyalty were not operative in today's family. Issues of loyalty then arise surreptitiously and unexpectedly. In many families the child's delinquent acts bring out a sense of family loyalty in defiance of society, so to speak. We have seen, for instance, that even repititious stealing at school may have its paradoxical, unifying effect on the family. In defiance of the school, i.e., the representative of the social system, family members often covertly endorse the child's denial of facts.

It is likely that a rethinking of family loyalty may be the first step toward reforming social values so that free society may survive. The questions of exploitation and fairness will have to be examined from time to time on a relational loyalty and reciprocity basis rather than according to predominantly economic criteria. Economic justice is, of course, important, but it can also be used as a materialistic escapism from human reality.

As long as political and social processes are viewed in terms of competitive success of individuals and groups, every revolution is bound to yield to an even more pervasive and subtly exploitative suppression. Only through transcending the power competition model can we hope to arrive at a genuinely improved social equation. Defining the criteria of fair reciprocity between nations, racial groups, boss and employee, contracting partners, etc., could ultimately bring more satisfaction to either party than successfully exploiting the other.

We suggest that no social group, i.e., family, union, race, religion, or nation, could have a better preventive investment in their relationships than through a focused study of the basic currency of their reciprocal exchanges within and outside the group. The maintenance of balance in relationships does not require equality among the partners. Relationships among unequals can be balanced, provided the partners can, consciously or unconsciously, face the accounts of reciprocity and are able to adjust the asymmetry of exchanges to compensate for the asymmetry of advantages.

The therapeutic implications of the system concept of balance and imbalance in relationships are bound to alter the therapist's operational values and principles. The principles of openness, insight, directness, encounter, etc., while valuable within their own range, become more limited goals. Open confrontation with the ledger of relational reciprocity is our first task, but it is only a means for designing a strategy of actively rebalancing relationships. Then, knowledge of the self and increased assertiveness find their place in the context of accounts of fairness and justice in close relationships.

6

Parentification

Although references to parentification have been made earlier, in this chapter we will deal with its systemic and loyalty implications in more detail. The term parentification sounds unfamiliar to those not involved in treating families, since it has been mainly used as a technical concept for describing a facet of pathogenic family dynamics. Yet the term describes a ubiquitous and important aspect of most human relationships. It is suggested that parentification should not be unconditionally ascribed to the realm of "pathology" or relational dysfunction. It is a component of the regressive core of even balanced, sufficiently reciprocal relationships.

By definition, parentification implies the subjective distortion of a relationship as if one's partner or even children were his parent. Such distortion can be done in a wishful fantasy or, more dramatically, through dependent behavior. For example, parents may wishfully enlist their child to strive to become a genius, or they may refuse to act responsibly in crucial decisions. If the act of falling in love is always partly based on imaginary parentification, then most marriages can be considered as subsequent life-long contracts for balancing this fantasy with responsible and giving marital mutuality.

In fortunate instances the extent of marital parentification follows a symmetrical pattern. It is easier to tolerate the other's demand if I can also demand of the other. Also, to some degree every child must be parentified by his parents at certain times. Without this, he would not learn to identify with responsible roles for his future life. The internalization of the image of the self as a potentially giving parent is an important step towards emotional growth. On the other hand, if couched in an exceedingly guilt-laden atmosphere of obligation, such

151

internalization may constitute a bind which traps the child in prolonged compliance with unilateral demands for parentification.

Rather than condemning every manifestation of parentification, the family therapist should be interested in its dynamic significance within the balance of relationships, in order to assess the degree of its inappropriateness. If one adult parentifies another—for example, a mate—the distortion usually occurs through a fantasied, often unconscious, regression of the self to a childlike position. In comparison with the self, the mate appears as one who should be obliged to be a provider, defender, or nurse. If an adult parentifies a child, the distortion of the relationship progresses one step further. The generation differential must be actually reversed. The person of the child first must be transformed into that of an imaginary adult. Why is so much effort spent in this way: What does an adult gain by the parentification maneuver? What effect does it have on the child who is being parentified?

The emotional gain derived from the parentification maneuver is intimately connected with basic possessive needs. An imagined infantile dependence on the other can gratify one's needs for security. Furthermore, the fantasy of retrieving a parent revives old wishes for healing grief over the loss of one's infantile reliance on ever-giving, all-powerful parents. The pain of facing the early losses can recur with every new separation. No doubt, even the most mature adult needs periodic relapses into dreams of childhood fulfillment and is tempted to use a current relationship as a substitute for possessing a parent. Conversely, a relationship becomes emotionally significant for us to the extent that we can invest it with regressive fantasies of infantile fulfillment.

Although our concept of parentification is expressed in essentially possessive (oral, dependent) terms, we are aware of other, e.g., aggressive or sexual, implications of parentification. The parent can relate to his child as if he were a generational equal instead of being of a different generation. Long-pent-up, unsettled resentments can be vented onto the child in displaced retaliation. Heterosexual (Oedipal) stimulation between parent and child has traditionally been viewed as one that occurs across the generational boundary. Using the child as an equal partner for the parent's own sexual needs will become incestuous at the point when the generational boundary is violated and adult-to-adult type sexuality is channeled into the relationship.

This analysis of the relationship structure does not replace clinical study. In our experience, incestuous relationships have a devouring, destructive, rather than truly heterosexual, motivation. We have found that besides an individual parent acting on his sexual or destructive urges, there are determinants in the parent–parent and total family interaction that condition aggressive and sexual exploitation of children within their families.

Some degree of unconscious parentification is probably a part of every parent's attitude toward his child. In this sense it is an attempt to prevent the parent from being emotionally depleted. However, under certain circumstances the parent's need to parentify his child gains consciousness and even obsessive emphasis. We have seen cases in which mothers reported that they had enjoyed picturing a certain child as a miniature grown-up, from birth on. In other instances, the parent's first glimpse of a baby's features sets it up as a candidate for a life-long scapegoat role, apparently triggered by its physical resemblance to the parent's parent or sister.

POSSESSION AND LOSS OF LOVED ONES

Possession versus loss of loved ones is the key dimension in the deeper experience and meaning of family relationships. The interlocking system of object-possessive needs of individual members contributes to the emotional foundation of the family as a unit. Man's greatest satisfaction is connected with entering into a relationship, and his greatest pain with unrelatedness or the threat of losing an important relationship. As the chance of raising a family is the most universal source of anticipated happiness, the prospect of losing one's child, even through the child's growth and maturation, can lead to the most penetrating grief.

The child who is able to make a move toward separation must sooner or later face his guilt and the awareness that his parents will experience grief and hidden resentment over his move. Ultimately, the process leads to the obsolescence of the older generation. This existential fact must be recognized as the major source of stress in family life, regardless of one's theoretical orientation to the psychology of relationships. Dynamic object-relations theory, especially as elaborated by Klein, Fairbairn, and Guntrip,[49] has developed the concept of internalization and reexternalization of relationship patterns as the main mechanism for telescoping of the child and parent aspects of family relationships. As I recreate my past attitudes toward my father in my relationship with my son, potentially I become both father and son. At any moment when I copy my father's fathering attitudes, something also revives in me my hungry child self who used to be held and supported by his parents. Thus, in a sense, my child who has made me a parent can also make me a child. Generally speaking, any close relationship offers the challenge of resolving the ever-recurring antithetical dialectic of alternating subject and object roles in the two participants: We receive by giving and vice versa. We cannot possess others without also being possessed by them. One of us has described earlier a distinction between *functional* and *ontic* dependency.[12, p. 37] Functional dependency is based on particular caretaking functions, while ontic dependency is inherent in our psychic being. Psychologically speaking, we "live" on relationships, and we are as secure as our relationships with other people permit. Loss of a meaningful relationship always implies the ontic disconfirmation of one's person.

PARENTIFICATION AND ROLE ASSIGNMENT

Therapeutically and theoretically, family relations or individual psychology can be approached on two levels: the overtly observable factual aspects and the covert, dynamically determinative forces. It is always easier to describe and study the overt role distribution in families. However, in family therapy we often discover a paradoxical ratio between the two levels, wherein the overt role assignment only helps to disguise diametrically opposed deeper motivations.

The structure of our inner commitments to a relationship interlocks in hidden ways with that of the partners, forming a complex balance of unconscious group forces and obligations. Since the beginning of the family therapy movement, various authors have made attempts at describing the structuring of deep commitments that bind family members. Some covertly structuring forces have been referred to as "family myths." Apart from the conscious, cognitively formulated myth, we can find precognitive, nonverbal, and less conscious patterns of relationships which do not yet deserve the name "myth." Parentification is one of those structuring relationship patterns which have overt role assignment as well as internalized expectation and commitment characteristics. We first turn to the role assignment aspect of parentification.

MANIFEST CARETAKING ROLES

Marital choice is often based on a covert fantasy of attaching oneself to someone who will be like a wish-fulfilling parent. In a well-balanced marriage mutual parentification expectations tend to form a more or less symmetrical pattern. "If I can be babied by you, I shall in turn be like your parent at other times."

At times the caretaker role of young children is overtly demanded by the regressive behavior of the parents. We have seen a 7-year-old child dial the number of the police while his mother screamed for help, as she lay on the floor, half-choked by the boy's father. Often we see the preadolescent child move back and forth as a pendulum, reassuring one parent after the other while they keep stressing their hopeless incompatability and divorce. As a general rule, full evaluation of the motives for any parental strife is impossible without assessing its impact on the emotional growth of the children. For instance, the parents' threats of divorce can halt the emancipation efforts of their adolescent or young adult children.

Even when children are not charged with overt caretaking roles, they may function as cementing agents, holding their parents' marriage together. We are not referring to the conscious effort of many parents at avoiding open conflict in the presence of their children. One of the most impressive learning experiences we have had from family therapy was to see how extensive, tactful, and thoughtful devotion can be unwittingly extracted from 3- or 4-year-old children of a disturbed marriage. In initial sessions children may act up to screen their parents' problems from the view of strangers. Later the children may visually or verbally express their worries that the parents' fighting might lead to separation, divorce, or even homicide. They step in to help the underdog and to cheer up the depressed one.

Children of the ghettos have been described as prematurely charged with parentlike responsibilities. Pavenstedt[68] describes families in which the 3-year-old child warms the milk at midnight for the baby while his mother lies drunk in the next room. Apart from such extremes of functional exploitation, however, it is not certain that reality-determined premature adult functioning has a crippling effect on the child similar to that of guilt-laden exploitation of the child for emotional rather than realistic needs. In fact, in many families the "republic" of the sibling world can be a considerably more reliable source of trust and security for the younger child than the dependent and unpredictable parent. The mutual reliance among the siblings can then prevent any one of them from being harmed by the infantile behavior of immature parents. In these families the development of basic trust is anchored in reciprocal parentifying functions among the siblings rather than in the performance of parents.

SACRIFICIAL ROLES

Sacrifice is a universal element of religious and ethical bonds in all early civilizations. It is the foundation of the covenants among groups of men or between man and his gods. However, the important contributions of the victim are often overlooked. When a child, for example, Isaac in the biblical story, is to be sacrificed for God, our first reaction is horror over the cruel exploitation of a weak and innocent child by powerful adults. Indeed, the traditional interpretation of Isaac's near sacrifice is couched in terms of power and obedience. God demands from Abraham that he sacrifice his son. He obediently complies, to the point where God, impressed by his loyalty and faith, relieves him of the duty of actually committing the act. Moved by Abraham's loyalty, God, who has power to erase nations, promises his loyalty to Abraham and his descendants.

It is easy to see here the traditional reinforcement of the father role through God, the superfather, and overlook the major contribution of Isaac the son. Isaac, we are told, was not a passively coerced, obedient victim. According to Ginsberg's account in *Legends of the Bible*,[46] Abraham did not hide from Isaac the purpose of their trip to the mountain, and Isaac willingly carried some of the wood for his own sacrificial fire. Abraham did not have to use force to compel his son to accept his fate. Isaac didn't even try to resist his cruel death.

Furthermore, Isaac not only did not question his father's decision to commit the sacrifice, but he took it upon himself to advise his father to tie his hands lest he shrink and jeopardize the sacrifice. In addition, Isaac showed concern about what his parents would do in their old age without him, their precious son. Here is the victory of family loyalty over power and fear. The real hero is the son who acts as if he were a responsible father to his own parents at a point when he anticipates being offered as a sacrifice by his father. Without his active compliance, an important contribution to the covenant between the Hebrews and God may not have been established.

Willing self-sacrifice is the basis of the cohesive force of most great religions. Just as Abraham's obedience to God in submitting his son as an offering became an important component of God's covenant with the Hebrews, the willing sacrifice of Christ is the key element of the Christian covenant. This is emphasized in the following interpretation from the *Encyclopedia of Religion and Ethics*: "This new covenant . . . the Christian gospel . . . is contrasted with the Mosaic law as the former or old covenant. Like the latter, it was sealed with sacrifice—even the blood of Christ, who by His voluntary obedience and submission unto death has rendered the older sacrificial system superfluous and becomes the mediator of a new . . . covenant."[52, p. 219]

We have often observed that the individual who offers himself as a willing victim becomes the source of the greatest social power. In contrast to the exploitive aspect of self-sacrifice, we are impressed with its importance for social cohesion. A martyrlike, self-sacrificing parent, most frequently the mother, can prove to be the most forcefully binding and successfully controlling influence in the family. The same principle must apply to the sacrificially parentified child. It is natural for a therapist to react to the scapegoated child in the family as a victim who needs his active help to be rescued from the oppressors. It is, however, more accurate to describe the victim as both a willing collaborator and, in effect, a winner.

Sacrificial roles can be filled either by "bad" or innocent individuals. Isaac in the biblical story is clearly an innocent victim, as are some "sick" members in contemporary families. They may be respected, pitied, and often overprotected in certain regards. The willing cooperation of the innocent victim of scapegoating is difficult to understand without an insight into the emotional rewards derived from compliance with the family's hierarchy of demands and commitments. While the goat is sadly abused victim of human beings, the human scapegoat is often superior to his exploiters through his sensitivity and capacity for caring. A delinquent boy, for example, may be described as completely irresponsible, submersed in destructive actions, and a severe drug addict. However, this boy could be the one who has remained with his mother after his father has separated from her and all other siblings left home. His delinquency and seeming irresponsibility can be balanced through ethical values on a more meaningful level of relational bookkeeping. Through his availability to his mother, he shows excessive responsibility, carrying it for all other separated family members.

In certain families the sacrificial victim becomes "bad" according to the moral value system of the family. The delinquent or offensively rebellious juvenile is a typical example in this regard. Their passionate hatred of the traitorous act may enable the other members of the family to reinforce their sense of solidarity and righteous devotion. Often the same pattern of rebelliousness is evoked, through specific mechanisms, in several generations of a family.

NEUTRAL ROLES

Aside from the manifestly caretaking and scapegoat roles, many apparently silent roles contribute to parentification of children. One such role is that of the *well sibling*. Initially, the well sibling is described by the parents as the paragon of health and good performance. One could assume that he has escaped the pathogenic system. On closer observation, however, the health of this child is discovered to be a myth; often he is found to be suffering just as much as or even more than the designated patient. He may be a poor performer at school and quite detached from the world of his peers. He may have a shallow existence, neither subject in his own right nor real object of the family members' intensive strivings—neither a "giver" nor a "receiver." Behind his well-preserved facade he may be struggling with feelings of emptiness, emotional depletion, or depression. It seems that the well sibling's contribution to the loyalty system of the family is to play certain prescribed premature roles and not to live an age-appropriate life. This function may provide reason and organization to the entire chaotic family.

A 19-year-old sister of a 17-year-old delinquent girl was described by the parents as a symbol of family loyalty and proper behavior. She was a good student and a religious scholar. She did not like participating in the family therapy sessions, but whenever she did come her presence was a beneficial one, i.e., the parents' uncontrollably vicious attacking of each other and of the designated patient was kept within bounds. The family's behavior then approximated some degree of dignity. As she opened up later in therapy, this superficially calm well sibling turned out to be desperate to the point of considering suicide, because she viewed herself as a hopeless social failure, never to become capable of romantic love, marriage, or parenthood.

Often the full value of the well child's contribution is not realized until his physical separation from the family. One daughter, a well sibling of a chaotic family, became highly incapacitated while attending college out-of-town. Later she reported that while attempting to study she kept thinking of her parents' miserable marriage and of the effect her absence might have on their capacity to manage.

PARENTIFICATION AND PATHOGENICITY IN RELATIONSHIPS

The practical implications of parentification for a relationship-based psychotherapy are too numerous to be mentioned here. We have discussed the parentification inherent in many cases of juvenile delinquency. Viewed in the context of relationship theory, the hypochondriac or psychosomatically ill person has the mental set of meriting care or being dependent on a parent surrogate or nurse. In certain couples the mates take turns in being ill and enforcing a caretaking, nurturing attitude on the part of the other. Family treatment of school phobia often reveals a hidden parentification in which the parent has the fantasy of being cared for by the truanting child. A mother whose much older mother had spent more time on business than on childrearing had the wishful fantasy that her 10-year-old daughter stayed home from school only to supervise her housekeeping practices. A severely psychotic adolescent provided parental concern towards both parents to a point of complete emotional self-exhaustion: The boy of 16, who had been described as beyond psychotherapy and a mere custodial case, obliged his father, asleep in the chair in front of the television, by picking him up and carrying him to his second-floor bedroom every night. Parents who batter or kill a child often do it under the power of an unconscious fantasy of getting even with their allegedly rejecting parents.[73, 28, 65]

SYSTEMS OF COMMITMENT: THE RELATIONAL FOUNDATIONS OF PARENTIFICATION

Patterns of interaction in a relationship system such as the family are governed by compromises among expectations, aspirations, constraints, and obligations. Each parent brings into the marriage the normative value orientations of his family of origin. As he tries to live up to these values, he also tries to make the mate do likewise. As an individual, each one enters marriage with conscious and unconscious expectations about the marital relationship. Their love and respect for each other and for their joint enterprise of procreating a new family helps to temper their fierce demands and bitter frustrations. Out of the compromise between their expectations and obligations arises a set of values and a dynamic ledger that will govern most of their interactions as founders of a new nuclear family.

As particular value configurations develop in a relationship system, they become focal points of the members' commitments. One of the many possible value formulas may be stated as follows: "Neither my husband nor I care for our parents, they are all horrible." Another formula might be: "If you don't touch my family, I will leave yours alone." Another example is: "We have a good marriage, but it is a pity that our two children are constantly at war with each other." Such value formulas have innate ethical characteristics in that, in addition to being informative statements, they represent an internally felt censuring and prescriptive authority which guides the members' behavior. For instance, the children whose parents assume that they rather than the parents have all the conflicts will unconsciously comply with these expectations.

It follows from our framework that ethical values are psychologically deeply interwoven with the ledger of reciprocity in relationships and with the person's commitment to relationships. The fourth command-ment of Moses says, "Honor thy father and thy mother: that thy days may be long." Ethical behavior is inseparable from feelings of loyalty. Most of our ethical orientation originates from our internalized rela-tionship with our parents. Freud[40] in his formulation of the superego intimated its role as both a guardian of moral values and a surviving internalized parental love object. It follows then that many of the so-called irrational aspects of marital "fighting" result from the conflict between internalized values which originate from each spouse's early formative relationships, on the one hand, and the ethical expectations of their marital and parental roles in the new family, on the other.

Ethical "accounts" are the most forceful determinants of conduct because their effect is channeled through internalized commitments in each member of the social system rather than through outside coercion. Social structures enforced by even the most suppressive external power are usually shorter-lasting than structures built on loyalty and commit-ment of the participants to values. This is proven by the greater survival capacity of religions as compared with dynasties or empires based primarily on political and economic might.

In families as well, parents hope to inculcate in their children not just a mechanistic submission to their power but an internalized commit-ment to the value of the family's merit ledger. Accordingly, compro-mises regarding loyalty commitments based on accrued merit or obliga-tion constitute much of regulatory activity and competition for leadership in families. Only from an extremist ethical viewpoint can families demand an uncompromising loyalty from their children. Cer-tain forms of such indoctrination lead to unyielding family symbiosis, while its lack leads to a vacuum of commitments, an anomic state of the family. Autonomous growth follows, therefore, from both integrity based on recognition of a balance of committedness and capacity to separate.

THE ROLE OF CHOICE IN COMMITMENT

Parentification is an expectation within a family system, and its target is chosen according to complex determinants. For instance, it usually is not one parent who elects the scapegoat but the family system as a whole. The choice is determined by previous phases of family relation-ships and by the developmental background of each family member. Members of a family may be seen taking their turn at being parentified. The more rigidly this role assignment is confined to one individual, the more damaging it will prove to be.

Loyalty to the family can be considered a competitive choice when outside involvements are considered. The question of preferential commitment becomes more important, the more the scope of significant relationships is limited. "Symbiotically" clinging families constantly test the commitments of their married children: Are they loyal to their mate or to the family of origin? The parentified child is in an especially difficult position in considering new commitments like marriage or parenthood. Not only may he violate the loyalty of belonging, but also the commitment to caretaking.

COMMITMENT AS A SYMMETRICAL PROCESS (DIALOGUE)

The law of symmetry in commitments demands of two partners an equal capacity for input of trust and reliable performance. The seeming asymmetry of an ungrateful child–parent relationship, for example, is often balanced by covertly accumulating, enormously strong obligations. While ordinarily the child repays part of his indebtedness to his parents through commitment to his own child when he becomes a parent, the parentified child is seldom released from his obligation. The more pronouncedly martyrlike the mother's attitude, the stronger will be the guilt-laden loyalty bind for the child. Feelings of guilt and obligation becloud the child's natural devotion to the parent and lead to deep-seated ambivalence. Since the possessor of one's unconscious loyalty commitment is often overtly resented and despised, "symbiotically" bound schizophrenic young adults are often violently hostile to their mothers. The mothers, in turn, take such hostility easily and with little concern over losing their child's loyalty. These parents know better: The child's violence documents his unchanging involvement and interminable devotion.

COMMITMENT TO SOCIETY AT LARGE AND PARENTIFICATION

It is possible to see areas of relative overcommitment and undercommitment in both small and large social systems. Dictatorial systems tend to despise and attack the values of family commitment and expect the individual to overinvest in the values of the revolution, the party ideology, or religion. Religious devotion is also often seen as selective loyalty commitment. The institution of celibacy was founded on the notion that commitment to family life diminishes the priest's devotion to the church.

The crumbling of a political organization is often preceeded by a noticeable decrease in the members' commitment to its ideology. A comparative vacuum of commitment developed in the later stages of the Roman Empire, in the Catholic Church during the Renaissance, in Weimar Germany, and probably in the areas of nationalism and religiosity in the United States today. A vacuum of political committedness can, at least temporarily, invite excesses of the least desirable kind: human sacrifices in the arenas of Rome, large-scale witchhunts and religious persecutions prior to the Reformation, Nazi inhumanities in Germany, and anarchy, violence, and radical extremism in the United States.

Another outcome of declining commitment to pervasive ideologies of society-at-large may be increased investment in the family. There has been much talk about the "child-centered" nature of contemporary American life. Whether this is an accurate characterization or not, there is a widespread tendency toward overloading the life of nuclear families with expectations for excessive commitment and satisfaction. This overloading is probably connected with a diminishing commitment to the extended family, religion, and nationalism, and also related to a generalized feeling of alienation in modern man. We believe that a tendency toward defensive parentification represents one manifestation of such overloading of the nuclear family.

COMMITMENT AND "SYMBIOTIC" DEDIFFERENTIATION (FUSION)

Overcommittedness and undercommittedness have a quasiquantiative (comparative) and a qualitative aspect. In a quantitative sense, one can be overcommitted because he has less investment in other relationships at a particular time. In a qualitative sense, one may be overcommitted because he has no capacity or freedom to shift commitments or even to become an independent person. People with amorphous identity tend to be endlessly tied to symbiotic, never-changing relationships as if their personality boundaries were coincidental with those of their families. Symbiosis is based on an obligation to remain eternally devoted to one's family of origin; lack of individuation or differentiation fulfills this obligation.

While every successful attempt to bind a child to the family through guilt-laden loyalty delays the child's maturation and leads to infantilization, on a more significant level it also parentifies the child. A parent's symbiotic clinging to his child originates from the parent's lack of maturation and self-delineation vis-à-vis his own parents. The unconscious attempt to retain one's parents through the magical device of undifferentiation and eternal immaturity leads to a symbiotic possession of one's children. The state of undifferentiation of personalities and the state of consecutive overcommitment to the relationship go hand in hand. Yet overcommitment of a symbiotic type does not require visible interactions or overt acts of loyalty. Semingly meaningless self-destruction, unfounded violent attacks on the parent, delinquency, or psychosis in the offspring may all result from inalterable, fateful unconscious devotion to the parents.

LOYALTY COMMITMENT AND MORALITY

The patterns of parentification in families illustrate how obligations operate in shaping relationships among members. Generally, parentification attempts do not become pathogenic until they begin to seriously handicap a child's development. What have been described in Chapter 3 as "systems of loyalty commitments" represent one of the relationship patterns underlying parentification. The parent–child relationship is itself an important instance of a loyalty system with its bookkeeping of merits. Both parent and child are expected to invest in the obligation system in order to make it function optimally. Initially the mother gives incomparably more love to the baby; however, the baby is expected to "mortgage" his loyalty as a long-term investment into the commitment system. The parent gets certain types of psychological returns on his emotional investment from the growing child, but under normal circumstances these returns are psychological rather than tangible.

The following quotes from a letter written by a mother to the fiance of her latently schizophrenic daughter illustrates some of the raw emotions aroused by the impact of the offspring's contemplated marriage on the loyalty system:

"Dear Jim, it seems that I've a little straightening out to do again . . . Mildred has been a thorn in my side ever since she was born. As soon as some unsuspecting dope takes her off my hands the better. I'll sing and shout believe me . . . The other day very smartly Mildred told me she had nothing to be grateful to me for or to thank me for. I replied that she should thank me for the breath she was breathing—for if it hadn't been for me she would have only been a dream that never would have materialized as my husband never wanted any children. So me having a family was like putting money in the bank, not financially but figuratively speaking. I am now beginning to collect my dividends or interest on my deposit of one named Joe by him having a family and giving me, or blessing me I should say, with grandchildren and believe me when I tell you, besides respect, grandchildren is all I expect from any of my children."

In these intensely emotional excerpts it is easy to find elements of denied pain over anticipated loss ("I'll sing and shout believe me"), ethical expectation of loyalty, financial analogy to investment of caretaking and expected returns, and a cultural stereotype ("besides respect grandchildren is all I expect"). The tragedy of the parent on the eve of her daughter's marriage is that the event is experienced as treason instead of being considered as evidence of successful maturation.

The ethical bondage flowing from such guilt-laden loyalty to one's family of origin is the source of "symbiotic" clinging and a variety of individual symptoms, e.g., delinquency. Unending symbiotic bonds which captivate psychotic or severely neurotic children are usually founded on the fear of committing treason against an obligation. Furthermore, the ethical imperative of the loyalty bond may shift the emphasis from an *ordinary* to a *loyalty* type of morality. The kinds of morality underlying these two injunctions shape two types of superego development in the children.

Another area in which parentification is used for balancing the transgenerational ledgers of merit is marital relationships. The attempt of a parentified mate to secure a return on his investment may lead to tragic disappointment or even a wish for revenge on the part of the indebted beneficiary.

A 48-year-old mother of several borderline psychotic children kept repeating the most hateful thoughts toward her 72-year-old, parentified husband. In one session she attacked this serious and mildappearing old man with open death wishes, stating that on the day of his death she would wear a red dress and laugh. In a few days this man was in the hospital with a stroke and died within 10 days. His wife did actually come in laughing and wearing a red dress. Subsequently, she slipped into a psychotic depression of several months' duration.

The background of this grotesque "voodoo" death wish was pertinent to our concept of the transgenerational accounting of parentification. The wife grew up grossly rejected and neglected by her parents. At the age of 20 she married a man of 44. It is apparent that she related to him as a second father; he in turn became repulsive to her whenever he started making sexual claims. Concurrently, the husband became the displaced target of resentment toward her parents.

From the viewpoint of the parentified person, parentification is an overtly exploitative maneuver. The exploitation of a child is of a double-binding type: He is expected to be obedient, yet behave in accordance with the ostensibly superior or senior position he is cast into. Although he is recognizable, at least covertly, as a willing victim and a source of strength for the family system, he pays for his assigned rank by his captive role. The great cost of such captivity is arrest of individual development and autonomy.

In the face of the crippling influence of parentification on a child, how can parents remain unaware of its detrimental implications? We do not want to turn the clock back to the one-dimensional parent-blaming attitude which occupied developmental psychology for some time. To-day's parents, whether they are affluent or poor, certainly have much to cope with, relying on minimal support from their extended families. Nevertheless, it is curious how well protected and seemingly blind parents can be in denying their responsibility in the parentification of a child.

The answer may partially lie in a specific unconscious displacement mechanism. If I, as parent, carry within myself a long-standing guilt for having deserted my parents, I may have the illusion of repaying my debt through exaggerating my loyal devotion to my child (as if he were my parent). This displacement of the object of my devotion helps to diminish my guilt: I am reducing my old debt by paying excess devotion to my child in lieu of my parents. The giving aspect of my displaced loyal devotion will consequently mask the demand and exploitation inherent in my overreliance on my child.

IMPLICATIONS FOR THERAPY AND CONCLUSIONS

In exploring the various aspects of parentification, we have found it to be a ubiquitous phenomenon, since it is based on fundamental posses-sive needs and obligations of human beings. It represents an effort at recreating one's past relationship with one's parent in a current rela-tionship with one's children. As long as the parentification attitude does not affect the freedom and growth prospect of a child, it can be consid-ered within normal boundaries, especially if it is reciprocally available to all participants.

Parentification becomes of pathogenic significance if it is connected with the causation or maintenance of disabling patterns in any individ-ual, especially a child. Therefore, its recognition is important for the individual therapist and essential for the family therapist. Disguised parentification is a factor inherent in many forms of individual "pa-thology." An arrest of a child's development e.g. through brain damage, may contribute to parentification, in that the family's possession of the child is prolonged. By becoming and remaining disturbed, a child may shield the relationship difficulties of the parents. Even delinquent behavior may coincide with the child's being parentified, since the child's actions may bring unconsciously wished-for parental (or rather, grandparental) substitutes into the picture, e.g., police, court, and school authorities. Through his behavior, the child answers the parents' own need for limit-setting authorities. His "badness" is then covertly condoned through subtle rewards and messages.

Since we did not include parentification in the conceptual framework of individual pathology, we will not discuss its "cure." We prefer to talk about "liberation," which is essentially a *political* rather than a *medical* concept. Such a view is necessitated by the "institutionalized," character of multiperson familial ledgers of obligation and merit. We believe that such liberation, freeing and individuation can be attempted in individual therapy; skillfully conducted family evaluation interviews can enlighten the individual therapist in this effort.

The effect of family therapy on parentification can be divided into two phasic processes: the immediate transference effect and the long-range working-through process. One can almost automatically assume that a symbolic substitutive adoption takes place in the minds of all family members, even within the first session. As the parents begin to transfer and invest the therapist with parental significance, the parentification pressure on the children tends to diminish noticeably; consequently, the index patient is likely to improve symptomatically. This early symptomatic improvement has its treacherous aspects. The family members may experience an improvement in the general emotional atmosphere and may decide to discontinue treatment. In these cases the improvement usually does not last long. In turn, the family members, by rejecting the therapist, may attempt to use him as the bad object, as a substitute for their harsh parental introjects. They may use the abortive treatment experience for confirmation rather than change of their system, and continue to shop for alternative forms of treatment as subsequent crises arise.

In those cases in which the family has courage and strength to continue treatment, a whole new spectrum of dynamic dimensions becomes available to work on. The following are signs of progress towards "working through": The parents compete with their children for the therapist's attention as if he were a parent; the therapist is tested as to his feelings of partiality towards individual family members; the children begin to try out new, age-appropriate familial roles, and attempt to make their parents respond in a parental manner.

In conclusion, regardless of the therapist's theoretical orientation, he will be in a far better position to design his strategy and evaluate his progress if he learns to recognize the signs of parentification in the relational dynamics of families.

7

Psychodynamic Versus Relational Dynamic Rationale*

RELATIONAL AND PSYCHOANALYTIC CONCEPTS: CONVERGENCES AND DIVERGENCES

Relational theory constitutes a challenge to contemporary individual dynamic (psychoanalytic) psychology. The challenge is not aimed at the substance of Freudian thinking in areas where its validity is evident. In directing our inquiry at the conventional limitations of the theory, we intend to invite attention, debate and we hope for an eventual gain for both fields: individual and relational theory. Monothetical, one-dimensional conclusions, we believe, deserve to be challenged by the rejuvenating dialectic of the relational viewpoint.

Certain of the original Freudian concepts were couched in terms of 19th Century scientific thinking which stressed the fixed dimensions of an emerging rational order of things. The rapid growth of technology and medical-biological knowledge encouraged the young Freud to embark upon building a "science" of the mechanisms of dark unconscious realms of the human psyche. Without such courage and intellectual devotion to bring order into chaos, our knowledge of human phenomena would not have developed to its contemporary stage.

One vulnerability of the classical Freudian position concerning therapy was that it was cast into a basically cognitive framework: unconscious mental functions should be made conscious. While the integra-

*Parts of this chapter are reprinted with minor changes from Boszormenyi-Nagy I: Loyalty implications of the transference model in psychotherapy. Arch Gen Psychiatry, 27:374–380, 1972. Copyright 1972, American Medical Association. Reproduced with permission.

tion of affect and striving into insight which followed as a therapeutic rationale of the later stage of theory was a more comprehensive construct, the goals of integration were either not spelled out or were put into an essentially cognitive language. Only later and gradually did structural concepts of the basic personality emerge as noncognitive and non-pleasure-based dynamic determinants. Ferenczi, Melanie Klein, Fairbairn, and Guntrip were among the pioneers of an object-relations-based personality theory within psychoanalysis.[49]

Fairbairn and Guntrip have formulated the basic psychology of the individual according to the *intrinsically object relational* propensities of the mind. Accordingly, man's built-in need for certain patterns of relationships determines the development of personality from its inception. This school of thinking is probably one of the most promising avenues for the expansion of psychoanalytic theory, because it faces the need to broaden the scope of phenomena to be explored. Nevertheless, even within this psychoanalytic school, relationships are considered only from the point of view of individual psychic needs and regulations. The emergence of an existentially more appropriate relational dialectic had to wait until the theoreticians of the family therapy field came onto the scene to explore and concern themselves with multiperson relational balances and accounts.

The consideration of the existential totality of relationships introduces a focus on ethical rather than psychological issues. A psychologization of the sphere of interpersonal obligations tends to help denial of the ethical-existential component of one's responsibility to his fellow. The integrity of fair reciprocity in the dealings of two human beings cannot be adequately reduced to an ego-superego relationship, just as it cannot be equated with a purely religious view of man's primary obligation to settle his transgressions against his fellow through sole restitution to God. The family therapist has to recognize the vitally dynamic nature of the issues of retributive justice or the balance of fair reciprocity in relationships. It is important to separate this ethical aspect of relationships from an ethical evaluation of individuals according to degrees of righteousness or wickedness.

Reality testing is one concept which cannot be divorced from a relational dialectic without committing a grave error of over-simplification. Stressing a capacity for objective evaluation of the "outside world" could easily be confused with a view that close personal involvements can also be tackled as parts of an outside world. Can it ever be boiled down to subjective versus objective reality testing whether one continues to be available to an aging sick parent or considers him as economically a non-productive burden? We believe that the essence of the solution of such questions does not lie in the extent of cognitive objectivity or effectiveness of coping, but in the courage and ethical sensitivity of one's responding to a call for integrity, an integrity that lies in the totality of a life-long parent-child relationship, rather than in any one person. The reciprocity of loyalty is inseparable from the historical ledger of merit-accounting among family members.

The question of evaluating the context and nature of reality for decisions and actions leads us into considerations of motivational theory. We realize that our relational view of motivations cannot be a reductionistic one though it may have predilectional dimensions as intrinsic guidelines.

NEEDS VERSUS MERIT AS MOTIVES

The original theoretical position of psychoanalysis stressed the drive or instinctual organization of behavior and mental function. The theory often sounded as if it were aimed at subordinating human relations to the conceptual dichotomy of drive-subject and drive-object. In doing so, consideration of the *object's own needs* was routinely omitted, rather than included as a significant input.

The relational structuring of loyalty is only partially reducible to the existence of drives, hungers, and needs of individual members. Drive or instinct theory is based on a conflict or power model. Competitive struggle can exist between psychic systems or individuals. Yet while I try to make the other an object of my drives, what happens to his needs to make me or someone else his object? What if two of us competitively make the same third person an object of similar or different drives? What if I want to make you an object of affection and you want to make me an object of destruction? Freud's concepts of the primal horde, drive cathexis, penis envy, and mastery by the ego are all illustrations of power oriented, energy-related constructs. On the other hand, merit as a motivational concept has a multiperson structuring which is anchored in an ethical context. While the ultimate reality of needs is biological survival, the reality of merit is in the existential history of a group. As in families, in the history of nations or religious movements the motivational determinative force of merit is immeasurable. Abraham's willingness to sacrifice his son in obedience to God served as the basis of the covenant which was believed to have pledged God's loyalty to his people. Christ's sacrifice revolutionized the merit of millions of people subjected or condemned for centuries. The self-sacrificing acts of a nation's heroes and the allegedly vile acts of their enemies determine the motivations of countless generations of young men who are born into each idiosyncratic merit context. According to Shakespeare, Romeo and Juliet were caught in an "ancient grudge" between families which can be buried only with the death of the "pair of star-crossed lovers."

The relational structure of loyalty encompasses the network of merit accounting in the history of a group. A child is born into a situation which is predetermined by the ledger of merit and obligation of previous generations. We all know cases in which a mother is determined to avoid exploiting her children the way she was exploited in childhood and in which, by the trick of unconscious motivation, she finds herself doing exactly what she hoped to avoid. The child is caught in the parent's struggle for balancing an injustice and becomes himself a scapegoat for previous injustices.

Although we suggest that retributive justice and merit accounting constitute important determinants of motivations, we agree with Ricoeur that motivation theory is not a true causal theory. Need and behavior can never be put in a simple, classical cause–effect model. Consequently, we do not claim that retributional merit dynamics should replace all individual theories of motivation. We readily acknowledge the multiplicity and relativity of the determinants of individual and collective human behavior; we see our goal in the ultimate integration of individual psychology in the context of relational systems dynamics. Loyalty obligations, while important contributory factors, alone are not sufficient causal determinants of short-range behavior patterns; people can deny their obligations, consciously or unconsciously.

Another key concept of the Freudian approach is the contrast between *conscious* and *unconscious* determinants of motivation. In the structural phase of theoretical development attempts were made for formulating a systemic whole of the individual's unconscious strivings as an anthropomorphic force: the Unconscious, the Id. This helped to draw attention to the unifying, self-regulatory and goal-directed function of man's—and every animal's—basic nature. The survival of the individual and of the species are given their appropriate psychological tribute perhaps for the first time in history.

The family therapist can hardly avoid noticing "mechanisms" which are outside the members' awareness and at the same time seem to have predictable determinative effects on the family. This raises the question: can we speak of an unconscious organization of motivations on a multiperson, system level? A number of early attempts at formulating the deeper structure of family relationships explicitly relied on the individual model of unconscious functions borrowed from Freudian psychodynamics. The psychodynamic model was an obvious choice for explaining multilevel motivations, even though interactional systems are on a more complex system level; their covert or unconscious aspects could not be reconstructed from a summation of the unconscious functions of individual members. Taken collectively, all the dreams and fantasies or sodium anytal confessions of all family members would still not reveal the configurations of unconsciously shared motivational patterns of the family.

Yet it is unquestionable that members of a family do develop a dovetailing complementation of each other's unconscious dynamics no less than each other's conscious goals and strivings. Hierarchies of obligations, collusive defensive and exploitative patterns found in families, while not definable in individual psychological terms, include and are based on and interlock with the unconscious needs and commitments of all individual members.

We believe that a broader, more inclusive ethical attitude is the clue to understanding the difference between the individual and relational dynamic viewpoints. As though the individual viewpoints had the "egotistic" ethical premise that shrewdness equals ethics: all I care for is my own maximal success and gratification. On the other hand, our relational point of view assumes the existence of genuine concern for at least a few closely related individuals. The whole range of dynamic theoretical concepts can then be reviewed from the dual vantage points of these two ethical attitudes.

One such concept is the important one of *internalization*, a process that could easily be taken as having its endpoint in the individual. Whereas traditional psychoanalytic ego psychology looks upon the process of internalization of "object relations" as determined by the inner rules of the mind, social systems theoretical "purists" in the family field would tend to discard the concept of internalization. The present authors' dialectical theory of relationships places the phenomena of internalization in the context of the deeper expectations of the give-and-take of the person's current relationships.

Classical psychoanalytic theory conceived of internalization as a defensive psychic mechanism, ultimately serving the individual's struggle for the control of instinctual impulses. More recently Sandler and Rosenblatt stated: "It is perfectly consistent with psychoanalytic metapsychology to link the expression of an instinctual need with the shape of the self-representation, or, for that matter, with the shape of an object representation."[77, p. 135, 136] These authors add however: "The representational world is never an active agent . . . it is rather a set of indications which guides the ego to appropriate adaptive or defensive activity. It may be compared to a radar or television screen providing meaningful information upon which action can be based."[77, p. 136]. In contrast with the intrapsychic point of view, the key issue for a theory of relationships is: how does the process of internalization interlock and remain connected with an active engagement with relational partners;

therefore, in what way is the internalized object also an "active agent" and representative of the needs of the "objects" of my needs?

Viewed in complete isolation from the systemic context of live relationships, the process of internalization in itself is of limited interest for us. We view it as a mere conservation process: The live relationships of the past get transformed into relational programming for the future. For us the concept of symbolic, internalized representation of the other has to be reviewed and broadened from the conservation point of view to one of "convertibility." The child's indebtedness to his parents can be converted into a punishing superego. If accountability for action is assumed to be one of the deepest common substrates of relational, i.e., psychic determination, internalized object relations can be considered like a foreign currency or personal checks into which payments for obligations can be made, at least temporarily, with a convertibility as long as the exchange rate remains stable or the bank account is good. Our assumption of the existence of a human world with its own rules of justice goes far beyond a mere learning model of internalization— it presumes a constant flow between internal and interpersonal dynamic forces: ". . . interaction reinforces paradigms of self–other relationships that have been postulated to be operating as 'internalized I–Thou patterns' within the psychic structure of an individual." [61, p. 199]

A dialectical reappraisal is needed to redefine the significance of internalization. It is through the bookkeeping of merits that the unity between internal (psychological) and external (interpersonal) relational events can be restored. We have shown that internalized relationships essentially serve to sustain the justice of earlier interpersonal ties and that seemingly interpersonal interactions can be exploited to settle issues with the internal agents. For all practical (dynamic) purposes the internalized other is an active participant of the bookkeeping system. Whereas monothetical, traditional dynamic theory chiefly wanted to trace the historical origins of the needs that manifest themselves in the projection (externalization) of an internal set of drives upon an irrelevant relationship, a dialectical exploration should look for the "relevant" aspects of the seeming distortions of current relationships.

The concept of retributive or reciprocity dynamics gives a new meaning to the mechanism of *projections*. Rather than deriving the need for projections mainly from a dynamic struggle between impulses and impulse control, the retributive theory assumes a repayment or revenge mechanism which is unconsciously guided by the sensed imbalance of the accounts of the person's past. As growth is inevitably connected with certain amounts of frustration, it is difficult to define objectively at what point a child begins to feel abandoned and therefore intrinsically exploited by those who have raised him. Nevertheless, an intrinsic subjective quantification of give-and-take must constitute the basis of the account which then must be settled through all the person's subsequent relationships. At times the imbalance accumulates as a result of one's growing indebtedness.

Once the individual feels that a long-term, unsettled account has frustrated him throughout the years, the necessity and a sense of justification will arise in him to try to balance the account by "paying it back" even though through inappropriate acts, enacted towards a variety of inappropriate others as substitute culprits. The truanting child may not realize that "he takes it out" on the school system in displacement from his family of origin. As an adult, he may pathologically depend on his spouse whom he can torment and accuse in displacement. As a result, others will tend to treat him as one whose thinking is distorted, a maliciously sick, paranoid person. Yet in a way, he is merely following the logic of retributive justice, satisfying a need to balance a past account.

An important question is: why the displacement? What is preventing insight and recognition of distorted perceptions? We can assume that the initial fogginess of memories (amnesia) about one's early development explains only part of the seeming randomness of the choice of a displaced target. One could also ask: why not retaliate against the family of origin? We suggest that an important explanation lies in what we call *double accounting*. By this we mean that whereas the person feels exploited by his parents, he also feels indebted to them. Exploitative parents can simultaneously appear martyrlike, suffering, and unhappy. The resulting ambiguity through its subtle and unresolvable indebtedness may set up an ethical injunction against any revenge on the parents.

Originally, Freud's *theory of instincts* represented an inherently interpersonal construct, insofar as it recognized the importance of the choice of another person as drive or love object. However, in reducing the other to the role of drive object, Freud chose to disregard the repertoire of characteristics of the patient's significant others. Initially he was interested in the truthfulness of the patient's historic accounts of his maltreatment by significant others. Subsequently, his interest shifted from the interpersonal to the intrapsychic structures and mechanisms.

Any relationship theory must be explicitly interpersonal though not necessarily psychological. It must avoid the asymmetry implicit in the drive-subject and drive-object models and recognize that using the other as a target of my needs represents only one side of a total relation-

ship. Without consideration of the other's needs, therapeutic exploration will be limited to the context of unilateral use of others, and in all
likelihood reinforce exploitation.

The transition from the classical Freudian model to that of relationship theory is to be found in the theory of the *superego*. Through the
internalized dialogue with his superego, the child retains dynamic reference to the value systems of important others or of society as a whole.
Thus while the person of my parent and not only his values survive on
the internal stage, as his needs become represented through my superego, they become to some extent my own needs, since I want to live
at peace with my conscience.

According to the traditional psychodynamic scheme, the person is
viewed in constant dynamic dialogue and search for a balanced reciprocity not only with his superego but, simultaneously, with real others
currently surrounding him. His superego–ego relationship determines
his guilt feelings. Yet, as Buber[25] stressed, whether he feels guilty or not,
a person may have committed an act against his fellow and thus may
have harmed the justice of the surrounding human order.[25, p. 117] Psychotherapy may help erase "neurotic" guilt feelings, but it cannot undo
the factual consequences of a person's having abandoned or betrayed
his friend. Actions have more consequential interpersonal impact than
thoughts, feelings, fantasies, and other "psychological" occurrences. In
our terminology actions become registered in the group's ledger of the
accounts of reciprocity or of justice.

Sandler and Joffe have stated: "It is both theoretically and clinically
important that from the point of view of psychic adaptation there is no
such thing as an unselfish or altruistic love or concern for an object (that
is another person). The ultimate criterion in determining whether or
not a particular object relation is maintained or striven for is its effect
on the central feeling state of the individual."[76, p. 89] This statement
seems to ignore the mutually reinforcing feedback that takes place
between two or more persons constituting a relational system. Furthermore, we assume that one's obligation to altruistic concern is codetermined by one's position in the up-to-the-minute balance of the multigenerational chain of reciprocal give-and-take. The extent of my
altruism will in part depend on whether I have a positive or negative
account on the balance sheet.

The use of the term "unselfish" is, of course, crucial for our consideration. What are the ultimate criteria for judging whether "symbiotic"
relationships are selfishly or unselfishly motivated? If I cannot separate
from my aged and sick mother because her condition causes concern
to me and increases the guilt level of my loyalty to her, am I selfish or

unselfish? How much does a given individual owe to his mother for parenting devotion received in early childhood? After what extent of repayment can I be considered unselfish or altruistic vis-à-vis my mother?

The family therapist is bound to wonder, what will be the outcome of the ongoing feedback process among the various family members' "altruistic" caring motivations for one another? In family sessions one can observe chains of expectations and individual reactions as they unfold in multiperson patterns. One of Freud's individual-based concepts which promises to be the most useful in constructing relational theories was spelled out in the early stages of conceiving his structural theory. Freud[41] postulated that group psychology is related to a shared, extrapolated superego-like function of all members of a group. Interestingly, to our knowledge there has been no further systematic elaboration of these concepts in the literature.

Another example of the inherently dialectical relationship between manifest and covert motivational structures of an individual psyche is the classical Freudian concept of *reactive character formation*. This concept assumes an inverse relationship between visible character traits and their exactly opposite need configurations in the deeper, unconscious motivational realms of the psyche. For example, a protective or oversolicitous overt-parenting attitude is regarded as covering up for and defensively mastering deep-seated hostile intentions. However, it is important to consider more than these two system levels for our purposes. The concept of reactive character formation was anchored in the individual, while our interest is in the dialectical programming of multipersonal relationships. For example, through unconsciously collusive arrangement, members of a family may act in concert to display both aspects of their motivational antithesis without individually experiencing ambivalence. The overtly righteous members can vicariously participate in the delinquency of the other member and feel morally superior to him at the same time. At times even the fact that one member openly sympathizes with the delinquent may enable the others to condemn him without guilt over their invisible complicity.

The question can be raised: Does the concept of disloyalty add anything new to the concept of *ambivalence*? Both concepts connote split commitment. The ambivalent person hates the one whom he also loves, whereas the disloyal person does not honor his commitment owed to a person or to the system. From the viewpoint of the psychotherapy process there is another similarity between the two phenomena. As one examines his ambivalence, for instance toward his mother, and shares the feeling with the therapist, implicitly he commits disloyalty to his

mother. Despite this implicit disloyalty, however, the traditional therapeutic view has regarded the dynamic significance of ambivalence to
be the person's confrontation with his own feelings. The arousal of guilt
over ambivalence is traditionally explained on the same basis: the patient's confrontation with his true, although often repressed feelings.
The therapeutic process of increasing awareness is then thought of as
mainly of an intrapersonal consequence, governed by ego strength on
the one side and anxious need for repression on the other.

Disloyalty, on the other hand, is related to the action dimension and
is anchored in the order of the human world. The extent of loyalty
actually owed depends on the ledger of past and present actions of the
other. Loyalty or disloyalty in turn are also expressed in actions. The
ambivalent attitude is cast in the ambiguity of love and hate; the disloyal act implies obligation and repudiation of obligation. In the multiperson system field of family relationships one's ambivalence to his
parent cannot be isolated from the question of loyalty to the parent.
The therapeutic relationship inevitably becomes a challenge to existing
family relationships and through its implicit disloyalty aspects it may
significantly increase the guilt over ambivalence.

SUBSTITUTIVE BALANCING

Given our view that accountability of justice is the main principle of
dynamic programming of relationships, we have to examine its relevance to psychological phenomena described as *projection, displacement,* or *redirection.* Common to all these concepts is the assumption
that they connote "inappropriate" channeling of dynamically meaningful impulses and attitudes into a cognitively false reality context.

Taking the child's position in his family as a prototype, he has three
options for repairing his suffered injustice. If the child feels unjustly
treated and hopelessly overwhelmed by the power of the adult world,
he can: (1) revolt against the parents themselves, (2) if that is not feasible, turn his revenge inappropriately against someone else; or (3) try to
swallow his feelings of hurt. Option (1) obviously plays an important role
in delinquency and overt intrafamilial aggression. Option (2) can develop into a long-term coping measure which creates a pervasive satu-
ration of the child's future life with angry, "inappropriately" retributive, possibly paranoid tendencies, anchored in his past. Option (3) often
leads to withdrawal, depression, and turning aggression against the self
or to other secondarily "symptomatic," "pathological," or "character"
patterns.

One relationship can be used or manipulated to balance the injustice of another, earlier relationship. For example, a spouse or even a child can be unconsciously parentified by the alleged victim for the purpose of settling his needs for retribution against his parents. From the point of view of the psychology of the individual, this can be defined as inappropriate externalization or projective identification. The traditional view of this type of relational "pathology" is that its inappropriateness is unconsciously determined and therefore it is assumed that an increasing awareness or insight should help uncover and consequently modify its pattern. Accordingly, once a person of sufficient "ego strength" is shown how inappropriately he uses his current relationships as if to settle the accounts of his past, he should be able to correct the "distortion." The growing, increasingly realistic ego then is supposed to develop more appropriate outlets for instinctual or impulse gratification.

Our position adds two major theoretical departures, both dynamically and therapeutically. First, we assume that *substitutive justice seeking* is a relationship dynamic in its own right which lies between the person and his world, and not between the person and his impulses or internalized representations alone. The balance of all members' subjective justices amounts to an implicit yet objective system characteristic. Second, we assume that there is a quasi-ethical gain in protecting one's loyalty to one's parents at the expense of subsequent relationships. It follows from the concept of primary loyalty to one's family of origin that the greatest "sin" is to hurt that primary and therefore preferential commitment. Here lies an important dynamic determinant of all types of persecutory and paranoid attitudes: Displacement of retaliation serves psychic economy: One may attack someone else or the whole world in the noble pursuit of retaining one's loyalty by not blaming one's parents. The parents' alleged harmful acts get revenged in absentia.

The relationship with the therapist can be caught in similar balancing efforts. We owe the important concept of transference to Freud. He discovered that patients tend to repeat early infantile attitudes and expectations toward their doctor as though the latter were the original parent.

Since the main framework of classical psychoanalytic theory was phrased largely in cognitive terms, transference manifestations were usually considered as distortions of perceivable reality. In other words, the patient's self-deception concerning the nature of the patient/doctor relationship was described as a cognitive error, a distortion in perception and thinking. When the patient makes the analyst the target of repetitious infantile cravings, he unconsciously deceives himself, and consequently one goal of therapy is to correct this distortion. Family system therapists, on the other hand, are more interested in the existential implications of the transference aspects in all close personal relationships. Transferred attitudes and expectations carry the continuity of past unresolved obligations and expectations of family systems and signify factual events and truth rather than fictive deception.

References have been made in chapters 3 and 4 to the motivational significance of merit as contrasted with needs. Merit transcends the individual or psychological framework as it constitutes a dimension of ethical, loyalty and justice accounts of relational systems. We would like to examine the phenomena of transference, a concept central to psychoanalytic theory and practice from this viewpoint.

Traditionally, transference has been viewed in a need-determined, dynamic framework. The individual, based on his repetitious, regressively conservative needs can utilize the therapist, the family members or any other significant other as screen for his need-determined transference "project." From the perspective of the economy of fulfillment of his psychological needs, the person can ultimately either exercise futile repetition or accomplish a necessary utilization of the transference relationship for change and growth.

The merit viewpoint regards transference phenomena within the structured system of familial obligations and credits. Accordingly, every new engagement in relationships impinges on the person's position on the familial merit ledger. Real or apparent disloyalty to the other members of the family may create imbalances in relationships which can feed back into the need-gratification equilibrium of the individual involved in therapeutic transference. Positive transference means the wishful fantasy fulfillment of having good parents; negative transference gives the patient the opportunity to punish the therapist while saving the real parents. Positive transference, thus, always implies disloyalty to the real parents, while negative transference restores loyalty, at least implicitly through denial of the loyalty to the therapist.

Therapeutic change which occurs in the context of positive transference, i.e., wishing to please the therapist as a substitutive parent, itself impinges on loyalty to one's family of origin. Insofar as illness and failure sustain one's loyalty to the familial commitment to no change, relinquishment of the symptom opposite to a stranger can mean the ultimate of treason. By the same token, symptomatic improvement has always a connotation of disloyalty towards one's family of origin, and in our experience it matters little whether the parents are alive or dead. Transmitted intergenerational pathology is one form of persistently loyal bookkeeping through substitutive balancing within the family system. The further away from the source of and reason for the obliga-tion, the less it is known to the participant and the more the system becomes blind and pathogenic.

LOYALTY IMPLICATIONS OF THE TRANSFERENCE MODEL IN PSYCHOTHERAPY

Let us trace the implications of our dialectical relationship theory from general considerations of its contrast with individual psychological theory to a topic central to psychoanalytic theory and practice: transfer-ence.

MULTIPERSON VERSUS ONE-PERSON STRUCTURING OF MOTIVATIONS

There are widespread misunderstandings about the real issues that emerge from family or relational therapy as contrasted with the indi-vidual approach. One of these is the belief that the relational approach focuses only on visible interactions and implies only a superficial inter-est in the structural aspects of individual family members. Another is the myth that the confidentiality of a one-to-one therapeutic relation-ship is *sine qua non* for therapeutic depth. Throughout the years, we have come to a conviction that the essence of the family therapy ap-proach lies in a motivational and loyalty commitment in the therapist–patient relationship. The fact that the therapist sees the overtly symp-tomatic and other family members separately or conjointly is dynamically much less relevant than his intention to be concerned with every family member's emotional well being and growth. The main indication for exploring or initiating treatment on a family basis resides in the therapist's capacity for "multidirectional partiality," i.e., his inner freedom to take turns in siding with one family member after another as his empathic understanding and technical leverage require.

In this chapter we are not trying to consider how the phenomena of transference differ under conditions of family therapy. Instead, we wish to ask the psychotherapist to consider the merit of certain theoretical and strategic implications for individual therapy, including residential therapy of children. Freud's monumental contribution of the concept of transference helped us to understand the patient's hidden structural-ized personal commitments as they become externalized and displaced to the therapist. Understanding of the patient's inclination to personal-ize a seemingly technical relationship became one of the main indicational criteria for undertaking psychoanalysis. The next logical step in expanding the scope of knowledge is to include the context of the patient's current close family relationships. We can ask ourselves: Do the patient's personal subjective commitments to the therapist have hidden family loyalty implications? Furthermore, if the answer is yes, we must determine how important these loyalties are for therapeutic success. We will focus on guilt over disloyalty to the family as a chief source of resistance to treatment and change.

Anna Freud in her book *Normality and Pathology in Childhood* remarks: "In periods of positive transference the parents often aggravate the loyalty conflict between analyst and parent which invariably arises in the child."[38, p. 48] From the vantage point of the family therapist, it is of even greater significance to recognize that every step toward change or improvement impinges on the child's unconscious commitment to family loyalty. The mere establishment of a strong transference, whether positive or negative, triggers guilt over violation of unconscious family loyalty ties. Transference as an attempt at temporary adoption, aside from being an externalization of intrapsychic patterns, must be antithetical to existing child–parent ties and should not be considered exclusively in the isolation of the therapeutic relationship.

Loyalty can mean many things; we define it for our purposes as one of the multiperson structuring forces which underlie relationship systems or networks. Multiperson relationships include but supersede the psychological organizations of their individual members. In the language of systems theory, such organizations have a causal or motivational contribution of their own, just as water has different properties from the sum of the properties of hydrogen and oxygen.

It is well known that direct therapeutic work aimed at dimensions of relationship systems is extremely complex. Repetitious archaic patterns which are evoked in individual therapeutic transference neurosis and studied privately, as if *in vitro*, must be understood in an integrated pattern, interwoven with "real" interpersonal interactions. In an embittered marital feud both husband and wife lose perspective to the extent that they fight each other and the shadows of one another's internalized relational world. The dynamic point of view pictures life as a process which takes place in a field of constantly changing forces.

Classical psychodynamic theory has elucidated the conflicting forces of internal need configurations and the ego's attempts at mastering external reality. To change a personality in a certain direction has been the traditional frame of reference of individual psychotherapy. Transference phenomena, as Anna Freud has stated, must be viewed as part of a "whole complicated network of drives, affects, object relations, ego apparatuses, ego functions and defenses, internalizations and ideals, with the mutual interdependencies between id and ego and the result- ant defects of development, regressions, anxieties, compromise forma- tions, and character distortions."[38, p. 5]

Some of these concepts are individual-based, while others refer to dyadic relationships. The family therapist must broaden his scope from dyads to larger relationship systems, and to consider each member of the system from his unique vantage point as the center of a universe. In short, the therapist of families and relationships in general must distinguish among three levels of relational systems:

I. purely intrapsychic (e.g., ego–superego, self and voice, self and imagined persecutor, etc.);

II. internal aspect of interpersonal (e.g., one's loyalty to a parent or mate); and

III. existential aspect of interpersonal (e.g., the fact of one's having or not having parents, siblings, etc.).

Relational phenomena which pertain mainly to one of these levels may interlock with and obfuscate phenomena or expectations on the other levels. Much confusion and irrelevant, unproductive struggle can occur between family members due to their own and the therapist's confusion regarding the relational level upon which the essence of a problem lies.

Another difference between relational phenomena on levels II and III could be illustrated by talking about one's murderous, incestuous, etc. feelings towards one parent to a) the therapist alone or b) in the presence of the parent.

One of the least constructive points of view in current writing about the family approach is the assumption of an either–or, mutually exclu- sive relationship between individual personality dynamics and multi- person relational or system dynamics. Certain authors talk of a "discon- tinuous break" between traditional psychodynamic theory and family or relational models of motivational theory. Our own outlook has been dominated by a search for a creative synthesis of mutually complemen- tary and antithetical factors in evaluation of the human situation. The fact that we have new and valuable information on the homeostatic regulatory laws of relationship systems does not vitiate the necessity for understanding the individual person as a valid level of motivational system.

The next major development in psychodynamic theory might very well be the description of the deep dynamic structuring of multiperson relationship systems. Such language will borrow a great deal from the essentially intraindividual and partially dyadic orientation of classical psychoanalytic theory, but it also will have to integrate the conceptual achievements of relationship theory and extend the usefulness of both frames of reference. Such theoretical extensions will, naturally, have to deal with those frontier concepts which will make the transition from individual to relationship system theory.

INDIVIDUATION: DIFFERENTIATION OR ESTRANGEMENT

One of the myths frequently held by adherents of the traditional individual outlook involves overvaluation of physical separation as a means of individuation. We would not argue with the value or necessity of certain marital separations, divorce, or of the adolescent's moving out when ready. What we do question is the confusion of separation with differentiation as a means of maturation. Physically removing a schizoid young adult from his home, for instance, should not be expected to help as much towards his maturation as direct help with his dependent relationships in the family. Conversely, there is a widespread belief (or perhaps resistance) among professionals that treating the family members together amounts to a therapist's endorsement of the family's everlasting symbiotic togetherness. Actually, if the therapist is experienced and properly trained, working on relationship dimensions in a conjoint meeting offers more hope for individuation than does physical separation.

Confusion may arise from not distinguishing between individuation and severing relationship ties. The former has been defined as: "whether and from which point onward a child should cease to be considered as a product and dependent of his family and should be given the status of a separate entity, a psychic structure in its own right" (Anna Freud[38, p. 43]), and is a question of psychic boundary formation. The latter is often beclouded by a personal myth, based on some combination of escape, denial, internalization of loyalty, or ostensibly hateful warfare.

The use of catch phrases like "he is old enough to move out of his parents' house" and "for some people it is better to have a divorce" may hide the therapist's own unresolved relationship with his family of origin. The therapist's capacity for facing his own family relationship will determine whether he devises a strategy for separation or a method for conjoint exploration and therapeutic confrontation. Such a problem is posed by the following excerpt from a husband's statement in a first marital session:

"It really doesn't matter to me, Doctor, how my parents feel or what they do. I don't hold a grudge, but the truth is they have never favored me. I started working at 12, and when I needed their help most they didn't put up the money which would have kept me out of jail. Now I have a record, and it keeps me from executive-type jobs. For years I used to see my parents only once in 6 months. My trouble is a severe drinking problem. I love my wife, but I don't come home from work until 2 or 3 A.M. Actually, I have no emotion left for anybody. I sit in bars and drink to the point of unconsciousness. For the last 2 years I go to my mother's about twice a week. I only go there to help my father with things like insurance on his car, on his house, and things like that."

Some therapists would hear disinterest and distance in this man's description of his relationship with his parents; others, on the contrary, would be impressed by his paradoxical interest in visiting his parents twice a week as an emerging potential for exploring hidden loyalty ties.

INTERNAL VERSUS CONTEXTUAL CONFRONTATION

Whether it concerns a child or an adult, the relational theorist is adverse to a consideration of intrapsychic structures in isolation from the context of actual relationships. The family therapist is not only curious about the effect of the relative's behavior on the patient, but will extend the patient category to include the relative's own outlook and the transgenerational account of intermember obligations.

Freud expected the patient to have the capacity and courage to face his own internal psychic structures and internalized relationships. Relationship therapy demands courage to face up to the ghosts that reside in actual relationships. If I tell about you in your presence, you will observe my reactions and I will witness yours. What are the risks and potential gains for each family member in talking about one another and asserting their points of view in one another's presence?

Aside from dealing with one another's exposure of frightening or shameful experiences, the family members collusively maintained pathological attitude is less likely to remain hidden if exposure is bilateral. Private and shared family myths are more likely to be revealed in the context of conjoint exploration. Unconscious vicarious gratifications in the other's destructive acts and covert manipulations of roles are apt to be uncovered in family therapy. The nature of the alliance between family and therapist is thus quite different from the traditional situation in which an individual is expected to confront his unconscious mental structures in the presence of a therapist. The relatives not only become copatients, but their interactions become directly observable rather than merely described and acted out through transference to and countertransference elicited in the therapist.

Experience has shown that a single conjoint session can reveal striking, relevant pathogenic interactional patterns which could not be uncovered during months of separate, collateral individual therapy. Many cases of school phobia attest to this. A 17-year-old girl was treated individually in one of the prominent training institutes as a psychotic. Two weeks after her transfer to the Family Therapy Division, she and her stepfather revealed the existence of a 6-month incestuous relationship. In subsequent family therapy the entire family of four made great progress, and it was discovered that the mother needed long-range therapy.

In examining the transference aspects of individual and relational dynamic approaches, we must consider a further expansion of our theoretical horizon. As our point of view progresses from relatively impersonal formulations of psychic mechanisms to subjective experience and meaning of exchanges among people, we must consider not only psychological reactions, but also the ethical and existential entanglement of human lives. Concern and responsibility for one another are important dimensions inherent in every close relationship, even if they are in a partially unconscious structural realm. The therapist who wants to liberate the patient from his concern for or guilt-laden loyalty to members of his family may succeed in removing certain manifestations of psychological guilt, but may at the same time increase the patient's existential guilt. Buber[25] distinguished between guilt feelings and existential guilt. The latter obviously goes beyond psychology: It has to do with objective harm to the order and justice of the human world. If I really betrayed a friend or if my mother really feels that I damaged her through my existence, the reality of a disturbed order of the human world remains, whether I can get rid of certain guilt feelings or not. Such guilt becomes part of a systemic ledger of merits and can only be affected by action and existential rearrangement, if at all.

SYMPTOM AS LOYALTY

A key consideration of the deeper structuring of relationships concerns the role of "pathology" and "symptom" in the unconscious loyalty to one's family. Insofar as the pathogenic family system is supported by the regressive needs of all family members, the most overtly symptomatic member can be viewed as a victim of his loyalty and of an unconsciously shared agreement to avoid hurting any member through anyone's personal change. A child may cover up the parent's regressive needs by school phobia, or a delinquent adolescent may try to balance a "yo-yo"-like marriage in which the parents take turns threatening to separate. It is logical to assume then that the symptomatic member, most often a child, is made increasingly guilty as he undergoes symptomatic improvement. In an existential sense, the more he improves his function the more he is bound to harm the order of his human world. This is more probable if his therapist promises confidentiality and a separate alliance; the familial betrayal becomes even more pronounced. Inasmuch as transference amounts to a trial and temporary adoption, its occurrence further magnifies the feelings of betrayal and becomes a source of psychological guilt in addition to the existential guilt inherent in symptomatic improvement.

We must add that family therapy experience has shown the strength and intrinsic healthiness of many an overtly symptomatic family member. His role is to bring outside attention and potential help to the entire system. He may be the only one who does acts which can effectively lead to change. This also explains why so frequently the initially symptomatic, designated patient member has a better prognosis than the silently pathogenic parents or well siblings. (See Framo[37])

TRANSFERENCE WITHIN THE FAMILY

References have been made in chapters 3 and 4 to the motivational significance of merit as contrasted with needs. Merit transcends the individual or psychological framework as it constitutes a dimension of ethical, loyalty and justice accounts of relational systems. We would like to examine the phenomenon of transference, a concept central to psychoanalytic theory and practice, from this viewpoint.

Traditionally transference has been viewed in a need-determined dynamic framework. The individual, based on his repetitious, regressively conservative needs can utilize the therapist, the family members or any other significant other as screen for his need-determined transference "project." From the perspective of economical fulfillment of his psychological needs, the person can ultimately either exercise futile repetition or accomplish a necessary utilization of the transference relationship for change and growth.

The merit viewpoint regards transference phenomena within the structured system of familial obligations and credits. Accordingly, every new engagement in relationships impinges on the person's position on the familial merit ledger. Real or apparent disloyalty to the other members of the family may create imbalances in relationships which can feed back into the need–gratification equilibrium of the individual involved in therapeutic transference.

In therapy, transference as a technical device is a means of changing a person's patterns of reacting. It is also a bridge between my habitual past reactions and my present or future ones. As I reexperience and act out past patterns toward the therapist, I can take a necessary distance from everyday interactions and begin to break up the repetitiousness of my "pathological" cycles. The essence of transference is not a cool, objective cognitive experience, nor is it chiefly a behavior modification process of a learning type. Instead, it is an emotionally charged, relational experience with subjective excitement of promised fulfillment and feared, though painfully familiar disappointment.

All of our emotionally significant relationships are embedded in a transference context, at least when transference is defined in a broader sense. As I fall in love with a woman, she may become a mother transference object to me. As my relationship with my boss becomes personalized, chances are that I discover how I begin to reexperience some attitudes that I had toward my father, older brother, or grandfather as a child. As therapists begin to see families rather than isolated individuals, they are soon struck with a different climate for therapeutic transference. The chief reason for this is the fact that family relationships themselves are embedded in a transference context; the family therapist can enter the ongoing transference relationship system rather than having to recreate it in an exclusive therapist–patient work relationship. As the therapist gains access to the system of intensively charged deeper family relationships, he obtains a position which surely demands a specialized skill, but he also obtains new leverage, based on the mutuality of relationship involvements among family members.

Since Freud, psychoanalytic theoreticians have been curious about the individual determinants of a patient's capacity for developing intensive therapeutic transference. Such capacity in patients has long been viewed as a main condition for psychoanalytic treatment. Recently, attention has been paid to the instantaneous capacity of certain psychotic patients for symbiotic transference. The analyst abstracts and condenses repetitious, regressive relationship attitudes into the therapeutic relationship, hoping for the emergence of a technically accessible transference neurosis. The family therapist on the other hand, is interested in same tendencies *within* family relationships. He must examine the multiperson system determinants of a person's intrafamilial transference involvements and his capacity for "transferring" relational attitudes from his family to outsiders. We prefer to include members of the family of origin of both parents in any family we have in family treatment. Frequently, the parent–grandparent relationship becomes the focus of observations and a target of possible intervention. Such parent–grandparent relationships are richly interspersed with feedback processes between so-called current reality and long-suppressed or repressed early longings and disappointments.

CLINICAL ILLUSTRATION

The family therapist assumes that regressive aspects of the lives and actions of family members constitute one of the main components of the family's loyalty system. Each member's investment of sacrificed growth is repaid through the other members' tolerance of his regressive gratifications. Such subtle, partly unconscious interlocking between personal needs of members and the idiosyncratic value system of the family builds up the context of familial intimacy. As individual psychotherapy or analysis redirects repetitious acting out through transference to the person of the therapist, the family's loyalty system becomes threatened. The threat is even greater when the patient is a child because the child is usually sheltered in a more dependent position than are adult members.

One of the most enlightening experiences in the practice of family therapy pertains to the amount of solid contribution of even very young children to family loyalty. The extremes of parental dependence on children can best be seen in cases of overwhelming parentification of children. Yet even if we disregard these extremes, few children fail to get the messages, "Never trust anyone but your mother" or "Your mother is your only real friend," either explicitly or implicitly.

The case of a 10-year-old boy and his family is illustrative of such situations. The staff of a private residential school invited us as family therapy consultants in their effort to broaden their psychoanalytic, individual treatment model in which the boy was seen by a psychotherapist and his mother had long-distance telephone conversations with a social worker. The child's problem was presented as an irritating retardation of motoric performance combined with an obsessive focusing on detail. The life of the family revolved around his slow responses. The parents reported that it took the boy hours to go to bed, meals were taken extremely slowly, and the boy could hesitate for a long time in deciding on which side of the closet to hang his shirt. It was easy to see the family's despair over this behavior and their wish for a change, at least on a conscious level. Psychological testing revealed good intelligence, and the boy's motoric system was found to be well coordinated. His 7-year-old sister was a very quick, vivacious child. (Unfortunately, no data were collected on the contributions of the well sibling to the pathogenic family system.)

We omit the description of the intrapsychic dynamics of this boy, to focus on relational factors: The workers assigned to this case reported that the parents were intellectually active but emotionally rather detached people. The father was a chemistry professor, and the mother, who had wanted to become a social worker, ended up studying sociology. The mother once was hospitalized for psychiatric reasons for 3 weeks and had subsequent neuropsychiatric treatment. She was desperately determined to regard her child's problem as essentially an organic one, and she recalled having been traumatized in a clinic where, as she alleged, attempts had been made to make her feel like a "rotten mother." She did not like to talk about her family of origin which she had years earlier left behind in another city. She stated that she saw her cold, "neurotic" parents once or twice a year. Her relationship with her parents was superficial; she could not be spontaneous with them. She claimed she did not trust professionals either. All she wanted was help with her son's slowness. Yet, paradoxically, she would talk once a week up to an hour on the telephone with the social worker, from a distance of almost 400 miles.

The workers had the impression that the child's father was an extremely aloof and passive parent and that his only assertion manifested itself in his final insistence on sending the boy to a residential school. Although there was little reported about the father's role in the pathogenic family system, it was easy to postulate that the parents in this isolated nuclear family did not have many resources for vitality of human relationship. Thus, the stage was set for a subtle parentification of the children.

The boy's therapist stated that the marked slowness of the child's behavior was also exhibited in school and that there had been only one situation in which it seemed to be almost completely absent. This happened during an excursion in a house outside the school's realm where the boy took his meal at a normal pace. They also reported an interesting observation. On the occasion of a school excursion the boy appeared to be enjoying himself greatly. When his family visited several months later, he made them drive through the same itinerary as the school wagon had gone, in the hope of conveying a similarly happy experience to his family. The therapist added that the boy could also recall that he had done likewise on a number of occasions at home, e.g., he made his parents drive through the same route as he and his uncle had driven earlier in a happy mood.

The child's capacity for giving to his parents was a striking feature, considering the lack of personal warmth in their own relationships. To view a child as a family healer—when his symptoms demonstrate a devouring oral demandingness and tiring anal obsessiveness—certainly appears paradoxical. Yet we can assume that the parents were able to use their child's symptoms as an escape from dealing with their own unresolved problems with their families of origin. Furthermore, on an existential level, the child's misdirected life energies revitalized the stale marital relationship. The sick child provided an agenda around which the parents' weak identity could crystallize.

A gratification inherent in parentification consists of the parents' utilizing the child to unconsciously undo their own early object deprivation. Early deprivation, as we know, can lead to a never-resolvable need for symbiotic clinging, with no capacity developed for individuation and separation. The more the child is caught in his own symptomatology, the longer the period of implicit posessive gratification for the parent. The parent can defend himself against insight into such dependence on his child's pathology, as above, by a rigid insistence on the organic nature of the condition. In this case, it was reported that the mother always had been preoccupied with viewing her child as organically damaged, from the first few months of his life. The social worker reported that most of their long conversations on the telephone were arguments whether the child's condition was organic or not.

On a deeper level, the child's behavior revealed a great extent of concern for his parents. Through covert messages it must have been conveyed to him that even though his symptoms irritated his family, his illness prevented his mother from facing her own depression, loneliness, and hurt feelings. Even in cases in which a parent's previous psychosis or conflicts are never openly revealed to a child, the child nevertheless has anxiety and responds with familiarity to belated revelation of the secret.

If we assume then that homeostasis of the pathogenic system is regulated by loyalty-bound regression and arrest of development, we can expect the child's guilt to increase to the extent he lets his parents down. Leaving them behind to struggle alone at home already borders on disloyalty; if in addition he would improve symptomatically, it could amount to psychological treason. Guilt over his familial loyalty is not simply a regressive fixation, anchored in an internalized situation; it is, rather, validated by interpersonal reality of the parents' own messages. To keep his guilt down and also to protect his parents, the child has to appease the system by (1) preserving his symptom and (2) trying to help his parents through sharing with them everything he can enjoy in life. Thus, it would be unrealistic to expect the child to progress too far in the face of actual disloyalty and mounting guilt over it.

In the case above, this model seemed to be at variance with the traditional model of the school's therapy team. They aimed their strategy at having the child invest the therapist with sufficient transference to gradually undo his fixated patterns, so that with the therapist's guidance he could begin to acquire new patterns of behavior. As they pointed out, this happens in a great number of residential treatment cases, although it is often reported that the effect does not last long beyond discharge. The family's influence seems to reverse the therapeutic change. It is as if the transference parent's (the therapist's) approval were antithetical to the real parents' needs and wishes. As family therapists, we felt an intense frustration over the lack of availability of the parents in this setting; they would come to visit only four times a year. How can we as consultants suggest methods to affect the system under such circumstances? Once again we notice the severe handicap that institutionalization can place on the family approach.

CONCLUSIONS

The logic of our loyalty model supports a possible use of the transference situation which is aimed to diminish the guilt caused by the patient's disloyalty to his family of origin. What if the strategic motto were, "How could you and I, the therapist, work as a team to help your family?" rather than, "How could I be a better substitute parent, so that you can use me for growing up emotionally?" If the first formula is followed in practice, the therapist can, by listening to the child's own description of his family experience, design ways in which the child can help his family and in turn be permanently helped. What is required is the therapist's concern for helping all the other family members, each as his own patient. The means then can be developed even though the contacts between child and family may be limited (e.g., visits, phone calls, correspondence).

Specifically, it would follow that the therapist must obtain clues to ways in which the child can help the parents. The child may be surprisingly aware of such possibilities and eager to discuss them with someone who is willing to recognize his role as a desperately eager family healer. In such instances it is easy for the therapist to offer an alliance for developing strategies for more effective help for the family. In cases in which the child is not aware of his leverage as a potential family healer, the therapist first has to explore and verify what the child's own notions are regarding his family role, and encourage the child's thinking by giving recognition to the hidden loyalty in his concern about his family. Using his role and therapeutic leverage in this manner, the therapist can considerably diminish the loyalty conflict implicit in the child's transference-determined devotion to him.

In considering the above strategic formula for therapy, we do not want to underestimate the goal of increasing the autonomy and functional effectiveness of the individual patient. However, whereas in the traditional individual approach the goal is accomplished chiefly via the transference relationship to the therapist and by learning of new patterns, we suggest an additional dimension of exploration: the loyalty implications of both transference investment and subsequent symptomatic change. This would require that the therapist include the loyalty investments of all family members as a major dynamic determinant in the patient's capacity for lasting growth.

In summary, the family therapist is not satisfied with the theoretical view that therapeutic transference should be considered in isolation from loyalty commitments within the patient's family. Consequently, he is likely to encourage new avenues for involvement among family members. Working with such an open relational system gives the therapist far more leverage than would a consideration of the transference relationship in isolation.

The traditional practice of isolating therapeutic transference investments from family loyalties implicitly assumes a liberation of the child from repetitious feedback chains of family interaction. The exclusive, confidential alliance between therapist and patient implies a formula: With my help you may defeat your pathogenic forces, your repetition compulsion, and (especially if the patient is a child) the influences of your pathogenic family environment. If, however, the therapist includes into his design family loyalty as one of the system determinants of repetition compulsion, by the same logic he will have to include the relatives' welfare in his contract for therapeutic alliance. All family members will then have to receive help in order to maximize the potential for change in everyone. We have learned not to trust the signs of a child's or adolescent's angry wish to abandon his anxious, constraining, guilt-provoking, parentifying, or infantilizing parents. We prefer to search for the underlying antithetical guilt-laden loyalty and to consider the structure of the paralyzing existential guilt which follows disloyalty to the system. We cannot fully understand the structure of the guilt-laden loyalty without knowing and being concerned for all members of the relationship system.

8

Formation of a Working Alliance Between the Cotherapy System and the Family System

Each family that accepts referral for family treatment must be studied in its own unique context. Family psychotherapy can be considered as a contractual arrangement between the family and therapists for an ongoing examination of all family members and their interaction, with the goal of benefiting the family as a whole. In forming a working therapeutic alliance with a family, there are complex demands on family therapists. Therapeutic alliances with individual patients have been discussed from the viewpoint of ego structure, defenses, and motivation.[48] However, establishing a "contract" with a family—a multiperson system—requires a different dynamic formulation. The manner in which the family has functioned in the past needs consideration, but a revision of techniques is required to ensure that all its members become engaged and committed to the therapeutic process.

Families readily evidence their psychological need to assign roles and project blame within as well as outside the family. Often, the underlying desire of family members is to repair what they feel are violations of family loyalty, and they rarely question whether the family system is impeding growth and maturation. If these and other factors are not dealt with quickly and continuously, the therapists and therapy will be assigned the "incompetent" role and the family will abruptly terminate treatment. Hollender[54] emphasizes that in forming a therapeutic alliance with an individual, the patient first has to want to learn what is at the root of his problems; secondly, how can he then modify or change his behavior; and finally, does he have the willingness and capacity for this work. While these essentials are still applicable with a family, the nature of commitment to family therapy is a more complex and fundamentally different process. The multipersonal system aspect of family functioning is the real issue. Consideration must be given to the whole homeostatically changing system in which, functionally, one individual may appear overadequate, but is just as dependent on the collusive system as the overtly underadequate member. Furthermore, the "well" functioning family member may become the most symptomatic one for a period of time, thus radically altering the definition of the problem. The therapists have to communicate the message to all family members that therapy ultimately may bring help and relief for the underlying pain rather than solely for the "symptom" or symptomatic individual that brought the family into treatment.

Ambivalent, possessive, warring-loving family relationships are riddled with recognizable fears of incest and murder, or the opposite fears of overwhelming loneliness or annihilation. Family members often bring with them an atmosphere of extreme hopelessness and have rarely trusted anyone outside of their family. Although they may appear guarded and suspicious, this is not always due to fear of the outsider. It is difficult for them to believe that anyone would or could help them. Underneath they feel unworthy, undeserving, and hopeless. Searles[78] writes that such feelings in a patient can often produce a protective screen towards the therapist. Family members may wonder whether the family therapists will "enter into" the family system, and if so, will they be annihilated or driven crazy? Can the therapists be strong enough to withstand onslaughts? Who would willingly enter their family's arena? Who could possibly like or understand them? They want and yearn for a different family life with some degree of emotional security. Are the family therapists strong enough to help them bring about such a state, or do they feel that therapy will lead to a more disorganized state?

The rigidity of some family systems and the intensity of ambivalent feelings with which family therapists may be confronted must be understood. Complex repetitious patterns of behavior are maintained so that the relationship system can be continued without change. From the therapists' point of view, these seemingly meaningless patterns serve many purposes. They may amount to a defense aimed at the control of frightening impulses. On one level, it is evident to the family that its methods have been ineffectual with regard to the designated patient. Family members tend to view the patient as the cause rather than the result of the unbalanced relationships within this family. Yet as they give the histories of their nuclear and extended families, they describe generational suffering. Exploration of these connections may be resisted, or even consciously refused. One woman said, "Why open Pandora's Box? It might get worse than now."

The therapists must be aware of the family's need for reassurance that the family loyalty system will be either restored or rearranged so that all can survive. The young member attempting to emancipate himself from a pathological family system may be regarded as a traitor who will cause the dissolution of the original nuclear family. Healthier families are not as threatened by emotional separation and can adapt more successfully.

Hope must be continuously found and fanned by the family and the therapists within the pathogenic family. It must be connected with the specific areas of strength and health which exist in all families. The therapists must convey that while they are aware of the family's suffering, they are strong enough to help them strengthen and rebuild the healthy areas. In other words, the therapists must use their strength to help with the relational tie-ups which deter or interfere with individuation. This can occur only if each family member makes a commitment to the therapeutic process in which the entire family will be involved.

REFERRALS

Prior to the formation of a working alliance the therapists should ascertain the attitudes of the referring professional and what he may have conveyed to the family. Was family therapy presented as a therapy of choice, or was the family sent as an end-of-the-line referral, or because the patient was deemed unsuitable? Was it presented as an opportunity for all family members to gain for themselves as well as for each other? Does the family feel individual therapy was eliminated because they are hopeless, their problems too severe, that they are not really treatable? Was the referring professional ambivalent regarding family therapy as a method of treatment? What types of problems are referred? Are only those families with a psychotic member selected, or those with a delinquent member, or perhaps with psychosomatic illnesses?

It is critical for the family therapists to be aware of how the family has reacted to the referring person, and to be alert to why the family thinks it was referred for this form of therapy. Do they think they could benefit from a joint therapeutic effort? Every family member should participate in the discussion of expected gains and desirable goals. If these issues are not discussed, understood, and overt resistances removed, the family will be unable to form an alliance with the therapists and will not accept treatment.

From the beginning the therapists must convey optimism and conviction regarding the therapeutic gains that can evolve from therapy with an entire family. Moreover, the cotherapy team must then help the family discover in themselves sufficient hope and strength to effect change. One of the most important facets of an initial contact with a family is that the therapists express a demand for commitment to therapy, even though it will require painful exploration on the part of all family members. This insistence on exploratory effort is one of the most important growth-producing therapeutic factors throughout the entire process of treatment. The family's general, preliminary apprehensions and resistances concerning treatment shall be brought out as directly and openly as possible. Such fears then can be dealt with specifically and in greater depth when the family brings up definite issues with which they are struggling.

DESCRIPTION OF THE FAMILIES: INITIAL PROJECTION OF PROBLEMS OR SOLUTIONS

Individuals with so-called strong egos may be dissatisfied with themselves, with their marital–parental roles, and because of disturbing symptoms seek individual therapy. By contrast, in some instances where marital therapy is requested, the alleged marital problems may cover over a deficit in the parent–child relationship. A marriage counselor related a situation in which a couple never mentioned problems with their son until he attempted suicide. To study one subsystem of the family—namely, the marital or parental—rather than both is to overlook the functioning of the entire family. Adults who say there are problems only in a symptomatic child or children initially do not perceive those problems as emanating from unresolved conflicts among the family members. The child's problems are presented as if all other existing conflicts within the family were unrelated or secondary. This possibly explains the readiness of some parents' to offer the child for individual treatment. Often other solutions are sought, such as boarding school, military academies, jails, and psychiatric institutions. Any of these avenues aid and abet the parents' need to protect or cover up the family problems. By assigning the "mad" or "bad" label to the symptomatic child, the parents unconsciously hope to demonstrate their own normality and that of other siblings.

While such solutions may temporarily appear to relieve the acute tensions that exist in the family, experience demonstrates that underlying conflicts are not resolved. When a family "extrudes" a member, this postpones and arrests those aspects of the growth process which evolve from their relationships with each other. The conflicts which have existed may lie dormant. This knowledge has repeatedly been confirmed in instances where one child has been removed from the home and shortly thereafter a second or third child becomes overtly symptomatic.

Consciously, parents say and do mean that they want to give their child a better opportunity to grow up with less suffering and deprivation than they have experienced. The impetuses for growth, namely, continuous individuation and separation at appropriate age phases, are consciously sanctioned. However, observations of many families indicate that the underlying or unconscious ledgers of commitments seem to be pulling them in an opposite direction. Symbiotic, infantilizing relationships are covertly reinforced. Bowen noted that any attempts to move out of such a family system are experienced as disloyal and threatening to the heart of the family system which has as its core an "undifferentiated family ego mass."[20, p. 45]

While the families request help in changing, and therapists conceive of themselves as change agents, the unconscious, collusively shared family goals may be diametrically opposite. If a scale of family "belongingness" can be visualized, there can be "overcloseness" at one extreme, and at the other, feelings of isolation, intolerable aloneness, annihilation, or as one father described it, "swinging in outer space." Unless the family therapists can help a family to accept themselves as the change agents, a therapeutic alliance is not formed. If a family consistently projects its problems and solutions outside themselves, they may bring themselves to the sessions, but there is no commitment to a therapeutic process of growth.

INITIAL STEPS IN THE WORKING ALLIANCE

Three main issues must be presented and discussed with the family: time, fee, and commitment. These may seem elementary issues which are taken for granted. However, each issue, as it is clarified with the family, begins to reveal how much or how little family members have seriously considered the demands of such an undertaking. For example, all family members have to face possible modification of school or work plans so that they can regularly attend the weekly session. The family should know that additional sessions can be scheduled if needed and that the therapists have time available. They need to know how cancellations for illness and vacations are dealt with. Any matters that might interrupt the therapy sessions need to be reviewed openly. They should be informed regarding the therapists' vacation plans or missed appointments. If one family member is ill, they need to know whether it is expected that the other family members will attend the session. The cotherapy team and the family must be clear about the inevitable absences on either one's part and how this will be handled regarding appointment and fees.

Time and fee have a common denominator. Has the family considered in terms of months or years how long the work may take, and in consideration of their financial situation, have they faced the possible financial cost? Will it come from weekly income or does there need to be a consideration of resources? Many families have said that treatment could be undertaken only if they were to use money being saved for the children's college education. Which will be given priority if the family is faced with such a choice?

These issues reveal whether the family has planned realistically about entering into and remaining in therapy. In general, the family members need help in realizing how important a priority treatment must be given in this phase of their lives.

DIAGNOSIS AND PROGNOSIS

THE FAMILY'S CAPACITY FOR WORK

Family therapists have not attempted to reach consensus on which families they will treat or what kinds of families are most suited for family therapy. They have accepted families with one or more symptomatic patients, e.g., families with an adolescent member diagnosed as schizophrenic and a depressed parent, and families who are referred where the adult is depressed and a child has a school phobia. Many of these families could be described as less individuated and separated, or symbioticlike. There are many reasons for lack of established indicational criteria for family therapy. Chief among them is the lack of a definition of "family pathology."

Patients most suited for family therapy are the ones who reveal a capacity for facing problems within the family rather than focusing only on presenting symptoms. A person with an obsessional neurosis may be told that he could profit from being psychoanalyzed, but he may not accept such a recommendation or even be found to be sufficiently motivated.

CONSENSUAL AGREEMENT

In discussing a family's capacity and commitment for work, family therapists have developed some criteria. In addition to recognition of the designated patient's problems, it is important that each adult and other siblings see themselves as also needing help. What does each one specifically hope to gain for himself as well as for the other? From the beginning, each family needs to reach a consensual agreement regarding what has been missing for all of them in their family, e.g., mutual understanding, privacy, inability to talk without threats or running out. Even though needs are different for each person, considering age phases and sexual differences, there are common denominators: human needs for acceptance, understanding, and respect regardless of age or sex differences. In addition, each must accept the role of patient, i.e., be aware that he is an active participant and contributor in helping to resolve the problems.

The initial, expressed wish for change cannot be entirely relied on as a basis for future symptomatic or structural change, nor can it be predicted at this stage whether a family will be able to tolerate or even profit from the experience. It is only after a prolonged evaluation phase of several months that a family reveals its capacity for facing basic issues and trying to understand each other's feelings. Although resistances are continuously discussed, some families still find the work too painful, difficult, or threatening. Others who appeared willing to try are found too fixed and rigid, "calcified." Some families are soon satisfied with removal of symptoms, while others find strength within the family to work towards structural change.

The clinical illustration which follows indicates a preliminary consensual agreement this family reached about their mutual needs for conjoint family therapy. It was obtained from each family member's direct participation rather than from behavior reported on by a family member. The children's presence rapidly and directly clued the therapists into the fundamental areas of family conflict.

In a family session, the three children, two boys and a girl, constantly interrupted their parents' discussion. Teasing was concentrated on the youngest sibling, a girl of 11. Each parent supported the other in affirming that they were extremely close and affectionate and all would be fine except for their son's stuttering. The parents "lived for their children" and wanted to give them a completely different life than they had experienced. This was expressed by the mother who was the family spokesman.

At this point, the daughter vigorously complained about her brothers, saying that she never had any privacy. When her girl friends came to the house, one or both brothers either insisted on being included or broke up their games. When the family was asked about privacy in the home, the mother began to weep, saying she never has time for herself. The children never let her have time alone. In the morning or after dinner they come into the bedroom to dress or watch TV. They never want to go to sleep. The husband said he tried to relieve his wife as much as possible, but the children did not listen to him unless he becomes abusive. He knew his wife's nerves were bad. They never had a conversation without the children either interrupting verbally or making demands to be helped with things they readily could do for themselves.

The mother said that perhaps she was overperfectionistic about the house, expecting too much from the children and being after them all the time, but she just could not stand their noise and messiness. The father agreed that he too found the children to be too careless and thoughtless with all the things he provided. He continued to be supportive of everything his wife mentioned, but it was said in a quiet, parrotlike way as if he was most fearful of incurring her wrath. The children said, "Mommy hollers and nags too much."

This was most painful to this overperfectionistic couple who struggled endlessly to be the ideal parents. Finally the parents agreed with the children that the entire family did need more physical privacy and opportunities to be able to talk to one another without constant interruptions. They all decided that by coming as a family they could work on these problems and other conflicts which were only implicitly referred to (i.e., the marital incompatibility).

SYMPTOMATIC RELIEF

When we refer to a family's capacity for work, we are referring to several factors: One is being able to eventually explore and begin to work through those aspects of arrested emotional growth which are structurally connected with a shared postponement of mourning as well as individuation; the second is facing the invisible patterns and accounts within relationships and finally, to see the unsettled obligations. From an individual viewpoint, Anna Freud stated, "If, by "mourning" we understand not the various manifestations of anxiety, distress, and malfunction which accompany object loss in the earliest phases but the painful, gradual process of detaching libido from an internal image, this, of course, cannot be expected to occur before object constancy has been established."[38, p. 67]

The shared aspects of struggle with a postponed mourning process can be conceptualized in multipersonal system terms. Boszormenyi-Nagy[14] conceptualized family pathology as "a specialized multiperson organization of shared fantasies and complementary need gratification patterns, maintained for the purpose of handling past object-loss experience. The very symbiotic or undifferentiated quality of transactions of certain families amounts to a multiperson bind, capable of preventing awareness of losses to any individual member. Another aim of the "symbiotic" family organization is the prevention of threatened separations. Separations can occur on interpersonal–interactional and on structural levels."[14, p. 310] This can be a long, painful process which could eventuate in basic, structural change in a family system. For some families the reliving and reexperiencing of the "mourning process" is too painful. For this reason they may remain in treatment only up to the point where there is symptomatic relief and some minimal shift in family equilibrium. Specifically, the family may terminate treatment at the point when symptomatic improvement occurs in the designated patient. For example, when a child with a school phobia is helped to return to school, the family is satisfied with this result and is unwilling or unable to explore additional areas of family pathology. This goal and contract for it is legitimate, regardless of the therapists' scale of values.

INITIAL REALITY AND TRANSFERENCE REACTIONS TO COTHERAPISTS AND TREATMENT: RESISTANCES

Awareness of their suffering in the form of symptoms in one or more members brings the family to therapy with the wish for relief. This is the motivating force which impels them to try to form a relationship with the therapists, whom they hope will direct them so they will become free of disturbing symptoms.

However, there are fundamental factors in the formation of the new relationship which have to be considered before such goals may be achieved. On the conscious level, the therapists may be viewed as experts and benevolent professional authority figures. While reality is a major component, transference attitudes toward the therapists must also be considered.

Greenson defines transference as "the experiencing of feelings, drives, attitudes, fantasies, and defenses toward a person in the present which are inappropriate to that person and are a repetition, a displacement of reactions which originated in regard to significant persons in early childhood."[48, p. 156] Manifestations of transference in family therapy are manifold, and they involve member–member as well as member–therapist relationships. Members of the more disorganized families readily reveal the wish to have the therapist assume the omnipotent role. Boszormenyi-Nagy writes that, "In family therapy the most important transference attitudes and distortions operate between family members, not between patient and therapist as in individual and group therapy. The current close relative is the most important reincarnation of the internalized objects of one's infantile self."[15, p. 416]

The family may appear helpless, and evidence feelings of extreme hopelessness: "Just tell us what to do and we will do it; we are desperate, nothing works, you are the expert." This must be countered and such magical wishes deflated, since quick, easy miracle cures cannot be produced. These attitudes must be replaced by the therapist's insistence that it is the family members who must work for increased understanding so that they can change. Other families wish to make the therapist a "judge" of who is right and who is wrong, who is good and who is bad. One couple demanded in the first session that the therapist state whether the husband was loyal to his wife or to his family of origin. Another family talked endlessly about "nice people" and shortly put the therapist into the category of "not-nice" people because she inquired about angry feelings in their family. These kind of demands and reactions have to be dealt with directly and continuously from the outset.

FAMILY EXPECTATIONS

Most families seen by the authors have generally functioned on an overly involved, symbioticlike level. The families therefore may have a very different perception of themselves and their goals, compared with the perception of what would have to occur for further maturation to ensue. The goal for some families is to return to the previous, symptom-free stage rather than recognizing that it was a poorly individuated, stagnant family system. In individual terms, Searles[78] defines symbiosis as "an intensely gratifying . . . mode of relatedness . . . which allows each participant to luxuriate in feelings of infantile satisfaction as well as in omnipotent mother fantasies." He adds, "despite its torment, [it] affords precious gratifications also."[78, p. 16] Bowen approached symbiosis from a family point of view and used the term "undifferentiated ego mass." He conceives of a "fused cluster of egos of individual family members with a common ego boundary. Some egos are more completely fused into the mass than others. Certain egos are intensely involved in the family mass during emotional stress and are relatively detached at other times."[21, p. 219]

Families refer to those members not designated as patients as being well, independent, adequate, and successful. It is a painful process for them to become aware that under the facade of superficial efficient functioning there may be fragility and inner unmet dependency needs.

AMBIVALENT ATTITUDES

Yearnings for gratification of dependency needs exist side by side with fears of engulfment, destruction, and abandonment. Family members often vacillate as a result of their hating–loving feelings towards each other and may include the therapist. They equally fear closeness and distance. The therapist must constantly be alert to and deal openly with excessive fears that circulate in a collusive way among the members of the family, but which are usually attributed to only one member. Otherwise its family members readily project onto the therapist their own fears of destructive rage, dependence, inadequacy, or weakness. If they feel "blamed" by the therapist, then they must rid themselves of her.

The therapist has to demonstrate a warmth that carries with it interest, consideration, and hopefulness to encourage the family to continue to explore the causes for their suffering. However, it is equally important that the therapist remind and, if necessary, demand that family members be aware that it is they who carry responsibility for their child and each other's behavior, within as well as outside the treatment situation. The therapist is "in charge" of helping them to face the balance of relationships and to find understanding; they must remain responsible for themselves. For example, in one situation the mother had always been in touch with the school personnel. She was asked whether she could let her husband be "in charge" in future school contacts and arrangements. In another instance the father was sure the family therapist intended "to pin him to the wall." At each session he was reminded that he was in charge of and responsible for his family's behavior; if any "pinning" were done it would be without the therapist' help. (Humor was used to remind him he was a foot taller and 60 pounds heavier and not very pinnable.)

SUPEREGO EXPECTATIONS

Family members often treat each other harshly, critically, and take turns blaming each other. Similarly, they seem to expect that the therapist will also be a blamer and find them bad or inadequate. Such a family style develops as a result of a lifetime experience of blaming and being blamed. Other families place the causes of difficulties outside the family system onto school, police, hospital authorities, etc. They expect the therapist to accept such projections which serve to avoid being held responsible for their behavior and its consequences. The therapist's strength is constantly tested to see whether she will respond as the critical, accusing, blaming–approving internalized objects, or whether the therapist's attitude can remain constant, holding out for understanding as well as responsibility on the part of the family. They need to hear the therapist's firm but noncritical response to their seemingly destructive behavior. At times casual chastizement on the part of the therapist is experienced as a wished-for form of caring. One family formulated a plan for a son's summer employment but did not follow through. When this was pointed out, the family rapidly made the additional plans and then sought our approval and recognition of their ability to be responsible. However, despite the best efforts on the part of the therapists, some families are able to scapegoat the cotherapy team instead of each other. They close ranks and unite in getting rid of the undesired parental substitutes represented by the cotherapy team. Since this is primarily an unconscious process, they may not be able or willing to analyze the reasons for such rapid, firm decisions.

CURRENT RELATIONSHIPS USED AS PARENTAL SUBSTITUTES

A marital partner or a child may unconsciously comply with a mother's need to have a parent substitute. At some point, however, the child, though loyal, may feel overburdened with this inappropriate role and become symptomatic. The family will turn to the cotherapists as a substitute for the parentified child, expecting the mother to be accepted by the therapists as the helpless, nonchangeable dependent adult. They would stay in therapy endlessly if the therapists accepted their unchangeability; the pathogenic family system would then be in charge of the therapy process and the cotherapy team.

All kinds of excuses, justifications, and rationalizations may accompany their attempts to resist treatment. A young, married woman who received superior ratings as a school teacher refused to cook or shop for food since she considered this beneath her. Her husband and child carried these responsibilities for fear of upsetting her. She seemed to expect the therapists as well as her family to be completely accepting of her passive, dependent attitude that it was beneath her dignity to fulfill this aspect of a woman's role. As long as the family members accepted her rigid expectations of them, there was little possibility for change or growth in this family.

The therapists are thus often experienced as "alien bodies" who seem to demand change when the demand for change does not arise from within the family. If there is not mutual agreement by family members and therapists on issues to be clarified and changes desired, then the therapists are experienced as disruptive, nonunderstanding forces aligned against the family, who therefore must be extruded.

COTHERAPY TEAM AS A SYSTEM

REACTIONS TO A FAMILY SYSTEM AND ITS EFFECTS

The cotherapy team's initial reaction to the many different kinds of families evaluated plays a significant role in the formation of the therapeutic alliance. Whitaker[91] puts it more strongly when he says families have to make a connection with him before he can invest himself.

Individual therapists as well as family cotherapists must have capacity for empathy, compassion, and trust. However, additional dimensions must exist in the cotherapy team. One is a capacity for complementarity. This requires an unusual amount of flexibility and creativity between the cotherapists. The loyalty system provided by the cotherapy team should be more balanced and a better model for the "pathogenic" family system than a single therapist could be. A well-functioning therapy team enables its members to act with sufficient reliance on a supporting and complementing companion. One therapist could be mystified by and painfully excluded from a collusively hostile family. Two therapists can turn to each other and exclude the family while regrouping their forces for a more successful approach.

Ideally, a heterosexual team permits each individual to function more comfortably in his or her life-long assigned biological–emotional role. However, mutual trust and respect must also exist in order to confirm the differences between masculinity and femininity. Additional demands are made on the therapy team: Specifically, one therapist may enter into and remain supportive of the family symbiosis, dependency needs, their seeming helplessness, and their excessive demands on the therapist. If so, the other therapist can remain free in a session to help his cotherapist and the family members emerge from this level of relating. He may "disrupt" the splitting techniques that the family is attempting to use on the therapy team. One therapist must remain firm and strong for progression, growth, and individuation, while the other therapist may temporarily accept and support the symbiosis. An early frontal approach or any defensive relational "mechanisms" would deny the family members' right for tact and consideration. Both therapists are available to the family for sympathetic listening, interest, and for increased self–other understanding. In any session, one may respond actively on a verbal level, while the other is passively alert but listening and noting nonverbal behavior. This too is a complementary position.

If the family competes for the attention of one therapist and the other is ignored, this might cause team splitting if both therapists are not alert. There must be mutual trust between the therapists. Although each therapist takes a turn moving in and out of the family system, discovering the family's hidden strategies, the two therapists still must remain continuously available to each other. Only as a united team can they be facilitators of the therapy process.

The cotherapists' needs and reactions to any family system indirectly determines whether a treatment situation will develop. Ideally, all therapists are psychologically available to all families who request help. However, extremely strong countertransference reactions may be produced regardless of the degree of self-understanding, and it may be advisable to refer a family to other family therapists. In the experience of the authors, such reactions have not necessarily arisen with the severely disorganized, depressed, or acting-out families, but more often in response to families that relate on a superficial manner or appear extremely manipulative. For example, one father had spent 10 years in a reformatory. He came to therapy because of delinquency on the part of his son. He expressed the wish for change in his family's life style, but upon further exploration the degree of denial and projection was so extensive that the therapists were continuously stymied. Their reactions were mocked and laughed off, and the distancing maneuvers made it impossible to reach the father. The therapists felt as if they were being "conned"—that the father's capacity for truth searching was too limited. It was necessary to accept the fact that this defense which had carried him from boyhood was untouchable and therefore unchangeable. Other families are so calcified that even though they might be willing to come to therapy forever, efforts to help them change would be wasted. It is not easy for therapists to face or accept their own limitations, especially when young children are trapped in seemingly irreversible family situations.

Two clinical illustrations in the evaluation phase are described and contrasted from the viewpoint of family therapeutic techniques. The S family illustrates a family's capacity to develop an alliance with the family therapists. The B family is unable to do so despite the intense suffering and commitment to a goal for all. In addition, the B family appeared more rigidly fixated at a symbiotic level of involvement with each other. The major difference of these families does not lie in the severity or seriousness of the symptomatology of the designated patient since all family members shortly reveal a variety of symptoms. It is rather that all members of the S family accept some individual responsibility as contributing to the pathological functioning.

The S family all agreed that issues were never faced directly, since each person withdrew either physically or emotionally. They wanted and needed to learn to cope differently with each other. By contrast, the B family continuously centered their unhappiness on the father's difficulties. Even while enumerating their individual symptomatology, they persistently denied seeing any connection with the total family problems. Their resistance to examining all their relations was further revealed in their refusal to bring in the maternal grandmother who lived in their home and was a central figure in the family constellation. Loyalty to the underlying symbiosis between maternal grandmother and her daughter was so strong in this system that it became impossible for them to remain in treatment.

CASE PRESENTATION: THE S FAMILY

The S family consisted of Mr. S, age 52; Mrs. S, age 49; Robert, age 23 (armed services); Sam, age 21 (college-dropout); Tom, age 16; Ruth, age 14. They were referred after Tom had had brief individual therapy. Later he had been picked up by the police for glue sniffing and possession of liquor in a car. Subsequently, he was transferred to a psychiatric hospital but was not participating in his individual or group therapy sessions. As the parents stated it, family therapy was "an end-of-the-line hope" for them.

In the first sessions, Mr. and Mrs. S described the family situation. Mr. S was a handsome, slightly obese man whose position as an executive in a national chain of woman's apparel stores required that he travel a great deal. He was rarely home during the week. On the weekends he either drank excessively or stayed away and went hunting or fishing. His health was precarious since he had had two heart attacks.

Mrs. S was an extremely attractive looking woman whom the family agreed was a very conscientious mother. "She was always there." On the surface she appeared very warm, sensitive, and very adequate. She felt that all decisions and responsibilities were placed in her hands.

At this time, Robert and Sam were not living at home. Both had been in and out of private schools from the age of 15. Robert had completed college and was now in the service. Sam was in the process of dropping out of college and was applying to a domestic job program. There was also the possibility that he might be drafted into the armed forces.

Ruth was described as the family worrier. She was doing poorly in school and had few friends or activities. She said she worried about her father's health, her mother's loneliness, and especially about Tom's delinquent behavior.

In the early sessions, there was consensual agreement that either there were explosive outbursts or family members gave each other the silent or walk-away treatment. It soon appeared that there was a difference in the way females reacted to conflict. Mrs. S and Ruth were the overt worriers who were chronically depressed. Mr. S and his sons primarily used the stay-away or run-away method as their way of avoiding conflicts. The family described their life as being on a "roller coaster"—their family life was a series of ups and downs for all. There were constant explosions and great fear that someone was on the verge of being out of control. Mr. S said, "Life was like being on the edge of a precipice, or other times when they tried to settle issues, instead of clarification resulting, it ended in dilute, dilute, dilute."

Tom and Ruth agreed that "Mother came from a family with a bossy father." Both parents tried to be "boss" in this family, but it resulted in each cancelling the other out so that no one was in charge.

Promises were made to be broken. The only time they were a real family was during the periods of Mr. S' heart attacks and convalescence. These were periods of peacefulness, closeness, and full cooperation between family members. As soon as Mr. S returned to work it changed back to detachment and isolation, except for the explosive moments.

In the initial session Mr. S said psychiatry was low on his value system, but since they were desperate they were placing themselves in the therapist's hands. In his family of origin he was the only one who had not been separated or divorced. Some members of his family had at times been hospitalized, drank excessively, had difficulty in functioning in their work areas. He and his wife had separated for a brief period. They had consulted an attorney concerning a divorce but eventually had reconciled. Their marital relationship had been rocky for a long time. Their older son also had serious difficulties. However, it was Tom's recent incarceration which had shaken all of them into facing the seriousness of the family's difficulties.

The Contract with the S Family

This family readily agreed that time and fee were no problem for them. What had to be sharply defined and reflected back to them was that they could not simply place themselves in our hands. Tom and his problems could not be handed over as had been done when he was in individual treatment. The contract and requirements for family therapy were different. Could each member work hard, contribute, and gain for himself, as well as help each other? Their pattern of running away was reflected back to them. This had been the inevitable solution in the past. Could this be changed? The fact that they had not separated or used divorce as a solution to their difficulties was an indication of their underlying loyalty to each other. However, their main method of solving problems was to seek solutions outside themselves. For example, if a member had school difficulties he was sent to another school. External authorities such as police or even psychiatrists were used to control behavior rather than to face the lack of control within and between themselves. Could they work on this lack in understanding each other or try to meet needs that were being expressed in behavior that led to serious consequences?

The therapist reflected back to them doubt about their capacity to stay in treatment, basing this on their past history. Could they see each other differently or try to find alternatives or constructive solutions to conflicts? Mr. and Mrs. S openly agreed that this had not been possible in the past and were not sure they could tolerate treatment. Ruth pleaded with her family to try. She wept endlessly, and said there was no alternative: "Everyone in the family has to learn to give in, to try harder." Tom reflected the hopelessness of the family system and said he could never talk to his father, and that he would never go back to that house which was not a home. Mrs. S wept and pleaded with Tom not to talk like that. Mr. S in an effort to control both his hurt feelings and anger tried to cover it by humor. Then his helpless feelings poured out: He didn't know what his part was in all of this, but he was willing to try; maybe he could learn to be a father, although he wasn't sure that he could change.

These early evaluation sessions were extremely difficult and painful for the family members who had used avoidance as a main defense in the past. Robert and Sam, who came home briefly from the service or school, attended one or two sessions. They described a family myth, "using tact rather than telling the truth to each other was the best way to cope with one another." Their remarks expressed their feelings of discouragement and supported the family's symbiotically restrictive relationships. Overtly they presented themselves as separated or individuated young adults, but in reality they were not functioning adequately. Despite their intelligence and pseudosophistication, the underlying feeling that they transmitted was one of hopelessness and failure.

In these initial sessions, the family's run-away syndrome was brought up as the alternative recourse to coming for family therapy. The purpose was to help them be continuously aware of their special form of resistance to continuing and to changing. They were thus helped to talk about their wish and need to flee versus staying to face the hurt and suffering each one was experiencing. They had a need to flee for a brief vacation, which provided them and the therapist an opportunity to discuss their need to run away and try to deny the degree of conflict and tension within the family. The vacation was to be used to decide about Tom's future after they had signed him out of the psychiatric hospital. When they returned they admitted that no decision was reached and sheepishly expected the therapist to reprimand them with, "I told you so." Upon their return they were again confronted by the therapist's doubts that they could resolve problems or conflicts by any other method than by flight to which they still resorted. This seemed to help them temporarily resolve their ambivalence about remaining in family therapy. They expressed a renewed determination to work towards change. As a result of using the therapist as a parentlike authority who remained firm but responsive to the continuous series of trouble and emergencies, all family members showed essentially improved functioning.

CASE PRESENTATION: THE B FAMILY

Living in the household of the B family were Mrs. B, age 42; Mr. B, age 44; George, age 16; Leonard, age 14; and Mrs. B's mother, age 66. Mr. B had been in individual therapy off and on for the past nine years. His therapists and internist felt his reactions were not true depressions. The past summer he had been hospitalized with a heart condition. He felt that neither individual therapy nor any medications had relieved him.

Mrs. B was the only one in the family who appeared asymptomatic. She wore a neck brace throughout the sessions after she recently collided with an automobile. Two years ago she had taken a job as a caseaid.

George was the designated patient in the current referral. The school counselor had told the parents that although he had college potential, his marks were such that he would not be recommended for college. He also lacked self-confidence, avoided any social situations he was invited to, kept his feelings to himself, and appeared emotionally estranged from the family.

Leonard had seen a child psychiatrist because of his general immaturity, hypersensitivity, and feelings of inadequacy. In school he had been achieving passing grades. Generally he felt he was not accepted by his peers.

About nine years ago, Mrs. B's father died and her mother came to live with the family. Mrs. B was an only child. At that time Mr. B had his first depressivelike episode and had continued to be depressed. His income remained at a high level because his partner covered his workload during his brief absences from business.

The family described themselves as a very close group. The parents never went out except on rare occasions with their sons and maternal grandmother accompanying them. The grandmother kept house for them. All agreed this was very helpful except that no one liked her cooking. After supper she retired to her bedroom, only leaving the house for brief shopping trips with her daughter. Each evening, the parents and children retired to the parents' bedroom to watch television.

The family stated that any attempts to converse with each other resulted in loud and noisy arguments with the sons usually siding with Mrs. B. She constantly cautioned them not to upset Mr. B or the maternal grandmother. While Mr. B was consulted on important decisions, the two women ran the household quietly and efficiently. The parents did not feel there was any lack of privacy; however, they could not understand why, when George was upset, he would walk out on them, retire to his bedroom, and lock his door.

In a typical session, Mr. B sat in a curled-up, fetuslike position and in a whimpering voice would start out by saying how depressed he felt, lonely and empty, and that no one believed or sympathized with him. George, sitting tall and erect, in an authoritative voice would berate his father for not trying harder—that he just felt sorry for himself. Mr. B would look hurt and respond, "You mean it's all in my head and I don't really feel terrible." George would say to the others, "If he would try to act like other fathers he would feel better." Leonard would try to placate his father by modifying George's comment. Then he pleaded with his father to go out and do things with Mrs. B or with him. Like a very little boy he would half-whisper his words, become silent, and was ignored. Or tears would often well up in his eyes and when asked if he could talk about his own feelings, he would only shake his head in the negative; his hand gesture was one of hopelessness. Then Mr. B said, "You all gang up against me and don't understand that I want to stay home and read." Earlier he said that he was unable to concentrate and had no energy to do any chores or drive his sons anywhere. The children simultaneously said, "You seem to be able to do those things you really want to!" Mrs. B then pleaded with the three of them to stop talking this way—that all of them should be more sympathetic about Mr. B's depressions. This silenced any further efforts to explore perceptions of each other, or to voice their unfulfilled wishes for any change. If the therapist reflected the mood that *all* of them seemed sad, unhappy, and lonely, they quickly shut off the therapist by bringing out or pursuing a subject which was extraneous to the immediate feelings being expressed. For example, Mrs. B would say, "Why wouldn't George attend a social dancing class? All the other boys in the neighborhood were going." There was little sensitivity or awareness of his shyness and fearfulness about associating with girls. This theme would be pushed until he would squirm, blush, and finally become tearful. These comments seemed to only reemphasize his feelings of being different from boys his age rather than being experienced as encouragement or being supportive.

The father and Leonard came to Mrs. B's immediate support despite the fact that at any moment they would be confronted by her with "You aren't acting grown up; why aren't you; why can't you be like other males?" Neither Mr. B nor the sons could say anything while she was pushing, belittling, and reemphasizing her disappointment in them. The dual message was clear—be adequate, be strong like I am, otherwise you are nothing. If George would say that wasn't the issue, he had difficulty either saying why he was disagreeing with his mother or speaking directly to the issue.

In the past when Mr. B was not feeling well he would go to work but telephone his wife and talk to her for hours. He would cry and complain that he could not concentrate on his work, that he was useless and no good. Despite her endless listening, he said that she never really heard what he was saying. He was angry that she had gone to work, feeling that in the evening no one had the attention of anyone because they constantly watched television. Mrs. B said that all four were constantly together when not at work or in school, yet they didn't understand each other. Despite brief, episodic flareups, their real (angry) feelings were "swept under the rug," meaning these were primarily turned back on themselves.

In the evaluation phase which lasted about a month and a half, Mr. B insisted that his depressions were the sole cause of all the family problems, and the family readily agreed. Despite this, Mrs. B, George, and Leonard would cry openly as they described their friendless, inactive, isolated lives which they said were so different from other families. This was then immediately denied and they refocused on Mr. B's symptoms.

The family described Mrs. B as being like her mother: good, overgiving, a martyr. She lived for her family as her parents had lived for her. She said no sacrifice was too great if it would only help her husband and sons. However, in the session when she cried and spoke about herself, she said she felt overburdened with all the care and responsibility that had fallen on her shoulders after her father's death and her husband had become ill.

Her husband and sons had never heard her openly complain, and all immediately vowed they would try to be more helpful to her. It was after this session that the family seemed to "close ranks" and shortly thereafter terminated treatment. It was in the final session when Mr. and Mrs. B came without the children that Mr. B said that he was sexually impotent. He also told his wife for the *first* time that he had always been very angry about having his mother-in-law living with him. Mrs. B silenced Mr. B by saying the lack of sexual relationship did not really bother her, and that she knew Mr. B did not mean what he was saying since he loved and appreciated her mother as much as she and the children did. Like a small child, he did not seem to dare refute his wife. As he smilingly accepted being chastized, he also agreed with her that family therapy could not help them. Mrs. B in effect had disconfirmed her husband, and he permitted this.

Upon reviewing the sessions it seems that the cotherapy team was unable to find the leverage which might have enabled this family to tolerate family therapy. The implications of the self-confrontation that emerged were too painful for them to face. In the past, they had been loyally successful in denying or minimizing the anger which permeated their relationships, especially regarding the maternal grandmother. The family could not permit open discussion regarding her presence in the home.

While they said they wanted to understand each other better and improve each one's functioning, particularly Mr. B and George, it became apparent after Mrs. B complained about being overburdened that further exploration was too threatening. Termination occurred despite the fact that neither Mr. B nor Leonard had made gains in their previous therapy.

The need to maintain the status quo of their denial-based system was too strong—despite the suffering of all the family members. It seemed that the overly close alliance between Mrs. B and her mother was untouchable and needed to be maintained as an absolute requirement of basic family loyalty with which all family members colluded regardless of "cost." In this way, Mrs. B could overtly continue her role of the strong, overadequate one who needed to baby and overprotect the "poor sick males."

DISCUSSION

These two families illustrate some of the major aspects that need to be considered in attempting to form a therapeutic alliance. Both families revealed overt symptoms in many members of the family: depression, learning problems, adolescent rebelliousness, alcoholism, and marital strife. Both families were suffering and not satisfied with a member's functioning in and outside the family situation. The problems of the designated patient brought both families to the treatment situation, and there was recognition that the other members were directly and indirectly involved in the family conflicts.

The S family was able to make a commitment to treatment, but the B family was not. The B family overtly agreed that there were multiple problems in the family, but then focused on Mr. B's depression as the single cause of their difficulty. They did not deny their overinvolvement with each other but instead were overly gratified with their extreme closeness. There was a united stand to deny that needs were unmet or that underneath was loneliness. Hurt or angry feelings were denied or minimized. They could not tolerate the exploration of the causes of their underlying symbioticlike functioning. The confirmation of this was seen in their agreement not to discuss Mrs. B's mother's presence in the home; Mrs. B's relationship with her mother was protected by the nonexploration. Mrs. B and the rest of the family preferred to "extrude" the therapists, regardless of the possible psychological cost to all of them. The problem of Mrs. B's insufficient psychological separation and individuation was perhaps projected onto the therapists after the therapists indicated that the maternal grandmother should eventually be included in the sessions.

By contrast, the S family shortly moved from blaming and scapegoating one member to accepting that all of them were contributing to the family's dysfunctioning. They shared the unsatisfactory pattern of retreating into silence or walking out as a safety valve, but agreed that it resolved no conflicts or issues. The loneliness that resulted through this distancing mechanism was equally intolerable to all of them. Even though the parents' executive functioning was minimal or nonexistent in both families, the B family was unable to face this, while the S family recognized that it was a goal to work toward.

While the problems in both families were equally serious, one family exhibited sufficient strength and capacity at least to begin to explore the causes of their suffering. With the B family, the therapists may not have been sufficiently skilled in helping them overcome their underlying fears of confronting their unbalanced relationship patterns. There is much need for increased understanding and skill in dealing with families who appear as symbiotically meshed and fixated as the B family. It still remains difficult to understand all of the possible mechanisms which enable one family to enter into and remain in treatment.

CONCLUSIONS

The formation of a working alliance depends on several basic factors: Most important is the family's capacity to commit each individual member to actively exploring the accounts of their unbalanced relationships and to reach a consensual agreement regarding at least one or more goals. If a family persists in the idea that they are coming only for the designated patient, without actively committing all members to a process of change and examining all relationships within the nuclear and extended family, then the degree of resistance will be so intense that the therapy process cannot continue. Some families even terminate after one session because the prospect of such an exploration is intolerable. Other families come a few times, as if going through the motions of "exploring" and being evaluated; because an instant "symptomatic cure" does not develop, they will also terminate. They cannot accept the premise of the child's or adult's problems being interlocked with other family conflicts. Even though the therapists try to help each family member to accept that there may be gain for each family member, this does not sufficiently help them overcome their underlying mistrust, anxieties, and fears regarding the therapist and the therapeutic process.

Some families stay in treatment for brief periods during which symptomatic improvement does ensue for the designated patient. These efforts and results should not be minimized or ignored. However, neither should this be confused with structural change which could take place on a multigenerational level; indebtedness and the underlying despair, pain, and rage over having been exploited remain untouched and unbalanced in the parent–child, marital, and grandparental relationships.

If the regressive forces remain hidden or invisible, with the family being strongly fixated on maintaining the symbiotic or overdistanced relationships, the therapeutic process will be experienced as threatening and intolerable, and therefore will be rejected. The therapists are experienced as "intrusive strangers" and are not given sufficient opportunity to instill or renew hope for improved family relationships. There are as yet no proven guidelines or objective criteria by which therapists can determine in advance which families will be capable of forming a working alliance.

Some families have more capacity to trust the therapist's reassurance and recommendations that the family explore and remain in treatment. The degree of suffering or despair within the family does not necessarily facilitate or guarantee an alliance being formed; however, it does connect directly back to their past and present experiences with their family of origin. Specifically, it ties in with the rebalancing of loyalty commitments and indebtedness in the multigenerational relationships, which includes nuclear and extended families plus the in-law system.

In cotherapy the team relationship is of course a powerful factor in the engaging of families in the therapeutic process. If there is not enough essential trust, respect, and capacity for openness and differences, the family can then split the team and scapegoat or parentify one team member against the other, which inevitably leads to rejection of the therapists. If there is too much competitiveness or rivalry between the therapists, this may also feed into the family's resistance. The family may challenge the unity of the team as well as each therapist's individual strength and ego boundaries. However, as stated earlier, despite the therapists' skill and experience, some pathological family systems are stronger and more powerful than the therapists in resisting openness and change. In such cases, all efforts are of little avail in forming therapeutic or working alliance or of helping families to remain in treatment.

9

Family Therapy and Reciprocity Between Grandparents, Parents, and Grandchildren

If one accepts the premise that it is essential to study the interconnectedness between an individual and his family system, then the boundaries of the family must be extended to include the interlocking between a nuclear family and families of origin (including the in-laws). From the field of gerontology and now from our own clinical experiences with families, it can be confirmed that the idea of the isolated or totally independent nuclear family is a myth. The aged parents have not abandoned their adult children or grandchildren, and in turn the younger generations have not abandoned their elders.

In the clinical or treatment sense, the nature of these relationships, specifically the intensity and depth of involvement between the three generations, has been an insufficiently explored territory. The literature reveals that in a few selected instances grandparents have been included in a conjoint family session, but there is little reportage of continuity of treatment and the effects it has had upon all the family members. Many research studies have revealed and confirmed that there has been responsible intergenerational behavior in the external and material sense: The aged are cared for financially and physically. It is the emotional quality and meaning of these intergenerational relationships and the effects they have on each generation that remains the clinical frontier.

In this chapter, illustrations will show, for a variety of families, how the families of origin are initially described by an adult daughter or a son-in-law. Techniques of helping the family to accept and include the grandparents in sessions will be discussed. Also described will be the purpose and potential aims of the initial interviews and how they are fully discussed with the adult parents in advance of such sessions. Included will be the various forms of communication that take place between nuclear and extended families: the letters, telephone conversations, and visits to each other's home. Wherever possible, the authors will attempt to illustrate the deep, existential impact that the three generations continue to have on each other. In Chapter 12 a single case will be presented, in its various phases of treatment, sometimes focusing on the younger adult parent and child systems and the marital system, as well as on the effects the original family systems have upon each mate.

The authors postulate that the major connecting tie between the generations is that of loyalty based on the integrity of reciprocal indebtedness. It may be expressed in the form of physical caretaking, telephoning, visiting, writing, showing interest, respect, and concern. Sometimes it is only expressed in the form of concrete services, although services may be combined with emotional attachment and involvement.

In past centuries, loyalty and indebtedness were freely discussed by families and by rulers, and its form of repayment concretely defined. Whether it concerned a king, a feudal lord, the mayor of a town, or head of one's own clan, physical survival was guaranteed provided there was the economic and political proof of one's loyalty. Portions of crops and other earthly goods were automatically shared with the rulers, who then implicitly guaranteed protection to their loyal subjects. These goods were forms of payment of duty, obligation, allegiance, and respect.

In old extended families, the oldest male was the owner of all property rights, who ruled through unconditional loyalty of all other members. In present-day families, economic or protective factors remain important but do not play as significant a factor as the psychological ties. Families that are able, do carry physical responsibility for their members, but an individual's survival is not necessarily contingent on his family's support. Local, state, and federal governments have when necessary stepped in and guaranteed physical caretaking of the sick or aged.

We are concerned with the manifestations of loyalty based on indebtedness and reciprocity. Loyalty and the multiple forms of its expression is a healthy or unhealthy force which creates the connecting ties between past and future generations. Even if these ties are overtly minimized or denied, a person remains deeply and unalterably committed to the repayment of benefits received and is connected to blood relatives. The struggle for all adults is to balance the old relationships with the new: to continuously integrate the relationships with one's early important persons with the involvement and committedness with current relationships, namely one's mate and children.

Some nuclear families are emotionally so "tied" to a family of origin that they not only live next door to one set of parents, but in at least three reported instances have made a tunnel from one house to the other in order to remain one big "happy" family. A son-in-law or daughter-in-law appears to be completely accepting of such a family arrangement. The lived-out symbiosis is clearly evident: Individual assertiveness, attempts to physically or emotionally separate, or critical comments are immediately stifled. That person is considered ungrateful and disloyal. In one such family, the mother and 8-year-old daughter shared the same phobic and hysterical symptoms, and the husband who had been raised in foster homes was passively compliant in visiting and being with his in-laws five or six nights a week.

Other nuclear families present themselves as detached, independent of, and not interested or involved with either family of origin. Often they express it as if it were a mutual, "agreed-upon" rejection. Geographic distances are readily used to reinforce their separateness and state of complete independence on anyone but themselves. They may at first accede that there is some contact, but describe holiday visits, phone calls, or letters as being nonpersonal or on a superficial level. Religious reasons are used or differences in ethnic or political background are also used as excuses for detachment.

In the initial phase of treatment, when these families were asked about the maternal or paternal grandparents, the initial responses are most frequently that there is minimal contact. "We don't or can't rely on anyone but ourselves." "Our problems are only that bad or sick child; if it weren't for him everything would be fine." Just as other serious individual and marital difficulties are hidden behind a "designated" child's problems, so initially are hidden the strong involvements and attachments to each one's family of origin.

If the therapists explore the presenting picture of the three generational relationships, the usual response is "There is nothing to discuss!" If asked about wishes for improvement, the usual reply contains a "hopeless note." This may even be disguised by open laughter at the therapists as if it were an insane notion: "You must be kidding, you don't know my parents or in-laws—they always were impossible and always will be," or, "They are so old-fashioned they wouldn't ever understand." At first the mate might readily agree with the spouse's comments. Despite the attempt to minimize the therapist's exploration, it is apparent that the area is a charged one—the voice tones inevitably rise with great intensity. If the children have been restless or noisy, a deep quiet falls in the room. Factual justifications for "noncontact" pour forth, and for the time being no further discussions of the subject seem possible.

One or more family members may immediately switch the subject back to a member in the nuclear family as the prime source of all difficulties. Someone, usually a child, is currently the "bad," disappointing, disrupting object. Looking at it from an individual therapy viewpoint, this child or several of the children do have problems, whether they are delinquency, learning or behavioral problems in school, bedwetting, or fire setting, etc. All the multipresenting complaints about any individual have a validity. Even the parentified child who until recently had been good, conforming, and supportive of his parents in the home —helping, doing chores or carrying responsibilities for the siblings— may now be changing and described as rebellious, lazy, or indifferent.

As discussed in other chapters, these problems can be viewed as only a child's intrapsychic difficulties. However, family therapists view the presented, visible symptoms as indicative of problems in the multigenerational family system. The thesis is that a child's symptoms are also representative of the hidden and unresolved conflicts between several generations of the same family or between both families of origin. One person's symptoms may be a mask behind the serious marital difficulties; conversely, marital difficulties may be a disguise of a child's problem.

THE INDIVIDUAL AND HIS FAMILY RELATIONSHIPS

First, unresolved conflicts from an individual point of view will be discussed. It will be followed with multigenerational theoretical and clinical findings. In family therapy what is being dealt with is loyalty obligations between each and every member, and repayment of one's indebtedness.

Whether the early, parenting figures in a child's life were nongratifying or overly frustrating, in reality or in fantasy, or one or both parents were not available because of desertion or death, the individual may be left with feelings of being worthless, inadequate, and lacking self-esteem. When dependency needs remain unmet and object constancy has been impaired, the individual is left with inner yearnings to be loved, appreciated, and approved. This underlying yearning may be consciously or unconsciously denied or minimized, and may be covered over by feelings of anger, resentment, rejection of others, or even feelings of numbness. However, there remains an eternal search for the good, beloved objects or parental surrogates who understand, who comfort, and who are completely accepting of behavior, even though it may be infantile and destructive. In many individuals the anger and disappointment about the original important objects are projected outside the self onto a husband, wife, child, or any other important but available person.

All individuals at times experience ambivalent attitudes, but the important aspect of ambivalence is not only the frequency and intensity of such responses, but the continuous and fundamental reactions in these close relationships. One can change friendships and employers, but within one's self is always carried a major ongoing feeling—whether one has received adequate loving, acceptance, and recognition of worth by one's past and current family members. Whether the early relationships were experienced as good and loving or bad, destructive, and inadequate, the individual is left feeling obligated and needing to repay. Repayment can be directly expressed towards one's aging parents in a kind, loving, and supportive manner. Revenge for unjust treatment may come out in the form of depreciation, ridicule, or even neglect. Possibly, it is upon one's children that the repayment takes place: Or feelings toward the bad, hated objects of the previous generation are externalized and projected onto one's children. There may be real physical and emotional neglect of the aging parents and in-laws.

The in-love phase and early marriage renews the hope for the "idealized" parent who will make up for or provide that which one seeks and eternally needs. If the expectations and demands are overwhelming and impossible to fulfill, it then becomes inevitable that the marital partner is a source of frustration and disappointment. The next available important targets become one's children.

Most parents will readily state that they are determined to be a better parent to their children than their own parents were to them. They may minimize or deny their own feelings of deprivation and make efforts to give their "all" to their offspring. What happens though to their own unmet hungers? They may overtly become the all-giving, sacrificing, martyrlike parent. This not only inevitably produces guilt feelings in the receiving child who feel that he must overpay for what is given in such a selfless manner, but more importantly, the child feels forever bound to live up to the parent's expectations.

All their life such individuals are left with a sense of indebtedness or obligation which can never be repaid. The strings attached to such martyred giving has endless repercussions. Even if they physically separate, marry, and have a family of their own, they are left with guilt feelings and the sense of being overly obligated lingers on. Even though the parent has urged marriage and parenting, the implicit message may be that the child is an ungrateful, unappreciative deserter. The deeper feelings are, "If I gave so much, how can you ever leave me when you owe so much." Jealousy or resentment of the chosen mate may be equally disguised or minimized. In some families, the guilt feelings regarding a child's indebtedness towards his parents are so exaggerated that there is no hope for repayment. The children remain forever in fixated positions in these loyal, guilt-laden relationships.

Other major facets must be taken into consideration, such as how one can give when one has received so little. In one situation, a young woman was having great difficulty with her boyfriend who happened to be of a different religion. Her mother was only able to berate her daughter about the religious aspects of an interfaith marriage. When her daughter wanted to discuss the fundamental aspects of her poor feminine identification and sexual difficulties, her mother avoided these areas. Because of the mother's own nonmaternal identification and unsatisfactory sexual relationship, she could in no way then be helpful to her daughter. In much "overgiving" there may be a subtle resentment that my child is getting more than me while I am still "hungry."

Essentially, such giving is a doing, material giving, or preaching–lecturing relationship, so there is no personal sharing of one's private worries. This does not refer to discussing private, intimate sexual experiences between generations, but to other fundamental issues of the relationship, e.g., male–female identifications and differences. The child may appear ungrateful and even reject this pseudogiving and relating. The adult parent may feel caught in a bind that feels like a repetition of the bind he experienced with his own parents, and will be hurt, angry, and depressed. The old yearnings can no longer be denied or minimized.

NUCLEAR AND EXTENDED FAMILY RELATIONSHIPS

The old hopes, to be loved and understood and cared for, may be unconsciously repressed. Then a hopeless giving up ensues, and each marital partner feels trapped in an intolerable guilt-ridden position. Some mates describe themselves as feeling numb towards their family of origin.

The children in such families are tuned into the underlying despair or depression in both parents. Moreover, the unresolved conflicts between the grandparental generation and the parents are fully known to the children, even though the parents believe it has been kept a secret. The children also know the full nature and extent of the marital battles. They are keenly aware that what was unresolved in the past is now being played out and transferred upon themselves. They make endless efforts to protect or be available as objects of gratification. The parentified child even when adult may continue to try to "make up" or "give back" to the aging parents. These children have been labeled the "burden bearers" by Brody and Spark.[24, p. 83] They try to comfort, reassure, and be a substitute good, loving parent. The other children also may be struggling, albeit in a negative way, to bring life and excitement in the hope of recharging the hopelessly stagnant, nongrowth-producing aspects of their parents' marriage. The ones who try to avoid these roles or to escape such family systems inevitably become the scapegoated "bad or mad" children. Thus, one child postpones his own maturation, and the other fights for it, but his family interferes with and misinterprets his behavior as if he were a disloyal son or daughter.

All family relationships contain some aspects of reality dimensions: An infant is a completely demanding, helpless person; the husband–father is a wage earner and protector. It is this reality, as well as the transference, within all close relationships with which family therapists are concerned. Whether one feels disloyal or not indebted to one's parents, the fact remains that there is implicit expectation of some form of repayment. If repayment is denied or minimized, the underlying feeling that one experiences is guilt. It is in this area—of balancing out in reality one's obligations to the family of origin, mate, and children —that family therapists must address their work. To fulfill their role as change agents for all three generations, family therapists must concentrate their work with nuclear and extended families. The course that must be pursued is an examination of the interlocking nature of reciprocal giving between the individual, the nuclear family, and both families of origin.

IN-LAWS AS A SYSTEM OF BALANCE

In addition to studying the situation in the three-generational context described, it is also of paramount importance to understand the unity and/or disharmony between one's original family system and its in-law system. Each family system has its own prescribed code of reciprocity in doing, relating, exchanging—giving and taking under the category of being loving. The importance of this area in treatment has only begun to be explored. Two strangers meet, fall in love, and marry. It is a standing joke, "I married you and not your family." Our clinical experience places that phrase in a completely mythical or fantasy category.

An in-law is an intruder. The common expression, "we've gained a son or a daughter," is more often a wish than a reality. Beyond the individual considerations of whether the young couple will complement, support, and fulfill each other and their children's needs, there still are essential issues of how the families of origin will be included or excluded. How much is it possible to face and deal with the codes and accounts of reciprocity in any family? For example, how will the grandparents on each side of the family be experienced and supported? One family of origin may be very expressive of affection and aggressive feelings. Other families are reserved but equally loving and supportive. There are families who are steady, reliable, upward striving, but nondemonstrative either physically or verbally. In some, there has been chaotic, disorganized, disruptive behavior, e.g., abandonment and multiple divorces. On a continium—just as with individuals—there are families that are overly symbiotic, smothering, and protective, compared with families that emphasize detachment, overadequacy, and complete independence—as if this was a realistic possibility.

Opposites do seem to attract each other, and yet in the close daily contact of family life these attributes may become the very source of what is irritating and unacceptable in a relationship. Compared with what one has anticipated, though perhaps needed, the mate's family style cannot be absorbed or integrated because it is too different from the world of the family of origin. An in-law and his family can shortly become the scapegoat for the other family system. A daughter- or son-in-law is not merely a rival for the parents' affection and support; the value system and way of life of the in-law are targets for attack, depreciation, or rejection. The emotional aspects may be symbolically expressed in terms of money, occupations, religion, and ethnic background, but the underlying dynamics remain essentially the same.

What we are dealing with is balancing of loyalty and indebtedness within families: Who does what for whom? How is it experienced? Who repays what and when? It can be translated into various terms, e.g., a system of justice or of merit accounting: "I have given the best years of my life to a husband, to children, and what have I received in return?" In mechanistic terms it can be described as input and output. In any ethics, there is the credo: As I give so shall I receive.

The families referred to us often appear as if they are in limbo or in a state of emotional bankruptcy. Family homeostasis, as discussed in the literature, usually refers to the current state of a nuclear family system.

It is our intention to extend this concept of homeostasis to include not only the two-generational dimension of loyalty and indebtedness, but also the multigenerational and in-law arena.

The clinical illustrations of this chapter reveal not only wishful distortions and projections, but also the unsuccessful attempts to cope with these unsettled accounts and hidden commitments. For example, one fascinating aspect is the wish to be adopted by one's in-laws. This phenomenon may introduce such ramifications as unconsciously placing an excessive demand on the aged in-laws and rivalry with one's mate for sharing his parents. It can also be used as a defense for not working through or facing one's commitments and responsibility to one's own family of origin. A double blow may be experienced by the marital pair when the "adoption myth" is exploded by the nonadoption of the in-law.

INCLUSION OF GRANDPARENTS IN SESSIONS

In our efforts to include the grandparents whenever feasible, several major aspects have had to be kept in mind. This will be spelled out more explicitly in our clinical illustrations, but the first factor is to interrupt and not permit the "blame syndrome" to continue. Constructive and growth-enhancing aspects of the relationship are the sole concern and goal. Angry and resentful feelings are inevitably expressed between the generations; such confrontations provide an opportunity to begin to break up what has been projected or externalized onto the other person. A mutual dialogue is encouraged so that the aged parent can reveal his own past, as well as current longings. The hidden accounts of both exploitation and unrequited merit must be balanced with loud claims.

In this dialogue, however, there is never a reversal of generations; An aging parent, though becoming more dependent or physically incapacitated, still remains a parent. As stated by Spark and Brody, "in feeling though the adult child may be old himself he remains in the relationship of child to parent. He does not become a parent to his parent."[80, p. 200] In conceptualizing development phases beyond genital maturity, Blenkner[8] has postulated the phase of "filial maturity." This is characterized by the mature adult's capacity to be depended on by the parent, and marks a healthy transition from genital maturity to old age. Thus it is not "role reversal," but fulfillment of the filial role to one's parent that implies resolution of earlier transitional phases.

Often, it is incorrectly assumed that a person who is in the aged or grandparental phase of life cannot change or modify his familial relationships. However, in some instances the grandparents may be less rigid and fixated than a younger family member. Moreover, most aged parents remain committed to their offspring and grandchildren, which helps the three generations to face the nature of the current relationship and obligations rather than the internalized, early distortions regarding one's parents. Whether the older parent was in reality or not a frustrating, nongiving person, there develops a renewed hope and opportunity for clarification and improved relating. Much that was unknown or unclear about the older person's circumstances may be shared for the first time. This can lead to a new understanding and mutual compassion between the generations. Rejection and distancing can be minimized or removed to a degree that was originally not anticipated by any family member.

The grandchildren, who may have been carrying the brunt of the negative transference feelings of one or both adult parents, are very eager for a reconciliation with their grandparents. It not only helps free them of the scapegoated or parentified role, but it renews their hope and provides them a model for reconciling their conflicts with their own parents. The children are often devoted to their grandparents, but may have inhibited these feelings because of their sensitivity to and wish to protect their own parents. One 7-year-old boy sat on his father's lap and pleaded with his father to take care of the grandparents, just as he is being taken care of by his father. The young father at that point leaned his head on his son's shoulder and cried.

In overgiving to one's children there may even be neglect and indifference to the physical and emotional needs of the aging parents. Each generation may be caught in a mutual, destructive, hostile bind. No one is able to discharge his obligations in a manner appropriate to his age or phase of life. The aged are "left out," jealous, and resentful of the grandchildren; the young adults do not receive the needed support and recognition from their parents or even from their children. The children are guilty about overreceiving or taking that which they feel should be shared with their grandparents. The adult children feel that their parents and children are ungrateful. In the sense of the nonbalancing of the "record," all three generations are suffering.

These loyalty feelings, though often seemingly unconscious to the adult child, are reexperienced or acted out in the nuclear family system. Unless such feelings are faced, the underlying source of the guilt feelings modified or changed, and past obligations met or paid, the adult child will continue having difficulty in balancing out his commitment and loyalty to his mate and offspring. While part of this is similar to individual therapy, our goal is extended to actually changing the existing relationship between the generations. The intrapsychic conflicts or infantile strivings for gratification from important persons in the past, which are being acted out within the family or acted out upon society, are dealt with in the present, here-and-now relationships.

What in the past was considered hidden in the unconscious of an individual, available only through dreams, slips of the tongue, and other psychic mechanisms, are now viewed differently. The aged parent, the adult parent, and children are the transference objects upon whom infantile hungers are being expressed. Instead of focusing on how infantile strivings and attitudes are transferred to an individual therapist, the family therapist attempts to utilize the disruptive, regressive, negative behaviors expressed in the relationships *"in vivo"* in order to rebalance and change the family relationships. As postulated by Boszormenyi-Nagy,[18] this concept of reconstructuring family relationships differs from the concept of individual dynamics in the sense that the multiperson dynamics of the family include but supersede individual dynamics.

TECHNIQUES AND COMMENTS REGARDING THE INCLUSION OF AGED PARENT(S)

As we became aware that many families were currently still very involved with their families of origin, it was suggested that grandparents be included in sessions. As described previously, the initial reactions usually were negative: "Nothing could be accomplished; it is hopeless; they would be unwilling," etc. However, from our experience as therapists we have learned that the aged parents in many instances really feel left out. The therapy may be considered as a rival or a force which might further alienate or exclude them. Our families found upon direct questioning of their parents that they were willing and in most instances eager to come in. Each adult child was free to make the decision when to use sessions with his or her parent(s) and whether they wished to include their spouse. The aged parents came not only because they still wanted to be helpful to their adult children and grandchildren, but also because they too were deeply unhappy about the relationship in the present, as well as from the past.

At first there may be angry blaming, sometimes much mutual recrimination—which could be classified as confrontation between the generations. With the therapists' help this generally should not continue long. For the therapists, it is more important to glean the principles of credit–debit accounting between the generations. They inquire into the aged parent's early life, or sometimes the aged parent spontaneously turns to them as if wanting comfort and reassurance regarding their own early deprivations. In this sense the blame syndrome may be minimized, and family members are helped to see their aged parents in a more adult context. Instead of the adult child feeling helplessly or dependently angry or unjustly treated, as he may have from childhood on, a new dimension may be opened to him. As stated previously, a reversal of generation does not take place, but rather the adult child is confronted with a need to repay or care for his parents in a different and perhaps more responsible way than he was treated.

Primarily these family therapy sessions stimulate a renewed hope for more positive relationships and improved reciprocity, so that past grievances or destructive behavior can be modified. The adult children who now have their own children are in a more advantageous position to identify with their aging parents—differences can be reconciled and past emotional debts and obligations resolved, whether in an emotional sense or also in factual, though not necessarily material, giving. Each generation is afforded the opportunity to list their grievances and complaints—the eventual goal being to reach some new level of relating between them. This may consist of reclarification and modification of certain fixed attitudes, but most important is modification of the behavior. Grievances which have a reality basis are explored and sometimes rectified and guilt feelings are thereby lessened. Even after several sessions with the aged parents, feedback is continuously brought in about the ongoing contacts. Where aged parents live in other cities, the family members continue to report on their communications by phone, letters, and visits. The way is always left open for further sessions if the adult son or daughter wishes to reinvite parents. Interestingly, the son-in-law or daughter-in-law and especially the now grown-up children seem eager and openly interested in any forms of reconciliation that can occur. They usually speak very directly and openly regarding the nature of the intense conflicts between the generations. They are tuned into the deep love as well as the hurt and despair of each generation. The children or the spouse are generally caught up in feelings that it is they who are being used as objects for "retribution"; they are therefore eager for the grandparents as well as themselves to escape this bind.

No matter how vindictive a person may have felt or still feels, the therapeutic goal is not mere recognition, confrontation, open expression, and thus a continuation of the negative relationships, but is focused on mutual clarification and reconstruction. The adult child and his parent are provided an opportunity to break destructive chainlike patterns of relationships which may have continued for several generations. A young child's depth of understanding can best be illustrated by the following:

The child's mother was saying that her aged mother was slipping. The maternal grandmother purchased two coats and kept asking people in her apartment building which coat was more attractive. The grandson, age 13, turned to his mother and said, "it is very simple. Tell grandma which coat you think she looks best in and then take the other coat back to the store for her. That is what she always used to do for you!"

The children are so keenly aware that their relationships with their own parents could be much more openly loving and giving, if their parents could resolve some of their conflicts with the grandparents. In one family the parents spoke with ridicule and contempt for their aged parents and then had difficulty trying to figure out why their own children mocked and ridiculed them!

CLINICAL EXCERPTS FROM SESSIONS WHICH INCLUDE THE AGED PARENTS AND THEIR CHILDREN

First, excerpts from sessions were chosen to illustrate various combinations: adult sons and mothers, adult daughters and both parents, sessions which also might include an adult sibling. A second aim was to illustrate various types of relationships. It is hoped that the case material will also convey the vast difference between an adult child talking directly to his parent in the presence of the family therapists compared with "telling" an individual therapist about his family of origin. Most of the grandparents were in their fifties and sixties and the adult children in their thirties and forties.

FAMILY #1

The L family initially came because their three children were constantly fighting each other and the parents; one son, aged 13, was active in sports and on the debating team but spent four and five hours in the basement doing his homework; the son aged 11 had no friends and after school trailed after his younger sister and interfered with her girlfriends' games or spent part of the evening tickling and wrestling with his little sister.

The parents were bickering constantly over money and the children but mostly attacked one another's family of origin. Mrs. L felt her family of origin was perfect, cultured, and refined as compared with her husband's family who argued loud but clearly and then made up shortly thereafter. Mr. L kept insisting that no family could be as ideal as his wife pictured her family to be. He agreed that her family was above his in education, money, and manners but felt his own background was nothing to be ashamed of.

Since the maternal grandmother lived around the corner from the L family, there was constant and daily contact between them. Mrs. L made no decisions or purchases without her mother's consent. It was suggested that Mrs. L bring her mother for several sessions since it was thought that the overidealization of her parent's family was interfering with her commitment to her parental and marital role. All blame was placed on her husband, her difficulties as well as the children's.

The following are excerpts from four sessions: two between maternal grandmother and her daughter, and the third and fourth between the husband and wife.

Session #1: Celia L And Her Mother (Mrs. K)

Celia: I told my mother that we had reached a stumbling block—she knows that I am unhappy about my marriage and children.

Mother: My mother lived with us. I was an only child when she became a widow, she came to live with us. She took care of my daughter more than I.

Celia: I hated to sleep with my grandmother until age 10. Mother, I am cold and frigid and have no sex with my husband. In a dream I saw my grandmother in a beautiful nightgown and she was hugging me—her whole life was grooming me.

Mother: My mother's life was me.

Celia: You owed her so much, you couldn't baby sit for me—too much on manners. My mother could talk about me personally but she wouldn't. I was glad when my grandmother died so that I could talk with my mother. I must have been a rough, bad child. She grasped on me and mother you just stood by. If I lost my mother my whole world would collapse. I constantly have these bad dreams; they harm my young ones and I protect them. I was obese and very restricted with my peers.

Mother: I will never share my suffering with my daughter.

Celia: When my father died my whole world ended then. I was at age 14, ugly, hateful to my grandmother. My brother was the star. I've always had a lack of self-confidence. I had an empty life—my childhood was a blank.

Session #2: Celia And Her Mother (Mrs. K)

Celia: I had a phone conversation with my mother because she felt the whole thing had grown to a great enormous thing.

Mother: You were hysterical, mother help me you screamed!

Celia: Why am I so unhappy, did I marry my husband on the rebound?

Mother: All you want to remember are the bad things.

Celia: Grandmother impinged on my life. How did you and Daddy argue?

Mother: Only after you children were in bed. My parents never argued in my presence.

Celia: What do you think about my relationship with my brother, wasn't that abnormal? Why am I so cold sexually?

Mother: Where do your three children come in? I wonder if the third child didn't damage her physically?

Celia: Mother why am I abnormal? I was a nothing—when my brother's friends were at the house, I wasn't supposed to come into the living room.

(The therapists ask the mother whether she felt her life was fulfilled as a wife and sexual partner . . . if not perhaps she cannot give her daughter something which she has not experienced.)

Mother: You have driven your husband off by telling him that you don't love him. A wife should give in and you don't.

(The therapists encourage the women to try to share more of their personal feelings with each other as two adults. Mrs. K says she knows that her daughter needs her, but she never told anyone about the suffering she experienced most of her life.)

Session #3: Steve And Celia (Marital Pair)

Celia: When I left her, I was a much more grown-up woman—my mother isn't really a woman. I have to look for someone else to help me. She said after our last session that sex is like bitter medicine . . . in order to keep a marriage going . . . 90% of women don't enjoy it. She was honest but she is like a girlfriend. I am not satisfied with being a robot . . . my husband cannot give it to me.

Steve: My mother-in-law believes that the treatment is driving my wife crazy by trying to make her believe there can be sexual fulfillment. This is not true! I have not touched her for two weeks. She used to tell me that she finds me repulsive. I can make her respond (especially when on vacation), but I am waiting for her response at home.

Celia: I am afraid of him. He verbally abuses me and then wants sex and I can't. I have a physical need for sex at times but it isn't there when I am home . . . My grandmother slept next to me all those years; her breasts were removed for cancer and she was repulsive. I was cruel to her when she was dying. I was sorry about it, no I wasn't.

Session #4: Steve And Celia

Steve: Very unusual week even though there was much antagonism between the children.

Celia: I have been closer to my husband than at other times and yet he wasn't different. He made me feel that he needs me. You were right about my relationship with my mother. I feel like a liberated woman. I am not as dependent. I don't call her as much. I used to feel that I was forced to the wall . . . the same feeling I used to have about my grandmother who forced and forced.

Steve: The children are not used to seeing us this close; sometimes I get the impression they try to break up this closeness . . . they're not used to seeing us this way.

In the two sessions where Celia and her mother were seen together there was mutual projection, denial, blame, and disconfirmation. The symbiotic attachment was revealed between mother and adult daughter. Reference was even made regarding the great-grandmother and some of the effect it was now having on the fourth generation. In sessions prior to these two, Celia had described her excess dependence and commitment to her family of origin. But this was untouchable since Celia split her relational attitudes—her mother being idealized and maternal grandmother being the hated, smothering, and engulfing bad object. Her mother manipulated an alliance with her daughter instead of being able to face what was missing in their relationship. She blamed Celia's unhappiness on the husband or upon the birth of a child. She not only refused to share her own suffering in the past, but even continued to treat Celia as a child who was incapable of thinking for herself or making decisions. In turn Celia remains excessively and ambivalently available to her mother.

Celia's mother was honest when she described her attitudes about sexuality: That which she has not experienced as possible cannot be presented as pleasurable. Another major myth that needed to be penetrated was that Celia's family of origin was perfect or superior; in fact all families have their own human frailties and limitations.

Overtly it would seem that Celia was only excessively dependent and demanding of her mother's interest and concern. Her mother scapegoated the husband and his family of origin as inferior, crude, and too expressive of emotion; thus Mrs. K continued to bind her daughter in the old loyalty system. "We are one." This prevented the exploration of the issues of the merit of genuine giving and receiving in their family. But it would seem that she was as much a victim in her lifetime as Celia now felt she was. On the surface, the mother was perceived as the giving one, in time, interest, and materially. Even though Celia was now an adult parent, there was no balanced reciprocity in the relationship. Celia remained in an infantilized position, still yearning for a different closeness about which her mother stated, "I will never share my suffering with my daughter."

In the next session, Celia said that things had now changed between herself and her mother—she was more grown-up, independent, and now had been sexually responsive to her husband. This was a "temporary flight into maturity." Yet when once experienced it can become a repeatable goal. However, a great deal was still lacking. Another imbalance had now emerged, "she will be less dependent on her mother, etc." What did Celia feel she still owed to her mother? Her brother was described as cold and detached. Who else but Celia was available to take care of and be responsible for her mother in the form that her mother was available to her own mother? Celia's mother had nursed the great-grandmother through her total illness and into the terminal phase.

Balancing of the family system, as applied to Celia, would mean turning her relationship around to a point where her mother would be a receiver, in addition to her husband and children. The children up to this point had been overprotected and overgiven as if they were also helplessly dependent. Steve, who in the past was most frequently scapegoated, had to become capable of helping to reshape the imbalance. In having lost his own mother at a very early age, he had felt "adopted" by his mother-in-law until it became clear to him the degree to which it was negatively affecting his marital and parental position.

FAMILY #2

This family came because their son, age 14, was provocative, rebellious, and constantly fighting with his parents; the younger sister, age 12, had innumerable fears and for a period of time had much difficulty in going to school (poor peer relationships and very few activities).

Not only were there strained relationships between these children and parents, but also with both families of origin. When they were first married, they lived with the parents of Larry G. Later Mrs. G's mother not only helped them to purchase a house, but also moved in with them. The father of Mrs. G had died two weeks before they were married.

Sarah G worked part-time and insisted that the children carry their share of the household chores. However, while she constantly harped at the children for not being neat and tidy, Sarah herself not only dropped things all over the house, but littered the hallway, bedroom, and spare bedroom with papers and magazines that she refused to discard. As a child, even though Sarah's mother worked all day in a corner grocery, her mother picked up after her, waited on her, etc. It became apparent that unconsciously Sarah was attempting to get her husband and children to do for her as her mother had done.

Since Sarah's mother visited their home two or three times a week, the therapist's felt that this guilt-laden relationship might be directly explored. Her sister, Molly, also agreed to attend the session. Sarah said that in letters and on the telephone, Molly held her responsible for their mother's unhappiness.

Session #1: Sarah G., Sarah's Sister Molly, And Their Mother

Molly: I said I'd come . . . I was upset that my mother was going to be here. I didn't want her to be hurt by my sister . . . am afraid I might accuse my sister too badly . . . I feel concerned with the way you treat our mother . . . it is a thorn in our relationship.

Mother: Our relationship is gone . . . it doesn't bother me anymore.

Molly: I am angry . . . you come to my house and you don't say what bothers you . . . I wanted to help my mother and sister. In the past six to eight months I have tried to change my attitudes to my sister . . . less critical and warmer to you.

Mother: Sarah has no time for me . . . I can also feel out of place with Molly, you both are too busy, I am glad I am working (cries).

Molly: I always have a place for you . . . I wish my . . .

Mother: In 1952 I was very sick—You, Sarah had more important things to do. I always did everything for my children.

Sarah: But when I am there you don't want me to be there.

Mother: When my children needed me I was there; when I needed them they weren't there. To me to die makes no difference. There is no help for me . . . I am nervous . . . I can't stand possessive people, I am not . . .

Molly: I don't think Sarah's children treat my mother right . . . they reflect my sister's attitude . . . in your family you go out more for strangers; a sister you can shrug off, but with a friend you can be nice. You are two persons: (1) gay Sarah or (2) a strong domineering person.

Sarah: Between you (Molly) and Daddy nobody had a chance! My mother is an overgiving person and does not let anyone express their thanks.

Mother: I remember Sarah saying to me . . . I am not going to be your slave anymore.

Sarah: I have always been very fond of you (Molly) but I stopped confiding in you . . . you were too critical.

Molly: I am terribly angry . . . Sarah is not grateful to our mother.

Mother: I don't feel that you ever do anything for me . . . forget about love, just consideration.

Sarah: Oh, Mom, you don't think I love you! I feel, Mother, that I do for you just as much as you do for me.

Mother: I am glad for you then . . . and Molly you live out of the city and it is so easy to criticize from a distance.

Sarah: Mother you never tell me when you need me.

Mother: When I ask Sarah to come with me to buy a coat she has no time but when she wants me to go with her I am 99% there . . .

Session #2: Sarah And Her Mother

Sarah: I asked my mother to come back.

Mother: I am drifting away from my daughter . . . I used to love her (cries) I just couldn't stay away from her. It is better for her to drift away from me. I didn't want to say anything about Molly but I am not comfortable in her home either.

Sarah: It's better to talk about it . . . I think my mother wants me to say, darling, I love you very much, everything will be the same . . . Mother you say no when you really mean yes . . . you make me beg you.

Mother: I am ashamed . . . I felt bad in your house . . . I didn't sleep all night . . . I was miserable all day yesterday too. I am 70 years old . . . how much more can I live . . . my daughters have domineered my life since my husband died.

Sarah: I can't be honest with you because you don't listen or you change it all around.

Mother: You killed the love for you.

Sarah: You always say we were close . . . we always fought.

Mother: Because I was always doing things for you. (She relates how at age 17 she left her family and came to the U.S. Her husband had offered her a trip to visit her family but she did not want to go. She and a twin sister were next to the youngest of 13 children. Her husband's sisters were against their marriage . . . the sisters were unmarried. She had no one here except her husband and children. Always tried to help everyone. Very independent and even now is working; never likes to receive.) Sarah and I got along well when I lived in her house, but when she stopped working she told me that I want to take over her house, then I left.

Sarah: My mother and I always got along better than my Mother and Molly (Molly also asked her mother to leave her home many years ago). If I am weak and dependent you have me as a child. You can't take anything, any gift from me, Molly, or even from my father.

Mother: When anybody gives me something, I feel like I owe them something.

Sarah: I struggled very hard not to lean on my mother . . . the whole burden falls on me.

Mother: I cannot stand idle . . . I do the dishes everywhere . . . I do praise my daughter, she is good looking and intelligent.

Sarah: I felt better after the last session because this was the first time that my mother expressed her anger . . . we could be friends again.

As these two sessions unfolded, it becomes clearly evident that both sisters were intensely involved with their widowed mother. Their mother even at age 70 still saw herself as being the all-giving, self-sacrificing person, who never liked to "owe anybody something." Yet because of her aging process, health, and loneliness, she now needed as she put it, "consideration," to be treated as a person and respected.

Both daughters had been filled with guilt feelings as a result of having a parent who gave so totally of herself. In the second session, it became clearer that the aging mother was defending against her loneliness and the aging process by still trying to give even when it is beyond her physical and emotional capacity to do so. Did she overgive because of abandonment by her own family of origin? Her yearning to be taken care of by both daughters was implicit in her statements, "both of you are too busy." She bound them in guilt-laden relationships; yet she was able to recognize that it had been hard for her to take.

There was hard confrontation in these sessions, with the older-parent in a sense taking the initiative. This was the first time their mother was able to openly express to her daughters how hurt and angry she had been. Prior to this time so much was massively denied or minimized. Sarah reported subsequently that she and her mother now no longer beat about the bush! When her mother visited in their home she would tell her daughter, son-in-law, and grandchildren exactly what she wanted or needed. For example, she used to insist on doing all the dishes. Now she could say, "I'm too tired," or "I will be glad to help too." The children and the husband confirmed the changes that had developed: "Everyone is more open and free with each other." The old sulking and tension between Sarah and her mother had greatly diminished.

Session #3: Jack G (Husband Of Sarah G), His Sister Lisa, And Their Mother

Jack, while functioning economically as an adequate and responsible individual, was constantly ignored or depeciated by his wife and children. In the sessions which had included Jack and Sarah and their children, the adolescent son would mimic and mock the parents in a clownlike manner. Inevitably the sessions ended in much noise and shouting between the parents and children. Jack seemed to be merely an echo of Sarah permitting her to finish or overlap his comments.

In the sessions that follow, with Jack, his mother, and sister Lisa, he also appeared to be defensively pleading for their approval. Jack could not be direct or strong either with his family of origin or with his wife and children. He made empty and hollow threats and felt much of the time like a "bad little boy." At this phase of therapy Jack had become aware of his position and did struggle to improve his relationships. Jack tried to move from the passively dependent role he had with his family of origin as well as with his wife and children.

Jack: I want to talk to you Lisa . . . you don't really like my wife and children . . . that puts me in a position on whose side should I be . . . I don't like my kids caught in this situation.

Lisa: I don't dislike you but I don't like your wife . . . she is a different person. I guess I am not family-conscious enough. I'd like the children to be close. Our lives are very different . . . Our friends wouldn't interest you and vice versa. I have gotten 20 years older, but Sarah hasn't. I don't feel comfortable in your house and I don't think you or Sarah feel comfortable in mine. I think you are very relaxed parents as to children's safety . . . you let them ride a bike among cars.

Mother: Jack was a worrisome child . . . he would come home straight from school and wouldn't eat until Lisa was home.

Jack: I was the favorite child.

Lisa: I was my father's favorite. I used to wish that I was a boy. I used to look up to my brother as big brother who was smarter than anybody.

Mother: It was very evident that my husband showed preference for Lisa's children, and I used to point out that it was wrong.

Lisa: My husband is super-responsible, and if I don't call my mother for two days he would remind me . . . maybe he adopted my mother.

Mother: Lisa's husband used to say, "if you, Lisa, ever leave me don't go to your mother's because that is where I am going to go."

Jack: My mother believes I only call when I want something. We are still on a mother and little boy level . . . whether I am a bad little boy for not calling you.

Lisa: Sarah's house is dirty, I can't eat a meal there ever again. My brother is not strong enough to make his wife keep things neater and cleaner.

Session #4 (Following Week): Jack And Sarah G

Jack: I was very depressed after last week's session . . . I didn't get anything out of it . . . my sister wasn't really honest. My wife does function on two levels with the house . . . it is operated on a party level. Yet the session last week has helped me with my relationship with my mother . . . also between Sarah and my mother. My sister has changed a great deal. My brother-in-law dresses up very neatly . . . he would like to be an upper-class WASP. He is very successful in business, inherited a lot of money from his father. I had for the first time in years a very long conversation with my mother after the session.

Sarah: I felt much better about my mother-in-law. In the past I was much prettier than Lisa and my family was financially better off than my husband's. Lisa and her husband would have separated years ago if her husband had not had therapy.

In the session with Jacks' mother and sister, it appeared at first that his sister Lisa scapegoated Jack's wife and his children as the reason for their overdistanced relationship. "Sarah is a dirty housekeeper. You are very relaxed parents as to the children's safety." As the session developed, the split between Jack and Lisa was brought out into the open. This was due not only to sibling rivalry, but clearly resulted from the fact that each of their parents had shown open preference towards the child of the opposite sex. In addition, Lisa had been refusing to carry any responsibility for her aging mother. After their mother was hospitalized for a heart attack, Jack had to confront his sister with her noninvolvement and nonresponsible behavior towards their mother. He moved from the "bad little boy role" to becoming directly available and responsible for his mother and also holding his sister to carrying her share of concern and interest along with him.

More importantly, a radical shift developed between Jack and his mother which even included his wife. He reported that after the session with his mother, "I had for the first time in years a long conversation with my mother." This led to phone calls and mutual visits to each other's home, out of genuine interest and concern rather than out of guilt. In the past, his wife had to remind him to call his mother once a week. As a result of his wife no longer being scapegoated, a more positive reconciliation developed between the daughter-in-law and mother-in-law.

FAMILY #3

This family was referred because their two adopted sons were having academic difficulties and also were behavior problems in school and at home. This was a second marriage for Rose D: "As a wife and mother I am a failure!" At times she said that she had married on a rebound; she insisted that her parents pushed her into the second marriage. Initially, they had considered her second husband was a very acceptable suitor as compared with her first husband.

Even though Albert D was a very successful merchant, Rose complained that he did not trust her with money. She said her husband was miserly and saw him fundamentally as an absentee husband and father. She openly expressed continuous rage against Albert. When she spoke about other family relationships, namely, her children or parents, she would cry or sob in a very uncontrolled way. Her husband and sons were either annoyed or disgusted with her weeping, which they stated made no sense to anyone. No one felt she was mistreated.

The excerpts from the sessions that follow may begin to convey the mutual hurt between an older parent and her adult daughter. The dependency tie, albeit, coming forth in a negative way, reveals the commitment and degree of involvement with her family of origin.

Session #1: Rose D And Her Mother

Mother: There were a few things a few years ago that were wrong which I could tell my son-in-law . . . when his mother was seriously ill, he wouldn't be home and he left his mother in my daughter's care . . . I even had to bawl him out for not giving her enough money. My daughter was unhappy. She was an only girl . . . lots of people spoiled her . . . she made a pretty picture . . . my father was crazy about her . . . we wanted her to look good, my sister got the better things for her, clothes, etc. Rose resented when her brother sat on my lap. My son was willing to do things but not Rose. Later she changed and always wanted to be with me and go shopping. She turned unhappy when she had her first miscarriage; she wanted a baby. I was very happy for her (both mother and daughter cry). I myself wasn't crazy about having more children. My husband was always very considerate . . . I always came first. I don't lean on anybody. Do you, Rose, miss me?

Rose: I did but I still think it is better for you to work in my brother's business . . . I can't talk to my mother the way I used to. She has other interests now (cries very hard).

Mother: Maybe she got through school because she was so pretty . . . I had a sister who was very conceited. My mother was very cold to the children (at age one I was brought to the U.S.). My father showed me a lot of love.

Rose: I don't know what I want anymore . . . I don't know what is the matter with me!

Mother: Maybe Rose is a better mother than I was . . .

Session #2: Albert and Rose D and Rose's Mother

Mother: Rose saw me being taken care of when I was sick, and she doesn't see it in her marriage. I just realized last week how my not seeing Rose again was as if I died . . . I cried hard at home . . . Rose did you feel better after last week?

Rose: I thought that I did understand something. After I had felt that nobody really cared I started to build a shell around myself. I was asked if I did not receive love how could I give it to my children?

Mother: Who stopped giving you love?

Rose: When I talk to you on the phone you are not really interested . . . my husband is too busy to listen to me.

Mother: Would she be better off at work with you Albert?

Albert: I don't think it was good in my parents' marriage.

Mother: Why don't you let her splurge $5 or $10 on something?

Rose: I don't want to say things that may hurt my mother.

Mother: It would be better for her if she could say things.

Rose: It would be foolish to expect my mother to stop working . . .

Mother: I remember when she was a little girl . . . she would come to my bed when I was asleep. I thought it was a cat and kept kicking . . . next day she would want to pack her bag and leave home.

Session #3: Rose And Her Mother

Rose: I have been increasingly depressed since I have been coming here. My mother thinks it may be due to a change of life. I don't cry during the week . . . but I do feel unhappy. I don't like crying in front of my family . . . I have a tremendous inferiority complex. There may be something that could just hurt my mother and I shouldn't say . . . that you didn't want me . . . children.

Mother: I said in the beginning I didn't want children . . . you have been wanted since you were born.

Rose: You have said it many times, that you didn't want children. I liked to go to grandmom's house because I was liked there.

Mother: God may have punished Rose maybe because of the way I was . . . I didn't want more children . . . I didn't want to have a dozen kids as they had it at home.

Rose: You have always said that I was a bad kid. I know what the problems are but I can't overcome it. My mother always told me I can't do anything (be a nurse, etc.) that's why I feel inferior. Did you encourage me when I wanted to do anything?

Mother: When you wanted to be a nurse I discouraged you because of the way you were.

Rose: You always told me I was too dumb.

Mother: Your school record was never good . . . she passed her tests, but . . .

Rose: You kept telling me how incapable I was and I did believe you down the line.

Mother: She only wanted to get married and I was afraid of (she used to get so depressed . . .) I rather let her get married than have something happen.

Session #4: Rose And Her Mother

Mother: If I had only known that she was that hurt about my saying that I had not wanted children up to the time she was born . . .

Rose: I was discouraged in growing up when I wanted to do anything.

Mother: She was more interested in dressing . . . material things . . . Whenever I wanted something from my daughter she always said no.

Rose: I do know I am a lousy cook, lousy housewife . . . children don't like it, my husband eats out . . .

Mother: I felt that Rose was a lot like me, interested in something but now I see it isn't so.

Rose: My mother is stronger.

Mother: I face every problem without getting panicky. You get a lot more done.

Rose: Nothing is too much for my mother and everything is an effort for me. I've tried to be a good mother but I didn't do too good a job.

Mother: She did too good a job! My husband kept the children in line . . . I wasn't fine with my children, but my husband wouldn't permit them to call me "she." I am not sentimental, I don't think about birthdays.

Rose: I would like to be stronger and less sensitive. My father was raised in an orphanage, maybe that's why home was so important for him.

Session #5: Albert And Rose And Rose's Mother

Rose: My vision has already been affected by the cataract. Robert (son) was real sweet yesterday . . . first time he acted like a son for a long time . . . it made life very pleasant . . . He was fifteen on Saturday. My mother and I got close to each other when I got a divorce from my first husband. She gave me tremendous moral support . . . neighbors may have thought I was a tramp.

Mother: The neighbors thought she should hold her head down and I didn't.

Rose: I couldn't imagine how someone could ever hate their mother. I hate my sister-in-law. My father did say something that hurt me deeply . . . but I would never say it in front of my children . . . he accused me of being promiscuous as if that was why I was marrying my first husband. (She then was asked if she could recall the last time she was angry at her mother.) When Robert was a baby I once told my mother never to come to my house again.

Albert: My wife does cry instead of getting angry.

Mother: The only time I recall her being angry (age 13–14) that she saved some money for a Mother's Day gift which she didn't buy but she gave me the money nevertheless, "here is the gift!"

Session #6: Rose And Her Mother

Mother: I never thought there was a problem in communication between me and my daughter.

Rose: There was a time when I confided completely in my mother, but then I was hurt because you just weren't interested. I felt that you were just glad that I was married and you didn't have to give up your involvement in business . . . I was hurt, inside I was (cries) even before my brother's child was born.

Mother: Married life is funny; there are things you have to take and things you have to give.

Rose: You hurt me with another thing . . . your attitude . . . to give my grandmother's earrings to my niece who was named after my grandmother.

Mother: (referring to her daughter's inability to have her own children) You can't go against God . . . you should still feel happy about having what you have (cries and blames herself for not having helped her daughter more during a pregnancy which terminated in a spontaneous abortion).

In one very moving session, which occurred later, Rose sobbed about having an infantile uterus and being unable to get pregnant and give birth to a child. Rose felt her mother could not possibly know how deeply hurt she was. Her mother also sobbed and replied, "I would even have had the baby for you if such a thing were possible."

In these sessions, the mother and daughter perhaps for the first time shared their own unmet needs, misunderstandings, and resentments.

Rose's mother had been one of 10 children, with little or no affection ever displayed in her home. She did not want her daughter to grow up conceited like one of her sisters. She presented herself as the solid, reliable person, "I face every problem without getting panicky." It was the mother who told her daughter Rose that she must learn to give more of herself to her husband—"that is what marriage is!"

Rose felt lonely and confused. It was better for her mother to continue working in her brother's business and yet she always had felt in the past and now even in the present that her brother was the winner —at least as far as their mother was concerned. Rose's reaction to her mother's job was to experience it as if she had really lost her mother. In turn her mother said," I just realized last week how my not seeing Rose again was as if I died."

It was as if Rose's mother felt that she still owed her daughter a great deal; and responded to her daughter's needs and demands as if she were still a little girl.

As time passed and her mother became available in interest and concern, Rose began to work toward finding something in which she could excel. She became rather expert in buying and selling antique jewelry. Now a shift developed between Rose and her mother, but more importantly between all three generations. With Rose moving out of the overprotective role with her sons and not nagging her husband about his hours of business and money making, the family could be more available and spontaneous towards each other than they had been in the past.

FAMILY #4

The family was referred because both a son and a daughter were having severe academic problems, with the school questioning whether they would be promoted. Both children had superior intelligence. Alan, age 14, was the most apparent target of his father's rage and disappointment. His father saw him as lazy, uncaring, a talker and not a doer. Ruth S said that her husband Bob continuously put Alan down just as he was "put down" by his father and brother. There was a perceptible overcloseness between Alan and his mother combined with overprotectiveness. In an early phase, Bob S said he felt left out of his family and did not like this position. His wife was more available to the children than to him. Susan, age 12, was also a target, but both parents, while concerned about her learning difficulties, were not as equally disappointed or angry as they were toward Alan.

Session #1: Ruth S And Her Father And Mother

Ruth: I was somewhat hesitant to ask my parents to come. Tensions that now exist must have been there before.

Father: I remember you as a favorite child of good fortune . . . recipient of everybody's love from birth on. You were a beautiful child . . . charming, kind. People reacted favorably to you. For awhile we were very poor; when Ruth was five we had to live in one room.

Ruth: I was always very protective of my younger sister Betty. I was shy, had trouble making friends.

Mother: Betty did feel that she was adopted.

Father: There was no relationship between my family of origin and my wife's. My parents had very little social life . . . They had a different background from my wife's family and looked down on her family. They objected to my wife in every way; felt that she took me away from them. There hasn't been any relationship with my family. I just accepted it.

Mother: You didn't even like your mother before you knew me. I loved my parents.

Father: My parents were cold as fish and I liked my in-laws; liked their warmth . . . my parents had 10 children.

Ruth: I always had tremendous esteem for my father, but I didn't go to my father for . . .

Father: I may sound authoritarian at times. I come to the essence of a question.

Mother: Yes, but you are a cold person like your family.

Ruth: We are not a kissing family. Am I still trying to prove myself to my parents. I ask Mother, "does Daddy know what I have done?"

Mother: You and your father have the same need . . . to have everybody love you . . . There has been too much make-believe that it was a family. One of my husband's problems has been his fear that I'd leave him.

Father: The children were the cement to keep us together. I don't think they had a fear of divorce. I used to feel that my wife had two daughters on her side against me.

Mother: I felt I was building him up for the children (cries).

Session #2: Bob And Ruth S

Ruth: My parents have been going through a stressful period of their marriage in the last months. Maybe coming here has helped my father. I never was able to talk to him. At age 21 when I was going steady with a young man, I suddenly realized the lack of communication with my father.

Bob: I have remained deliberately distant from them . . . I didn't want to be in the customary son-in-law position. I must have felt that Ruth was a person that needed . . . that I needed. I love her now more than when I married her. My mother-in-law has no endearment; she is selfish. I needed a family. I saw them as an interested couple but they weren't.

Ruth: I wonder how my parents have been holding me back. What am I still doing . . . The only one changing is my husband. I am confused.

Bob: I feel now we, both of us, attack a problem together. My wife is still wrapped up in the children, her parents, and not herself.

Ruth: Maybe I am just a diplomat.

Session #3 (Next Week): Ruth, Bob And His Father

Father: My wife died from cancer when she was 46 years old. Bob had always been more of a student than his brother. I am concerned about both of my sons . . . the other one has made the best of it. I tried to bring the brothers together through business. Bob is more culturally interested; my other son is more like me. Bob is more ethical . . . he is more like his mother, more truthful. For me in business, a little white lie . . . but he criticizes me for it. In the early years the two brothers were fighting more, but I used my money to bring them close. Bob is in the same business as I am with a loan from me; Joe is in a different kind of business which I helped him to get started.

Bob: It was difficult to grow up because my father wanted to determine what he wanted in his house. I did as much as my brother when we were younger —worked in a factory, was in the army, too.

Father: You think you did! American boys don't know what real hardships are.

Ruth: They talk about present only . . . in our early marriage there was much struggle between them. I wonder about Bob's childhood. I was most interested in my father-in-law saying that Bob dropped out of college because his father could not pay.

Session #4 (Following Week): Bob, His Younger Brother Joe, And Their Father

Joe: My family has been having troubles too, and we've talked to psychiatrists. I'm the one with a temper . . . Bob once hit a cigarette out of my mouth about 20 years ago. Used to have to fight for him. I think he has high blood pressure—suffers from nosebleeds. We are complete opposites—he is educated . . . different associates . . . school meant very little to me. Our mother was in the house constantly . . . Bob and I slept together and best times were when either he or I were sick and we had to be separated. I got more than Bob . . . in being the baby of the family, my mother would recite verses and play games with me even when I was too big for it. My mother's father and her sister were educated, so much so that my father wasn't supposed to eat with them as if he were a peasant. Her sister felt that my father was a poor choice of a husband for her. I got more attention from my mother, but Bob was siding more with my mother and helped her.

Bob: My mother told me to go into my father's business when she was dying . . . she wanted me to protect my father.

Joe: I don't think Bob lived enough of his childhood, he always acted 10 years older . . . He never dated singly like I did. I married at 18 a girl who was 18

. . . Bob didn't marry until he was 29 and then married a girl of 22 . . . who acts like a schoolteacher. Can't stand the way Bob dresses, puts on a big front.

In the session which included Ruth S's parents as well as her husband, many important dimensions are revealed. Not only was Ruth still struggling to get her parents' approval, but she was still unable to have a personal conversation with her father. Coincidentally, she had a similar complaint about her husband. Of greater significance, Ruth was revealed as clearly identifying with her mother who "had to build up her husband to her children." In both families then, the children could not directly discuss anything with their father, and channeled things through the mother as though the children needed protection from their fathers. By using such mechanisms these women lived vicariously through their husbands and children, thus avoiding facing their own lack of identity. Bob S described it very clearly when he said, "my wife is still wrapped up in the children, her parents, and not herself," also implying that she was not available and committed to him as he would like her to be.

In the sessions between Bob, his father, and brother, one saw that Bob was clearly assigned and accepting the role of the parentified child in his family of origin. While he was identified with the women, it was evident that his mother and maternal aunt were the educated and intellectual members of the family. However, the brother made a significant comment," I don't think Bob lived enough of his childhood." In addition, he was committed to carrying out his mother's dying wish, "to go into his father's business in order to protect him."

The S children were caught in a passively negative bind with the parents in being nonacademic achievers. In addition, Bob S experienced his son as a rival for his wife's interest and concern. The repetitive component also came out in the form of the father constantly putting his son down. Ruth had stated that when she first married Bob she felt her father-in-law was constantly doing the same thing to her husband. Between the deprecation on his father's part and his mother's seductive demandingness, their adolescent son was bound in such a way that he cannot freely concentrate on his school work.

CONCLUSIONS

Whether the first, second, or third generations are objects of constructive or destructive attitudes and behavior, the family therapist must face and work with the mutual involvements, loyalty ties, and feelings of indebtedness between the generations. The reality is that intergenerational continuity does exist.

The excerpts from the sessions were used to try to demonstrate that in many families there are pathologically prolonged and intense emotional attachments between the adult children, aging parents, and grandchildren. The blood tie or bonds of loyalty to one's current and extended family kin and the effects on each generation should not be disregarded. Whether it is implicit or explicitly stated, families and society in general are aware that there is a code that expects emotional and/or material payment and repayment between the generations.

In working within a three-generational context, family therapists may have a unique opportunity to relieve aged parents, adult parents, and children from being scapegoated as objects for all the anger and hurt feelings over alleged or real exploitation. Each generation may be helped to face the nature of the current relationships, exploring the real nature of the commitments and responsibility that flows naturally from such involvements. They are provided an opportunity to face internalized, early distortions regarding their parents. This is accomplished by helping the older parents describe in their children's presence much that may have been unknown or unclear about the circumstances of the suffering which is handed down in various ways, generation after generation. This seems to lead to an increased reciprocal understanding and mutual compassion between the generations, as compared to the hurt, unilateral blame syndrome which may have existed until the present.

In addition, the grandchildren who may have been carrying the brunt of the negative charge of the unsettled "accounts" of one or both parents may be freed of these roles; they are the most eager beneficiaries of such reconciliations between the generations. They are not only helped to be freed of the scapegoated or parentified roles, but it renews their hope for age-appropriate gratifications and provides them with a model for reconciling their conflicts with their parents now and in the future.

The hoped-for goal then is that in facing each one's accounts of loyalty and indebtedness to his family of origin, a more satisfactory balancing of committedness and loyalty can take place towards his mate and children. If these relationships can be more adequately or responsibly dealt with, then there is a greater possibility of an integration taking place, even with one's in-laws. Though there may be differences in ethnic or religious backgrounds, or of an economic or social nature, or merely differences in style of speaking and expressing feelings and actions, by working in a three-generation context, the differences may eventually be experienced as complementary rather than being used as pretexts for negative or hostile ways of relating to each other.

Whether one is an aging parent, an adult child, or a child, one struggles continuously with dependence and independence, burdens of loyalty or disloyalty. Family members continuously search for support and acceptance; whether and how it is given or received depends on how all family members can resolve the unsettled balances of their past and present relationships.

It is necessary to restate that the inclusion of grandparents in the therapy sessions also may have negative implications. While the parents express the wish for more openness and reciprocity between themselves and the grandparent, they may be unable to use the opportunity for such explorations. The despair or the need for revenge or retaliation may continue to be so strong and fixed that neither person affords the other any possibility of change in the relationship. As a matter of fact, there were even a few instances where the grandparent and parent slipped into a collusive alliance against the therapists. Prior to scapegoating the therapists, the son-in-law had been held responsible for all of his young wife's unhappiness. In these instances, it is not possible to work through the negative feelings which have been transferred upon the therapists, and the family withdraws from treatment.

There are other instances where the grandparent is brought into the session and despite months of careful, preliminary preparation regarding purpose and plan, the grandparent is "handed over" to the therapists. If the therapists were to accept the role of "explorer" with the grandparent, it would again lead the therapists into being scapegoated as the "attacker or exploiter" of the older person. The parent could also use this as justification for remaining in a passive position, implying "proof" that even the therapist cannot reach the grandparent.

Often as much may be accomplished through telephone conversations, letters, and the holiday visits of the parents to their parental home. These aspects must be included in the treatment approach regardless of whether the parents attend one or more therapy sessions. The process of change between parent and grandparent is as gradual, as difficult and full of resistances, as the marital or parent–child relationships.

It was previously mentioned that many older persons have gladly and willingly cooperated in and outside of the therapy sessions; we have also found the complete opposite to exist. Some grandparents have experienced the therapists and the therapy as rivals, competitors who threaten their roles and spheres of influence. Behind the scenes they disparage or criticize any gains or efforts that the nuclear family do begin to make. Messages are brought to the therapist: "We don't know what we are doing; we have crazy ideas." All efforts by the nuclear family to bring in the grandparents are rejected. Offers by the therapists to make home visits may even be turned down.

The therapists can become readily and unduly discouraged if they do not fully perceive this area of family relationships as one frought with "extreme touchiness." It requires great sensitivity to know when and how to introduce the idea, how to stay with it, and when to accept that the family cannot open these relationships for exploration. For some families it is emotionally impossible to bring the grandparent(s) to the sessions. It remains a fixed, untouchable area within the therapy process. The inability may be on the family's part—or upon the lack of skill and experience of the therapists. Whether it is one or the other, both areas are most essential ones to be further studied and explored.

10
Children and the Inner
World of the Family

CHILDHOOD IDEALIZED: BASIC TRUST AND LOYALTY

When adults are asked to recall the essence of their childhood, a glazed look may come into their eyes as they attempt to recapture a time of life which retrospectively may seem primarily pleasurable. They focus back to the hours of play and make-believe. Universally, play is defined as that aspect of childhood that is a time of fun and lack of responsibility. Adults were considered as resources for having basic needs fulfilled and met: Physically, the children were fed, housed, and sheltered; emotionally, they were comforted and protected. The adults were experienced and perceived as either active participants or observers of their children's play—laughter, running, jumping, and climbing —all the ingredients which characterize the picture of the carefree life of children.

While playing is primarily pleasurable, it also is the child's pathway to learning the meaning and value of close, intimate relationships and mastering his related life experiences. Basically he is discovering what his own needs are and how to obtain gratification; yet simultaneously he is also learning about the needs of family members to whom he is fundamentally or ontologically related. Ideally, what is being learned and developed in this earliest phase in the relationship between parents and children is a capacity for mutual trust and loyalty commitments based on the laws of reciprocity and fairness. This can evolve only when parents have also experienced trust in their earliest object relationships, which comes as a result of having their physical and emotional survival needs adequately gratified. Both the children and parents perceive and are perceived as valued, important, and loved objects within a family. Erikson defines basic trust as emanating from the mother's relationship to her baby, "in the unmistakable language of somatic interchange, that the baby may trust her, the world, and—himself." He continues, ". . . mistrust is accompanied by an experience of "total" rage with fantasies of the total domination or even destruction of the sources of pleasure and provision; and that such fantasies and rages live on in the individual and are revived in extreme states and situations."[35, p. 82]

During the first year of life, since the child is totally helpless and dependent, few demands or expectations are made on him. Generally he is permitted to nurse freely, to experience the pleasure of feeding and being fed, to eat or not eat, to smear or squeeze his food, to play with or reject what is offered. However, from the time a spoon is placed in his hand, the mother is beginning to convey her expectations that he will eventually learn to use the spoon as a tool for feeding himself. Under ideal circumstances, the child tries to please his parent and works toward self-sufficiency. The patient and understanding parents provide the circumstances, the stimulation, and approval which encourages him to learn and master this phase of his growth process. Too much pressure and impatience or excessively early expectations regarding his performance may slow or impede this process towards self-sufficiency.

Twentieth century American parents have been flooded and bombarded through the media of radio, television, magazine articles, and professional persons—teachers, physicians, etc.—to strive to be parents who have ideal children. The idealized goal is spelled out clearly: A child should have a life space of his own, to grow and develop into an independent, self-sufficient, autonomous person. In some phases dependency needs may be ridiculed, minimized, or overtly denied. Psychic separations are socially expected and reinforced via school, work, and marriage.

This climate is an opposite extreme compared with the historical past. Then a child was considered of less import to his father and family than the cows or oxen that were owned. In Ancient Rome, the state gave the father the power to practice infanticide or sell his children into slavery. Children and sometimes women were considered as commodities to be used for the physical survival of the family and clan.

The idealized version of childhood and the ideal goals of childrearing have been taken seriously and striven towards by most American parents. These same kinds of idealized images are anticipated even in the marital relationship. While the values and constructive aspects of such idealism should not be minimized or ignored, they must be tempered with the facts of human frailty and vulnerability, particularly as it is experienced in family life. Otherwise, marital partners, parents, and children may be flooded with a sense of failure as they become aware of not living up to the family or society's expectations. What is ideal and wishful must be integrated with what is a possible reality.

This chapter describes how some children and adults relate to one another and deal with emotional separations in *the inner world of their family life*. By studying in vivo all the relationships within families, family therapists have had an opportunity to learn about new and different dimensions which the study of an individual isolated from his family cannot reveal. Some readers, whether lay or professional persons, may respond by saying, "they are sick families, sick adults, sick children." Family therapists may be seeing only those segments of the population who are more troubled, having multiple symptoms, are less able to cope with their family relationships, and having difficulty with school and legal authorities. However, the authors' viewpoint is that we are dealing with universals in families. All close relationships contain conflicts which entail struggles for closeness and distancing, for likeness and for differentiation, for being bound and for being separate, for dependence and individuation. As Stierlin states it, "the ability to maintain and to re-establish a sense of separateness or distance against the diametrically opposed inner forces that drive us toward fusion."[83, p. 358]

There are families which may appear organized and functioning well, yet upon close examination may not be encouraging or tolerating closeness and intimacy. Other families are clearly symbiotic, chaotic, disorganized, or fragmented. It is of utmost importance that the degree of tension and conflict in all the relationships be studied in trying to diagnose how incapacitated the members may be within the family. Many families may function adequately despite disturbances and conflicts. There are periods when there is less struggle and turmoil. They may never need or seek help outside their nuclear and extended family relations. For others, however, because of their children's problems, school or legal authorities must confront the family regarding malfunctioning of one member and then refer them for professional help.

The purpose of this chapter is to encourage the reader to study family relationships from a different and more comprehensive vantage point. It is essential to examine and compare ideals as well as overt and implicit myths that each family creates regarding expectations of loyalty of its family members, and also to become aware how some of these factors are incorporated in our social institutions. Family therapists are also aware of the healthy, constructive, life-giving resources which exist to some degree in the reciprocal exchanges within the families which they have studied. These factors are used to enable family members to grow and to find creative gratification within the family and in the world outside. It is the regressive, fixated, exploitative, escapist, and guilt-producing aspects of family relationships which family therapists are called on to help with—to unlock, unscramble, break down those walls between family members which create feelings of being lonely and full of despair.

Most families come to treatment with a troubled or symptomatic child who is blamed for being lazy, inconsiderate, bad, or mad. The family's complaints are made on a conscious, rational level. However, our experience with troubled families has revealed that the child's conflicts are directly connected with the interlocked, collusively unconscious, or denied processes which disrupt and interfere with growth of all the family members. It appears as if, in order to survive emotionally, both parents and children, husbands and wives, do exploit each other and are exploited in their efforts to have unmet dependency needs fulfilled. There is a conscious and unconscious compliance to avoid exposure of the basis of unmet reciprocity between all family members, caught in emotional webs that may even produce a kind of psychic strangulation or appear in the form of suicidal behavior. Even those adult members who have geographically removed themselves or believe they are emotionally separated have been found to be emotionally loyal, interlocked, troubled, and nonindividuated to a greater extent than they believe themselves to be. Despite their most conscientious intentions to have a family life different from their family of origin, they find it may not be as they had wished. One 23-year-old married sister who came to help her truanting, drug-taking 15-year-old brother said, "I could just as well be back living in my parents' home. My husband is an alcoholic like my father and we fight all the time. I nag and scream at my children, just as my mother did with me and my siblings." Thus in remaining unconsciously loyal to her family of origin she cannot comfortably commit herself to her present family.

Stories about children from past history fill us with horror and dismay when one recalls that children were bought and sold like cattle; that children who were considered bewitched and bedeviled were placed in chains and put into prisons with adult beggars, thieves, and murderers; that children were also burnt at the stake. Such physical abuses and practices are no longer permitted or condoned. Our statutes are filled with laws stating clearly what is no longer acceptable and is punishable legally as well as morally. Industry is no longer allowed to exploit forced child labor. There are voluntary and governmental agencies who are enpowered to step into family situations to "rescue" abused children.

Family therapists do not see many neglected or physically abused children unless the court or private agency makes such referrals. Physicians have become acutely aware, active participants in stepping into situations which have been labeled the "battered child syndrome." The main social practice has been to separate such children from their families and place them in institutions or foster homes.

Our families come on a more voluntarily referred basis, having accepted the school counsellor's or physician's recommendation that their children do need psychological help. The clinical material in this chapter illustrates situations where the "abuses" are translated and transacted in a psychological form within families. The endless varieties can be only briefly described. The purpose in presenting these clinical abstracts is to show that children as well as the adults are caught in a pathogenic family process of loyalty and are compliant participants in mutually destructive interactions. Each family member, regardless of generational or sexual differences, does suffer, despite the fact that all families are overtly dedicated to a better life for all.

A FAMILY SYSTEMS POINT OF VIEW

Family therapists are groping for a vocabulary to define what they see and understand. Many family areas need to be translated into a teachable body of knowledge. They have found that a broader and deeper understanding comes from reversing the traditional order of study—investigating the histories of families of origin as well as those of the nuclear family system, and observing how they have accomodated to or interfered with the functioning of family members with regard to generational and sexual differences. To repeat Boszormenyi-Nagy's[15] notions, what is being explored within the family system in connection with emotional growth are those aspects of a postponed mourning process which a family member may have denied in order not to reexperience painful feelings attached to past lost-objects; moreover, such systems also are attempting to impede experiencing emotional loss and separation within the current family.

The focus is on multipersonal structures of expectation, motivation, feeling, and thought. The nuclear family system consists of two major subsystems whose functioning must be studied, namely the marital and parental system. It has been found that symptoms in one subsystem may be reactions to or caused by unresolved conflicts in the other subsystem. However, the study of one individual, one dyad, or triad does not reveal how the needs of the remaining family members are being met. All the relationships in a family must be examined to ascertain the nature of the involvement and the effects this has on each member. Emotional overinvolvement reveals symbioticlike relationships. At the other extreme, total physical neglect leads to nonsurvival. The studies of Spitz[82] showed early emotional noninvolvement can produce irreparable damage; such children showed a seriously decreased resistance to diseases and an appalling mortality.

The historical material regarding the family of origin and the current nuclear family will reveal the overt quality of the marital and parental relationships. Of more fundamental import is studying the covert implications. What were the role assignments in the family of origin? How are one or both parents unconsciously carrying out this assignment in their current family situation? Have they remained unconsciously loyal and bound to unsettled balances of indebtedness within their family of origin, yet living out the guilt feelings by projecting them onto their children? A marriage and a new family mean additional commitments and demand a shift from the family of origin. Has the "indebtedness" been paid, or are young parents still carrying feelings of guilt about psychologically and physically separating from their parents? How do they attempt to meet their aging parent's needs, while simultaneously attempting to adapt to the emerging needs of family members within the current family?

As stated earlier, children need a life space of their own, to play and to learn, to be permitted to be a child. In pathogenic family systems, by contrast, children are used as objects upon whom many conscious and unconscious feelings and attitudes are projected by their parents. Thus, children are perceived as sources of life-giving strength; as objects of loyalty or disloyalty. They may be caught in a power struggle between the parents or even between the parents and their family of origin. Children may be perceived as stimulators of conflicts, to be blamed. They may be experienced as sources of dependence who are rejectors as the parents may have felt rejected. Yet, children remain eternally loyal. They may appear exploited by their parents, but on some level children—out of loyalty—unconsciously comply with the parent's need to exploit them.

Although family therapists emphasize the family system's effect on the children, they are not unaware of individual motivation and phase development. As Waelder defined his principle of multiple function, for the individual, "psychic phenomena as a rule have many determinants. . . . Behavior served several functions, or, as one might also say, that it was at once responsive to many pressures or was a solution at once for many tasks. . . . Reality-directed behavior can be expected to serve instinctual demands too. . . . [Behavior is] not the result of one all-pervasive motive but as the outcome of many, usually conflicting forces."[86, p. 56-57]

As an illustration, one young girl after the onset of her menses became unable to attend school. Her school phobia was certainly motivated by individual as well as familial factors. On an individual basis, there was her fear of growing up and controlling her sexual strivings, competing socially with other girls in the boy–girl situation, reworking Oedipal feelings, etc. Her academic performance was not yet affected. However, on a multiperson system level, this school-phobic daughter was also responding to her parents' fears about sexuality and child rearing. The mother had suffered a postpartum depression after the birth of the daughter. The couple then decided that they would never have any more children. The three of them were locked in a position where no one could make a move without the other; the mother eventually did volunteer work at her daughter's school as one way of getting her to attend school. The father's business was attached to the family home, so that the three of them were continuously together through the days and evenings. The concern about their daughter also helped to mask their extreme loyalty and dependence on the wife's family of origin. The daughter in attempting to control her own impulses was also unconsciously placed in a position to control her parents' behavior. It was the daughter who each night would decide whether the family pet would be sleeping in her parents' bedroom or with her.

SYMPTOMATOLOGY IN CHILDREN AND PARENTS

Symptoms in a child are traditionally viewed as manifestations arising from internal conflicts regarding mastery of age-phase developmental tasks and ambivalent feelings toward internalized or reality objects. The family therapist's view is that difficulties are codetermined and that symptoms appear as a result of conflicts in interpersonal relationships. There is a conscious and unconscious interlocking between systems—individual, marital, parental, and the extended family.

Families that do not have very stable structures may experience changes connected with growth as similar to psychic loss of an important object. They feel so overwhelmed that they are unable to digest, adapt, and reintegrate themselves even to a previous level of functioning. If the underlying family structure has been shaky, then the impact of a new loss or change is likely to produce chaos and more disorganization. Even a family with a more stable structure, with higher levels of differentiation, may be overwhelmed when faced with cumulative demands of biological and emotional maturation.

A first conjoint family session with the F family reveals manifest symptomatology in all family members. They are an illustration of a very labile family system, who are chronically unable to cope with changes occurring within or outside the family. Even when extended family members were available for emotional support, they functioned minimally. Previously they had not been in such a disorganized or chaotic state as they appeared at this time. When the extended kin were no longer available, they then attempted to manage by using the children as substitute parents. The children were parentified and scapegoated simultaneously as a way of dealing with all their intrapsychic and interpersonal conflicts. The reality stresses of physical illnesses and the death of a parent must also be viewed in the context of the entire family system's difficulties.

The crucial breakdown was stimulated by their adolescent daughter's attempts to "run away" from her family, to escape her role of parentification. Even though she ran away from home, she made sure that she did not get too far removed: she became impregnated. This not only brought her back to the family fold, but added more disaster and despair to the family. All family members were caught in a loyalty bind to each other and with their families of origin. The guilt-producing mechanisms were pervasive as they had been passed on from generation to generation, so that all of them were reduced to a state of chronic despair.

When Mrs. F was in her eighth month of pregnancy, her father who had been suffering from cancer died. Several months after the birth of this first child, a daughter, she had her first severe depression. She received out-patient shock therapy. Subsequently, she developed a cancer phobia, continuously developing new physical symptoms for which doctors found no organic evidence. Within the next few years, Mr. F began to drink excessively and subsequently lost his business. At that time, he complained of pains in his chest and saw a cardiologist who suggested that he see a psychiatrist. Again, there was no organic basis for his symptoms.

The family decided to move to another city where a sister of Mrs. F's was living. Mr. F found a job there. This move not only was a geographic change for the family, but it was a cutting of a more fundamental tie for Mrs. F; she had spoken on the phone to her mother at least three times a day if they did not visit each other in person. Mr. F's new job entailed working many evenings and part of Sunday, so that Mrs. F and the children were alone a great deal. The children and the parents described it as follows: "Our mother used to lie on the sofa, complain about her endless ailments, filled with fears that death was imminent; in the evening she regained her energy, ran out night after night, to play cards." Mrs. F said that this was the only time she had a few hours when she was free from fears and feelings of depression.

When her sister or mother was not available to help Mrs. F, the children would have to fend for themselves as well as take care of their mother. Anne, now 15 and the designated patient, described how frightened she used to be when she watched and listened to her mother's complaints. "From as far back as she could remember." It was assumed that she should care for her mother and her two younger brothers and be responsible for household chores. When Mrs. F. had to have breast surgery, her sister did help all of them; but since she also had young children, she could not fill in as their mother had. Besides, Mrs. F said the relationship with her sister was a stormy one. They would explode and weeks of silence would ensue between them.

When Anne was 13, she was minding her brother David, age 7. He ran into the street and was struck by an automobile, but fortunately was only bruised. The family did not openly blame Anne. However, shortly thereafter, Anne became a chronic runaway. When she became pregnant she was aborted as a result of medical and psychiatric recommendations.

Mrs. F said that her husband was a steady worker but was "happy-go-lucky like a child." He put his wife first, took her from doctor to doctor and worried about her health, but left all responsibility and management of the home and children on her shoulders. The parents mutually complained about the children's lack of respect for them and that Anne had changed from being a good compliant child, to a fresh, impudent, irresponsible adolescent. The children said they used to be terrified about their family situation; now they either no longer listened to or laughed off their parent's complaints and demands. In one session, Anne and Louis seemed to pay little attention when their parents talked; they whispered to each other, giggled, were openly flirtatious and seductive with each other as they snuggled close or touched each other. David was made to sit next to his mother. Mrs. F said they tormented him: "They call him faggot, peg-legged, skinny; telling him he is dumb, that he can't get along with any children his own age."

Anne's running away and pregnancy was the most recent stress with which this family had to cope. Anne's behavior could be viewed as adolescent rebelliousness and sexual experimentation, but seen in the context of her family and their multiple crises, had a broader and deeper basis. This family had had major stresses in a span of about eight years: death of a parent caused by cancer; loss of employment; uprooting of family ties and support in moving to a new city; mental illness; breast surgery. The basic structure of this family was not very stable; faced with multiple stresses, it is understandable that they became more confused and disorganized. To have viewed this only as intrapsychic problems of an adolescent girl rather than including the multigenerational interlocking would be overlooking very fundamental elements.

ASSIGNMENTS OF ROLES TO CHILDREN

In pathogenic families, one or both adults and all the children are assigned and assume inappropriate generational and sexual roles and stereotyped characteristics. Instead of being experienced as distinct entities, with the full human range of feelings and attitudes, they are responded to as if they were part persons, having only singular characteristics. Brodey states that "the constellation of roles allows internal conflicts of each member to be acted out within the family rather than within the self, and each family member attempts to deal with his own conflicts by changing the other."[23, p. 392]

The children who overtly appear good, quiet, and conforming—the "well siblings"—are generally assigned the role of parentification. Such role assignments are shifted very readily. However, it is more often the "bad" or negative characteristics which are emphasized. Unconsciously, children are expected to be adult, with the adults acting childlike, particularly in the sense of abdicating essential, executive functions (as well as sexual ones). Parents who are unable psychologically to be parents may try to justify their inabilities under the guise of permissiveness, of being democratic and nonauthoritative. Parentification of children may ensue as a result of parental inactivity, inertia, or chaotic behavior—which amount to emotional abdication by the parents. The feelings which permeate the relationships in these families are depression, despair, rage, or sadness—feelings which may or may not be consciously experienced or expressed.

In situations where children are assigned the role of scapegoat, as seen in various kinds of delinquent behavior, it is the schools, social agencies, and medical and legal authorities upon whom the children must rely to help contain their self-destructive behavior; they cannot rely on their parents for such controls. In addition, the child's efforts may also be viewed as indirectly attempting to bring help to his chaotic family life. Such behavior needs to be understood as inverse loyalty to one's family. These social institutions are used as parental substitutes, in many instances for the parents as well as for the children.

Many of these children may appear "detached," both physically and emotionally, but experience with them, in the full context of their family life, reveals that they remain covertly loyal to their families. Even though their behavior may have negative repercussions, it is their way of trying to relieve the suffering of their parents, as well as their own. In this context, delinquency—with all of its negative components —may be an unconscious effort to bring some life back into the family. On an individual level, chastisement, criticism, or even severe punishment are preferred to the noninvolvement or nonresponsiveness they have experienced within their families.

These acts are in marked contrast to more balanced parent–child relationships. Even when a child is labeled good or naughty, or a mischievious one, the reference is to one aspect of his behavior. He still remains free to be a child, pursuing childish interests and activities. Emotionally, he is slowly learning to identify with parents of the same or opposite sex. Emotional responsibility for himself and for others slowly evolves as he masters age-appropriate tasks. Even while helping to take care of household chores and siblings, it is done under the supervision of the adults who carry full responsibility. It is a preparation for his future life role. In a balanced relationship, the child's autonomous growth process is stimulated and encouraged; for the parentified child, who too early is overburdened with adultlike attitudes, growth is interfered with and disrupted.

PARENTIFIED CHILDREN: THE FAMILY WORRIER

A daughter cannot attend school since she accepts overburdening emotional responsibility, as well as the physical care of her siblings. This is in response both to her mother's underlying depression and to the emotionally unavailable father, who unconsciously sanctions his wife's need to be cared for by the daughter. Studied in an individual context, this would be labeled as a school phobia. In another instance, a mother's continuous hypochondriacal complaints keeps the children in a constant state of anxiety. Their hyperactivity and tenseness is a reaction to her complaints of pains and illness and fears about dying. Each child may respond somewhat differently, depending on their age and position in the family; eventually such a mother manages to insure that at least one if not all of the children will never leave her alone. Children are unceasingly loyal and will assign themselves as physical and psychological guardians to one or both parents if they sense insatiable, unmet needs for comforting. These are the parentified children.

THE AGGRESSIVE OR SCAPEGOATED CHILDREN

One or more children in a family are described as though they are uncontrollable aggressors who cannot be managed by their parents.

These children are often scapegoated into this "bad" role assignment. Often they come into conflict first with the school authorities, and then the law. Their behavior within the family may or may not cause overt difficulties. In some instances their reactions to family tensions are acted out away from the family. Although cultural factors may influence the form of the expressed behavior, the essential causes are found in the underlying conflicts and tensions within the family system. Erikson[35] refers to this type of behavior as a negative identity which is preferable to that of being ignored, detached, and a nonobject in a family. From our point of view, desperately aggressive behavior by a child is absolute indication for family exploration.

CHILDREN AS SEXUALIZED PARTNERS

Another form of the "bad" child role is enacted by children through delinquent sexual behavior within or outside the family. Seductive, incestuouslike relationships or overt incest is frequently found in severely disturbed families. Children of the same or opposite sex are used as a substitute for a marital partner. In many instances, sexual relations between the marital pair occur infrequently or have been discontinued altogether. This develops as a result of the mutually experienced hurt, anger, and disappointment by the marital partners. The "other" had originally been selected as the idealized person who might make up for the emotional deprivation to which they felt they had been subjected; often, as a result of disappointment in this need, sexual disinterest may become mutual. If one partner does continue to have sexual interest but is continuously rejected by the marital partner, gratification may even be sought with one's child.

When incest occurs in a family, it indicates the lack of generational and ego boundaries in all members. Usually there is collusion by the nonparticipating adult as well as the siblings—such secrets are usually not secrets. This collusion may be conscious or only partially outside awareness. The act of incest does not necessarily bring a family for help; often it has been occurring for a number of years. It seems rather that in many cases legal or psychiatric treatment is sought when pregnancy is a possibility or danger appears either in the form of homicidal or suicidal threats. Ego boundaries are diminished, controls within the family system have weakened, and the question of physical as well as emotional survival now plays a paramount part.

The relationship reveals the adult's desperation, since psychologically he is being murderously destructive with his child. Aggression in this form is a psychological murder of the self, as well as of the child. In such instances a child is not perceived as a child but as an object, to be used and exploited for dependent and retaliatory motivations, and for narcissistic self-gratification. Revenge against the rejecting or indifferent marital partner as a motive is secondary when a parent has an overt adult-type sexual relationship with a child.

Why does a child cooperate and become a partner in such an incongruous relationship? Fear of punishment does not sufficiently explain a child's cooperativeness; neither does the element of pleasure that body contact can produce. The authors hold the opinion that a child accepts such a role because of the unconscious, collusive loyalty expectation that to act otherwise might result in psychological loss or nonsurvival of one or both parents. It may be the child's supreme effort to help create some boundary for a parent which in turn would hold the family together. Again, the loyalty issue is revealed as a profoundly essential ingredient to explain such relationships.

In some families, the acts of incest not only span several years with one child, but in some situations includes other siblings. With his or her own growth and maturation, the child may become more resistant. Other complications may develop where there are overt or covert homosexual-incestuous relations or where intense rivalry or jealousy develops, followed by the threats of murder.

In one family, it was the law that gave the option of family treatment or incarceration. The father had been sexually involved with his daughter and two sons over a period of several years. The wife stated during the initial session that, while she really did not want her husband to go to jail, she could not accept that the children should lose school time. She also was sure that the children, ages 6, 8, and 11, had already forgotten the sexual experiences with their father. Under the guise of being affectionate, or assuming that children are not aware or capable of understanding, parents proceed to use their children as direct or indirect sexual objects.

THE FAMILY'S "PET" CHILD

Another category of family role assignment is one in which families describe the child as perfect or ideal. This varies significantly from the parentified child. The function of the parentified and loyal child may be that of family mediator or "healer" as defined by Ackerman, [1, p. 80] or to be the martyred "burden-bearer" as referred to by Brody and Spark.[24] The pet is described by the families as the carefree or nonsymptomatic child. They cause no overt troubles. They may act clownlike, do silly, annoying things, or tease, but it never is done with serious intent to hurt or make anyone angry. They are rarely taken seriously. It is as if these children exist to bring the family lightness and laughter. They may also be depicted as good students. This child's goodness and nondemandingness is frequently used as a model against the siblings who express their hostile feelings. But close to the surface the child's affect is one of sadness and depression.

The child that has been least studied is the family pet. He is rarely brought for treatment. In reality there is no real position for him in the family; usually he is the baby or the youngest of many siblings. For the family he is in a sense a nonperson, and his sense of worth or importance is very minimal. The needs and inner feelings are negated, denied, minimized, and disconfirmed. The virtues or assets which the family ascribe to the family pet may have a basis in reality: He is often affectionate or cute or funny despite the fact that this is a facade which may hide his own feelings of emptiness. An animal pet, while affording companionship or protection to its owners, has one major family function: to constantly and loyally reflect back affection and acceptance to its masters. Studying a pet child in the context of his family reveals that the emotional needs of these children are overlooked; their underlying self-esteem is poor, and they constantly yearn for a place within the family. Their social-life capacity may be minimal. The pet child may later move into the role of parentified child as an older sibling leaves the home.

CASE ILLUSTRATION OF THE BAD, SEXUAL OBJECT; THE SCAPEGOAT; THE FAMILY PET

The J family came to therapy because of their concern over Joan, age 16, an artistically talented girl who was acting out sexually, sniffing glue, and failing in school. The mother had read letters in her daughter's bedroom which confirmed her fears that Joan was getting into serious difficulties. Since this was a family that felt they had been able to give their children much time, energy, and material advantages, they could not understand why Joan was "bad."

They complained about Joseph, age 19, because he was such a complete bookworm in college. He had no friends, no outside interests, participated in no sports. Something was wrong, but they had never considered that Joseph was deeply unhappy and worried, and very tied to his parents' "apron strings." He was the object of scorn and belittlement by his parents and siblings. That he was so isolated, detached, and schizoid was not perceived as a signal to this family that Joseph needed as much help as Joan.

The family pet, the "darling" of the family was Susan, age 10. No one had any complaints about her. They unanimously agreed that all the family conflicts had left her untouched. If the therapists asked Susan to speak directly to an issue which had been raised, one family member "automatically" answered for her. The answer always was that Susan didn't know, it didn't bother her, she couldn't care less, etc. When the therapists asked why she was not permitted to answer for herself, Susan would begin to weep for the remainder of the session, without a word coming from her. In response to her tears, family members would try to humor her out of them; Mrs. J said, "it is ridiculous, Susan had no reason to cry." It was as if they unconsciously silenced her because they could not bear to hear that she too might also have worries and troubles. Thus Susan remained loyal to her family by going along with disconfirmation of her total being. By treating Susan almost as a nonperson, her own wishes, fears, and needs as a 10-year-old girl were made to appear nonexistent.

ON THE INTERLOCKING BETWEEN A CHILD AND FAMILY SYSTEM

Some family therapists such as Bowen have stated that those children who are left out of symbiotic dyads and triads may be able to leave the family arena of conflict with less emotional impairment than the symptomatic child. Such deductions came from studying families who had a schizophrenic adolescent. The siblings were described as somewhat detached or isolated, but their functioning was on a superior level than the disturbed, designated schizophrenic member.[20]

As family therapists began to treat families with preadolescent and younger children, additional significant data were obtained. While the designated patient brought them into the treatment situation, Friedman found that the "well" siblings were also symptomatic or only temporarily symptom-free.[45] Other members might become acutely symptomatic soon after the designated phobic child returned to school. It was as if one family member had to automatically fill the vacuum that had been created when the "bad or sick" child showed improvement.

Each of the children are assigned roles that seem to have definite functions in the family: Third, fourth, and fifth siblings move in and out of the bad or sick role, or two daughters may share the parentified role. In the pathogenic family system, each family member is not experienced as a whole, distinct entity, having his own needs which are age- and sex-approrpiate. Children are treated as bad, worthless, perpetual infants or "as-if-adults." The family pendulum swings from one extreme to another. Overinvolvement, excess infantilizing, excessive expectations, too extreme detachment, etc., are all labels which at some point can characterize the functioning of pathogenic family systems.

CHILDREN AS FAMILY REFEREES OR JUDGES

The A family was referred by the school counselor because both children, John, age 14, and Helen, age 12, were disrespectful and acting defiantly towards teachers, the counselor, and school principal. Also, they were doing poorly academically.

From the first session, the parents were constantly bickering with each other. They used various means to depreciate and humiliate each other: name calling, laughing and interrupting, and making snide comments to the therapists. Mr. A felt that his wife was too lenient and tended to baby both of the children. Mrs. A's response was to laugh at her husband, to say he was too hard and unfair— that he didn't know what he was talking about. Mr. A was asked whether this represented what went on in the home. He said this was mild compared with when they both let go of their tempers. Mrs. A was the one who becomes physically abusive. Several years before this referral, Mrs. A had attempted suicide because she felt, "it was all so confused and hopeless."

The therapists made efforts to discontinue the round-robin bickering and try to help them focus on parental and marital issues. They tried to comply with the suggestion that they discuss money or the wife's poor housekeeping efforts, but it was impossible for them to do. Within seconds, one parent would turn to one or both children and ask, "am I right or wrong?" "Am I telling the truth?" "Did he or didn't he say that I am a liar?" The children took turns refereeing the fight, or took sides, or appealed to both parents to stop talking. They constantly changed their seats, sitting with one parent, moving to the other parent's side or moving completely out of the circle towards the back of the room. One way the children could stop the parents was to start bickering between themselves, using their parents' words and manners. The parents were surprised when the therapists commented that, "since the parents in this family do not seem to have consideration for each other or know what respect means, how would the children be able to show it to school personnel?"

LACK OF SEXUAL IDENTITY: SEDUCTION OF CHILDREN

The G family was referred because Ted, age 8, was displaying impulsive behavior in school, was unable to concentrate, and was failing academically. His behavior with his peers was like that of a 4-year-old, having temper tantrums and demanding his own way. His sister, Lillian, age 13, was obese, unkempt, and had no friends.

The parents were asked about Ted's problem in falling asleep; they had mentioned that they took turns lying down with him and often sleeping with him through the night. Mr. G said they no longer were taking turns and he felt Ted was doing better; Mrs. G said the situation was getting worse; both children confirmed that there had been no change in managing Ted's bedtime demands. Lillian stated that she could not see how anything was going to change because neither parent could insist Ted stay in his own bed. If they would not come in his, Ted would go into his parents' bed.

Spontaneously, Lillian added that she no longer allowed Ted to come into her bed or get physically close to her. When asked why, she responded, "you know, like in Playboy magazine." Fearful that she may have revealed too much she said, "maybe it's just natural curiosity." Ted was asked for a reaction to his sister's comments: "It is just that I have scary thoughts."

Each parent said, after all, Ted is still just a baby. The therapists picked up the reference to the magazine filled with pictures of nude females. Again Lillian answered directly to the therapists, "my brother and I used to wrestle on the bed, but I know we are too big for that anymore." She knew he was not a 2- or 3-year-old baby anymore.

Mrs. G guessed that Ted had seemed overly curious, so recently she began to lock the bathroom door; lately she wore pajamas instead of a nightgown when she lay down with him. Mr. G turned on his wife and said loudly, "see I told you he is growing up!" When asked about his participation in this nightly ritual, he could see no problem in his lying with his son.

At this point, the husband and wife began to bicker with each other, both arguing that Ted is just a baby and that Lillian's ideas about sex are ridiculous. In seconds this was diverted to the fact that neither parent could accept the opinion of the other. There was mutual blaming of the other, while insisting that each one was helpless in the situation. They could not face the fact that the children had directly and openly revealed the incestuous seduction that each one had participated in.

Mr. G said he guessed there could be something sexual in all of this, but he couldn't remember how he felt when he was the age of his children. "His parents told him nothing about the birds and the bees; yet he had siblings of both sexes." Mrs. G said her husband was even more embarrassed than she to talk about this subject. Lillian again in a loyal way tries to protect her parents, "it must all just be natural curiosity." When she was asked about her own curiosity, she said she went out and bought a book which answered all her questions about sex.

Ted was asked again about getting into his parents' bed and sleeping between them or about his parents taking turns sleeping with him; He responded, "no one ever asked me how I felt about it." Mr. G interrupted Ted and said, "maybe there have been some of those kind of feelings between me and my son." This time Mrs. G became protective and insisted, "it is all maternal." Lillian turned to the therapists and said that sometimes she had been aware that her brother got her "excited." At this point, Ted said he had to go to the bathroom and ran from the session.

The therapists said that it did look like sexual feelings were expressed either between the siblings or parents and child. Mr. G said, "maybe it is because there is nothing between my wife and me." The children had heard the quarreling and bickering in and out of the bedroom, had heard the endless threats about separation and divorce. They had heard Mr. G plead with his wife that she go to bed early, but she stayed up doing the laundry and ironing.

In this session, incestuous feelings were not relegated to fantasy. There was open stimulation and seduction taking place. Lillian was able to use the therapists for confirmation in her adolescent struggle for sexual identity. The parents were so involved with themselves that she had to use a book, or turn to the therapists to help her with the incest taboo. Talking directly with this family might have given the children reassurances so that fears need not be expressed in nightmares, insomnia, firesetting, and enuresis. Ted was encouraged to no longer participate in the nightly ritual. At this phase, the parents could not be used as superego-like controls, since the parents' concepts of privacy and sexuality were distorted and ineffectual.

In a later session, Lillian struggled with her father over the fact that his touching her in a certain way did disturb her: Both parents' angry and discomforting responses to Lillian's comments confirmed that they were aware of sexual implications.

DEPRESSION IN CHILDREN AND PARENTS

Depression is defined as aggression turned against the self. In individual terms it occurs as a reaction to the loss of an emotionally significant object, or of a personal ability or attribute. The individual reacts as if it were a loss from his own self-image as compared with a loss of the object. Depression in infants, namely anaclitic depression, has been described by Spitz.[81] It manifests itself as weepiness, apprehension, withdrawal, refusal to eat, sleep disturbances, and eventually stupor. The term "anaclitic" refers to the "leaning-on" quality of the infant's relationship to the mother, as the person who nourished and cared emotionally for him. The causal factor is the loss of the mothering person without provision of a suitable substitute.

Depression in young children is rarely recognized as a separate clinical entity; the child may look sad, be clingy, and whiney, but pediatricians and families do not categorize these children as being depressed. In disturbed families, the underlying affect between all family members may be depression. Other symptoms may mask the underlying depression, e.g., school phobia and learning disabilities. Depression may be denied by one or both adults, but the children experience such feelings for they carry the burdens and worries of their parents.

The F family illustrates underlying depression, although the manifest symptom that brought the family to treatment was Janet's school phobia. Janet, an only child, age 15, had not been able to remain in school during the past year for more than a day at a time. It had started the previous spring as she was graduating from junior high school. This was also the time of the onset of her menses.

After Janet's birth, her mother had a postpartum depression during which she was given shock treatment and was hospitalized for several months. The parents had mutually agreed not to have any more children because they felt it was a risk to Mrs. F's health. The nuclear and extended family were in constant and daily contact; the business was in the home. Mr. F felt that he was looked up to by his in-laws and was constantly consulted in family matters as if he were a son. "I was adopted by them."

Although the grandparents felt Mr. and Mrs. F were too indulgent with Janet, there had never been open conflict about any family member. Janet was constantly making insatiable demands for more extravagant indulgences and was watched over and infantilized in other areas. She had been described as a moody, obstinate child who had difficulties with her peers since elementary school, but was an excellent student academically. The major socializing forces for this family were constant visits back and forth in the homes of relatives.

In the session, as Janet wept, she screamed that she should never have been born! She described feelings of deep inadequacy and lack of self-worth and confidence. The parents were bewildered by these statements—all three wept openly. Mrs. F said that at times she had felt this way about herself—but Janet's comments were inexplicable. They loved and adored her, and rarely refused her demands; she was so pretty, so smart!

Janet in reality was in charge of her parents, pulling, pushing, and manipulating, and constantly testing them as adults. This combined with the fears that all three had about her growing up, sexuality, parenthood—and separation. Mr. and Mrs. F were emotionally as much a part of their families of origin as they had been in the past; the only difference was a geographic one: they all did not live in the same house together. Because Mr. F felt adopted by his in-laws, he was completely accepting and supportive of the overinvolvement that continued on a daily basis. For them the overcloseness might be termed ego-syntonic, since the entire family was in complete agreement that this is how family life should be. No one was ever in a position to make an autonomous decision or act independently.

Janet had previously been in individual therapy, but refused to continue: She had barely been able to leave home to attend school. Her rebellious and demanding behavior could be construed as typical adolescent efforts to emancipate herself from her family. However, refusing to go to school, in the context of the relationship of this family, revealed that behind Janet's symptoms were the family's feelings and problems in separation. Specifically, the mother's memories about her postpartum depression were activated at the time Janet began to menstruate; the father's feelings of helplessness and inadequacy were also revealed as they recalled the period around Janet's birth.

For a period of time, all three were severely depressed. Janet would withdraw into her room, cry, refuse to eat, and rejected their efforts to comfort her. It was not until the parents moved in two major areas that a decided shift took place in this family: One was that her mother forced Janet to go to school even though it meant the mother was a volunteer worker in the school system for several months. This not only helped Janet, but Mrs. F became much more outgoing and friendly with her coworkers. The second major area centered on the family talking more freely with Janet about dating and boy–girl relationships. This led the family to talking about marriage and pregnancy. In Janet's presence, the parents reviewed the circumstances of her birth and shed a different light on the subject.

Janet had always felt that somehow her birth was resented or that she had in some way seriously interfered in her parents' relationship. What was eventually clarified was that it was her mother's own fears about being a competent and responsible parent. The greatest change then evolved: Because of the problematic infancy, the parents were always trying to "make up" for something they felt Janet had not received. In reality, what Janet desperately needed from them was more trust so that she could be self-sufficient and self-reliant, and their permission for her to experiment more freely with her peers without having to report every detail. A final shift was symbolized when the parents could take a holiday with each other—away from Janet. In other words, Janet's emerging maturity coincided with the parents' working through further separation from Janet and their families of origin.

HOMICIDAL AND SUICIDAL THREATS TO PARENTS OR CHILDREN

Clinicians have studied the histories of individuals who have either attempted or succeeded in suicide or homicide. Homicide or suicide reveal the individual's extreme despair, loss of ego boundaries, lack of controls, and feelings of worthlessness, regarding the self and significant objects. While threats of suicide or homicide do not carry the finality that the act itself produces, they can create guilt feelings and an atmosphere of terror for all family members. Such threats imply a tremendous pathogenic double bind in such family situations: One must consider who is the potential murderer, who is the murderee, as well as what is "needing to be murdered" in this family. The threat of murder highlights a seriously unbalanced state of justice and obligations in family relationships. Needless to say, all lives are endangered physically and psychically when such threats or actions occur.

In the Mc Family, when Mrs. Mc found herself choking her oldest daughter, age 4½, she then ingested pills. Before becoming unconscious, she telephoned her mother who rushed over to the home. She was hospitalized because of the suicide attempt. When Mr. and Mrs. Mc were seen with their four children, ages 4½, 3½, 2, and 5 months, the children had vacant, stuporlike expressions on their faces; the observing staff compared them to soldiers who were still in a phase of shell-shock as they came off a battlefield. The children seemed to avoid contact with both parents, as if expecting little comfort from either one.

Mr. Mc reacted with denial regarding the seriousness of the entire situation, either as far as his wife or children were concerned. He stated that his wife was exaggerating her desperation: He was perfectly contented with their home life. The birth of the last son was a result of what Mr. Mc described as his wife's "excessive motherliness." However, shortly after this child's birth, Mr. Mc agreed to have a vasectomy. His comment about this was that he felt nothing but great relief about this procedure. Mrs. Mc overtly had also accepted her husband's decision.

As the family dynamics unfolded, it became evident that Mrs. Mc was in daily contact with her mother, and confided more with her about the marital and parental conflicts than with her husband. There had been endless discussions about separating, and Mrs. Mc said she knew her mother would welcome her back. In essence, while Mrs. Mc complained that her husband helped very little, emotionally he was excluded by his wife and mother-in-law.

They then revealed that both maternal and paternal parents had objected to this marriage—first, because of the mixed religions, and secondly, because they were too young. Both were the youngest in their families of origin. Their efforts in defying the paternal wishes were now resulting in failure.

However, of greater significance than their immaturity was the fact that each was steadily told and felt that they had been disloyal to their families of origin. They were unable to reconcile their individual and marital feelings with the fact that both sets of families were disappointed in them. Mr. Mc's mother told him, "he had made his bed, etc.; don't come complaining or crying to me about your wife!" It seemed that the marital failure was a need, albeit an unconscious one, to prove that their parents were right and they were wrong. In other words, they were remaining unconsciously loyal to their families of origin. This did not negate Mrs. Mc's depression and despair as an individual. However, studied in a family context, additional dimensions of loyalty to the family of origin are revealed.

THE ENEMY–ALLY SYNDROME

In the G family, Mr. G made homicidal threats toward his wife. In the sessions without the children, he denied his wife's accusations and insisted they were figments of her imagination. Each one of them would talk to only one of the therapists, as if pleading for belief that the other person was mean, vicious, belligerent, selfish, inconsiderate, and worthless. Neither would listen to the other marital partner or to comments by the cotherapist. This was a continuous attempt to split the team, to gain an ally in supporting the seriously disturbed behavior.

Description of their behavior in the home by one parent was chronically at variance with what the other said. Mr. G would refuse to look at, or talk to his wife, or he would pump the children for information about the bad things his wife had done to them while he was at work. Then he would become violently angry and would not listen to any attempts by his wife or even the children to clarify the distortions about her being a "neglectful mother." Mrs. G would become so upset and helpless that she could only cry, and then withdraw into silence. All their energy went into justifying their own behavior while simultaneously "blackening" the other.

At the therapists' insistence, the children were brought back into the sessions. They not only confronted their parents with the open talks about separation and asked what would happen to them—particularly since they were adopted —but, more urgently, there had been an episode when the father had thrown the mother to the ground and was choking her. When the oldest son, age 7, could not physically remove his father, it was he that threatened to go to the phone and call the police!

The inclusion of children in the sessions clearly reveals their awareness of the extent of their parents' own need for parental controls. Secondarily, it provides the children with an opportunity to abreact and express their fears regarding such traumatic experiences. If the children perceive the therapists as outside resources to trust and rely on, or as potential persons who can help "parent their needy parents," the children are reassured. But primarily, they no longer need to fill the role of family rescuers or mediators, a responsibility which should be carried by adults.

CHILDREN AS CAPTIVE OBJECTS

Some marital pairs form such a fused or symbiotic relationship, speaking and acting for each other, that they create an emotionally tight island as far as the children are concerned. The parental relationship appears "insulated" and the children's emotional demands and needs are experienced as an "intrusion." The children's physical needs may be met, but their feelings are minimized, ignored, and disconfirmed. They grow up in an atmosphere of confusion and frustration which does not permit any sense of their personal worth or identity. Through their loyalty children remain in a captive state—becoming more and more demanding of recognition. Parents may even describe these children as insatiable, while in reality the children are being starved emotionally. One sibling in such a family may give up the effort to make himself heard or seen, or he tries not to "rock his parent's boat" and channels his despair by being a "parentified child." Even these efforts by the child may be rejected or go unrecognized by the symbiotically fused parents. Another child continues to be aggressively demanding and a complainer, spending his efforts in trying to break up the "island fortress." In terms of psychic energy, he cannot be a dependent child and pursue his own life work, such as learning in school.

The H family was referred after Joan, age 13, had been briefly hospitalized when she had threatened to kill herself or her father with a knife. Previously, she had been in individual therapy. Mr. H had had his first psychotic episode during college and a second one during his wife's first pregnancy. Ellen, age 17, who had previously been an excellent student, had dropped out of her junior year for some months because she had suddenly become "boy crazy." Mrs. H said her reason for marrying Mr. H was that "she needed a cause and he was it." She saw herself as the constant mediator in the family.

In the initial phase of treatment the sessions would begin quietly, but within a half-hour, Joan would either be sitting on her father's lap—snuggling like a small baby or being openly seductive. Mr. H would in turn pat and stroke her, saying he had no idea whether she was being a small baby or a seductive female —but making no effort to remove her from his lap. Ellen said Joan was like a prostitute manipulating her father in order to get more allowance from him. At other times, if Joan were being complained about, she would stand in front of her father, calling him vulgar names, attempting to provoke him into a physically abusive response. She would even taunt him by saying she wished him dead. The conflict was so chaotic that Ellen often put her coat over her head, curled up on the seat, and went to sleep. The therapists consistently urged either parent to restore order since it often appeared as if all the people and furnishings would become a part of the chaotic behavior. Ellen at times became a part of the screaming, threatening disorder.

Mrs. H would sit in her chair, in a stony silence, making no effort to interrupt the hair pulling or fist fighting. However, on a nonverbal, seemingly nonparticipant level, Mrs. H vicariously participated in the excited frenzy. Even though the therapists continuously held her responsible, for a long time she did not hear us; she sat passively by, with a bland expression on her face, as if a helpless spectator watching crazy behavior in an arena.

The sessions illustrate not only interlocking, unconsciously punitive feelings—as revealed by the members' murderous and incestuouslike behavior—but are examples of weak or overlapping ego boundaries between family members. It seemed as if the behavior had to be repeatedly reenacted until these essential themes were exhausted by all family members. Questioning the meaning of the behavior or direct requests for more control by the family were of little avail in this initial phase.

The rape–murderouslike behavior was not modified until there was a direct shift in the marital relationship. This began only at the point when Mrs. H actively intervened between her husband and children while simultaneously beginning to express her inner feelings of rage and despair about herself. As Mrs. H said, she had to open her own Pandora's box, facing the fears and anger and role of mediator. This had to be connected directly with her husband's and daughter's overtly disturbed behavior. Her inner feelings of badness and worthlessness were also projected onto the other family members. Through her martyrlike attitudes and behavior she was able to initially deny, minimize, and negate her own feelings. The children, as well as Mr. H, were loyal but captive objects in this psychoticlike family system. Even as the girls willingly complied with the needs of the parents, their own needs as growing adolescents were unmet. They were experienced as demanding intruders in their parents' relationship.

CHILDREN AS SACRIFICIAL OBJECTS

Kempe not only helped bring child-abuse problems to the public's awareness but was instrumental in getting most of the states in America to pass laws to protect these children. He writes, "usually these children are very loyal. They come to accept the parent's image of themselves, believe they are bad, and deserve what they are getting. This attitude persists for a long time and surfaces later in life when these children become parents and batter their own children."[58, p. 53]

In families where parents have experienced early object deprivation or may have spent formative years in one foster home after another, or in institutions, there seems to be a need to parentify even a very young child:

In the instance of a 4-year-old girl who had been beaten and hospitalized, it was the maternal grandmother who had accepted the care of the child, even though the mother felt she had always been rejected. Mrs. K had been one of eight children. She felt that she had always made strenuous efforts to please everyone in the family, particularly her mother. Her oldest unmarried sister, Joan, had assumed the emotional and economic leadership in this family. Mrs. K described her mother as a person who had always kept her feelings to herself, taking a spartanlike pride in not getting involved in anything her husband or children said or did. Her father was pleasant but ineffectual. Joan was the one who assigned chores and tasks, set the rules and regulations for her siblings, and administered the punishments. Mrs. K felt that she managed to totally alienate her family when she married a man of a different background. Mr. K also felt that his family was rejecting of him and his marriage.

In the marriage, Mrs. K was overburdened with total care and responsibility for the home and five children. Despite holding two jobs, Mr. K was completely passive and dependent on his wife. Neither Mr. or Mrs. K were able to openly express their feelings towards each other, or to face how intensely hurt and isolated they were by their family's rejection of their marriage and children. All the anger and resentment was channeled onto their only daughter, age 4; the other children ages 5, 2, and 1, who were sons, they described as completely "good and compliant children." In reality, they were seriously cowed and submissively frightened little boys.

Each parent was caught in a negative loyalty bind by feeling not loved and trusted in his family of origin, and was unable to transfer sufficient trust and loyalty to the marital partner. Both felt at times that their families had never wanted them to be born, or that they had been treated as an unwanted burden whom the parents had wanted to extrude as quickly as possible. They had lived in a state of chronic rage, which they now channeled onto their demanding and dependent daughter: She was described as excessively provocative and rejecting toward her parents. It was as if they attempted to use this child as a sacrificial object—that is, if all badness were carried within this daughter, she was the one to be extruded. Then perhaps their families of origin would see the good in them and love them as they wished to be loved.

CONCLUSIONS

Adults who have not adequately worked through their emotional separation and guilt feelings may remain unconsciously overcommitted and loyal to their families of origin. Their children may then be used as substitute objects of gratification for the parent's unmet dependency, aggressive, or sexual needs. The parents may even attempt to pay off their indebtedness to their own parents by martyrlike, guilt-producing giving to their children. They overgive time and effort to their children and neglect their aging parents, so that they appear uninvolved or even irresponsible towards that generation.

When children are not permitted to be children, to pursue and gain mastery over their interests and work (school), then they feel overresponsible and attempt to carry parentlike functions. These are overburdening roles for children. If children are emotionally needed, then out of deep loyalty to their parents, they accept such inappropriate roles as the parentified child, the scapegoat, or the sexual partner.

The histories of these pathogenic family systems reveal that prior to children being used as substitute, parentlike objects the early marital relationship was frought with disappointment, anger, and despair. The marital partner was expected to be the long-sought, unconsciously idealized parental substitute. It is often after this relationship is frustrated that the children are turned to as a new resource. Underlying these efforts are the parents' attempts to ward off reexperiencing the psychic pain regarding past lost-objects—as well as to deter current emotional separations. Thus, to adequately understand the phenomena described in this chapter, it is necessary that they be viewed in a multigenerational context. The blurring of generational and sexual differences between parents and children is best explained on the basis of the underlying loyalties that exist in all families. In more healthy families, coexistent loyalty to one's family of origin and one's nuclear family is more aptly balanced. In pathogenic family systems, excessive psychic loyalty to one's family of origin is unconsciously maintained, at great cost to the marital partner and to one's children.

When children are treated in the inner world of their families, new and different dimensions are revealed. In conjoint family therapy, where children and parents are in simultaneous treatment, there is an opportunity to discover new connections which might not be accessible in the treatment of an individual child or adult. While the child or adult's psychosexual level of maturation is taken into consideration, the family therapist is aware that the conflicts are primarily connected with the interlocked, collusively repressed, or denied processes which interfere with growth and maturation of all family members.

In the traditional theoretical and treatment approach to children, the parents are regarded as either inadequate and unsatisfactory or potential resources for the child's dependent needs. What is overlooked is that more frequently, the parents' own unmet dependency needs are a part of the same relational dynamics. A biological parent is not automatically parental. Unless the parents' needs are met, they are emotionally unavailable to their children.

Observations from our clinical practice has taught us that, in turn, the children attempt to be parentlike substitutes to their own parents. They assume roles which are inappropriate in terms of age and sexuality, in attempting to fulfill the parental vacuum. Family therapists see the effects of being a parentified or scapegoated child: depression, learning and behavioral difficulties, psychosomatic illnesses, accident-proneness, suicide, and battering. The child is in a complex dilemma: He is unable to be a child in that he must repress or deny his own needs. He must try to postpone his own course of growth and development. His loyal attempts to meet his parents' needs are met with ambivalent responses because he cannot totally replace the grandparent and undo the original injustices done to the young parents.

The parents are in an even more complex situation. Marital and parental relationships result in additional demands and commitments, as well as a shift of loyalty ties from their family of origin. How is their "original" indebtedness being handled? Are they unconsciously denying their previous attachments and commitments while remaining guilty over their psychological and physical separation from the families of origin? Three levels of need exist and must be balanced: one, that of the aging parents; secondly, the self and the marital partners; and finally, those of their young children.

A study of the forms of pathogenic parentification and scapegoating of children in families yields important clues for the therapists' roles. The therapists are forced by the children to look at the parents through their eyes and are tested as to their competence to assume the burdens which the children have been carrying. The parents, in turn, are themselves in need of parenting, while simultaneously anticipating that the therapists will parent the children. This reversal of vantage points offers rich learning and challenge for transference manifestations. It is our thesis that the multigenerational approach provides family therapists with the most important clues and dimensions for handling the complexities with which they and the family members are faced.

The process of therapeutic change is also placed in a new context as a result of the multigenerational focus. The deprived child, parents, and grandparents are in a sense equally suffering and equally in need of therapeutic intervention. The therapists' strategies in the course of treatment must be based on the interlocking of each member's specific guilt over unpaid obligations that exist between the generations. The therapists must be appropriately available to each person's reality and transference feelings and needs. Symptomatic relief may ensue as a result of treatment of an individual child or adult, but in order for basic or structural change to occur within a family system—for reversal and rebalancing of destructive processes—the multigenerational treatment approach must be given full consideration.

11

Intergenerational Treatment of a Family That Battered a Child

Brutal assaults of parents on their children, such as in battering, burning, and incest, are indications of serious pathological conditions within families. Child suicides, accident-proneness, and psychosomatic illnesses also fall in this category. Although the theoretical and clinical implications of battering families is focused on in this chapter, we suggest that the multigeneration treatment approach is applicable in other situations. The trauma to and the reactions of the children are of prime importance; however, in order to produce symptomatic and structural changes within families, the marital–parental and grandparental relationships must become the central focus of consideration. In other words, what is examined and treated is the interlocking dynamics of both families of origin and the nuclear family rather than only individual psychodynamics.

The emotionally "battered" child and his parents have been studied intensively and extensively. Findings important to the clinician's understanding of the child's psychosexual development have been well described in the literature.[33] Family therapists have moved from this individual level to a consideration of the symptomatic child as a signal of a family's need for help. Treatment of the child is undertaken in the context that the entire family is in need of help. Therapists have learned that the designated patient's symptoms mask marital, multigenerational, and other parent–child conflicts. Where it is feasible, a multigeneration treatment approach has been considered as a more advantageous method in facilitating change and growth for all family members.

Family therapy literature has provided little information regarding treatment of physically battered children and their families or the intergenerational treatment concept. There have been many studies of the

275

extended family; most of these have been done from a sociological point of view, from psychological tests administered to older family members, and from histories taken in individual sessions. Experience which actually included the aged in conjoint family sessions has been minimal. As reviewed by Spark and Brody,[80] other authors are not describing the "inner world" of relationships which exist between nuclear families and their families of origin.

Family therapists have rarely encountered physically battered, neglected children. Families with these types of problems have primarily been in contact with physicians and hospitals, social agencies, and legal authorities. In addition to the laws that have been enacted to protect such children, social institutions have been made available to supplement and carry out the legal recommendations. This is in direct contrast to the emotionally disturbed children, where persuasion by school counselors and teachers, physicians, and other professionals is paramount in making referrals for treatment. Where feelings are carried into action as in the battered-child syndrome, it is obvious that problems exist. The seriousness of the problem cannot be as readily denied or minimized by the family as when a child is labeled emotionally disturbed.

A brief review of efforts by people who are engaged in this area is offered. It is hoped that the family therapy approach will add dimensions to the already existing findings and efforts. Several initial questions can be raised: First, to how large a segment of our population does the term "battered-child syndrome" apply? Second, is there a specific definition of this syndrome or is it a vague and nebulous label? Finally, in a multidiscipline approach, what efforts have been successful, and what additional facets need to be considered which might yield greater success?

HISTORICAL AND RESEARCH DATA

In the early 1900's a Society for the Prevention of Cruelty to Children was formed in both New York and Philadelphia. These societies were instrumental in the development of children's rights and the passage of laws to protect children from undue physical neglect and cruelty. Departments of public welfare and courts have played an equally paramount role in placing such children in foster homes and other child-care facilities.

In the medical field, it took the efforts of pediatricians, radiologists, and pathologists to confirm that a child's physical injuries were due to other than accidental means. Findings of Caffey,[27] a radiologist, and

Silverman,[79] a pathologist, are examples of pioneering contributions to help confirm the diagnosis, "other than accidental means." In 1961, Kempe, at the annual meeting of the American Academy of Pediatrics, used the term "the battered child syndrome," which fortunately took hold and resulted in interest and activity on the part of pediatricians, social agencies, the legal profession, police, lay organizations, and legislatures.

The significance of this particular issue is pointed out by Helfer and Pollock, who state that, "in 1966, 10,000 to 15,000 children in the United States were severely injured by non-accidental means. It is estimated that 5 percent of these children were killed and 25 to 30 percent permanently injured." They continue, "the true incidence of child abuse is not available since many cases are not reported or go unrecognized."[53, p. 11]

As research studies of other conditions have revealed, no single significant personality type produces specific symptoms or behavior. Parents who physically neglect or abuse their children represent a wide range of personality types—usually various combinations of schizoid, hysterical, or obsessive–compulsive traits—and no one type is an indicator of potential child abuse. Psychological testing has indicated a wide range of intelligence, from dull, normal, to superior. This confirms that the family as a whole should be the criteria and focus of study.

All socioeconomic levels are represented and most of the parents appear superficially to be well adjusted. Reiner[72] states that, "social class differences do not protect children from [physical] neglect and battering and their residue of physical and social retardation. The parents' manner of presenting themselves differs and it is difficult to believe that neglect or battering could exist without the backdrop of poverty. In the financial upper segment of the population, neglect symptoms may be more subtle, phrased in psychosomatic forms."[66, p. 33, 34]

Morris and Gould state that, "studies of the neglected, battered child and his parents can help us solve the riddle of social retardation, too often disposed of by diagnosing it as a social or maternal deprivation and poverty. Social retardation is an active, destructive, interpersonal process. Expressed in parental role defect and incapacity it is the cause of much physical and mental illness."[66, p. 34]

FROM INTRAPSYCHIC TO RELATIONAL CONCEPTS

A child may become the target of a parent's intrapsychic conflicts, externalized and acted out upon the child. Johnson and Szurek[56] made a significant contribution in describing this phenomenon. Philbrick[69] found that neglect and abuse may be an action language of the parent, a call for help.

Another aspect that has been described is that of role reversal. Morris and Gould defined this as "a reversal of the dependency role, in which parents turn to their infants and small children for nurturing and protection." The child is parentified, that is, he is needed and attempts to be a substitute parent to his parents. "In the neglected battered child syndrome, the parental concept of role is fixed at satisfaction of earliest interpersonal needs—the infantile, explosive, uncontrolled feelings and behavior that antedate ego development. These parents seem to have perceived and experienced their own parents as unloving, cruel, and brutal."[66, p. 31]

As described by Fenichel,[36] some of these battering parents have an archaic, animistic conception of the world, based on a confusion of ego and nonego, of self and no-self—a kind of reverse identification where the outside world becomes the whole sum of existence and self at any point in time.

Boardman[10] approaches this behavior from a learning or educative point of view. She emphasized the "high danger of wishful thinking and of the clichés, 'learning one's lesson' and 'giving another chance' . . . [and that] the recurrent battering . . . shows that these parents do not learn. This nonlearning and lack of response to threatened punishment suggest a pattern of behavior so fixed that self-preservation has become secondary."[66, p. 33]

FAMILY SYSTEM POINT OF VIEW

The available literature on child battering makes reference to relationships; in searching for meaning behind the violent behavior, causes are attributed to particular sets of psychological circumstances within a nuclear family.

Helfer and Pollock describe two conditions: "The first is a particular pattern in which children . . . are expected to satisfy . . . the parents' emotional needs. One manifestation of the pattern is an insistence upon a high level of performance from extremely small children. The pediatrician may note that the mother insists on expectations of behavior from the [small] child far beyond his chronological age. Older children in these families are often very skillful at supplying emotional support for their parents. This pattern goes [far] beyond the enforcement of . . . excellence for the children, because what is actually required of them is that they understand and sympathize with their parents' needs for affection. . . . If no gratification is received from the child, the parent responds with frustration and rage. . . . The second set of circumstances is the presence of an additional type of stressful situation for the parent. The battering parent often feels unable to receive emotional support from the spouse or other relatives. Because the parents have a large residue of unfulfilled emotional needs themselves, they are extremely sensitive to withdrawal of such support from their environment."[53, p. 17] In turn, the parentified or scapegoated child willingly cooperates in attempting to meet the parent's needs.

It is our hypothesis that the problem requires a multigenerational approach rather than being considered the acting out of intrapsychic conflicts of an individual. Family therapists have made enormous strides by their consideration of the nuclear family as the unit of health and disturbance. In further extending the unit of study and treatment to the extended family systems, deeper and broader dimensions are revealed. Our approach is to build a bridge between individual personality dynamics and the multiperson relational or family system dynamics. As stated by Boszormenyi-Nagy, "multiperson relationships include but [in a sense] supersede the psychological organization [of an individual]. . . . The relational theoretical point of view [does not study the] . . . intrapsychic structures [of an individual] in isolation from the context of live relationships."[18, p. 375, 376]

The essence of family therapy lies in the concept that loyalty commitments constitute important motivational factors in every close relationship: husband–wife, parent–child, and including the aged parents and adult siblings. Restated, the essence of each one's existence is interlocked with all important others. Loyalty and indebtedness to each important other is the major force which underlies relationship systems or networks. The family therapist is concerned with the emotional well-being and growth of all nuclear and extended family members.

In the treatment of all family members, each individual not only faces his internal psychic structure and internalized relationships, but in addition must face the ghosts that reside in his actual, live relationships. In individual therapy, attitudes may be concealed by an individual, but in family therapy they are more likely to be revealed when all family members are present to discuss problems. Unconscious and vicarious gratifications, destructive acts, and manipulation of roles are more readily revealed through behavior in family sessions. When all family members are present, interactions become observable in vivo as compared with an individual indirectly describing relationships or having them revealed in transference phenomena with an individual therapist.

One of the main resistances in individual treatment may be connected with that of family loyalty and obligation. The parentified child or even the scapegoated grandparent may move out of such an assigned and assumed role only if he knows that the other persons are being supported and helped in the growth process. A family member may remain loyal and available to his family of origin by remaining in a locked position which helps support the family homeostasis. His symptoms may be the cry for help for his whole family, which unconsciously wishes to defer or prevent emotional separation and individuation. Often such individuals are unable to fully commit themselves to their marital partner until they are able to rebalance and repay their indebtedness to their family of origin.

In those families where children are consciously or unconsciously equated with the grandparents' roles, many of the parent's unmet dependency needs have been channeled upon the children. This has the effect of parentifying and scapegoating everyone in a locked, overclose involvement, with important others being rejected or locked out so that they appear nonavailable for emotional support.

Based on these premises, we must take into consideration the three-generational dimensions—e.g., the yearnings behind the hurt and angry feelings that are unconsciously transferred from the parent to a spouse or to children can then be directly connected back to the original sources. In other words, the multigenerational approach provides new opportunities to modify and change those relationships which presently appear hopeless, unyielding, and nongratifying. In the family accounting system, then, the injustice of parents having been emotionally abandoned or exploited may be corrected and rebalanced. Behind the acts of aggression on the child lie the accumulation of feelings of helpless rage over having been exploited. Retaliation and revenge is thus reenacted upon the provocative, challenging child. Guilt feelings may be modified or decreased through discharging one's emotional obligations in one's close, personal relationships. For instance, if a young mother and her mother should become available to each other and discover new or different levels of relating, it stimulates more gratifying responses between all family members. It may free and change the family system from a stagnant level of relating and nongiving to a more spontaneous one of sharing and being emotionally supportive.

TREATMENT CONSIDERATIONS

Exploited individuals who try to rebalance the impact of their formative relationships through child beating are frequently difficult to treat. Despite their fear of the law and subsequent consequences, they may show little overt remorse or guilt over their actions. Even after discharging their feelings in such aggressive action, they remain critical and angry towards their children. Professionals and neighbors or friends are repulsed and frightened by the display of such parental violence; in addition, they have little desire to be involved in the moral or legal processes.

Despite this, professionals from many disciplines have taken active steps towards the healing and protection of these children. They are aware of the need for corrective measures, especially in view of the history of repeated beatings of the same or other children in the family. The need arises to find more effective methods of prevention and treatment of these recurring patterns. Individual therapy has not been sufficiently successful with character-disordered and borderline individuals. Temporarily the use of foster-home placement, homemaker services, and other community resources must still be used and considered; but for more permanent changes, multigenerational treatment may provide more economical and meaningful long-term possibilities.

A therapist or other professionals i.e., homemakers, pediatricians, or social agencies can provide only a temporary resource for emotional support. Such people may temporarily carry the authoritative or superego-like role for the family who is unable to function effectively on this level. One young woman stated it very graphically when she told a nurse, "one kiss or words of praise from my mother was worth a hundred from any other person!"

In the case that follows, as we examine the relationships between the child, the young mother, and her family of origin, and the marital and parental relationships, it provides material not only from the past, but emphasizes what continued to be painful in the current relationships. We may understand the significance of "ghosts" from the past, but more importantly, her current life revealed that she was "shadow-boxing" with them in her present existence. By seeing all three generations together, these shadows from past relationships become live and open conflicts, and the means of resolving them become more accessible to the three generations. Each generation is helped to face having been exploited and indebted. These negative loyalty ties can be modified into constructive emotional involvement and repayment.

Another concern is the question of resistance. This applies to that hard core of seriously disturbed individuals who rarely request treatment for themselves. Their conflicts are unconsciously projected onto other family members. They cannot tolerate their feelings of anxiety or depression and tend to use "flight" to escape treatment. It is specifically in these situations that multigenerational treatment is more readily tolerated. From our experience, although initially the nuclear family resists the inclusion of the grandparents or the grandparents initially resist being included, we have eventually found an opposite reaction. The grandparents are often hurt and lonely as a result of past or current conflicts and their lives of rejection, exclusion, and exploitation. Because of this, they may become accessible and even eager to be included in treatment; this becomes an opportunity for everyone to rebalance accounts so family relationships can be improved.

Family therapists, by indicating their convictions of the value of this approach, stimulate hope that family relationships are changeable, regardless of the age or accessibility of the grandparents and siblings of the families of origin. This kind of participation depends on the therapists' capacity to be available to each family member and not to take sides against any individual. Individuals as well as their families test the therapists by including them as family members who could then be scapegoated in family alignments and splits. The family therapist must be strong enough to be included in the family system and be "for" every member, yet be able to remain outside in the role of the facilitator for emotional change.

ROLE OF CHILDREN

Children in these families are, in one sense of the word, "victims" of their parent's aggressive feelings. Young states that, "the children serve as a protective shield for this parent against the destructive behavior of the other. The more the children are the objects of parental abuse, the less the punitiveness may be turned against the passive parent . . . in effect the children serve as scapegoats."[94, p. 50] As conceptualized by Brodey, "by incorporating the ego-dystonic "irrational" side of the parent, the child not only gives to the parents a way to avoid inner anxiety" but a way to maintain equilibrium.[23, p. 397]

However, from a family or relational aspect the child's behavior is not only a reflection of his intrapsychic conflicts but also reflects his attempts to help his parents. The child is so tuned in to the marital and parental conflicts that in an unconsciously loyal way he permits himself to be used as the target for his parent's rage. As stated by Boszormenyi-Nagy, "the child gets caught in the parents' struggle for correcting an injustice and becomes . . . a scapegoat for previous injustices" done to them.[18, p. 377] The parentified or scapegoated child complies unconsciously in the behavioral expectations of the family.

In essence, the symptomatic child attempts to move out of his current phase of development but also expresses the need and hope for change in the family. The parentified child assumes premature responsibility for his family, often at the cost of his own emotional growth. The other children may be denying or repressing their needs and in effect supporting the regressive and stagnating aspects of the family system. In the case to be presented, Mary Ann was defiant, provocative, and challenging towards her parents, as one would expect of a 3½-year-old child in the anal phase of psychosexual development. On the other hand, as the parentified child she would try to help her mother in giving her younger siblings the bottle, setting the table, and removing soiled diapers. Her older and younger brothers were good, quiet children, who would passively withdraw from the parents' conflicts. It was Mary Ann who also gave much of the affection that was openly displayed. She was the one who most actively comforted her mother, father, and siblings when they were upset.

The foster agency and court placed her in the maternal grandmothers' home. She continued the same behavior there, to test and provoke limits as well as affectionate responses, even from her grandparents who had been emotionally divorced for many years. The major effort of treatment was to help her and her siblings give up these assumed adultlike roles and to permit them to be children. In order to accomplish this for children, it was first necessary that the adults' unmet dependency needs and unresolved negative loyalty ties with their families of origin and the marital partner be brought into awareness, then rebalanced by constructive involvement and repayment of indebtedness. If this can be accomplished, the children can then be parented by their parents, and the substitutive parents (the therapists, the foster agency, the homemaker, and the courts) can withdraw from their active involvement.

THERAPY OF THE CHILDREN

All the children were present in the sessions unless ill. No play material was brought into the sessions in order to directly observe the physical and verbal interactions between the parents and children, and between the siblings. The children were in general very quiet and from the therapist's point of view, too well-behaved. Any loud verbal interaction or physical restlessness on the children's part, although age-appropriate, was pounced upon by the parents. In the sessions, Mary Ann was very affectionate towards her parents and brothers: Many times she tried to hold the baby on her lap or would hold his bottle for him. None of her taunting, teasing, controlling behavior was reenacted within the sessions. But for many months after therapy began, the nursery school teacher and the grandparents did say that she was still very domineering and controlling with them. She showed no overt fear of her parents and did not appear traumatized from the beatings.

The therapist told the parents that they should continue to be in charge within the sessions, but it was not expected that the children behave as if they were in a classroom. Despite this, for a long time the C's gave menacing looks, used threats of punishment, and snapped their fingers for immediate obedience. However, there was much open display of affection, and the children, including Mary Ann, did not seem to be afraid of the parents. In the sessions, Mrs. C was like a martinet, even with Mr. C, who carried out her orders to diaper or feed the baby or take the other children to the toilet. At other times, Mr. C played with the children more like a sibling than a parent.

In other families with children this age, there is often hyperactivity, restlessness, fighting, loudness, crying, running in and out of the room, frequent trips to the bathroom, etc. The C children were much more subdued and passive, both physically and verbally, towards their parents and the therapist. Eventually they warmed up, showed off their Christmas presents and their new baby, were affectionate with the therapist, and brought her many drawings.

It was the children who comforted their weeping mother when she spoke about missing them. "The quiet was much more unbearable than the noisey, demanding racket of the children!" After about three months, the boys came home for weekends; Mary Ann could spend Sundays with her parents, and they were permitted to visit her at the maternal grandparents' home. The therapist had to help the parents cope with the children's insomnia, bedwetting, and other reactions to the separation. At first they blamed the agency, the foster parents, who were also in-laws, and finally were even angry at the children themselves. Their anxieties finally diminished, and they all settled down as a result of continued support by the placement agency worker and the therapist.

Naturally, there was even more anxiety about Mary Ann's trial visits and eventual return home. By the time she was permitted to go home, the school, grandparents, and Mr. and Mrs. C stated that she was now a changed child. In the sessions, she seemed freer and happier. Her brothers were also more verbal and physically active too. This was all simultaneously happening as Mrs. C and her parents and siblings became more available to each other.

Fundamentally, what helped all the children was to see their mother reshape and rebalance her previously angry or distant relationships into loving, participating close ones with their grandparents, aunts, and uncles. The children were no longer needed as targets for their parents' aggressive and unjust outbursts. Change in the relationships in one part of the family system in turn effected change in the relationship between the C's and their children.

CLINICAL ILLUSTRATION

The case material presented has many similarities to those described in the literature of the battered-child syndrome. However, in addition to the efforts to heal these traumatized children, what is emphasized are those dimensions that reflect therapy with the nuclear and extended family system. This in no way precludes other dimensions—individual, marital, and parent–child. We cannot give a complete picture of the total efforts to change these complex family relationships without also giving full recognition to the efforts and support of the child-care agency, the nursery school, the homemaker service, and the court.

In accepting the referral from the child-care agency, psychiatric hospital, and court, the specific requirement was that the entire nuclear family attend the sessions, and in addition that as frequently as possible, the maternal grandparents be included. (The paternal grandparents, who were divorced, refused to be included.) The social institutions acted as basic support for treatment, but more significantly, temporarily fulfilled the role of substitute parents. Although the treatment described spans a period of one year, Mrs. C has continued a telephone contact with the family therapist through the following year.

REFERRAL INFORMATION

Three months previously, Mary Ann C, age 4, was admitted to a hospital suffering from severe welts and bruises as a result of having been beaten with a belt and buckle by the mother. In addition, she had almost drowned in a bathtub which had contained baby oil, where she had been left alone. Her father found her in an unconscious state, and had used mouth-to-mouth resuscitation while waiting for the ambulance.

At first Mr. C said he had done the beating. Then Mrs. C was arrested, placed in jail, and subsequently transferred to a psychiatric hospital for evaluation. When Mary Ann was 2½ years old she had been hospitalized for a concussion. She had been whipped by her mother, who stated at the time that the child had slipped on a rug which resulted in the concussion. Both parents said their daughter had been a "bad" child from age 6 months and was an increasingly difficult discipline problem. Mary Ann would mimic, challenge, and aggressively defy her mother. She would tease and taunt and say things which Mrs. C said she had never dared say to her parents. They would have "killed" her if she had. A child-care service had referred them for treatment, but they did not follow through at the time. One year later the mother went to a child guidance clinic for a total of five sessions, but treatment was interrupted three months later when the child was beaten and hospitalized. The beatings had been administered by *both* parents, although Mr. C insisted he was forced to do so by his wife. Food was often withheld, and the child was placed in a closet any time of the day or night to "cool off." It had been suggested that Mrs. C put her in a quiet place when Mary Ann would not respond to her parent's efforts to control her temper tantrums. Mrs. C was defeated when she once again tried to establish herself as a good, loving, person, as a superior wife and mother. Mary Ann had challenged that image.

The C's were married when Mrs. C was 19, and six months later she gave birth to John, who was now age 5. Mary Ann, the designated patient, was 4, Jim was 2, Tim was 1, and the mother was again pregnant. In a recent contact it was learned she gave birth to her sixth child in the seventh year of her marriage.

MOTHER'S HISTORY

Mrs. C, age 25, was an attractive, articulate, obese woman. She was the sixth of eight children. At this time, still living in her parent's home was an older, unmarried sister and two younger siblings. Her father was a skilled mechanic who, although a steady worker, had frequently gambled away his earnings. As a result of this, Leona, their oldest unmarried daughter, not only remained as the more reliable source of financial help but had rescued the family home from the mortgage company. Although Mrs. C complained that her parents had rejected and exploited her, it was Leona whom she described as ruling everyone's life with an iron fist. It was Leona who dictated who would receive what and how they were to be treated by the other family members.

Mrs. C said she had been a good and obedient child who always got the "short end of the stick." She recalled that in her early teens she had generally felt detached from her family and had periods when she became so depressed that she even considered suicide. She recalled getting in a car, driving around for hours in an "amnesialike state," and wanting to smash the car and herself. A high-school graduate, she worked as a secretary until age 19 when she became pregnant by a man who was already married. When she confided this to Mr. C they married after knowing each other for just a few months.

She felt her family looked down on Mr. C because he was not a high-school graduate. Her family acted as if they weren't good enough for them and never gave either one any credit for their efforts. She was deeply hurt that at age 21, the family did not follow through on a tradition whereby each child was given $100 and a set of furniture when they married. She felt they were treated like outcasts. She wanted to have eight children just like her mother, despite the fact that she had a son age 5, Mary Ann age 4, a son age 2, a son 11 months, and was now in her fifth month of pregnancy. Her mother had severe migrane headaches. When Mary Ann was 2⅛, Mrs. C was hospitalized for studies since she also complained of headaches.

FATHER'S HISTORY

Mr. C was a short, slightly built man, age 26. His father had deserted his family and subsequently secured a divorce. Both of his parents had remarried. However, Mr. C's father had married a woman who was only five years older than Mrs. C. Mr. C had three half-siblings from this marriage. He did not want to repeat his parents' marriage or home life. He felt that his parents always expected him to do too much for them and in turn had exploited him from age 12 by always demanding or borrowing money from him. About his mother, he said, "she shows her coldness in a kind way." He had told his family about Mrs. C's first pregnancy, and thereafter she was never accepted by his family. He had been asthmatic from childhood on and even after marriage had to be hospitalized. He trusted no one and never had any close peer relationships.

MARITAL RELATIONSHIP

Mr. C held both a full- and part-time job but frequently became ill and was therefore unable to work steadily. Mrs. C was alone a great deal and insisted that it was not financially necessary for him to hold two jobs. They rarely went out together, and Mr. C resented that his wife objected when he went out with the "boys" after work. He turned over his money to his wife who then took full responsibility for payment of bills. They fought frequently and violently; on several occasions Mrs. C stabbed him with a nail file or knife, but the lacerations were described as superficial.

He teased her a great deal, which in turn infuriated her. During the arguments he called her all kinds of vile names and even insinuated that she was being sexually promiscuous. She would vacillate from being loving and affectionate to belittling and humiliating him. Mr. C described his wife as a nagging person and an overly meticulous housekeeper. Sexually he found her more demanding than he was. He did not want any more children but was unable to discuss this directly and openly with his wife. Mrs. C believed that he wanted her continuously pregnant so that she would not become interested in anyone else. Both felt mutually exploited by the other and by the children, that despite their efforts, there was no gratification or reward for themselves. There was frequent reference to separating.

INITIAL PHASE OF TREATMENT

Mr. C was very inarticulate in the sessions. He agreed with his wife that he always had difficulty in expressing himself. It usually came out wrong in the first place, and when he tried to explain, things ended in more hot water. Both of them were explosive with each other and with the children. However, Mrs. C felt that her husband's general nonresponsiveness was even more difficult than his anger. His work situation was experienced by Mrs. C as his way of staying away from her and the children. When Mary Ann became too difficult for her to handle, she would telephone her husband to come home from work. Both parents were collusive partners in the beatings.

In the sessions with the maternal grandparents, upon the urging of the therapist, Mrs. C tried to tell her mother about her feelings of loneliness as she was growing up; she felt her efforts to be helpful in the past were never really appreciated. The maternal grandmother sat in stony silence and turned her body away from her daughter. She said she didn't know what her daughter was talking about, and that none of it was true! Even after Mrs. C began to cry, her mother insisted that the only thing that was wrong with her daughter was that she had been "spoiled rotten." She had treated every one of her children exactly the same. She told the therapists that her daughter was not as patient and calm a person as she had always been with her children. The maternal grandfather agreed with his wife in a semicollusive way, despite the fact that they rarely spoke to each other and had not lived together as man and wife for many years. He worked in the same place as Mr. C and insisted that he did like his son-in-law.

After several sessions, the maternal grandmother refused to return, giving her severe migraine headaches as the reason. Mrs. C wept as she insisted everything was hopeless as far as her family of origin was concerned. She angrily told the therapist that there was no point in trying to pour her heart out to her parents and that nothing would change! She put the major blame on her sister Leona, whom she subsequently compared with Mary Ann. She felt that both of them were exactly alike in being critical and rejecting of her and that they were always trying to control and run the show. Yet she pitied her mother, whom she felt was in the full power of Leona's hands. She resented that her mother was used as a doormat and mistreated by Leona and her two younger siblings. In the meantime the child-care agency had placed Mary Ann in the maternal grandparent's home.

In addition, Mr. and Mrs. C insisted that their sons were being mistreated by Mrs. C's relatives, with whom they were now living. They wanted the children to be returned before the birth of the next baby. In the treatment sessions, the children were strictly and harshly handled by both parents. They snapped their fingers insisting that the children sit completely still, despite the fact that the room was large enough for children to move around in.

The major effort in this phase was to help Mr. and Mrs. C become more open and direct about their needs. Mrs. C tended to speak for and about her husband. He had difficulty in accepting that what he might say could interest anyone. The question of more children had never been clarified between them. Mrs. C was completely surprised to learn that Mr. C felt overburdened and overwhelmed with his current responsibilities. He said he was willing for his wife to have her tubes tied but retracted this later as being against their religion. However, he clearly stated that with each pregnancy his wife became more irritable and nervous.

SECOND PHASE OF TREATMENT

In these months, Mr. and Mrs. C began to be even more direct and angrily spoke of feeling exploited by even one another. Later, their life time despair over this exploitation poured out. There was still evidence of Mrs. C being guarded and suspicious of any questions directed to her by the therapist, but slowly she was becoming less defensive.

Mr. C had little contact with his family of origin; Mrs. C, while laughing at the therapists' continued urging that she visit and telephone her family, did do so. She reported the ups and downs of these contacts. Her father came to a few more sessions when he was able to take time from work. He showed much more active interest in his daughter, but more importantly became a constructive resource to his grandchildren (and frequently to his son-in-law).

Another major focus of therapy was the marital relationship. Mrs. C said her husband was good and kind but could not carry any responsibility. He left everything up to her, and she felt he leaned on her like a little boy. He said he had always been a loner, and now things were worse for him than ever before. "A man who is a child beater is considered as bad as a murderer." The men at work avoided him, and he even ate lunch alone. He began to pour out his past and present feelings of being unloved, being used and exploited, and being overworked and overburdened. When he complained, his wife turned on him to nag, belittle, and humiliate him, even in the sessions.

Both poured out their mutual feelings of despair regarding their increased isolation—which not only included rejection by their families of origin, but also included neighbors and the few friends that Mrs. C had made. This all was a result of newspaper publicity they had received. They felt as if they were outcasts, shunned like lepers!

In the sixth month of therapy the therapist and the director of the program offered to meet with the grandparents and their eight children on a Sunday afternoon in the grandparents' home. While Mrs. C's parents and oldest sister accepted the idea of such a meeting, the other siblings refused to attend and it was not held. Despite this, Mr. and Mrs. C had increased contact with the previously "unavailable" siblings, including one sister of Mr. C.

When the two older C sons were returned home, the parents were surprised at the children's reactions to the new baby and to themselves. The children had sleep disturbances, urinary incontinence day and night, and in general were tense and anxious. The C's did not connect these responses with the ordeal all of them had experienced, but blamed the maternal relatives for the children's reactions, as if they had been neglecting the nephews. The therapist pointed this out to them and then helped them to be more openly loving and reassuring toward the children.

Mary Ann had been admitted to a nursery school, and Mrs. C was afraid the teacher was too permissive when she learned that Mary Ann was permitted to play with water and mess with paints. The therapist explained that this would help Mary Ann to express her feelings in a more appropriate way. Initially, the school reported that Mary Ann was very bossy with her peers and difficult to manage. After several months, the court permitted Mary Ann to spend her weekends with her parents. She was no longer overdemanding, and her temper tantrums had decreased. From being considered a rebellious and rejecting child, the C's described her as now being loving and affectionate toward them. She tried to outmother her mother with the new baby.

THIRD PHASE OF TREATMENT

Mr. C, after having elected to have surgery for a hernia during his wife's last pregnancy, lost his job, complained of depression, and had psychosomatic complaints. His wife vacillated from being chronically disappointed and angry with him to pleading with him to be more available to her and the children. He struggled in his role as a husband and father, but he was desperately in need of "parenting" himself. He continued to insist he would leave if his wife's outbursts toward him and the children did not abate. He insisted that he had nothing left over for himself, either emotionally or financially, and that he was feeling as exploited now as he had been by his parents.

Mrs. C did not really believe that he was afraid she would lose control of her temper towards the children again. She thought he was afraid of his own anger and possible loss of control. She was very hurt that he did not accept the changes that she herself was experiencing, in feeling calmer and more loving with the children and towards her husband. The issue of additional pregnancies remained unsettled, although by now Mr. C was direct about not wanting more children. She had refused to have her tubes tied after the last baby was born, although the obstetrician had been willing to perform the surgery.

FINAL PHASE OF TREATMENT

Mrs. C again became pregnant, and Mr. C deserted his family. The phone calls to the therapist increased as depression and despair set in. Mr. C refused all offers even to see him separately. When Mrs. C expressed suicidal feelings, a home visit with her parents was quickly arranged.

The maternal grandmother, who previously had been a cold, disconfirming, defensive person in our presence, was now much softer and available emotionally. Together with maternal grandfather they urged Mrs. C to keep going and reported that everyone in the family would continue to help both emotionally and economically with furniture, bills, etc. For the first time, Mrs. C learned that her mother had also had her tubes tied. They praised Mrs. C for her housekeeping efforts and the way she handled the children.

The maternal grandfather even offered to have a talk with his oldest son about his son-in-law's behavior and to consider the possibility of having a man-to-man talk with Mr. C. They were very angry about Mr. C's behavior, but the grandfather thought his son would hold him back from letting his son-in-law "have it physically." From their previous position that the C family difficulties had no connection with them, they shifted to asserting that they would do all they possibly could for their daughter and her children.

The suicidal feelings were openly mentioned in this session, and it was at this time that the maternal grandmother became more openly demonstrative toward her daughter. She pleaded with her daughter not to despair—that Mr. C's leaving was not the end of the world for her.

From this point on, Mrs. C moved from a position of emotional paralysis to activity. She applied for public assistance, and went to her lawyer and into court to request support and to try to get Mr. C. to reconcile The child-care agency placed a homemaker in the home, and a sister offered to stay with her a couple of nights a week. When bill collector: threatened to take back some of her household possessions, her sister: and brothers offered to give her various items from their own households.

Because her father and the agency could no longer provide trans portation to the clinic which was 20 miles from her home, a transfer to another clinic for individual therapy was discussed and arranged (conjoint family therapy not being available). Mrs. C accepted this even though she continued to be in frequent telephone contact with the family therapist. She continued to talk about her progress with her family of origin. She attended a family picnic held at her parent's home, a first since she had left home. She bubbled with pleasure as she described her feelings of being accepted and loved by siblings and in-laws whom she had initially described as "cold, uncaring, and like enemies."

She reported that although her husband had not returned home after the birth of the sixth baby, she did have her tubes tied. All through the pregnancy she continued hope for a reconciliation. However, when she learned that he had moved in with another woman and her four children, she began to think about a divorce. Her parents had urged her to accept that she was still a young woman and that her life was not over just because Mr. C had left her.

In a follow-up telephone conversation six months later, Mrs. C reported that she had begun to hear from her sister-in-law that Mr. C was interested in a reconciliation. He began to visit her and the children, often crying as he hugged the baby, saying he was lonely and missing them. He offered money or to run errands for them, and for the first time gave a telephone number where he could be reached.

Since her last family therapy session and the birth of the last child, Mrs. C had lost over forty pounds. She openly expressed her wishes and made efforts through the court for reconciliation with her husband, which she believed was inevitable because both of them had changed a great deal. Specifically, she felt that both of them were now much less angry and explosive persons. However, she did not deny that she still was very hurt about her husband's abandonment. She felt that she was now strong enough to help him accept that both of them had been overwhelmed by the emotional and economic responsibilities regarding the children. For Mrs. C, one of the most surprising aspects of the current situation was when she learned that her mother-in-law and father-in-law were also urging that Mr. C return to his wife and children. For the first time, both families of origin were now being openly available and supportive of the marriage.

CASE DISCUSSION

Even though the maternal grandparents were not directly available for all of the treatment sessions, it is evident that through phone calls and visits to the parents' and grandparents' homes, a great deal was accomplished outside the treatment situation. Much was left undone due to the fact that Mr. C's family of origin consistently remained unavailable to treatment.

Nor can the fact be minimized that the already shaky marital relationship was disrupted when Mr. C left home. This can be defined as a negative therapeutic reaction. Despite his wife's changed attitudes in the marital and parental relationships and his in-laws' reacceptance, nothing counterbalanced his basic reaction of feeling used and exploited. His "unfinished business" with his family of origin interfered with his capacity to involve himself in a more constructive way with his wife and children.

Individually Mrs. C could be regarded as a very deprived, distrustful, paranoid person. She not only had strong unmet dependency needs, but revealed a split in object relatedness, with her mother being a "good" object and Leona being the "bad" one. Leona and Mary Ann were perceived as rejecting, controlling individuals, with the maternal grandmother being a passive victim ("a floormat") used and abused by other family members. However, Mrs. C ambivalently identified with her mother and was in competition with her mother and Leona/Mary Ann. Additionally, her choice of a mate was in direct contrast to her father and brothers, whom she considered as noninfantile or abandoning men.

On one level she attempted to prove that she was as competent and loving to her children as her mother had been, and also wanted to have eight children. While her mother's attitude towards her was overtly a nonrewarding one, Mrs. C yearned for a loving, shared closeness with her mother. Through the multigenerational treatment, the underlying core of rage and despair over being exploited—which was projected on all of the children (not only on Mary Ann)—was rechanneled and eventually reshaped with all members of her original family. Her mother's migraine headaches diminished as these two women shared many personal feelings about their lives.

It was as if Mary Ann was the externalization of Mrs. C's unresolved negative loyalty ties toward her parents. She had never openly revealed her "bad" self to them. In handing over Mary Ann to her parents, it was as if she were still hoping that they could then see her as the good, loyal daughter that she had tried to be. It was her perverse way of attempting to rebalance her murderous rage over having felt unappreciated and exploited in the past. Because these feelings had been hidden from herself and them, she had been unable to give them recognition for all they had tried to give her.

Both Mrs. C and Mary Ann in a sense were always trying to help their parents reconcile their marital difficulties. Another important change was that Leona, who had been in the "bad, rejecting object" role, became a main resource to Mrs. C and her children. Leona had been the self-sacrificing martyr who had deprived herself of a husband and children in order to care for and support her aging parents. Toward the end of treatment, Leona moved actively to mobilize her parents and siblings in emotionally and financially supporting Mrs. C and her children. As with the rest of the family, Leona moved out of the controlling "ogre" role and lessened her competitive efforts with her own parents, especially her father.

Mrs. C's father and oldest brother not only became directly available to Mrs. C and her children, but moved from being mere figureheads towards actively contacting Mr. C to help him become a more responsible male adult in his family. This was more than his own father had been able to do. Despite their efforts to "adopt" Mr. C, he was unable to trust them. It remained essential that his own family of origin should become available to him, so that he could rebalance his negative feelings with them.

In summary, therapy facilitated some reconstruction in the family. By focusing on the nuclear and extended family systems as well as the individual mechanisms, changes occurred on a multipersonal level. A basic shift developed in the life style of family members. The relationships were changed from detached, seemingly noninvolved, allegedly disloyal, disconfirming ones to more openly devoted and direct regarding the emotional needs of all.

THERAPEUTIC RELATIONSHIP WITH THE FAMILY

Both Mr. and Mrs. C and the maternal grandparents were initially hostile and mistrustful toward the therapist. This was quickly brought into the open, and the therapist stated that it was expected and understandable. They expected blame, which is what they had experienced from neighbors as a result of newspaper publicity and from people who had participated in their arrest, jailing, and placement in a psychiatric facility.

It was readily evident that the mistrust was from an even deeper level as a consequence of their earlier life experience. Both had deep feelings of worthlessness and inadequacy. The current situation confirmed their own feelings of "badness." Any comment or inquiry by the therapist was reacted to with suspiciousness and construed as "criticism." The therapist had to continuously reveal an accepting, interested, concerned attitude toward everyone, while holding them to changes in their relationships.

At first there was a great deal of projection of "badness" onto Mary Ann and the other children. The parents also attempted to manipulate the therapist regarding the legal placement of the children. It had to be clarified quickly that there were no direct connections with any future legal proceedings. Although psychiatric treatment was recommended as part of the legal process, acceptance of treatment as a family was a voluntary choice. The fact that the child welfare agency represented the family in court helped to separate the psychiatric work from the placement procedures.

A beginning essential trust was established toward the therapist after the maternal grandparents were included in several sessions, and Mrs. C became able to talk more openly with her parents about being exploited and unjustly treated. This was not easily accomplished, especially as far as her mother was concerned. She either appeared not to hear her daughter or completely disconfirmed her. When Mrs. C tried to tell her mother that she had always felt unappreciated for anything she had done to help at home, her mother's reply was, "you were just

spoiled and were always given everything you wanted." As the therapist helped the nuclear and extended family members to explore these
emotional myths, they were able to remove some of the barriers which
kept them from being genuinely involved with and available to each
other.

Another main area that at first was "closed off" was the marital relationship. They presented themselves as a loving, affectionate, sexually
intimate couple. However, after a few months of being forced to focus
on their own needs and obligations, in addition to the children's problems, they were able to bring out the disappointment (and anger) towards each other which had been minimized and denied.

The therapist frequently praised the family's efforts to communicate
directly with each other and with their own parents and siblings about
their yearnings and indebtedness. It was hard for them to believe that
anyone could really be interested in what they thought or felt. It was
as if no one really understood their loneliness or their despair or expected more control of their aggressive rage. Although the therapist
never "told" them what to do, discussed were alternative ways of meeting each other's needs—both parentally and maritally.

The couple were held to discussing for the first time the multiple
pregnancies and the excessive burden placed on both of them; finances
were discussed, with Mrs. C helping her husband learn to write checks
and pay monthly portions of each bill as it arrived. Another major area
centered on Mrs. C defining to Mr. C her need to have him available
to her and the children and proving she could manage on the income
from one job instead of his also working four or five evenings. She
interpreted his behavior as rejection of the family. Mr. C insisted that
this was his concept of being an adequate provider for his wife and
children. Subsequently they became aware that the both of them felt
exploited and used. He felt he got nothing after taking care of everyone
and frequently became ill and was unable to work on either job.

Mr. C openly identified his wife with his mother, whom he felt had
taken advantage of him, but he was unable to separate his wife from his
mother. He began to seek out the company of a paternal uncle who was
a bookie, with expensive cars and clothing and living a "carefree bachelor existence although being married." He felt rejected by his own and
his wife's family, and it was impossible to help him rework these feelings
despite his in-laws' efforts to support him emotionally. He remained
critical and defensive in all these various relationships. During his wife's
sixth pregnancy, he abruptly deserted his family and went to live with
another woman and her four children. It was as if he was so depleted
emotionally that he felt justified in abandoning everyone. Despite ev-

ery effort of the therapist to see him alone and the court's efforts to bring about a reconciliation, he refused to respond. Subsequently, he was placed in jail for nonsupport. He even refused to visit his wife in the hospital after the birth of the baby, although he signed the necessary legal papers to have her tubes tied.

THERAPIST'S REACTIONS

When this family was assigned, the director was informed that it would be accepted by the therapist on a "trial" basis. The anxiety that was generated was on both a personal and a professional basis. Not only did the therapist have to consider what would be stimulated within himself, but would need to be able to be objectively professional with persons classified as "would-be-murderers?" Would I tend to overidentify with the battered child and be resentful and rejecting towards the parents? Another important factor was the element of risk as far as the child's life was concerned. Having conviction about the efficacy of family therapy is one dimension, but would the family be able to tolerate and constructively use the therapeutic process so that when the child visited or was returned home he would be safe? In family therapy there are no objective criteria to estimate or guarantee outcomes.

In addition, the child-care agency, the court, and the psychiatric hospital, while being totally supportive of the effort, were also placing certain expectations regarding therapeutic results. In the majority of cases, families are required to make their own commitment to treatment regardless of the referral source. In this situation, the family was coming on the insistance of these medical, legal, and social institutions. It still was necessary to have the family make their own personal commitment to family therapy.

Although the family was continuously informed that the therapist had no direct connection with agency and court decisions, it was understandable that the parents constantly tested the therapist about decisions for visiting or the return-home dates of each child. The therapist found the parents and children physically attractive and pleasant, and overtly cooperative about coming for family therapy. It cannot be denied that there was excess anxiety and tension for the therapist and the family in the initial weeks. Being "accepted" into any one's private family life is no small task; however, this family had already been "intruded upon" by so many other professional persons that they were not eager to have another inquisitive stranger inquiring about them or their families of origin.

Initially the children were quiet, obedient, and tended to cling to their parent's sides instead of exploring the unit as most children do. Mr. C presented himself to the therapist as a small, dumb boy, as if he were a mild, meek, acquiescent individual who could only give monosyllabic replies. Mrs. C was tense, guarded, and replied to questions in a suspicious way: "Why was it important to learn anything about her personal, or historical background?" Sometimes, she acted as if she did not know the answer or implied she could not consider that there might be some connection between the marital and grandparental relationships and their extreme behavior toward Mary Ann. Both parents demanded that the children refrain from any movement or activity, although the therapist urged that they be permitted to act as naturally as they might at home. The parents snapped their fingers to demand instant obedience when any child moved or wanted to go to the toilet. They would bark orders, and push or shove the children instead of telling them firmly what they expected of them.

Overtly neither parent seemed particularly guilty or upset over what Mary Ann's reactions toward either one of them would be. Interestingly enough, in the sessions Mary Ann was affectionately loving towards her mother and father. While they never said Mary Ann "deserved" the treatment she received, they implied that her challenging, taunting, teasing, and provocatively bad behavior justified their punishment of her. It was as if Mary Ann was the aggressor and the parents were the helpless victims who had "appropriately" retaliated. The only subject that brought tears to the eyes of Mrs. C was when she spoke of feeling rejected and used by her parents and siblings.

As they described their lives, there had been no exceptional physical or emotional deprivation: Mrs. C was an excellent housekeeper; the children were well fed and clothed. The income was adequate for their standard of living. There were no severe health problems. Compared with other families seen in family therapy, there seemed to be no exceptional external pressures to account for their extreme behavior towards Mary Ann. Neither parent had been subjected to extreme physical abuse when they were children. As a matter of fact, the therapist found them to be very similar to other young parents struggling with family problems.

The premarital pregnancy had been kept a secret from Mrs. C's family, although Mr. C had revealed it to his family. Even the number and closeness of the pregnancies, or desire to have more children, did not seem significantly different from traditional Catholic families. The main discontent and complaints were focused on the behavior of their only daughter, the absence of Mr. C because of his holding two jobs, and finally on the degree of isolation and rejection by their families of origin.

In the therapy sessions held at the clinic or during home visits the therapist saw no display of excessive rage or violence between family members. The cold, stony facial appearance, rigid body posture, restricted verbalization, and seeming unreachability of the maternal grandmother gave the therapist one main clue to the degree of despair that may have been accumulating in the violent eruptions upon Mary Ann. Yet both grandparents had subsequently accepted the agency's placement of their granddaughter in their home.

For the first six months, Mrs. C was guarded and suspicious of the therapist. At times, Mr. C seemed to relate to the therapist like an inarticulate, passively compliant small boy. He was apologetic about his inability to read and write very well, which is why his wife had to write checks and handle all of the finances. At the end of one session, he spontaneously put his arms around the therapist and said, "no one ever wanted to know what I thought or felt. Whenever I spoke, it always came out the wrong way. I can't see why you keep saying it is important for me to talk about myself and my family." He said from childhood up to now too, that he had been laughed at, ignored, or exploited.

For many months, the therapist was regarded as an intrusivelike stranger who held the family members to increased and appropriate responses. It was necessary for the therapist to continuously define the children's behavior as being age-appropriate or understandable in terms of their traumatic experiences and enforced separation from the parents. Another illustration of the family's reaction toward the therapist was when the therapist came to pick up the grandparents to take them to their daughter's home (at the point when Mrs. C was expressing suicidal feelings). I had been politely seated in their living room, but was completely ignored by the siblings who walked in and out of the room, ignoring my greetings. It was as if I didn't exist.

As therapist I overtly stood my ground with them in a quiet and firm way, insisting and holding all of them to active reinvolvement with each other, within I felt tested to my own personal and professional limits. My major source of encouragement and support came from the director of the clinic. He especially reinforced my confidence when he offered to be my cotherapist on a Sunday afternoon if we would be given an opportunity to meet with the maternal grandparents and the seven siblings. The treatment of this family was a testing of our developing understanding and conviction about the value of the multigenerational approach.

The main gratification and reassurance came from observing the changes in the relationships. Despite resistances, discouragement, and risk of suicide and homicide, there began to emerge more positive feelings and behavior. Eventually, there was mutual acknowledgement of loyalty and indebtedness, and sincere concern and interest replaced the generational rejection and exploitation. The major rejection was expressed between Mrs. C's siblings, but now phone calls and visits were increased, presents were exchanged, and parties and picnics became total family affairs.

However, Mr. C was unable to accept his in-laws' efforts toward reconciliation. He remained too mistrustful, too rigidly fixed towards the idea that his wife and her family, like his own, would still try to exploit him. The therapist was not able to help him overcome his essential lack of trust in anyone. In this respect, Mr. C could be considered as having a negative therapeutic reaction since he refused to return to therapy. Nor could he accept being "adopted" by his in-laws. He remained in a negative loyalty bind with his family of origin, and retaliated upon his wife and children. Yet, in follow-up telephone conversations one year later, Mrs. C reported new hope for reconciliation: "I never thought I would live to hear my in-laws telling my husband to go home to his wife and children."

TREATMENT GOALS

Both Mr. and Mrs. C were immature, passively dependent, lonely, confused individuals who all their lives had felt emotionally abandoned and exploited by their families. It may appear as if at the conclusion of the treatment the family was worse off because the parents separated. However, one major improvement was that the children no longer were used as an arena to rebalance the parents' unfair exploitation. Behind the abusive behavior toward these children lay unresolved individual and marital conflicts which derived from negative loyalty ties to both families of origin. Their punitive and obedience-exacting expectations toward the children were modified and alleviated. The agency homemaker who was placed in the home reported, and we saw in the sessions, a much more accepting reaction towards the children's needs and demands. The three sons were returned home, and Mary Ann showed marked improvement on her weekend visits with her parents (and in nursery school too).

The greatest change developed between Mrs. C and her family of origin. She changed from a critical, hurt, angry, distrusting individual into a much more active, reaching-out, loving person. She not only began to make friends with neighbors, but she reestablished herself with a group of women with whom she had gone to school. The most marked improvement was not only with her children but with her

parents and siblings. After having rebalanced the accounts of exploitation she was open and responsive to their efforts to see her, be with her,
and help her with material things. She in turn became available to her
parents and siblings, moving from overdistancing to being actively interested and concerned about them.

Her manners and appearance became markedly different. From having an angry, sullen, defensive manner, she became more expressive of
affection and humor. There were many bad periods of despair; night
and weekend phone calls were frequent to the therapist, but she
"bounced" back more rapidly.

While she continued to express hurt and angry ambivalent feelings
about Mr. C's desertion, she remained hopeful that he would trust that
she had changed. She stated that he feared her uncontrollable temper
in the past, but now she felt very different about herself. She thought
it was his own fear of himself that kept him from returning to her and
the children. She felt that he really loved and needed all of them and
would eventually return.

CONCLUSIONS

In this nuclear family, the initial impression was that Mr. and Mrs. C
had been written off by both families of origin. Their cumulative rage
over the years of feeling exploited had been discharged with little
apparent guilt upon their daughter, Mary Ann. In different ways, both
of them felt that they had been used and exploited, or had been overavailable to their parents, and had received very little in return. Their
collusively hurt and angry feelings and despair from the past had been
mutually minimized or denied. The old arena of battle had been channeled and reenacted upon their children. The marital relationship had
been presented as a close and loving one. In turn they had become
unavailable to their families of origin and to each other.

However, the child beatings inevitably brought to the surface the
dimensions of their denied, unresolved, negative loyalty attachments
toward their families of origin. Both insisted that their families were no
resource in their struggle to meet needs in a responsible and constructive way. Nor were they willing or able to be available to their parents.
After the court entered the situation, the maternal grandparents and
siblings did take the children into their homes. However, each placement was frought with tension; even physical care was given reluctantly by the relatives. It was only in the course of family therapy that
these multiple dimensions were faced in depth. Treatment was focused

not only on the marital and parental relationship but also included the original family systems of both Mr. and Mrs. C. There was direct intervention in the inclusion of all important and available persons in their families of origin. The maternal grandparents were included in the sessions, home visits were made, and phone calls and letters addressed to the married and unmarried siblings.

As a result of opening these relationships to closer scrutiny of the denied debts and obligations—that is, the hidden loyalty dimensions— the therapist helped them undo the myth of hopeless unavailability. The therapists' interest and concern provided a model for all extended family members to face the desperate unmet dependency needs among the C's, as well as of each other. The multigenerational approach forced this family to reverse a destructive process that had existed for several generations. The emotional divorce between the maternal grandparents which had affected all the siblings to some extent was brought into the open. This provided an opportunity to become available with more involved and supportive behavior than they had shown each other in the past.

The therapist was used as a substitute parent in the exploration of the existing impoverished relationships. However, the therapeutic relationship can only be a temporary substitute for the live relationships by which families will be surrounded in their future lives. The reconstruction process included the "undoing" of fixations and unresolved accounts, but more essentially helped to rebuild the connections and hidden loyalty ties that existed between all family members. Rather than each one remaining hopelessly despairing or in guilt-laden positions, an opportunity was provided for restoring a more constructive and supportive relationship between the generations.

12

A Reconstructive Dialogue between a Family and a Cotherapy Team

The clinical material presented in this chapter will consist of excerpts and summations from the initial, middle, and terminal phases of family treatment which lasted 3½ years. Excerpts are from notes taken within the sessions. They reveal that the family was often chaotic, dispairing, provocative, and at times almost intolerably challenging to the therapists. Initially, the family appeared to be so disorganized that the therapists felt it might be impossible to effect change, but the clinical material will show that eventually there was real progress by everyone.

As excerpts from the three phases are presented, the authors will comment from several vantage points:

1. how the nuclear as well as paternal and maternal extended families were first revealed and the nature of the relationships within this specific family;

2. the way each family member viewed himself or herself as an individual within the family; how the family members saw each other;

3. the overt behaviors as transacted in the sessions, considered in the context of the hidden agenda; that is, the hierarchy of expectations and commitments toward each other and their families of origin;

4. the therapy team's methods in terms of their interventions and responses which enabled a mutual "adoption" to take place between the therapists and the family;

5. and finally, the resultant changes in all family members, not only from the point of view of the therapists, but more importantly as each member perceived his own and each other's growth; consensual confirmation on how many hidden, fragmentary aspects of each one's original family systems were integrated and brought together.

In other chapters, the authors have defined the fundamental concepts and the applicability of knowledge regarding visible and invisible loyalty commitments that exist in family systems. The concepts of loyalty in the current family and toward the family of origin have been discussed, including the ideas of indebtedness and reparations. Also reviewed were the connections between the hidden loyalty system and the assignment of roles such as scapegoating and parentification. Symptoms have been discussed in terms of their early disappearance in the designated patient, with other symptoms being reported in other family members. Family members reported new and more fundamental areas of difficulty which were not the ones that originally brought them to treatment. Many factors must be considered in the family context: generational dimensions and sexual differences are explored, since this is used to help a family define new goals for themselves.

Work with a multiperson organization such as a family places an inordinate demand upon all family members as well as upon the therapists. Even though the clinical material in this chapter will be discussed on the various levels mentioned previously, only major highlights can be touched upon. We had to learn a great deal from session to session. Even after termination there were many unexplained areas. Many transactions in sessions were overlooked, misunderstood, or had to be "unscrambled" as we did our homework in discussions between sessions. We had to wait for months at a time for additional material which illuminated a relationship pattern. Sometimes we had to "undo" our individual personal and professional reactions, or had to help each other to become reunited as a team in feeling and understanding. At times behavior in the sessions was so turbulent that there was not sufficient energy left over to be too concerned about the possible implication or meaning of the family's behavior.

In the long run, what helped this family and us was a rugged common denominator, namely, a mutual determination to face and to work through deeper relationship commitments. Eventually, we and the family could take pride in the family's progress as a result of this difficult but rewarding cooperative effort.

The work with this family and other families during these years enabled us to discover new and more fundamental dimensions and theoretical formulations about family relationships and their functioning via a family's hidden agenda—namely, that each family member's unconscious loyalty commitment to his family of origin structures the nature and quality of family relationships which are passed on in both attitudes and behavior, from generation to generation. The concepts of family loyalty and indebtedness helped the therapists and the family to understand the meaning of behavior not only within the nuclear family, but among the three generations.

At first a family may appear detached, indifferent, and noninvolved with both families of origin, or they will describe destructively negative behavior between the families. In the context of a family's loyalty system, a seemingly disloyal, drug-taking, defiant adolescent is not just a rebellious daughter who is trying to assert her independence from her parents. While the behavior is overtly self-destructive, it still is of functional value and, thus, one form of manifestation of loyalty to her family. Her behavior may bring excitement and life to the parents' detached, dead marriage; her negative behavior brings school and legal authorities, i.e., social resources which may help her and the family with the current family predicament. These authorities can be used as substitute parental authority, when a family is unable to provide it. Unconsciously, the child's behavior may be her way of forcing the parents to demonstrate care, concern, and involvement towards each family member. Manifestly, it appears as an negative or as a destructive mechanism. Underlying such efforts are the loyalty to a family system which helps restimulate life-provoking responses and increases involvement. The child is made to pay off a hidden, alleged, or imagined debt.

Before presenting the family history, clinical material and comments, we wish to make some general statements about the family and our early theoretical considerations.

The P family were a middle-class, upward-striving family, concerned with human values and family relationships which needed improvement. They were goal directed regarding education rather than being materially or possession oriented. They were an intelligent, physically attractive family, functioning fairly well in the occupational and economic world, but they maintained no social relationships.

In the inner world of their family, there had already been psychiatric hospitalizations of one parent and one child. There was isolation or overinvolvement, lack of personal differentiation, suicide attempts, and gestures of homicide. In the sessions there were at times violent, physical scenes. The streams of verbal vilification and depreciation seemed endless.

They described themselves as "four circles." They presented themselves as a detached nuclear family, who vehemently insisted that they had written off and in turn had been written off by grandparents and parental siblings in both families of origin. This myth as well as endless other statements were presented as unalterable facts. As treatment proceeded, relationships were eventually modified between nuclear and extended family members. Naturally, treatment helped the symptoms of the designated patient member first.

It is hoped that the material will reveal how these overtly negative loyalty attachments and commitments to the families of origin were affecting the functioning of this family. Beneath the wishes for change in their current relationships were unresolved yearnings for improved relationships with each one's family of origin. Change in all members of this nuclear family system simultaneously produced change in the extended family relationships. As they eventually became able to recommit themselves to each other with more supportive and responsible behavior, they were able in a constructive way to rebalance their loyalty commitments and obligations to their aged parents and siblings.

Fragments of sessions which have been selected illustrate how family members saw themselves and each other's behavior. A dynamically useful history was collected from the family as a group as they shared thoughts and feelings about each one's family of origin. Each family member described his feelings about the living grandparents and parent's siblings as well as feelings toward those who were deceased. (Mr. P's mother had died about 7 years previously, and Mrs. P's father had died 2 years previously.)

The sessions during the first months, and sporadically during the first years, were chaotic. At times the noise level was intolerable due to the yelling, screaming, slapping, punching, and crying, particularly between Anne and her father. This itself was a testing of the therapists' capacity to accept their infantile behavior. Even though the parents acted irresponsibly and tried to abdicate their executive role as parents, the therapists had to steadily demand that the family focus on specific issues. The first order of business was to insist that the parents take charge of controlling family members so that behavior and events in and outside of the sessions could be discussed. This was no easy matter, for they all talked at the same time and none listened to the others.

Noting Mrs. P's detached, seemingly nonparticipating manner during any melee, the therapists assigned her the pivotal position of quieting down the family members. This was done despite Mrs. P's insistence that she had nothing to do with provoking the violence taking place in the room. The seemingly endless, turbulent interactions eventually subsided after the therapists forced her to take an active stand instead of acting like a nonperson or outsider. Prior to therapy she was a peacemaker who kept her feelings and her needs to herself; eventually she was able to see that her nonresponses or fixed, inappropriate ones were unconsciously aiding and abetting the turmoil. It was as if some of the husband's and children's extremely impulsive behavior was enacted in order to get some kind of more controlling mothering response.

Even though the children made sporadic efforts to emotionally or physically emancipate themselves, it soon became apparent that they did not receive support and their efforts were undermined. Like iron to magnets, they continuously were pulled back into the family fold until Mrs. P became able to open her "Pandora's box" and express more genuine feelings in the sessions. In an early session, when asked why she was unable to reveal her inner feelings, she responded graphically, "there are boxes within boxes inside of me and if they were all to be opened, it would explode my marriage and my family."

It is our hope that the clinical excerpts which are only characteristic highlights will in themselves reveal the changes that took place. Illustrations of the therapists' participation and comments will be given, but the reader is reminded that much of our thinking took place outside of the sessions. In the early phase of treatment we often had to first recover our own equanimity and then, as a team, actively plan our strategy. There were even times when we did not know or care whether the family could work or even return. It often seemed a question of our own emotional welfare and survival relative to the therapy. But the therapy team and family began mutually "adopting" each other after the seventh session when the family started to show some functional improvements.

Lucille and Anne, who initially ridiculed and belittled the therapists, by the beginning of the second year brought us cakes and cookies baked especially for us. They also reported with tremendous pride any achievements, whether personal, social, or academic—demanding and expecting as much recognition from us as from their parents! This kind of give-and-take went on despite the fact that Anne continuously had a need to verbally deprecate the female therapist: "your make-up was the wrong color; your dresses were drab and never hip; your shoes were the wrong shape, etc." Often the greeting in the waiting room was, "drop dead, you old hag!" These comments, in addition to expressing loyalty to the family, implied that Anne was the spokesman for the family's negative way of expressing affection.

FAMILY HISTORY

The P family was referred for family therapy because the designated patient, Anne, now age 15, while in individual therapy had become agitated. She had picked up a carving knife, threatened to kill herself or her father and consequently was hospitalized. Her symptoms at age 13, which had initiated the original psychiatric referral, were: "temper-tantrums in the home, thumb sucking, stealing from her parents, intense feelings of inadequacy and self-depreciation, poor peer relationships, and a talent for manipulativeness." Of superior intelligence, her marks had slipped from A grades to failing in some subjects. She was described as emotionally and physically immature (no onset of menstruation).

Mr. P, age 40, was the youngest and only son in his family of origin (one sister was 8 years older, the other one 12 years older). He stated that his mother had put extreme academic demands on him, wanting him to be "my son the doctor." He described the relationship as a "harsh but indulgent one" and he felt that he had failed to live up to his mother's expectations. He always thought that his father was more interested in him, but they were never really close. He saw his father as an ineffectual man beaten down by his wife, a nervous person, who tended to isolate himself from his family. During his years at college, Mr. P had his first nervous breakdown and was given a leave of absence from the university. After being in the service for only a few months he was given a discharge because of his extreme anxiety and paranoid reactions. Eventually, he returned to college at night, working during the day, and did secure a Bachelor of Science degree. In the early years of the marriage, he continued to work towards getting a Master's degree in mathematics. However, during his wife's pregnancy with their first child, he was hospitalized for an acute psychotic episode.

Mrs. P, age 39, was a middle child, having a brother four years older and a sister two years younger. Her father had died two years previously. Her parents, like Mr. P's parents, had had a small, corner neighborhood store. The lives of both Mr. and Mrs. P were much affected by the fact that their parents had spent long hours in their shops. They worked arduously and had to continuously overaccomodate to customers in order to eke out security for themselves and their children. Mrs. P felt that her mother not only had been unavailable to her, but expected her to be very helpful both in the store and the home. Her brother was the one preferred by her mother, and her baby sister was the family "pet." She had felt closer to her father and felt protective toward him, although she considered him the weaker of the two parents. She described him as the "peacemaker" in her family of origin and now identified herself as the peacemaker between her husband and children. She had married Mr. P against her parents' wishes. Even though she described herself as the strong one upon whom everyone leaned, within she felt "unsure, perplexed, and at times overwhelmed and helpless." She gave the impression of a walled-off, tight, nonresponsive woman. She was caught in a negative relationship with her mother and her present family.

Lucille, age 17, a senior in high school, was presented as the "well sibling." The family felt she was the pretty one, socially popular, and academically a good student. There had been one brief period when she had become "boy-crazy" and her marks had slipped from A grades to C's. Upon graduating from high school, she was planning to attend a college in the city, but would be living in the school dormitory. The family perceived her as capable and independent, and anticipated no problems in the planned separation from her family. Her competence and independence shortly proved to be only a facade. Emotionally she was even more shaky than Anne, who was the symptomatic member. By the second school semester Lucille was asked to leave school because of her poor academic performance, unacceptable behavior with her peers, and the use of drugs. Lucille reported the appearance of various somatic complaints (skin problems, recurrent widespread neurodermatitis, hormonal (thyroid) imbalance, fainting spells, attacks of colitis, and menstrual difficulties).

FIRST YEAR

SESSION #1: FOUR CIRCLES: A BEGINNING

The crisis which brings the family is the psychiatric hospitalization of a member, Anne. The referral source had previously informed us about the death of Mrs. P's father two years earlier, which coincided with the original request for treatment of Anne.

The therapists begin the initial session by asking them to tell us what brought them to request family treatment. The emphasis is thus turned away from the designated patient as the sole focus. They are requested to give a presentation of the whole family and to include comments about each member.

Mr. P: Anne is so similar to me that we never hit it off.
Anne: My mother is a "blah!"
Mrs. P: We are four circles circling but never getting close. Anne feels no one cares for her. We never mesh. It is many times a contrived situation.
Mr. P: It was my circle because I've been away at school two to four nights a week; my life has centered around my studying and going to school. Lucille has launched off on her own, and now that she is dating acts like she is grown up and doesn't need us.

Mrs. P: I'm blah because I try to keep on an even keel amidst hostility and genuine hatred. My husband is inclined to violence.

Mr. P: I agree with my wife; she is the one who refuses to meet violence with violence.

Lucille: I want to come home to a house where people are smiling.

At the end of the first session, the therapists ponder "who is the sick one and who is driving whom crazy?" How can we help unify a "four circle" family?

SESSION #4: CURRENT AND HISTORICAL RELATIONSHIPS

The therapists note that the family seems to be more relaxed in our presence, but they are also becoming verbally and physically provocative. We are being tested, and our responses are being noted and commented upon. (Anne seems to be the leader in the crazy, provocative behavior that they have been revealing in the sessions. There is punching, hair pulling, scratching, and biting, mostly between Anne and her father. Chairs are overturned and doors are banged. The therapists ask them to compare this family life with life in their original families.)

Mr. P: I must admit that I get pleasure in fighting just as Anne does.

Mrs. P: My parents argued a great deal over the store. My mother was the boss, and I was my father's favorite. My brother and sister were allies and continuously fought me. No one protected me. My mother was on their side. (She almost cries as she talks about her father.) He never developed his potential. Although he was the weak one in the family, he is the only one who gave me the feeling that someone cared about me. I never wanted to be like my bossy mother and sister.

Mrs. P: My parents also worked hard in their store. My father was excitable, and the customers were always upsetting him. My mother was more stable and a better business manager than my father. However, she overworked and was a martyr who made others feel guilty. I therefore was always angry and guilty because of them. My sisters were 12 and 8 years older than me, and got out early; I was the baby and supposedly the favorite.

Anne: There is only deadness in this family.

The value of getting generational relationship history within the session is that all of them have opportunity to learn unknown facts about each other and to begin to express feelings regarding their guilt feelings and unresolved loyalty conflicts between themselves and both families of origin.

By securing historically diagnostic material, the therapists also begin to evaluate and tentatively hypothesize about some elements of the relationships which may have been transferred from the previous parent–child relationships onto the current ones. We notice that Mrs. P feels opposed to her own mother and plan to keep in mind how this can be affecting her role vis-a-vis her daughters.

Mr. P. affirms that he always felt angry and guilty in his family of origin as well as currently. Once the screaming, angry "baby" in his family of origin, he now appears to demand "parenting" from his wife at the expense of her needs as well as the children's. He asks the therapists how the sessions can be more productive for the family. The therapists respond by suggesting he try to restrain his disruptive behavior and take the leadership on important family issues.

In a session that follows, Lucille says the therapists are helping her to see her parents in a more human way. This comment is interpreted as urging the family to continue in therapy.

SESSION #6: PARENTAL NONRESPONSIBILITY

Anne comes into the session taunting and provoking her parents, especially her father. The therapists again insist that Mrs. P be more assertive in controlling Anne's behavior. Can they begin to change anything in this family? For example, can Mr. P. enable his wife to settle things directly with Anne without his interference? Then for the first time, Mr. P. tries to control his provocative behavior. Anne is finding for the moment that she cannot maneuver her parents, and turns on the therapists to demand that we tell her exactly how we can help all of them. The therapists direct this question to the parents, inquiring what they think some of their goals are for themselves. Mr. P says he realizes that when Anne is provocative, he responds sadistically; Dr. N agrees that it is a mutual need-satisfying relationship, but suggests that Mr. P consider why violence toward Anne gives him gratification: Where did this originate and is Anne the only person with whom he is angry?

We are being tested as to whether we will take over the parental function of controlling impulsive and explosive behavior and whether we can hold the parents to be more responsible. In addition, the family members' responses are inappropriate, closed, and dead-end which reinforces the frustration and nongratification of one another's needs.

The therapists, in pushing Mrs. P to be more actively responsive, do not accept her comments that she must play this self-denying martyr role for survival purposes. Mr. P is asked to support our interpretation, and again it is requested that he let his wife handle the provocation between Anne and herself.

SESSION #7: BEGINNINGS OF CHANGE IN THE SYSTEM

The family says that something is beginning to shift in the family. Mrs. P has a new and better-paying job. Mr. P has been told that he might be advanced professionally. However, it appears that Mr. P depends on his wife as his conscience for not completing his master's thesis. Lucille says that she is going to receive a second scholarship for college. Mr. and Mrs. P report that they are planning a vacation without the children, something they have not done for many years.

Mr. P: After the previous session, Anne had apologized to her mother in a more genuine way than ever before. Even the relationship between the children was more "sisterly." Anne was less rude and provocative.

The family members report various changes and improvements that have taken place. These must be considered as temporary or transference-like improvements rather than any structural or basic change in their relationships. Some families and therapists might accept the above change as a goal and terminate treatment. The therapists view this as the family briefly experiencing new hope and courage to face the more fundamental, hidden problems in the family system. Naturally, continued work can be expected only if the family members are so motivated.

SESSION #8: THE PEACEMAKER ROLE

Mrs. P: Things are more relaxed at home. I have a new job. Lucille has two scholarships and will be able to live in the dorm.

Dr. N: How do things compare with Mr. P's family?

Mrs. P: It always was difficult to visit with my inlaws. It was like it is with Anne: As soon as he was with his family, my husband would put on his mask of hostility and fight . . . because that is how his family was.

Mr. P: Even then my wife acted like a peacemaker, calming my family.

Mrs. P: This is my father in me, we needed to be peacemakers.

Dr. N: (interprets) Peacemakers need turmoil!

Anne: So my mother is more a troublemaker than I am because she needs us to make trouble to make peace.

Lucille: My father's family must have been similar to this one in that they didn't let strangers in. (to her father) How would you accept my husband if I got married?

Anne: We aren't ready yet for my mother to have a son-in-law. (It is obvious that everybody is unhappy about the prospect of Lucille dating and getting married, and Anne is the spokesman for the family.)

Mrs. P: My husband and I are going away on vacation for four days, our first in seven years.

Lucille: That is too much for me; two days would be enough with Anne.

This session indicates two points: that they have limited capacity to trust and let strangers in; and that they are limited in coping through peacemaking and cannot permit a genuine dialogue to take place. The therapists continue in not "taking over" but demonstrate their ability to "take it" while expecting the parents to assert themselves as parents.

Anne's statement prepares us for the immediate problems of separation—Lucille's leaving for college. However, the parents' vacation plans are symbolic of a beginning separation of the marital and parental issues.

SESSION #10: CHALLENGE OF THE "WELL SIBLING" MYTH

Lucille is away at school for one week, and although she says she is happy at school, she now has a bad itch all over her body. Both parents deny that they miss her in any way; Mr. P's tone implies that whether or not she is with them matters very little.

Lucille bursts out with anger regarding his lack of understanding about her feelings—as when he tore up a picture of the "Beatles" which meant so much to her. For years she has had all kinds of feelings stored up in her which they have never permitted her to express. She is sick and tired of being left out, ridiculed, and physically abused.

The therapists ask the family whether they have been aware that Lucille has felt that they never really listened to her and that she has felt left out? In this family, must a member restort to some form of violence to be heard? Lucille cannot talk to anyone! Even in childhood she used to sit alone while the other three watched TV.

The family begins to reveal that Mrs. P and Lucille have severe psychosomatic symptoms (colitis, dermatitis, menstrual difficulties). Of equal importance in this family system is that people do have to be violent in order to be heard; hurt or angry feelings are responded to with more violence rather than with compassion, concern, or inquiry into the suffering. Anne is the overt "carrier" of or stimulator for a crazy verbal attack in the session, which seems to be in response to Lucille's physical separation from the family.

SESSION #11: CONFRONTATION REGARDING DESTRUCTIVELY CHAOTIC RESPONSES

Lucille is absent. Anne tries her usual tactic of trying to provoke a fight; after getting no response she bounces out of the room.

Mrs. P: Lucille and I had a disagreement this weekend and although I sided with my husband, I really feel Lucille's accusations are justified. My husband goes into his daughters' bedrooms, prying and snooping through their personal possessions. (This is first time in a session that Mrs. P confronts her husband with her angry dissatisfaction.) He is impulsive and unpredictable. At times he threatens to kill himself or others—goes around muttering and cursing. It is hopeless because I cannot change him. Recently I am becoming the angry one and he the reasonable one. I have swallowed too much all my life.

Mr. P: I am aware that my wife does not turn to me with problems. I feel deprived of the opportunity to comfort her and also left out of the family.

The therapists note: Is there any middle ground between being an observer or being violent in this family? We also reflect back to Mr. and Mrs. P several other things we have noticed in the sessions: They do not have any direct or open conversations with each other. They seem to talk to each other either through the children or limit their remarks only to the children's problems. If someone makes a personal or meaningful comment, the others do not respond except with laughter, which in essence disconfirms the other person. Sometimes they seem to pseudo-agree but always place the tension or cause of their disagreement onto the children.

We continue to push the family to become aware of their inability to have a genuine dialogue with each other. Although Mrs. P begins to feebly confront the family members with her own angry feelings, she says in a session that follows: "if I were to open up, I am afraid of what would happen to my marriage and family!"

SESSION #14: TRANSFERENCE MANIFESTATIONS

As the therapists enter the room, there is a great deal of yelling and physical scuffling going on. For several months this kind of behavior had diminished.

Mrs. P: I have been thinking about Dr. N's comment from last week and want him to explain again why he said the family was not taking responsibility for their own or each other's behavior. (She is visibly angry towards both therapists.) I don't see how anyone would be helped by talking about how one feels inside.

Dr. N: It seems that your silence incites your daughters into acting crazy in the sessions. They need more appropriate responses. Your husband had stated several times that he wants you to talk to him too, to tell him how you feel about many things. In the sessions, you really act like a nonperson; that is, you never take an "I position" toward anyone or about any issue that is brought up.

Mrs. P: I have been upset by my daughter's reported escapades at college. (However, she reports this in a matter of fact tone, and says she has nothing further to say on the matter.)

Mrs. P refuses to elaborate upon her statement, and the therapists are unable to help her bring out a more effective response. The children then produce filibuster-like tactics. They become challenging towards the therapists and pour out amorphous anger towards all the adults. The therapists attempt in no way to replace the parental position of giving a more adequate response to Lucille's delinquent behavior at school. Instead, when the parents "abdicate" as they did in this session, this is again pointed out to them. The children, through noise and confusion, seem to throw up a protective screen between the parents and the therapists.

The sessions continuously amount to a test of our conviction that the parents need to take responsibility for the chaos and need to learn how to act as parents—specifically in defining their values toward their children and setting limits. The rage that is at times directed toward both therapists is a test also of our capacity to continue to handle the family with composure, while holding them to dealing with the children with firmness and strength.

We become aware that as we confronted, guided, and demanded more appropriate responses that Mrs. P is making attempts to move out of the passive-peacemaker bind. She begins to experience our efforts as interest and concern for her as a person.

However, this session also illustrates the parents' collusive ambivalence and resistance to the therapists' urgings that they take charge of the children's behavior and respond more genuinely. Although the family tries to scapegoat the therapists in response to their strong demand for more appropriate responses, they are not successful in making the therapists defensively counterattack. The children, in using filibustering tactics, try to protect their parents from the therapists' comments. The therapists are not readily silenced, although after many sessions they are left feeling battered and drained.

In a subsequent session the therapists are again challenged by the family's disruptive behavior and are told by Mrs. P that they are not trusted. Dr. N responds, "Where can you go from here? What is the risk to the family?" Mrs. P then states she will try to change her position with her husband in that she will no longer think for him or push him as if he were a baby.

SESSION #16: AMORPHOUS SEXUALITY AND LACK OF BOUNDARIES

The family is bantering about something which at first we cannot follow: the cooperation of Anne is to be rewarded by $4 . . . Anne then proceeds to sit on her father's lap, wiggling up and down, obviously stimulating him and herself in a physical way. The family looks at the therapists, trying to determine our reactions. Dr. N asks Mrs. P whether there is anything in this behavior between her husband and daughter that is upsetting to her, since by remaining silent she seems accepting of it.

Lucille: She's had similar experiences like this in the past.

Mrs. S asks Mr. P Are you caressing Anne as if she were a baby or as a young, attractive female? Is this incest or not? Is there anyone in the room willing or able to stop what is going on?

Finally, Mrs. P responds: She is annoyed by the lack of boundary between stimulation, affection, and what looks to her like incest. However, she says and does nothing to try to interrupt either her husband's or daughter's behavior.

Lucille: The sex goes 50–50 between my father and Anne and between my father and mother. Anne's a prostitute.

Anne then turns to the male therapist and aggressively asks him if he is jealous and would like her to sit on his lap. The therapists confront the family with the apparent discrepancy between behavior and affect. There is always excessive smiling and inappropriate laughter. Murderous talk and inappropriate sexual behavior are met with inappropriate responses. We tell them that we would not like to be a member of this family since any intense or genuine feelings are ridiculed, denied, or minimized.

Mrs. P: I will no longer continue to be used by my husband as I have been in the past at my own or the children's expense. (As she openly confronts Mr.

P, we see a beginning shift. Her martyrlike mask and composure are being dropped a little as she expresses more underlying resentment towards her husband. She is beginning to refuse to act like her husband's conscience.)

The therapists continue to be tested regarding their acceptance of this family's infantile, primitive exploration of each other. Although they repeatedly try to parentify us by manipulating them into taking over for the parents, we steadily hold them to facing how their need for affection is fused with incestuous touching, etc. The family is forced to differentiate between the two.

SESSION #22: TRANSFERENCE DIMENSIONS BETWEEN MRS. P AND THE THERAPISTS

There is a confrontation between Mrs. P and the female therapist. Mrs. P is asked how she feels Mrs. S could be more helpful to her. Why does Mrs. P fight so hard to hold back her feelings? Has she ever been able to trust anyone; does she have any close women friends? This is said to her at a point in the session when Mrs. P is fighting to hold back her tears as she speaks of being a failure as a woman, as a wife and mother.

Mrs. P: You would like to see me cry for your own benefit! I learned to hold back my feelings because my mother always said we will talk on Sunday, but Sunday never came. Or, if we sometimes talked my mother betrayed my confidences.

Dr. N: Does Mrs. P keep quiet in order to appear as if in control of everything; as if she always had to be the adequate and strong one?

Mrs. P: I don't know how I really feel inside about anything or anyone; for so long I have been submerged in Mr. P and living through him. Besides, if I let go I am afraid of getting a bellyache or of having a colitis attack. (This symptom is mentioned here for the first time.) I never realized that other people, even my family, experienced me as a detached person and were unable to get close to me. I would like to become more of an "I" but don't know how.

Mrs. P vacillates in a gamelike way with the therapists, "wait until Sunday and maybe I'll talk about myself." She fights hard to continue as a walled-off, insulated, nonreactive person. She feels this is the way she can keep peace in the family. To protect herself, she agrees with Mr. P, but the battles are fought through the children.

The therapists urge Mrs. P to directly express how she feels, commenting that words cannot kill! We push them to trust us about opening up instead of maintaining the family's failure game of holding back as if they would kill or destroy each other. Dr. N tells them that, "only by opening up can Mrs. P learn who she really is and what she feels and can then help herself and her family."

SESSION #26: MARITAL INCOMPATIBILITY REVEALED (SEPARATE SESSION WITH THE COUPLE)

Mr. P: We have achieved a middle ground. Our desires are different.

Mrs. P: Damn kids inhibit me. I can't relax. There are sounds; noises bother me . . . (Children are blamed and psychologically are in bedroom.) We should go out to a motel. Once a week would be enough. My mother had strong antisex attitudes.

The family is told from the outset that they are free to use the sessions to discuss their parental or marital relationships. Thus marital privacy is encouraged and the children completely accept being left out of those sessions. The initiative is left up to the adults as to how they will use a session.

Mrs. P reveals not only some of her fears and inhibitions, but the fact that the children's presence in the home is permitted to be a major factor in her sexual nonresponsiveness. Mrs. P states that Mr. P is not only "heard" before the children are, but that he shuts out the children by too much seductive behavior in front of them. He denies that this overstimulates his daughters.

In a session that follows, Mr. and Mrs. P are direct about their feelings toward the therapists:

Mrs. P: There is a flow from you. I call it alchemy. Catalyzing a better relationship that makes us feel happier. We make you frustrated.

Mr. P: I give you credit for infinite patience. We probably progress slower than you want us to.

Mrs. P: For one thing, it helps for me to be able to express my feelings here! We always allowed Anne to dominate the conversations.

This is a beginning recognition by the parents' of their own expectations and of the therapists' efforts to help them toward more appropriate marital and parental behavior. However, these words are promptly followed by a melee between Anne and her father. This reflects the ambivalent wish to change and the fear of change, since there was still a very long way to go from verbal praise to behavioral realignment.

In a later session, Mrs. P is more open about her ambivalent feelings toward Anne and her husband: "I love and hate both of them." Mr. P's response is that at least he is getting to know more about his wife and with whom she is angry. The therapists also help Mrs. P to connect such feelings back to her family of origin. We begin to introduce the possibility that she bring her mother to the sessions. The therapists try to help her face the fact that some of her reactions have been carried over from the past and are now reexperienced in current relationships. We question the validity of the hopelessness that she expresses regarding her relationship with her mother. Mrs. P agrees to consider including her mother and plans to find out how her mother would feel about coming to such meetings. Several months later her mother attends several sessions.

SESSION #30: REGRESSIVE BEHAVIOR AND MORE INAPPROPRIATE RESPONSES

Lucille: I am sick and tired of the other three fighting, especially Anne and my father—with my mother sitting there silently. I have been going thru an emotional drain last month. I am not able to sleep or look at a book in school . . . the words don't make sense. I take tranquilizers. I even fell and had a slight concussion. The crazy fights at home worry me. I even find myself fighting with my boyfriend. Lucille pleads with the parents, "if they disagree with something I'm doing they should tell me in an adult way instead of merely being sarcastically evasive.

The therapists again comment that Lucille seems to be asking her parents for limits as well as more direct responses of caring and concern. We ask the parents directly, can either one express genuine feelings of concern towards Lucille rather than being destructively critical?

Lucille withdraws from her previous efforts to cope with school, is failing academically, and has poor peer relationships. She reports that she has been experimenting with drugs, is fearful of pregnancy and veneral disease as a result of her promiscuity, and is being threatened with expulsion from school. She has never experienced the basic support or trust, encouragement, and guidance—those fundamentals which a child requires from parents in order to function adequately. The therapists cannot be substitutes for the natural parents. However, it is not until Mr. and Mrs. P can begin to rework their loyalty ties to their own parents that they can provide adequate parenting to their children.

SESSION #32: DOUBLE BIND AND LOYALTY ISSUES

Anne (in tears, turns to the therapists): Should parents laugh at their children?

Mrs. P: I try not to laugh ever since it was pointed out here.

Anne: I have no privacy. My mother went through all my drawers using as an excuse that she was looking for a sweater. Nobody protects me from being laughed at (cries even harder). The two people in the whole world who were supposed to love you ever since birth turn against you and laugh at you. They shouldn't speak for me and tell me how I feel or distort what I say. When I grabbed the knife it was because my father laughed at me! You may lock me up each time when they laugh at me and the same thing will happen!

Mr. P: I laugh so I won't kill! The murder is inside me. I don't know where it comes from. I'm trying to grow up and learn to listen.

The therapists continue to demand that each one not cut off the others' conversation and do not permit anyone to divert from the feelings and explanation which the person is giving. No one in the sessions is permitted to answer for another. Anger in this family also originates from not being permitted to express personal meaning.

Mrs. P seems to accept our comment that she is a martyr who acts as if she had never received sufficient love or interest; however, she finds in turn that her husband and children are constantly demanding that she be totally available to each one of them.

By contrast, Anne who was the overtly "crazy" family member, has been bound in the family system in a symbiotically loyal way. She reveals how she is held in—and accepts being in—an overinvolved, nonindividuated relationship with her parents. Lucille, by contrast is presented as the pseudoadequate sibling who would be able to separate emotionally and leave home physically. However, these sessions only reveal the different aspects of the family system's inability to encourage and support emotional growth and separation of the children. This is similar to both grandparents being unable to help Mr. and Mrs. P work through and balance out their loyalty commitments to the families of origin.

In sessions that follow, Mrs. P expresses resistance to change and obligations and to continuing therapy. She brings out thoughts of separation or divorce as a solution to her marital difficulties. We point out that if she wishes, she can keep "running away emotionally," but this has not helped her to find more gratification for herself.

SESSION #39: NEGATIVE ASPECTS OF INTERGENERATIONAL LOYALTY ARE REEXPERIENCED

Mrs. P: Recently I have been able to effectively shut my sister up. My sister talks incessantly "at me"—it is never a meaningful or personal conversation. As far as my mother is concerned it is hopeless. Nothing can change that relationship. My mother has a tendency to talk bad about everybody. I therefore withhold anything concerning myself, husband, and children so that my mother will not use it and be critical of them. My mother I can't trust, and I am the same way. I don't like myself either (she cries). I can't say I've done anything of which I can be proud (crying continues). I live hypocritically. I can make a good impression, but I can't back it up. I blame myself for the way the children have turned out.

Dr. N.: Is Mr. P merely an observer? Can you find a middle ground between violence and merely being in the passive observer role?

Mr. P: I want to stay away from the violent role at all costs. But I don't like the fact that my wife does not assert herself.

Just as the children have been able to reveal their feelings of hopelessness and despair, so Mrs. P begins to reveal more openly how hopeless she feels about her mother and siblings. As the two-generational maternal rejection pattern is more openly revealed, the painful feelings about the deprivation are reexperienced.

Mr. P. still continues to vacillate from being a passive observer to exhibiting violent, explosive behavior. He is not ready or able to explore his role in his family of origin, but again emphasizes a wish for his wife to change first in becoming more expressive of her feelings. The parentification of Mrs. P by her husband continues as long as he is unable to use the therapists' encouragement to examine his past and present passively dependent way of relating.

In an interim session Mrs. P states, "I can give the encouragement to my family, which I didn't get from my mother. I can't talk to Mrs. S as a woman because the others are present." Dr. N. comments, "Maybe it is the other way around; the need is so great towards Mrs. S that turning it off is the only way to handle it." Mrs. P counters this with, "I see no purpose in trying to change my mother. She has such tendencies to talk bad about my family so I don't tell her very much."

SESSION #44: THREE-GENERATIONAL DIMENSIONS OF MR. P ARE EXPLORED

Mr. P: I have changed and can now openly express that I love my wife. So much of the time though I don't know what to do; nor do I know what my wife is upset about.

Mrs. P: (cries): For the last three days all I hear is Anne saying how horrible she is, how badly she looks, overweight, and a fat slob. Lucille isn't interested in her family or heritage. (She recalls that Mr. P never comforted her during her pregnancies.)

Mr. P: I guess I am like my father who is going to take his feelings to the grave. I feel that my thoughts were never given enough weight or respect either by my family of origin or my wife and children. The only feelings I ever expressed were those of frustration or anger. My mother had some praise for me but never a smile. My father always held his feelings inside. (He recalls that his mother spent her last five years in a nursing home as a stroke patient who was unable to talk.) Never had a chance to improve my relationship with my mother who is now dead.

Mr. P begins seriously to compare his role in his current family with his family of origin. There also is evidence of system changes in his being able for the first time to openly express the fact that, while he loves his wife, there is still need for improvement between them.

SESSION #48: FOUR-GENERATIONAL RELATIONAL EXPLORATION (MRS. P AND MGM PRESENT)

MGM: I don't think that my daughter Ruth (Mrs. P) was neglected. She was a sickly child. I see my other daughter more often. She lives closer. Anne has a complex that nobody loves her.

Dr. N: Do any of your children feel that way?

MGM: I don't think so. My son-in-law didn't love Anne, didn't fuss over her as a baby. When I was 14 I came to this country and had to help my parents, the same as it was between my husband and me. Ruth didn't get along with her brothers. When she was born her brother was jealous. My husband left everything up to me. He couldn't control the kids at the table. I was the strong one. We were far apart from our parents. No warmth and no feeling in the house. My father was standoffish. I think I understood my children better than my husband did. His theory was that you shouldn't show too much love to the children. Maybe my children felt that I was like my mother who had no time for me. For my husband the customers were more important than anybody; (cries) even when the children were hungry and the food was burning on the stove, I had to go into the store.

This material reveals those aspects of the family system that resulted in splits between the parents and the previous generations, and specifically highlights the issue of the martyred mother—as if she were stronger and more concerned with the children than the father. Just as children have been parentified in one generation, it continues to be repeated and lived out in successive generations. The children are the targets for exploitation of the marital arena, with conflicts arising within the marital relationship remaining unresolved.

SESSION #49: THE PROCESS OF NEGATIVE IDENTIFICATION AND LOYALTY CONTINUE TO BE EXPLORED

MGM: I didn't hear anything new from Ruth last week. Ruth was grown up young; at 12 she was able to shop on her own. I had an older brother like Ruth, and both brothers seemed to be less responsible than their sisters. I can't see any improvement between my daughter and me. She tells me some of her troubles, but I know she does not tell me everything in order not to aggravate me because she is afraid I will get sick. My children didn't dare talk to me the way her daughters do—the kind of language they use! As far as Anne, I have seen it for a long time, she always felt her father didn't like her . . . maybe that's part of it. I never knew Ruth was an unhappy child.

Mrs. P: (crying) My father didn't try to get out of his responsibilities; he wanted to please his wife.

MGM: Ruth and my husband were closer than her sister and her father. He would even turn to Ruth with personal grievances against me in the later years.

Both Mrs. P and her mother continue to share their rivalrous and competitive feelings towards each other and the men in the family. This covers over the underlying despair and loneliness. Mutually, they reveal and share their negative loyalty commitments to their families of origin. In being bound to each other in a destructive mother image (just as maternal grandmother was to her mother), they are unable to be available as a constructive resource to one other or to their mates.

SESSION #50: NEGATIVE IDENTIFICATION SHIFTS

(Mr. and Mrs. P and Maternal Grandmother).

MGM: I had a headache this morning which I rarely have.

Mrs. P: I think that after my parents got out of the business that their marriage improved.

MGM: I loved all my children the same; if one abused the other, the abuser got the punishment. I feel that my daughter was too harsh with Anne. She was chastized whenever she made a face at Lucille . . . she may be sick because of that.

Mrs. P: Anne always created serious dissension, especially when the grandparents came to the house.

MGM: I tried to help; when my daughter was pregnant I was the one who signed my son-in-law out of the psychiatric hospital.

Mrs. P: Yes, this one time you helped, but the only one. Otherwise, you have critized me constantly by telling me that other people's children were better. Last week I learned how much I am displaying the same kind of destructive love as my mother . . . by not praising, taking good things for granted and critizing.

MGM: I had to make all decisions, my husband made me the boss, and I resented it. I learned here that my daughter thinks there is a wall between us.

In this third session with the maternal grandmother, the couple continue to review their similarities and begin to clarify some of the misunderstandings and nonavailability between them. Both of them have been overcritical with their mate and children. Although both of them scapegoat Anne as a "disrupter," they recall that in the past the maternal grandmother has also been helpful. Facing the fact that a "wall" exists between them helps to renew their hope of overcoming the distance and possibly becoming available in a more loving and meaningful way. If they can rework their relationship, then Anne will no longer need to be used as the "bad object" upon whom they project their lonely, hurt, and angry feelings. In becoming more supportive to each other, feelings of guilt and indebtedness are diminished.

In the sessions that follow, Mrs. P says she is more expressive towards her husband. They plan another vacation. Afterwards, they hold each other's hand and report it was a "honeymoon" vacation.

YEAR II: CROSSROADS OF CHANGE

SESSION #53: SYSTEM CHANGES IN THE MARITAL RELATIONSHIP

Mrs. P: The behavior of both girls is changing. Anne may be a scholarship winner; her grades are improving. They double-dated and talk to each other like two girls. I also received a new engagement ring.

Mr. P: We can enjoy each other better.

Mrs. P: We can work together on putting the children in their place.

Dr. N: Have you gained from the session with your mother and from seeing any other similarities in those patterns?

Mrs. P: My mother has started to blame herself for having been a domineering wife and mother who was less than helpful to her children. She also has realized how much resentment there was between my brother and me. At least I was able to express my yearning in my mother's presence, whether she heard me or not.

Mrs. S: Is there a sexual difference compared with the past?

Mrs. P: I am less distracted while making love. I have been bothered by the fact that the girls might walk into the bedroom.

Mr. P: I have learned to listen to the children's point of view. I think now before I shoot my mouth off. I feel that the children want guidance, am concerned about Lucille's promiscuity. My wife and I don't agree about all of this.

This session describes improvements in many areas. We are aware that these shifts and improvements may be temporary, but they do have the positive feedback of encouraging the family to continue to work towards increased openness and sharing. The sessions which include Mrs. P's mother help her face her need to project her feelings onto her children and husband. They also highlight the need to "balance the ledger" towards her family.

SESSION #54: FURTHER TRANSFERENCE

After a vacation period, they are asked whether they missed the therapists.

Mrs. P: There wasn't a definite lack. I try to filter out personal feelings. You two are "functional" human beings. Yet, I guess I was very angry at Mrs. S because she seemed to want to force a personal relationship. It has to terminate in a reasonable time, so it can't be a friendship. I have gotten something out of this as far as Anne is concerned, but I always have to be the fall guy! (cries) I'm supposed to open up my relationships, but I don't know anything about you two. (Anne starts to cry too, and says to Mrs. S, "Do you care about us?")
Dr. N: Is the yearning pushed back so that Mrs. P can't be hurt again?
Mrs. P: I can't get involved. I can't be concerned with myself and others too . . . to examine myself and look at you too.

Mrs. P fights hard not to reexperience the yearning to be loved, as though she will have to be rejected or lose a beloved person again.

In a subsequent session Mrs. P turns to Dr. N and says, "You are wise to keep silent—but at least you listen. My father and my husband never listen."

It is significant that Mrs. P says she knows nothing about our personal lives and Anne again asks whether we care about them. This material follows the sessions in which the maternal grandmother revealed a great deal of information and feelings about her past life. We have steadily encouraged more sharing and availability between Mrs. P and her mother—just as we continue to push for more appropriate responsiveness between the parents and their two daughters.

SESSION #56: SYSTEM SHIFTS AND SEPARATION ISSUES

Mrs. P: I did try to cope differently with things during this year; but I exceeded my way of coping and nothing has replaced it (cries). I don't feel I can make a decision about anything (doesn't know whether to let Lucille do as she pleases or make her do what parents want her to do). I feel like the "fall guy" in the whole situation . . . but I do want to tell Mrs. S. . . . Most anything you would say I would take as criticism!

Dr.N: What is happening to this family—feelings of loss?

Mrs. P: Definitely, I lost one daughter and am losing another and I want two of them (cries and is referring to children going to college). I sacrificed one relationship to strengthen another. It is too soon to cut the umbilical cord—for both Lucille and myself. I didn't have parents who wanted to help me . . . I had parents who didn't understand what I was trying to do.

Mrs. P begins to gain more awareness or insight regarding her feelings toward her parents and how those relationships affect or are transferred to the relationship with the therapists. She is afraid of reexperiencing her past pain about not having had parents who were available or interested in her or who understood her. However, she does remain in therapy, demanding we help her to cope more adequately with her current family relationships. While being openly critical and nontrusting of the therapists, she does reveal her dependency and involvement with us.

SESSION #60: CHILDREN AS SAFETY VALVES FOR MARITAL DISSATISFACTION

Lucille is having difficulties at school, missing classes, partying too much.

Lucille: They consider me a hippy . . . the drug scene, I don't need drugs, I can look at a flower.

Mr. P: (stands up) You have been missing school and messing up your status as a student.

Mrs. P: I feel betrayed by you. You talk out of one side of your mouth and act another. (Anne acts up, becomes verbally provocative and is hit across the mouth by her father. She cries and since her lip is cut her mother rushes her to the bathroom.)

Therapists: Is Anne an extension of her mother, and when Mr. P hit Anne is he hitting back at his wife? (At this point when Mr. P shows his anger, Mrs. P admits that he does carry the anger for both of them. Mr. P says he is not really supported by his wife. They are unable to be authoritative but can only still react with physical punishment.)

Anne: I still never get a response from my mother.

Dr. N: Lucille pours gasoline on fire by her behavior and Mrs. P says I see a little pink flame, then Lucille pours on more gasoline. (The therapists had the feeling of unmanageable anger on the part of Mr. P. If he really let go would he kill his wife?)

The children are still being used as the arena for both parents to act out their individual and marital frustrations. They reenact the generational aspects of their own unmet dependency needs as children— which had previously been responded to by physical or emotional deprivation or punishment.

SESSION #61: DESPAIR AND SUICIDAL THOUGHTS: THERAPISTS AS SCAPEGOATS

A special meeting is asked for by Mrs. P.

Mrs.P: I have been crying since the last sessions three days ago. Lucille is on LSD . . . I was hit on the head . . . my husband lacerated Anne's mouth . . . he receives the applause . . . I am the monster . . . you look at me for the answer . . . then there is no point in living . . . I never felt so completely alone . . . The roof caved in. Everything was my fault . . . my driving was bad.

Mrs. S: You used the word "betrayed."

Mrs. P: You jumped at it. You didn't accept it. You asked me what I need . . . I said confidence . . . I had not gotten any. You have destroyed my way of competence . . . you stumped it into tiny bits . . . I am being tossed about . . . took sleeping capsule at three a.m. I was tempted to take all of it . . . so completely alone . . . so completely responsible. I hate both of you . . . both frauds, pretend to help . . . take away all defenses, no substitute. Are you telling me what's missing . . . ? What have you done for me! I've let you break down all that I have.

Dr. N: Does loneliness lead to recollections of the past?

Mrs. P: No.

Mrs. S: Was there ever anyone to turn to? Can you let anyone comfort you?

Mrs. P: Nobody . . . I handled it better. There is no future . . . The only thing I could think of was Anne . . . she was trying to console me. I talked to my sister today.

Mrs. S: Did your mother say you betrayed her?

Mrs. P: All the time after I married. What do you both really have to offer? I am not coming back. What is it that my daughter needs?

Dr. N: Expression of your feelings.

Mr. P: We agreed that I express my feelings to the children when the excitement is high, but she controls herself.

Mrs. P: My mother was happy that I left . . . I concentrated on my husband's problems. I didn't want Lucille to repeat it . . . Betrayal . . . here we are trying all we can.

Mrs. S: Your mother didn't want to lose you . . . your mother said here you were her best child.

Mrs. P: I don't believe it.

Mr. P: Your mother doesn't want to go to your sister's house.

Mrs. P: No, because my sister is too excitable.

Mr. P: I am to blame, I shut her up by talking . . . there should be meetings without me.

Even though Mrs. P is extremely upset as the family situation spirals from crisis to crisis, she does turn to the therapists with her feelings of despair and helplessness. In addition, she seeks consolation from her daughter Anne and her own younger sister. She does not lean on or turn to her husband. The therapists, while showing concern and compassion, do not condone her wallowing in her professed helplessness. They also help her to connect such feelings with feelings of having "betrayed" or having felt disloyal to her mother when she left and married a man whom her family felt was "unacceptable." Mr. P. supports the therapists when Mrs. P is told that she as well as her daughter needs expressions of concern and support rather than condemnation and criticism. An essential issue that emerges periodically is trying to move out of this negative, isolated loyalty bind and turning to others in a more trusting and meaningful way. She feels unable to rely on her mother or husband as persons who could be leaned on or trusted—almost as if they did not exist.

SESSION #62: CHILDREN CAN BE DEPENDENTLY AGE-APPROPRIATE

Lucille was dropped by her college

Mrs. P: I am shook up. We have to go back and use restrictions. Lucille lost our trust.

Mrs. S: You have two babies back home!

Mrs. P: Cutting the umbilical cord too soon! I woke up in the middle of the night with palpitations, which is new. I'm tired because I haven't slept (cries). Anne hugs her: "I love my mommy."

Anne: Lucille, you never were a cuddly baby.

Lucille: I wanted to sit next to my mother from the beginning. I don't have anybody. I am lonely (cries).

Dr. N: When was the last time there was any show of affection between mother and Lucille?

Mrs.P: I don't know.

Lucille: Last year my mother was not feeling well so I tucked her in bed. (Mrs. P again expresses anger at Lucille about school, drugs, boyfriends).

Lucille: I'm a bad seed. Talking to my mother is like talking to a wall!

Mrs. P: I feel if I reach out I will be repulsed (touches Lucille's hand). I don't want to be hurt anymore.

Lucille's acting-out behavior appears to bring her back as a loyal daughter into the family fold. In one sense, both children are still seeking the "mothering" that they have never received. While there are tentative moves in that direction, Mrs. P also desperately needs the "mothering" she has never been able to receive from her mother. The interaction with Lucille in this session is a beautiful illustration of reciprocal parentification.

SESSION #65: CHILDREN AS SEXUAL INSULATORS

Mrs. P: I felt upset and worked up and dissatisfied, that is why I asked for an extra session.

Mr. P: You don't speak! If you have something to say, start!

Mrs. P: (turns to Mrs. S) Would you start to ask me questions.

Mr. P: You won't make up if there is a hurt feeling. It is like wall. It is there and it doesn't go away. I think sex is bugging you.

Mrs. P: So tell me! Last nite it was better. But for 20 years it was so-so. I can't enjoy sex when the kids are in the house (while giggling). I am afraid the girls will overhear or barge into the bedroom.

The children's availability still seems more gratifying than husband–wife love. Is Lucille's promiscuity with unacceptable young men connected with this, as well as the seduction between father and Anne? Anne sits with her father on the loveseat in the office and puts her feet on her father's lap. Interpreting this behavior, Lucille says it is sexual stimulation plus Anne's need for affection. Mrs. P states that Mr. P knows what is going on but enjoys it. Lucille then turns on Anne and says, "Who comes down stairs naked with your gown in her hands!"

The family continues to struggle to balance appropriate and inappropriate sexual responsiveness. Mrs. P turns to Mrs. S with questions as a way to avoid taking a firm stand with her husband and children about the overt seductiveness between them. The therapists again turn this issue back to the family.

In the sessions that follow, the family discuss their feelings about Lucille being dropped from school. Mrs. P resigns from her job in order to take care of her, since Lucille becomes both agitated and depressed. Lucille responds very well to her mother's administrations.

SESSION #68: INFANTILE–SEDUCTIVE BEHAVIOR CONTINUES

Mrs. P: After last week's session, I told my husband he could have moved to another chair away from Anne. (Anne is now apparently asking to be scapegoated, screams aloud, kicks Lucille, runs from the office as she slams the door. Her father runs from the office after her, threatens her, and demands that she go back to the room. Mrs. P ignores the uproar and continues to talk about colleges. Mr. P hits Anne again insisting that she take another chair. Mrs. P keeps trying to get the therapists' attention and tells her husband and Anne to do as they please. Lucille laughs while this is going on; Anne curses her father.)

Mrs. P: Anne, you are flexing your muscles.

Anne: Some loving wife you are, I mean some loving mother you are! (Mr. P again slaps Anne and pushes her into a chair.) Nobody hits me without apologizing! (chairs are upset and turned around.) Would you like to kill me now? I am paranoid! I ought to be locked up!

Mrs. P: Your feet were placed in a sexual way.

Anne: He placed them.

Mrs. P: He didn't, we watched you, there were no strings attached to your feet.

Anne: How do you know?

The family continues to test the tolerance of the therapists with their painful, chaotic, infantile, incestuous-like behavior. We remain accepting of their need to express such behavior in our presence, while holding the family members to facing the destructive nature of such acts. This in turn helps to diminish some of the anxiety and violence in the home.

SESSION #69: MR. P AND THREE-GENERATIONAL RELATING TO WOMEN

Mrs. S: Is there more in your Pandora's box?

Mrs. P: I think there is much more. I never appreciated my husband's remarks about the girl's sexual development. The only thing in my family was my hostile relationship with my brother . . . but no sex.

Mr. P: It came from my family. You are saying the feelings originated with me, but the action is not with me. I don't consider anything I did as incest! I am being seduced. I could move away from Lucille, but Anne follows. I either accept it or there is a violent scene. I am never sexually aroused.

Mrs. P: I disagree. Anne tries to be accepted by him and tries to please him through that sensuous or sexual approach. (Anne cries while this is being discussed, and her mother moves over to hug her.)

Mrs. S: What was the murderous punching of a girl's breast? Is that sexuality?

Mr. P: No. I never beat my wife, maybe that is the trouble.

Mrs. S: Do you hate women?

Mr. P: I may. At times I was very hurt by my mother. She had a knack for aggravating me. Turning up the radio when she knew I had to study. There were fights with my younger sister. I was a cute little toy as a baby. That period is a blank now. There was frustration, but I didn't turn to her with violence. I was masturbating since age five or six, and there was a lot of hatred toward women connected with it.

The deeper levels of fear, anger, and resentment toward females in the past and present are steadily being revealed by Mr. P. More specifically, the children continue to be scapegoated for the unresolved marital difficulties, as well as Mr. P's earlier conflicts with members of his family of origin.

SESSION #83: MORE DESPAIR AND CHANGES (MRS. S ABSENT)

Anne: Where is "something?" (pointing to Mrs. S's chair)

Lucille: Do you want to hear the good news or the bad. I feel depressed and have an ulcer. I have been crying for days.

Mr. P: I am disgusted, discouraged . . . I'll tell my reaction next week when Mrs. S is here. The only reason I am here is because Lucille wanted to come.

Lucille: I am a baby again; I am home sleeping with my stuffed animals.

Dr. N: Does Mrs. P also need to be taken care of?

Anne: My mother is as helpless as Lucille.

Mr. P: I am looking at troubles differently now than I used to, not that there are any more than before. (to Anne) There have been a lot of changes in you, and this has helped me to change.

Anne: This makes him weak.

The family still desperately needs Mr. P to take more initiative and assume the leadership role in the family. As long as he remains in the angry, passive-observer role he is experienced as "weak"—waiting for the others to change and grow.

SESSION #88: TRANSFERENCE DIMENSIONS

Mrs. P: When I talk about leaving it isn't Joe . . . I am talking about all of them and myself (cries). I can't take the drastic changes . . . he lacks maturity. I married a little boy . . . I don't want to be his mother . . . want to be his wife . . . I have given so much for him to finish school . . . I told him Saturday that he lets me down sexually . . . He should be responsible for my satisfaction . . . if I care for him, why can't I get sexually aroused? I hate myself when I am fat and vice versa . . . I am one personality outside the house and inside. In trying to build up my husband I put into a boy all my desires. He is able to function sexually any time . . . that is his safety valve. (She is asked why she brought up suicide.) Failure . . . I didn't become myself . . . put everything into my husband, as well as into Lucille, and it turned out otherwise than I wished it to be. I am jealous of you, Mrs. S, because you have achieved something . . . you have something you can call your own (cries). You've gone to college . . . became a social worker . . . your life . . .

Mrs. P, while openly expressing envy and resentment toward Mrs. S and her husband, still conveys very personal wishes for improvement in her own life. This is in direct contrast to earlier sessions where she presented herself as the detached, noninvolved peacemaker within the family. This is progress on her part; she more openly reveals her underlying suffering and feelings of lack of worth.

SESSION #96: SEPARATION ISSUE AND NEW RESPONSES

Mrs. P: Lucille doesn't consider herself as part of family (cries). She left last Friday and didn't return all weekend. I found her at my office on Monday, and then she came home with me. I told her that I wasn't going to put up with her acting like this.

Anne: She says she's living in a commune.

Dr. N: Is this a change?

Mrs. P: Yes, I took a stand . . . I can go to sleep and try to sleep . . . feel relieved (cries very hard).

Dr. N: Can you imagine a change in Lucille to the effect that now that she can't get a rise out of parents that she can change to a more constructive way of living? Is this a beginning or end for you?

Mrs. P: Beginning . . . I am going to be selfish.

SESSION #97: AMBIVALENT RESPONSE TO SEPARATION CONTINUES (TWO PARENTS AND ANNE)

Mrs. P: Lucille hasn't been here really . . . she assumed usually a sleeplike position.

Mr. P: Lucille deserted the family. We haven't seen her except when my wife got a glimpse of her walking in town. She looked well, neat and tidy.

Mrs. P: I am not too eager to talk to her . . . I don't want to reverse my stand. I am angry about Lucille looking successful in what she is doing.

Mrs. S: Why shouldn't you be able to call Lucille without compromising your position. (to Anne) How about your separation?

Anne: It's not coming up for another year.

Mrs. P: Lucille's idea of separating was let's be friends, to call, but always on her terms.

The theme continues to be the family's ambivalence about Lucille's living away from the family: Can she succeed on her own? They still reflect their feelings that extreme togetherness or explosive, destructive separation are the only possible responses. For a while the three members pull closer to each other at the expense of the expelled bad member, Lucille. This situation alternates with expression of open wishes for Lucille's destruction and that she deserves such punishment for leaving in a shameful manner.

YEAR III: RECONSTRUCTION AND TERMINATION

SESSION #104: MULTIGENERATIONAL CONNECTIONS

Mrs. P: My mother was operated on last week . . . malignant tumor . . . metastacized . . . the doctor told her it might be major surgery . . . I said she should be operated on so that she either gets helped or dies. He put a drain in . . . and unfortunately, her heart holds up well. I asked Lucille to come home. I can't go through this with a divided family (cries). (Anne asks Lucille, who has moved out of the house, to come home or at least stay overnight, which Lucille refuses to do.)
Mrs. P: The first impact of grief was mixed up with my feelings about losing two people.
Mr. P: You come home, Lucille, but nobody wants to pressure you to say I've told you to do so.
Lucille: I've paid my own doctor bills and put money into the bank. I have a good job. Although I felt that my mother was hurt. I needed to do these things in order to cut the apron strings . . . to make it on my own. I tried to do it in the dormitory. I'm not having a nervous breakdown or feeling depressed. I have the octopus feeling that my family could suck me in again.

Mrs. P, who overtly had been the child least close to her own mother, now is able to be the responsible "head of her clan." She has tried to escape her loyalty ties through making a project of her husband and children. After Lucille upsets the family equilibrium by removing herself from the home, Mrs. P then begins to experience guilt about her behavior towards her own mother. The three-generation references reveal the connecting links between grandmother and grandaughters.

SESSION #105: INDIVIDUAL SESSION WITH LUCILLE

Lucille: My mother is upset. I almost lost my job too . . . missed several days in going to doctor. I didn't tell the conditions of my living to my parents, but I couldn't because of my grandmother's illness. I am living with a boy . . . getting along very well . . . yet . . . he is like my father, very explosive.

Dr. N: Are you less self-destructive?

Lucille: Had LSD only twice since I left home. We don't keep any drugs in the apartment. We want to get another apartment . . . he is idealistic, I am the realistic one . . . he has outbursts . . . religious differences. I have a situation which is not the best, but I don't want to go back home . . . I wish I could get their understanding. I am horrible to my parents; I wish I weren't! I think Mommy has destroyed herself, and she just starts to rebuild herself . . . I don't want that to happen to me. I was angry at Tom when he assumed my parents were ogres.

At her request, Lucille is seen alone, only to reveal that she remains loyal and committed in a dependent way to her family. While having again physically separated, it is done in an ambivalent way and with a person not acceptable to herself or her family. It cannot be considered a constructive move towards real individuation or autonomy. She seems to be repeating her mother's pattern in that they both try to balance out their disloyalty in separating from family through self-sacrificing devotion to an inadequate young man.

SESSION # 123: THE DYING GRANDPARENT

Mrs. P: Lucille moved this week. The doctors don't tell my mother about her condition; my sister doesn't want her to know.

Dr. N: Is it a giving to her to deny that she is dying?

Mrs. P: I told my mother how I felt about my childhood and the recent years. My mother got upset and blamed everything on the store, the bills, the customers. I also reminded my mother about the time I had to go to the dentist and that I had needed her . . . The very next day we were holding hands and my mother commented that my hands were comfortable.

Mrs. P has been expressing both her hurt and loving feelings towards her mother as therapists have been steadily urging her to do. In response, her mother can share her loving feelings and they are available to each other in a mutually comforting way.

SESSION # 124: COMBINED INDIVIDUAL AND FAMILY SESSION

Anne: I can't stand my mother any more, and I can't get out of it . . . unless someone helps my mother . . . maybe she is afraid I'll get hooked on drugs like Lucille . . . that I'll get drawn into political situations . . . that I am going to cloister myself with girls and not accept dates.

Mrs. S: Do you feel responsible for your mother since Lucille is out of the house?

Anne: (angrily) . . . She married her husband!

The parents return to the session and Anne is encouraged to discuss things directly with her parents.

Mrs. P: Well, for one thing, we really don't have money for a private college and we are not going to pulverize ourselves; secondly, I am not sure of your motivations . . . you do cloisterize yourself.

Anne: I want to get away from you . . . are you afraid to let me out of your sight . . . that I won't be that sweet lovable daughter again!

Mrs. P: I think that Anne is talking traitorously (meaning that it comes at a time when Mrs. P's mother is dying). If you want to "pull a Lucille" . . . do it right now!

Anne: You are confusing me with my sister.

Anne struggles with her problems of separation and individuation, and the parents' response is again fear and mistrust. She tries to clarify with them that she is not like Lucille and needs to be considered and supported in a different way.

SESSION #129: SEPARATION STRUGGLES

Lucille: I still can't communicate with my mother . . . but I am not angry. At least my father has been sincere a few times in the last two years.

Mrs. P: (who had been silent) Lucille, I thought you were trying to console me.

Lucille: Yes, but I was afraid that you'll chop my head off. It is like going out with a guy and telling him that you love him but you don't because you are afraid that he will laugh at you.

Mrs. P: Try me!

Lucille: Alright, about my friend, John . . . you are saying that marriage would make it worse . . . you are saying we are playing house . . . I would like to go to you because it is a woman-to-woman problem.

Mrs. P: What is the basis of this relationship?

Lucille: How can I talk about love and trust? John and I love each other.

Anne: You are a dirty, sinful person, and I see no good in this.

Lucille: I just lost some hope Dr. N, my mother didn't defend me against Anne's stupid accusations.

Mrs. P: (to Anne) At least she is doing one responsible thing, and that is earning her own living.

Lucille: I am going to get hurt most because I am putting out.

Dr. N: Mrs. P, can you only express moral condemnation . . . does Lucille have other needs?

The therapists try to help the family move from a moral, condemnatory level of relating to becoming more responsive to Lucille's underlying problems regarding her conflicted, weak feminine identification.

SESSION #130: THREE GENERATIONS INTERLOCKING

Lucille: John and I are going through shedding the trappings and are looking at our relationship, which is painful.

Dr. N: What can be done?

Mrs. P: Blow it up!

Lucille: Can you and Mrs. S help me woman-to-woman or leave me the hell alone. You are still my mother.

Mrs. P: Dr. N said I gave moral judgmental responses . . . but where is my own self in it? (cries). I came to you with a failure, and now I have a bigger failure and what have I done?

Dr. N: What about your mother?

Mrs. P: My sister and brother-in-law had a fight and my mother, who is staying with them, heard it. So there was talk about my mother coming to stay with me. My mother got dressed and even though she had 103-degree temperature she kept insisting on going back alone to her own apartment. I told her to come to us. I don't want to quit my job again and just stay home with my mother . . . I need my job. If I take my mother, I wouldn't be doing it on my own. I am being pressured there, and here I am being pressured into seeing it through Lucille's point of view.

Dr. N: Could you express your anger rather than moralizing towards Lucille? Maybe it could help clear the air.

Lucille: Why should I get things straightened out for my mother? Yet, I argue with John about things in defense of my mother and her values.

Mrs. P: She is asking me to take something that's rotten from the beginning and make it look good.

SESSION #131: RELATIONSHIPS REDEFINED: THE DIALECTIC OF BEING BOTH DAUGHTER AND MOTHER

Lucille: My mother and I have had a breakthrough in communication. John got a job.

Anne: I'll have a job next week too.

Mrs. P: Maybe I am a little more relaxed in speaking with Lucille . . . avoid talking about John. I am going to bring my mother to my house. My mother said if she knew she had cancer she'd take enough pills to kill herself, and she only struggles for her children . . . "because she has wonderful children." . . . I kissed her when she said that. Lucille has even offered to take part of the nursing job.

Dr. N: Lucille, what are the problems between you and your mother aside from John?

Lucille: I never knew that my mother had opinions, otherwise she was talking through my father.

Mrs. P: Lucille now recognizes that I am an entity.

As Mrs. P shifts from her ambivalent, hostile relating to her mother, there is a concommitant shift between herself and Lucille. The moralistic, condemning feelings are replaced by closeness, concern, and a new awareness of each other.

SESSION #132: LOSSES ARE BEING FACED: FURTHER PARALLELS IN MOTHERING

Mrs. P: My mother and I have this thing going, "you took care of me when I was little and now I take care of you." My mother says she has wonderful children, should have had more. She tells me that I am a good nurse. I don't feel that all my life's pain was intentionally inflicted on me by my mother . . . whatever pain I inflicted on Lucille . . . I must have done it or else she wouldn't behave this way, and I know that I never purposely wanted to do it to her.

More changes occur after Mrs. P brings her mother into her home and takes full care of her mother in her terminal phase of cancer. She attributes this to Dr. N, who asked her whether she felt Lucille was hurt in a similar manner as she had been. The entire family participates in experiencing their painful feelings for the dying maternal grandmother. These feelings of loss are directly connected with Lucille's need for understanding and support regarding her efforts toward individuation.

SESSION #137: THE MOURNING PROCESS CONTINUES

The maternal grandmother is rehospitalized.
Mrs. P: I was reluctant to give up my mother . . . my patient.
Anne: Your baby!
Mrs. P: She refused to call me during the night . . . I think it is selfishness . . . close physically . . . there were a few opportunities for better communication . . . I hope there will be more of these . . .
Anne: I kissed my grandmother and she kissed me back, although she denied it the next morning . . . my mother is not the only one having experiences.
Mrs. P: I am less angry at Lucille about her present "living arrangements." I told my mother about it, and we discussed it. We agreed that the main thing is to help Lucille rather than be vindictive.

Mrs. P can turn to her mother as a constructive, supportive resource for coping with Lucille's behavior. The therapists also encourage Mrs. P to seek out Lucille, despite her daughter's seeming rejection, and together face the underlying needs.

SESSION #138: A SHIFT IN AN EXTENDED FAMILY MEMBER

Mrs. P: My mother is improving some and can leave the hospital in a week. My brother was here for five days, and I believe he is mellowing or else I do. He was always such a difficult person to be with—he was upset . . . at least I heard him talk about something other than his Cadillacs and money things.

Dr. N: Is it your mother's dying?

Mrs. P: Maybe it took the dying to get closer . . . I can't stop crying since Sunday (cries very hard) . . . I picked up Lucille, and John came along too . . . the most repulsive looking individual . . . a phoney . . . has no independent thought . . . a parasite . . . my daughter would choose this kind of individual to live with . . . an insult to her father. It may be a further attempt to hurt us.

Dr. N: This sounds like moral condemnation and anger rather than concern.

Lucille: Yes, his "party line" talk doesn't impress me. I agree with some of it because I have to live with it . . . I am not ready to get married . . . just playing getting married.

Dr. N: Why is Lucille insecure with boys who are higher up on the family value scale? Is this a stoning "scene," or can there be a climate created so Lucille can continue to explore her insecurities?

The improved relating between the P family members begins to carry over into extended family relationships. Mrs. P has consistently rejected her older brother, whom she described as sadistic, hostile, and indifferent towards her, her husband, and children. As a result of her renewed strength and self-confidence, she can reach out to her brother, and she states a "mellowing" has taken place.

SESSION #143: FURTHER CLARIFICATION IN THE MARITAL RELATIONSHIPS

MGM is having more pain. Mrs. P gives her injections for it, and feels the doctor ought to end it all if he can't help her mother. The therapists ask Mr. P about not responding to his wife in their private conversation two weeks ago.

Mr. P: I feel that what you said was a total rejection of me.

Mrs. P: On Saturday we had another hassle . . . I cannot take it, not that we should throw away 20 years . . . He said not much could be changed and walked away . . . then he returned and kissed me. It is extremely difficult for me to respect someone who walks around muttering, cursing, and putting on a false face . . . I am now less able to take things in my stride . . . I don't want it anymore . . . I am tired of making excuses for immature action.

Mr. P: If I didn't want to change, we wouldn't be here . . . I get no pleasure out of my mother-in-law dying in our house . . . If I can do anything for her it gives me the feeling that I am doing something valuable . . . few things I can be proud of. I don't know what my wife wants from me in the present.

Mrs. P: I need a man . . . someone I can look up to . . . someone who can take initiative to improve his job situation; the other is the sexual area . . . apologizing for his boorishness.

Mr. P, by actively participating in the care of his dying mother-in-law, uses her as a substitute for the nonmourned loss of his own mother. He is able to begin to resolve his own guilt-laden impasse towards his parents. In addition, the couple are freer to be more open and direct about their needs and commitment towards each other.

SESSION # 144: SEXUAL EXPLORATION CONTINUES

Mrs. P: Anne carried on something horrible last time. She hasn't had a date in four months . . . resented that Lucille gets some attention.

Mr. P: You need my support tonight.

Mrs. P: I feel weepy (sobs) . . . situation with my mother—opening those boxes, Anne attacking . . . I don't know what to do with myself. I have to defend but you just attack my statements . . . you are not with me . . . you're sitting there and smiling. He kissed me and touched me in the kitchen . . . with a leer . . . obscene . . . it makes me feel like a sexual object, not a person.

Mr. P: I wanted to convey love . . . after 20 years of sleeping together I am not allowed to touch my wife . . . I felt rejected.

Dr. N: How did your wife mean to improve the sexual situation last week?

Mrs. P: I feel disgusted when I am unfulfilled . . . and he is not trying to do what he could do to improve things between us.

Mr. P: Maybe you have it in the back of your mind that I am the person who is leering.

Mrs. P: He often interrupts near the climax, allegedly for prolonging the climax, and it is all spoiled for me . . . it is cruelty.

Mr. P: In the past she used to pretend orgasm . . . it makes me sad . . . looking back it probably saved me a great deal of pain, but at a horrible expense. Now I prefer that she tells me if she has no orgasm.

Mrs. P: Now I can get more hurt because I want it for myself, but most of the time I don't get it. (She expects him to know how to help her, but she is shy about telling him.) I feel if he is a man, I shouldn't have to tell him . . . he should know!

Both Mr. and Mrs. P continue to examine sexual attitudes and behavior from the past which have interfered with mutually gratifying sexual responsiveness. They both are now more open and direct about their individual needs and desires and can in turn be more available to the other.

SESSION #147: STRENGTHENED FAMILY RELATIONSHIPS

Mr. P: I feel I am more useful and needed as far as my wife is concerned. I feel frustrated about Lucille . . . I feel good about Anne and my own family. I am too busy being useful for hating . . . at least I see things I can do.

Dr. N: What are the goals and what are the accomplishments?

Mr. P: I personally am well out of the woods . . . I've gotten my bearings . . . equipped to deal with situations I didn't know how to deal with before . . . more capability to handle Anne than we had with Lucille . . . our biggest concerns: the immediate strain of death approaching my mother-in-law and Lucille in the long range—to get her out of what she is in now and in with different people.

Mrs. P: I just want to cry . . . I feel terribly frustrated with Lucille and what to do with Anne . . . I find myself lacking . . . Anne is coming along . . . Joe and I reach a better understanding, but for myself, I don't know where I am.

Mr. P: You gained a husband and lost two children.

Mrs. S: Is Mrs. P happy with the prospect of relying on Mr. P?

Mr. P: Did my wife lose her martyrdom?

Mrs. P: I am a little fearful . . . it is too good to last . . . I can't stand outside and look at the situation. (Dr. N then explores how Mrs. P and her mother are with each other.)

Mrs. P: The process of closeness continues. We are like one together on this.

Mr. P makes one of his strongest statements about his own progress. He has moved from the impulsive expresser of rage and the observer role to being more competent as the head of his family. As he grows stronger, Mrs. P begins to be more trusting and shows reliance on his judgment and actions. This is also intertwined with the changes in attitudes and behavior toward the children and extended family in both families of origin.

SESSION #157: DEATH OF MATERNAL GRANDMOTHER

Mrs. P: I approved of autopsy, thought it might help someone else . . . a most difficult decision to make. I no longer feel that I have to wait with talking about something until I get here for protection . . . feelings of self-sufficiency.

Mr. P: We are able to talk with each other more . . . Lucille says I can now talk to you alone better than in the office.

Mrs. P: Anne's social life at college seems okay . . . but goes with older people . . . In a way I think she is skipping a phase . . . she doesn't want the wildness of her age group . . . at the same age I was scornful of roudiness too . . . now I feel I missed out on something . . . I am no longer afraid to speak up . . . therefore we are closer.

Mr. P: I feel that you are not totally involved . . . little initiative on your part . . . it bothers me. There is not enough response to me as a woman to a man. You either suppress your sexual attitudes or you don't have any.

Mrs. P: It has always come naturally to you. It is difficult for me to believe that someone loves me the way Joe says he does. (Is Mrs. P's cautiousness still due to her life-long frustrations with her mother . . . Can she fully commit herself to intimacy or continue to fear being hurt and rejected?)

Mrs. P: In losing a mother I gained a mother.

Mrs. P's statement, "in losing a mother I gained a mother," symbolizes the essential change that has taken place throughout the family system. Closeness, tenderness, and intimacy have replaced the angry despair that permeated all of their relationships. While there remain areas for improvement, the family is filled with increased hope and confidence in being able to reconcile the conflicts which exist in all close family relationships.

SESSION #159: PROGRESS IS SUSTAINED

Mrs. P: Lucille is working very hard and is enjoying the course she is taking. Anne is interested in boys . . . enjoys making cookies for student gatherings. She picks on her father, but not like it used to be, and I influence her better than before.

Mr. P: (paternal grandfather is in nursing home) My father had attacks of memory loss and gets very confused about people and things. He calmed down after I talked to him for two hours . . . I really am getting closer to him.

Mrs. P: My husband gets so uptight and guilty over his father's condition that I was worried about the possibility of a heart attack.

Mr. P: I wanted to do this alone. My father never meant much to my wife.

Mrs.P: You cut me off. You were a great support with my mother when I needed you, and now you don't accept my support.

Mr. P: I wanted to be there alone. I wanted sex after the first visit to my father, but my wife was too tired.

Mrs. P: I wanted to help in a different way. When my mother was very sick, my husband and I had more closeness as well as sexual responsiveness.

Mr. P has become increasingly available and supportive towards his father. He defines his need for his wife's support in this area, but insists that it be different than it was towards his mother-in-law. However, there still is an increased sharing and confirmation of each other, despite their different responses to needs of their aged parents.

SESSION #163: THE MOURNING PROCESS CONTINUES

Mrs. P: brings in and reads a newly found short note written by her mother two months before her death in which she assured her "Dear Children" about her deeply felt love, which she said she couldn't express like other people. "After I am gone try to hold the family together," her mother tells Mrs. P. Mrs. P's reaction is that her own doubts about loving her mother may have hurt her mother, and this may have made it necessary for her mother to state that she had not been able to express her love like other people.

Mr. P: I was running away from my parents. There was too much . . . smothering.

SESSION #165: TERMINATION PROCESS

Lucille has separated from John and moved to her own apartment and found a new job.

Mr. P: I have been spending more time talking to my father about my childhood . . . slept in my parents' room until age 8 . . . I had a deathly fear of dark green leaves. Even today I can't eat salads.

Mrs. S: What are the goals?

Mr. P: You both have been stabilizing influence . . . where would we be without you . . . I am least concerned about Anne . . . Lucille needs help to check my own hostility . . . I got a lot . . . I get a whole life out of this. Now I can get up and feel happy in the morning . . . I see my wife in a new light, much better than I ever thought it possible. There is no fear of leaving you (therapists) . . . some of it is from habit. I still want things to be better. You served partly as parent, advisers, and friends . . . Lucille also said she doesn't need the two of you to talk to us or to Anne and vice versa.

Mr. P is the spokesman for the family in reviewing the gains that the family has made. In addition, he also confirms the basic trust and confidence that has developed toward the therapists. He does not minimize or deny feelings of anxiety and dependence towards the team, but asserts that the family is now strong enough to separate.

SESSION #170: LAST SESSION

Mrs. S: Would Lucille miss anything in not having these sessions?

Lucille: We have learned to talk, to joke about past bad things. We don't need these meetings now . . . At college time, I felt very miserable and couldn't talk verbally, but in action, to my parents . . . cosmic depression and dejection . . . All others were busy talking to a boyfriend . . . proud . . . pig-headed . . . I wanted my parents to feel sorry for me . . . a good spanking and lots of hugging. I get only that I was guilty . . . I did it to hurt you . . . guilt . . . guilt

... guilt ... one doesn't need to be hit in a condition like that ... I never realized how sheltered home life was.

Mr. P: Listening to this takes me back to where I was feeling myself.

Anne: My father and I talk more and argue less.

Mr. P: I will have a new job at the company ... handle my job better because of the changes within myself ... more confident ... know how to handle people better, spend more time working and less time churning ... I didn't miss my mother. I never really had her like my wife had her mother for a few months before her death. I shared her mother with her. When she got incapacitated, it was devastating ... my mother chose not to come to my graduation. I couldn't understand why a business appointment was more important for my mother ... I asked my sister about it and she said, "You got all of yours!" She was jealous of my parents giving money for my tuition ... I still have a lot of talk about my father, but it is not as difficult now.

A termination date had been set by the family and the therapists a few months ago. While there is awareness of "unfinished business," it is agreed that the family has made sufficient gains so that they can more adequately cope with each other. They are assured that we will be available if needed in the future and would like to hear from them from time to time.

SUMMATION OF FIRST YEAR OF TREATMENT

The P family is illustrative of a symbiotic family that was stuck together in a network of unchangeable and chaotic relationships. They vacillated between extreme togetherness or explosive destructiveness. The precipitating events that threatened the system, and which helped propel them into treatment, were first, the death of Mrs. P's father two years ago; secondly, Anne's symptoms which had necessitated a brief psychiatric hospitalization; and finally Lucille's plan to leave the family to enter a college.

On a family system level they exhibited impulsive behavior, inappropriate responsiveness such as laughing or meeting fear with angry, disconfirming comments, or as illustrated by Mrs. P, remaining silent and withholding inner feelings. Little or no affection was displayed except for sadistic sexual stimulation displaced from the marital relationship onto the children. Ties with their extended family were presented as hopeless, nonsupportive, and critical, or as being nonavailable as a result of death.

As individuals, Mrs. P and her mother hid themselves behind all the others in a guilt-producing martyr role. However, she represented herself as the adequate, reasonable peacemaker. Mr. P and Anne were presented as the family expressers of craziness in being physically and verbally violent. Lucille was initially the nonsymptomatic "well sibling" who was expected to leave home and do well. However, shortly after leaving home she revealed many severe psychosomatic symptoms; she began to fail academically and moved into the "delinquent" role.

By the seventh session, there were beginning shifts in the family system: Mrs. P received a better-paying job; Mr. P was promoted on his job; the parents took a vacation together for the first time in many years. The therapists accepted these as evidence of "transference-like changes" rather than structural ones. The family constantly struggled with the therapists to avoid taking charge of or being responsible for their own behavior or for that of one another. The therapists refrained from "taking over" while constantly demanding that the family members take charge and provide more genuine responses to each other. During this process we had come to realize that hidden and unresolved loyalty commitments to the families of origin were preventing the development of genuine and meaningful relating to one another. It tied them together in mutual exploitativeness as one another's targets for "inappropriate" externalization.

Until the therapy process began to uncover the dimensions of the multigenerational loyalty accounts, Mrs. P was not able to recognize and genuinely respond to her daughters or her husband's desperate need for more appropriate support. Even when the therapists interpreted Lucille's delinquent actions as pleas for limit setting, and encouraged genuine parental interest and concern, it did not help. Mrs. P even resisted responding to specific requests by her daughters until the therapists helped her in reopening and modifying her stagnant relationship with her own mother.

Mr. P was supported by the therapists in trying to move from "parentifying his wife and children," into taking responsibility for controlling his impulsive and explosive behavior. He became aware that he had continued to be the "excessively demanding baby" that he was in his family of origin. In having permitted his wife to take charge, he had denied himself the opportunity to share his feelings with all of them or to become the head of his family. He then tried to become a "silent observer" and to control his inappropriate sexual seductiveness towards his children. Mrs. P was more able than her husband in being the first to explore her negative loyalty ties to her family of origin and then correct it with her present behavior.

The therapists in the first year helped the family to bring out the multiple, hidden conflicts and unresolved loyalty ties that beclouded generational and sexual boundaries. We confronted the family with their inappropriate responses and inauthentic way of relating to one another. We connected the family's inability to trust their professional and personal feelings to the lack of trust that they experienced with their families of origin.

It was in the fifteenth session that a major turning point occurred, after Mrs. P talked openly about her lack of trust of the therapists. This was then turned back to the family, and Dr. N asked, "Where can you go from here? What is the risk to the marriage and the family?" Then Mrs. P set a new goal for herself and her family: "She would try to change her position with her husband." Implied in this was the affirmation that there would be renewed efforts in exploring new possibilities in all the relationships. By the end of the first year, this included the relationships with their families of origin, which we had not accepted as being "bad and hopeless." Mrs. P brought her mother to several sessions and began to explore the possibilities of removing the wall between them.

SECOND YEAR OF TREATMENT

During this year, several major events developed, such as Lucille being dropped from college and again moving out of the home, and Mrs. P's mother having another heart attack. The family continued to struggle with problems of emotional separation and inappropriate responses in the form of chaotic and seductive overstimulation. In addition to the bringing out of more irrational feelings of anger and despair within the sessions, there were sporadic areas of improvement and periods of quiescence. There was more frequent and genuine sexual intimacy between Mr. and Mrs. P. On a deeper level, both Mr. and Mrs. P continued to explore their negative loyalty commitments and guilt feelings regarding their families of origin.

In the family's relationship with the therapists, there was increased trust and acceptance of their dependence on us. They continued to test our capacity for accepting and supporting them while being aware of their remaining underlying despair. There continued to be setbacks and the acting out of destructive behavior toward each other.

After the inclusion of the maternal grandmother in several sessions, the therapists continued to keep a focus on that relationship and helped to bring out the underlying need for Mr. and Mrs. P to be parented. The relationships with the children continued to be explored, with Lucille being used less as the scapegoat and Anne the parentified child. The parents were being helped to use them less as targets and arenas for their unresolved conflicts. Specifically, both daughters were "babied" in the sense that they could be children who were needing concern and interest. However, behind most of this was Mrs. P's unmet need also to be mothered.

As more regressive feelings were channeled into the therapy sessions, they exhibited more adequate areas of emotional and behavioral functioning in the outside world. Anne received a scholarship; the parents had a vacation which they described as a second honeymoon. Mr. P moved from his violent, overly expressive position to a more thoughtful and observing role. He made more loving comments, in addition to demanding more appropriate responsiveness from his wife. However, there was need for more progress in rebalancing the relationships within this family and with their families of origin.

THIRD YEAR OF TREATMENT

Anne began to emerge as a genuine person. She now had more regular menses and brought up the possibility of moving out of the home and going to college. She felt her parents still thought of her as a child, even though they said they wanted her to have friends and activities. On the surface, the parents' main fear was whether she would follow in Lucille's footsteps of delinquent behavior. In the sessions, Anne had become less provocative and violent. She was less a target of her father's rage and was less protected by her mother.

After they learned that the maternal grandmother had a malignant tumor, the P's made the decision to have her live in their home. Mrs. P gave up her job and with Mr. P's help assumed a full-time nursing role. Grandmother and mother openly discussed Lucille's difficulties and her need for increased support. Mrs. P moved from the condemning and moralizing role into a supportive and encouraging one. There was much more open and direct affection and appreciation between maternal grandmother and all family members. As a significant by-product, Mr. P used his increased closeness with his mother-in-law to work through his own repressed and postponed feelings regarding his mother's death. His visits and conversations with his father were more frequent and greatly improved. When his mother-in-law was experienced as a substitute for his own mother, he became able to move from his previous guilt-laden impasse with his own parents.

During the terminal phase of the maternal grandparent's illness, Mr.

and Mrs. P and both children were able to express and receive the appreciation, concern, and recognition that had been "held back." There was not only support but great tenderness expressed towards the dying grandparent, in the physical nursing care and in the open, verbal exchanges that took place in those last months. It was after Mrs. P's mother died, that Mrs. P told the therapists, *"in losing a mother I gained a mother."*

In the last six months of treatment, Lucille, who had moved out of the home, also separated from the young man with whom she had been living. It had been an exploitative, mutually destructive relationship. Her parents in this period had changed from an initially accusatory, condemning, challenging stand to expressing supportively constructive attitudes which helped her explore the negative implications of that relationship. She not only moved into a new apartment in a more desirable neighborhood, but also enrolled in and was successfully completing a technical course. Lucille was able to be open and direct with her parents, as well as constructive for herself. She became available to Anne in a more "peer" level of relating as contrasted to the murderous, scapegoating rivalry that had existed previously.

Anne not only made good academic progress in college, but despite being two years ahead of her classmates steadily became involved with them in school activities. Her emotional separation from the family was done at a much slower pace, but in a less destructive and violent way than Lucille's. She gained a great deal of personal gratification and recognition in the part she played in supporting her mother and grandmother through the final phase of that illness. Her taunting, provocative behavior was replaced by directness and an emerging sense of humor. She fought hard to reestablish a different role in the family, and it was different from Lucille's rebellious adolescent stand. She was able to articulate her many fears about her emerging independent wishes and was even tolerant about her parent's lack of trust (because of Lucille's acting-out behavior). She remained cautious but was interested in dating, although insisting on privacy about her dating and sexual functioning.

Mr. P took more initiative and responsibility for the care of his father, who was now in a nursing home. He visited frequently and used as a model his wife's rewarding relationship with her mother—he began to have more personal discussions with his father. He was able to be very effective when his senile father had distorted and persecution reactions to the personnel and patients in the nursing home; this was reported with pride and gratification in the sessions. In addition, he was able to confront his supervisor about his professional status and salary and to secure a promotion which he felt was long overdue.

Mrs. P returned to work after her mother's death and secured a supervisory position which she found challenging and gratifying. She began to initiate social activities for her husband and herself and also to engage in "reconstruction" of their home. Her health and appearance improved, and included a loss of weight. There was increased communication and display of affection with her sister and her previously "despised" brother. She felt it was her responsibility to hold her family together and to carry on her mother's efforts in this direction.

THE FAMILY'S TRANSFERENCE AND REALITY RELATIONSHIP WITH THE COTHERAPY TEAM

The family therapy process addresses itself to four major areas of relationships: the cotherapy team; the marital pair; parent–child; the transgenerational accounts of loyalty and justice with the grandparents and siblings of both families of origin.

Before examining the last three areas, it is appropriate to focus first on the cotherapy team relationship. Ideally, a heterosexual team facilitates the process of delineating dimensions of the male–female roles— differences and similarities, complementation, and capacities for balancing closeness and distancing. There must be trust and respect: Rivalry, competitiveness, and power struggles can interfere with the smooth functioning of the team. However, to minimize the existence of such feelings and to deny that they break through at times would suggest that the therapists were superhuman. Rather, it is the way these feelings are faced and dealt with that is the significant point. If they are handled constructively, a model is provided for reconciling differences. Families are "experts" at splitting the team, and this must continuously be faced both by the team and by the family members. This is equally applicable where the cotherapists are of the same sex, although the form of such expressions vary.

Family therapists must have a capacity for multidirectional relating in order to be available to each member of the nuclear family, as well as to extended family members. But fundamentally, they must remain available to each other. They must be aware not only of the struggles that exist in their cotherapy relationship, also of one another's struggle with his own nuclear and extended family. This is not meant to imply that it must be a therapeutic relationship; rather, the main purpose is to help each other in order to be continuously available to the families that they are treating. This necessitates much discussion and clarification outside the sessions. Work with families is demanding, exciting, challenging, and rewarding; however, just as therapy with individuals impinges upon one's individual functioning, work with families places an even greater burden on family therapists.

Our capacity for relating to one other with openness and directness in facing intrateam conflicts, and for revealing genuine concern and appreciation of each other's abilities, in turn, provides the strength to respond appropriately to different kinds of families and the multiple problems they bring to us. It is, however, a difficult task to describe the nature and implications of the cotherapy relationship with the P family over the three years of treatment. Just as the family went through various phases in their efforts to rework their unresolved conflicts and hidden loyalty commitments, so too our relationship with the family had to undergo much stress, as we tried understand and help in the eventual reconstruction of their family system.

We were used in multiple and complex ways. Some of the family's responses to us were on a reality basis as authoritative specialists, while others were of a transference nature. They repeatedly tried to use us as substitute parents since at times we were the only adults available to them. The family was encouraged to live and act out their feelings in our presence, but we did not permit them to use us as direct targets of their aggression. While encouraging them to express themselves more openly and directly, we simultaneously tried to help them separate our "understanding" from acceptance of their nonparentlike, destructively hostile, and inappropriately seductive behavior. We interacted with them on a feeling level of concern and interest, but we also had to present ourselves as objects for identification. Regardless of their chaotic and provocative behavior toward us, we had to maintain a sense of calm and reason. While being sympathetic and compassionate, we had to continuously hold them to increased understanding as well as modification of their infantile behavior, in order to help facilitate the growth process.

In the beginning phase of treatment, it was essential that we help them try to establish some order of communication and to create an atmosphere of trust. Families like the P's have never had relationships with important others where the people were experienced as being genuinely interested in knowing what they thought or felt. The P's were suspicious and guarded, as if anticipating that they would inevitably be misunderstood, criticized, depreciated, devalued, and disconfirmed. As a result of their previous family life experiences, they were in collusion with each other and the children, and seemed to have written off all members of their original families. Despite the fact that we were aware of their scapegoating and parentification efforts, lived out on their children and on one another, we were not drawn into either condoning this behavior or blaming them. From the beginning we demanded that each person have an opportunity to express his needs, as well as to express reactions to the excessive or inappropriate responses. Mrs. P personified the family's withholding or condemning responses, while Mr. P was the impulsive, explosive, violent reactor. It was essential to hold Mrs. P responsible for becoming more open and appropriately expressive, to move out of the seemingly passive mediator role. Mr. P was encouraged to take charge of himself and the others in becoming a better observer and listener. While we focused on these levels, we also helped all of them to explore their underlying feelings and denied negative loyalty ties with their families of origin.

We made no direct efforts to "rescue" the children from these destructive binds except to focus on the despair and unmet dependency needs of both parents. We chose to "parent" the parents by holding them responsible for taking an active stand in exploring the meaning of their children's behavior and their own. It took tremendous control and discipline on our part to withstand the entire family's efforts to involve us as referees in their chaotic melees. They also tried to split the team by disconfirming one therapist's comments and turning to the other for an immediate answer. The noise level, confusion, and their scapegoating and blaming tactics toward one another and us were at times discouraging. Even though aware that we were being tested for our capacity to be trustworthy, to remain rational, and to be firm in our demands for increased responsible behavior, at times we inevitably revealed our discomfort and therapeutic despair. Sometimes they told us we were cold and inhuman. However, our efforts to be warm and spontaneous were met with anxiety and fear. Closeness forced them to re-experience the pain they experienced with important others. As Mrs. P described it, "she would have to lose us anyhow."

When we introduced the idea of trying to rework the relationships with Mr. P's father and Mrs. P's mother, it was at first ridiculed since they both collusively insisted that these relationships were completely hopeless. However, as their trust in our competence—and more importantly as people who cared—increased, Mrs. P slowly began to explore with her mother the possibility of attending a few sessions. She was surprised when her mother accepted the invitation. It required several months of work for her to overcome her initial anxiety and resistance to the thought that anything constructive could ever develop between them. She was helped to face the fact that her protectiveness was used to maintain "the wall" of isolation and despair that existed between them. We also interpreted to her that her negative feelings and loyalty commitment to her family of origin directly interfered with her being available and committed to her husband and children. The work in the sessions was continuously connected with such efforts. This was equally applicable towards Mr. P and his family of origin. Because of his illness, his father was not able to attend a therapy session. Despite this, Mr. P became available to his father and sisters as a resource when his father was hospitalized and later had to be moved to a nursing home. Additionally, with our encouragement, he initiated long personal conversations with his father about their past and current lives. These two, who had been comparative strangers to each other, thus became available to one another as a father and son for the first time in their lives.

The therapists continuously helped the family members to explore four dimensions: first, their responses to the cotherapists, second, the marital relationship, third, the parent–child relationship; and fourth, their families of origin. A shift in one area stimulated exploration and changes elsewhere. We were committed to the concept that basic change in parenting the children could develop only as a result of Mr. and Mrs. P resolving their own lack of basic trust due to not having felt "parented" themselves. We could be used only as temporary parents and as persons who were trying to help them rework the internal and external relationships with their own parents.

Guilt feelings and losses were reexperienced and worked through as a result of the family's increased commitment toward the therapists. They were encouraged and supported in facing their internalized, postponed, unmourned, or denied feelings regarding the parent who had died. However, the major portion of the work was in helping them face and rework in action the real-life relationships with the living parent and siblings. The therapists were perpetual targets for the family's rage and despair resulting from the past and present relationships. We had to be available for extra sessions when suicidal or murderous feelings were experienced. The children at times were loyal and overly protective of their parents and labeled us destructive intruders—or saw us as the withholders of love and concern for the family. At times the children aided and abetted the family's destructive process by permitting themselves to be used as targets for the scapegoating and parentification that the family needed. Essentially, however, the children's needs stimulated the growth process for all. After they felt more secure regarding our ability to "carry" their parents and to help them find constructive gratification of their needs, they moved out of the scapegoating–parentification roles and were able to be children with age- and phase-appropriate needs.

As the grandparent–parent, marital, and parental relationships became strengthened, the family members had less need to use the therapists as a resource for clarification, sharing, and proving. They now turned to each other and outsiders, knowing that each one's needs could be openly explored, and that the responses would be thoughtful and more considerate even though disagreement was at times inevitable. The old guardedness and impulsive, explosive responses were replaced by warmth, humor, and genuine availability. Intimacy and closeness were no longer feared or denied.

The termination phase was faced by the family and the therapists with the recognition that not all problems had been faced and resolved. The essential help lay in their awareness that the "process of change" must be continuously faced and dealt with as directly and openly as possible. Each one's continued strength depended on each other as a constructive resource, as long as they lived. We would remain available as consultants for any future crisis as the family moved toward increased individuation and separation.

Although as cotherapists we had worked together prior to treating the P family and had already established a valuable working relationship, this family demanded new dimensions of awareness and understanding about our relationship and professional work. Both of us liked the family's keen intellectual abilities and responsiveness; in addition, we identified with them on a personal–professional level, namely, in their determination to improve their family relationships and functioning. While at times their too lively and intensely destructive behavior was repulsive and overstimulating, we were able to "meet" them on the level of their perpetual yearning for improved meaning and relating as a family.

Finally, the family was completely responsible and cooperative about attending sessions, cancellations, payment of fees, and other "contract essentials." They helped us to increase our learning and afforded us the opportunity to explore new dimensions such as hidden loyalty commitments to their families of origin. The work in the sessions and outside with their families of origin provided us with new insights hitherto unexplored in our work with families. Their unfolding trust helped increase our strength and skill as family therapists, both in our teamwork and as individuals.

CONCLUSIONS:

MULTIGENERATIONAL RECONSTRUCTION AND THE DYNAMIC MEANING OF FAMILY LOYALTY AND INDEBTEDNESS

The major purpose in presenting the treatment of the P family has been to clarify our current framework of understanding and its clinical applicability to families. In addition to consideration of need, need fulfillment, and the concomitants of frustration, we have included our concepts of the interlocking reciprocity between the generations: The dynamics of loyalty and indebtedness of family systems include but supersede the dynamics and functioning of an individual. Inherent in all close and meaningful relationships are the fundamental elements of giving and receiving, of being treated fairly or unjustly, of taking without repaying, or receiving with no possibility of giving back. Martyrdom or overgiving and permissiveness, scapegoating, and parentification are illustrations of nonbalancing or nonmutual reciprocity within relationships. Such relationships stimulate feelings of guilt and perpetual indebtedness; they also produce feelings of despair, as if one could never settle family accounts—either through emotional interest and concern or by concrete actions.

Since we assume as a basic postulate that every child receives from his parents and implicitly owes them repayment, a parental unwillingness to receive is considered as detrimental as a parental inability to give. For example, the martyrlike parent can never be repaid for services. As a result, an atmosphere of filial indebtedness to the parent hangs perpetually over the relationship, without any possibility for actually balancing the accounts. The hopelessness of ever achieving reciprocity in such a relationship leads the child into deep despair. Instead of learning confident optimism about the nature of any human relationship, as based on reciprocity of giving and receiving, the child believes that in order to survive one must find substitutive ways for repaying for benefits received from the parent.

Acts of rebellion or escape through separation can never in themselves resolve the child's predicament. These measures just sink him deeper into guilt-burdened obligations. Many children become angrily ambivalent captives of never-repayable obligations. Their relationship to the parents may turn negative, but it never becomes basically disloyal as long as the child remains in the symbiotic obligation bond. In short, the guilt-bound, loyalty-trapped child owes the parent: (a) the symptom, (b) no change, and (c) no mixing with outsiders. In such relationships, an incapacity for repaying carries with it an arrest of receiving on the part of the child too. A seeming antithesis of receiving through giving resolves itself in the dialectic of normal parenting. The parent gives to his child but implicitly expects repayment, and the child receives but hopes someday to return benefits to the parent. In this, both parent and child are motivated not only by the actual day-by-day exchanges of their relationship, but by the entire family network of obligations.

In describing the dynamic chain of events during therapy with a family, we hypothesized, that unless all interactions are in some balance with the pressure of obligations, debilitating conflicts and arrest of development is bound to ensue. Unattended obligations tend to accumulate guilt. From Mr. P's background we can reconstruct the fact that his hard-working parents gave much devotion to customers in their grocery store and appeared devoted martyrs, yet were minimally available in a personal sense to the children. If the child is expected to repay the parents indirectly, e.g., through success ("my son, the doctor"), and if credit for his small services is held back from him, ultimately his thwarted personality development will become the only avenue for repaying the debt. Even expectation of success becomes exploitation under these circumstances. Mr. P ended up in a mediocre job, and he never seemed to be able to finish his education despite his good intelligence. In constantly postponing work on his master's thesis, he, the perpetual childlike person, complemented the protective, parentlike features of his wife. Mr. P's relationship with his family was pictured as a fixated, hopeless, and helpless condition, with sexualization of the fantasied overpowering, subjugating aspect of females coupled with a deep resentment of them. He claimed to have minimal contact with his surviving father and his two sisters. It was only later in therapy that it became possible to see resources in Mr. P's own unused capacity for renewed giving to his aged father.

Mrs. P was raised in a somewhat similar familial constellation as her husband. However, whereas in her family of origin her role was defined as a negatively defiant one, she became a protector and peacemaker. In one of the interviews which included her mother, we could see operative a life-long issue: Her mother described Mrs. P's father as irresponsible and unconcerned about the children. Mrs. P defended her father against her mother. At the initial presentation, Mrs. P appeared resentful of her mother, whom she said never had time to sit down and talk with her children. Once, while Mrs. P was cleaning up the house, she heard her mother say, "my children and my family don't help me with the housework at all." According to one statement, Mrs. P for some time had sought interest and concern from her mother, until at one point it became hopeless and it was clear that her marriage could then be a revenge on her mother's seeming indifference. Revenge on one's parent always encompasses its dialectical opposite: a signal for expressing desperate wishes through actions. ("Look how desperate I am. I hope you will respond to me.")

Mrs. P's choice of a borderline psychotic young man for a husband must have offered the combined opportunity to assert herself despite maternal disapproval and to become a rebel with a sacrificial "cause" —dedicated to self-sacrificing identification with her failing husband in an effort to help him. At the same time her mother kept implying that Mrs. P's marital choice made her a traitor. It is reasonable to assume that a portion of guilt not balanced by the self-sacrificing devotion to her husband was expiated through her lasting frigidity and disinterest in sex. It is interesting that her sexual interest and capacity for experiencing orgasm changed in direct proportion to her capacity for repayment, in offering to take care of her ailing mother.

We must emphasize that the lack of reciprocal give-and-take that was a personality characteristic of both Mr. and Mrs. P was not immediately apparent to us. More readily apparent were the features of their emotionally deprived developmental history and consecutive ego weaknesses. Should the therapists have accepted the traditional conceptual framework of ego weakness in the parents with resulting deprivations in the two daughters, they would have been led to a different course in therapy. Individual therapy with the daughters along with periodic supportive contacts with the parents would have been recommended, in the hope that we could at least work with the healthy core of the adolescent daughters towards their individuation and separation.

It was only the gradual unfolding of the full spectrum of relational structures that enabled us to set a goal of multigenerational reconstruction. Our insistence on working with the family and, later, including the maternal grandmother led us to the realization of available, dormant relational strength that needed therapeutic rechanneling. We tried then to connect the crucial points in the multigenerational patterns of arrested flow of reciprocity and impoverishment of basic trust among family members.

THE MAIN MECHANISM OF CHANGE

Assuming the principle of balanced justice and obligations as a key dynamic, it is psychologically impractical and uneconomical for a child simply to try to ignore and deny filial obligations of loyalty, even if the parent has been comparatively nongiving. The child will pay for such denial with paralyzing guilt, arrested personality development, and even disruption within his future family relationships. It seems that repayment of benefits was made more difficult in the P family due to the fact that Mrs. P's mother was unwilling to *receive* benefits from this allegedly disloyal daughter.

In concrete terms, our therapeutic strategy was aimed first at breaking the deadlocked mutual scapegoating between Mrs. P and her mother (which in turn was being reprojected onto her husband and daughters). The avenue in therapy was a gradual strengthening of Mrs. P in her nuclear family relationships to the point where she might undertake an active "giving" attitude towards her mother. The test of our hypothesis lay in the prediction of self-assertive responses by Mrs. P following each successive step in rebalancing the guilt-laden and denied daughter–mother accounts of obligation. Examples of such predicted responses were: (a) more capacity for accepting her husband, (b) increased sexual satisfaction, and (c) rearrangement of her relationship with her daughters.

One of the initial signs of change in Mrs. P was a conscious desire to stop her overly protective, mothering attitude towards her husband. We can assume that the basis of this pathogenic protectiveness was that it constituted one means for denying guilt over her nongiving attitude in her relationship to her mother. By the 48th week of treatment, Mrs. P was able to overcome her feelings of hopelessness and fear of being rejected again, and she could invite her mother to a family therapy session. In a third session, in her mother's presence, Mrs. P achieved a major breakthrough into their mutually scapegoating cycle: She stated that she had learned how much similarity there was in her own mother's "destructive love as mother" in not praising, taking good things for granted, and criticizing. The shared weeping, as the maternal grandmother described her role in her family of origin, also helped to reverse the "blame" syndrome.

It is interesting that three weeks later a great deal of encouraging change occurred in the family relationships, as if to confirm our therapeutic hypothesis. The two girls doubled-dated, and husband and wife planned a vacation for two for the first time in years. Mrs. P reported better sexual experiences and was given a new wedding ring.

It seems that another whole year had to pass before further progress could be made between Mrs. P and her mother. In the meantime there was a phase of nonprogression, consisting essentially of testing the implications of an improved reciprocity of giving and receiving among members of the nuclear family. Despite gains in other areas, Mrs. P appeared extremely nonresponsive and resistant to most overtures by family and therapists. She seemed indeed to replicate the destructively nonreceptive pattern of mothering: She was unwilling to give credit for the other's good will. In this period, Mrs. P did a great deal of testing of the therapists through blaming them as inhuman, "functional," nongiving persons. Lucille also continued to test her parents with a rebellious, self-endangering, "delinquent" behavior. Anne was forced to overrespond to her father in what was interpreted by the family as a "sensuously affectionate," semiincestuous way which had resulted either in seductive attention or violent rejection by her father.

Originally, Anne's symptomatic ways of "repayment" consisted of chaotic, borderline psychotic behavior, decline in academic achievements, and exclusion of all outsiders; her symptomatic improvement could be interpreted as a sign of her growing hope for new avenues of expressing filial gratitude. Toward the end of the first year Anne not only improved her grades but was reported to be a National Merit semifinalist. By the end of the second year she graduated *cum laude.* Concurrently, Anne began showing interest in boys. She lost her marked overweight, stated that she wanted to be noticed by the male therapist as a "lady," and began dating. With growing insight, she reflected on the balance of the justice of her world: "I have been the good kid, good student, fairly moral person, I don't hang out with bums like Lucille, and where the hell am I?" Several weeks later when Anne considered applying for college and moving away from the home, she implied that she could not get out of the home unless someone helped her mother. Anne then openly confronted her mother with her wishes. She asked whether Mrs. P was worried about her taking drugs and acting like Lucille, or was she just concerned that Anne would want to get away from her mother and would no longer be the "sweet, loveable daughter." Her mother responded by calling Anne's talk "traitorous" and adding: "If you want to pull a Lucille, do it right now."

It is important to understand the relational determinants of Lucille's protracted self-endangering delinquent behavior. On the one hand, it is consistent with individual theory to interpret this behavior as fulfilling Lucille's dependent needs for parental responses—albeit negative ones. She kept trying to provoke correctional responses from her parents, but they would not react until her extreme behavior of drugtaking and hippie living made them order her out of the house. One can easily view this rebellious destructive adolescent pattern as a means of separating and individuating, even though at the cost of pain to everyone. This seems to be substantiated by Lucille's comments in a separate individual session at a time when she was living communally with several most "undesirable" partners: "I am horrible to my parents. I wish

I wouldn't." Toward the end of the therapy when she was already returning to both her family and their middle-class living patterns, she stated, "At the college I acted to make my parents feel sorry . . . a good spanking plus a lot of hugging was needed . . . I was guilty . . . I did it to hurt you." However, aside from such self-motivated reasons, Lucille may have acted rebelliously to fulfill certain unstated expectations of the family system. In fact, at no point was she genuinely disloyal. She could always be counted on to perform essential services in connection with the needs of her parents and ailing grandmother. At times it appeared that she was obliging her parents by playing the scapegoated role. For a time after Lucille was expelled from the home, her father continued talking about his murderous impulses—turned now toward Lucille *in absentia*—and her mother expressed disappointment over Lucille succeeding economically while allegedly down in the "gutter."

GRANDMOTHER'S ILLNESS OPENS THE GATE

A rapid succession of rearrangements became possible with the discovery of the grandmother's cancer toward the end of the second year. With the prospect of continuing physical impairment until death, the possibility of action through offering care and services opened up. Mrs. P's continued hopelessness about changing her relationship with her mother was countered by the therapists: They referred to death as irreversible and encouraged her to do what was still possible while there was life. After some hesitation, Mrs. P took her ailing mother into her home, gave up her job, and became a 24-hour nurse for a patient who needed high colonic enemas, injections, and constant supervision.

She struggled with doubts and thought that her mother accepted her more only because she had become her nurse. However, as her mother's communication became open, she became more convinced that at this point her mother was ready for a genuine realignment of their relationship. She gave ecstatic reports after her mother stated that her children were wonderful—how she then kissed her mother and reassured her, saying, "You took care of me when I was little, now I take care of you." At one point she told us that her mother said that she would have liked to have had more children and that she did not believe Mrs. P ever hated her.

A major issue of justice is confronted when a person gains insight into his own tendency for projection and scapegoating. Most of her life Mrs. P seemed to be aware of her painful frustration suffered because of her mother's nonresponding attitudes, but only gradually did she gain consciousness of her own frustrating mothering attitudes. To the extent she turned the "action dialogue" with her mother into a positive giving one, she could then afford to face the unfairness of "taking it out" on Lucille or keeping Anne in the overclose, symbiotic relationship. In the session in which Mrs. P reported that she had kissed her mother, she also stated that she did not believe her mother had hurt her intentionally, nor that in turn did she hurt Lucille purposely.

It was in the subsequent session that Mrs. P gave up her job with the reasoning, "Now at least I know what I have to do and I am doing it." It is of great clinical and theoretical significance that the "feedback" process of reciprocal giving between mother and daughter stimulated other members to participate in the care of the grandmother. Mr. P reported that he did not deserve to be regarded as an unselfish helper of his wife: "I get a great deal out of this, my mother-in-law is my mother now." The full circle was completed when two weeks prior to her death the grandmother asked Mr. P's forgiveness for not giving him her daughter willingly, and her son-in-law returned her gesture with a kiss.

The whole period was marked with a quiet, almost mystical ecstasy over an emotional rebirth of the relationship. A few weeks before the death Mrs. P reported, "My mother said she never knew what kind of a person I was and she kissed me. I don't know when she last made an affectionate gesture towards me . . . my whole world is heaving." Simultaneously, Mrs. P became much more interested in obtaining a sexual climax. For the first time Mr. P was able to demand a work promotion and an increase in salary. Anne went out on dates more regularly than ever. Lucille began to look at her boyfriend more appropriately in a mature and critical way. Mr. P also showed active concern for his father's treatment while in a hospital. Finally, after her mother's death, Mrs. P made the paradoxical statement, "In losing a mother, I gained a mother." It seems that the gate of reciprocal give-and-take was opened and rebalanced before death could seal it shut.

In reflecting on the various system levels involved in the determinism of human action, we have emphasized the therapists' endorsement of action aimed at breaking the deadlocked hopelessness in a mother–daughter relationship. Specifically, we helped Mrs. P shift her attitude toward her mother from hopelessness over irreversible deprivation to actively giving. Since she must have attempted giving attitudes and actions on countless previous occasions before abandoning hope, we had to explore the factors which were now different. Some of these factors resided in Mrs. P and were reinforced as she was encouraged by the therapists and the nuclear family to change; others were in her mother as finally she was made capable of receiving her daughter's attentions. The psychological effects of guilt were major considerations in exploring the interlocking between relationship system and individual motivation.

On the one hand, it is conceivable that increased guilt makes one unable to receive, yet on the other hand, more inclined to try to give again and again. Therefore, Mrs. P needed an increased awareness of her responsibility for appropriate responsiveness towards her children, while her mother needed support for the justice of her situation, i.e., an exploration of the unjust features of her own earlier existence. Mrs. P became more giving after the discovery of her unjustness toward Lucille and her replicating the "destructive mothering" pattern. Her guilt and responsibility conceivably were sources of her renewed motivation for action, despite hopelessness. At the same time, when her mother was able to reflect on the hardships of her own childhood and her marriage, her account was in turn made more just and balanced because it became more humanly understandable. Also, by listening to the direct reproaches of her daughter and by her admitting her own errors, her guilt must have diminished. Furthermore, her age and incurable illness tended to increase her dependency and diminish her obligations while they increased Mrs. P's responsibility.

Perhaps it is least essential for us to mention Anne's role in the reconstruction of this family's account of hidden loyalty obligations. She was the family member initially designated as the sick one. Her despair created the initial family stress which led to her hospitalization and ultimately to family therapy. We can postulate that Anne's (and most ill family members') provocative, annoying behavior was more than compensated for by her sacrificial contribution, as far as the family's interests are concerned. We believe that as soon as her parents and sister began showing signs of meaningful therapeutic engagement and then undeniable movement toward change, Anne in turn was liberated from the obligation to fail. Gradually she was able to demand attention for her age-appropriate adolescent needs and to loosen her anxious concern and overavailability to her family of origin. The successful results eliminated the need for self-sacrifice on her part.

A model has been developed: Deprivation of parenting and resulting lack of basic trust was made partially responsible for a defensive withdrawal from two interlocking mother–daughter relationships, but lack of parental willingness to receive repayment from the child was viewed as an equally debiliatating factor. A full parent–child action dialogue presupposes giving and taking on the part of both participants. By selectively focusing only on the deficiencies of parental taking, we can anticipate a consecutive accumulation of guilt in the child who cannot repay. In cases where this situation coincides with, and is reinforced by, the child being scapegoated as "bad" and "ungrateful," the relational feedback system may reach a point of such impasse that the natural defensive outcome will be a mutual withdrawal. Withdrawal may, however, characterize only the visible one-ninth of the iceberg of the relationship. Underneath there remains a hidden commitment, often in the form of negative loyalty. In other words, if one can relate to one's family of origin only through being a bad object, one is likely to accept such a role assignment. The ensuing truncated dialogue will lack positive exchanges, and even negative exchanges will take the form of omissions rather than commissions. Without a renewed active initiative to inject an attitude of giving into the system, the chances of change are rather limited. Without change, the detrimental effects are bound to affect the lives of subsequent generations.

13

Brief Contextual Guidelines for the Conduct of Intergenerational Therapy

This chapter is not intended to be a full treatment of therapeutic "technical" rules. It presupposes the reader's familiarity with the general principles of psychotherapy and personality change, both on an individual and family relational basis. Nor is this chapter a summary of the therapeutic implications of the present book. Our practical therapeutic attitudes can be gleaned from reading the previous chapters. What we intend in this chapter is to review briefly how our general principles can be applied to the strategies of family therapists. We have been reluctant to call this a chapter on "techniques." We do not believe that the word "technique," or even the word "therapy," can do justice to that aspect of human dialogue which takes place between the family members and the genuinely helpful professional. We cannot agree with trends which seem to place psychotherapy in the framework of producing "measurable" results in the manner of industrial productiveness. Life phenomena must be understood in their contextual dialectic, rather than through monothetical, one-dimensional criteria of effectiveness. Therapy or healing pertains to a capacity for living and enjoying life: The patterns of invisible loyalties determine the relational context in which the individual is either enabled or hampered in his life aspirations.

In a causal sense, all psychotherapeutic success is more dependent on the "patient's" motivations than on techniques of the therapist, in contrast from the successful alteration of the structure of a building which requires mainly a good architectural design and suitable engineering implementations. It is one of the main limitations of psychotherapeutic success that most people have no inner conviction about the necessity of changing their life attitudes; they just hope to eliminate disturbing and painful experiences from their everyday living. The therapist's most important motivationally enabling leverages issue from the patient's close relationships.

ETHICS OF INDIVIDUALS AND RELATIONAL SYSTEMS

The practice of family therapy raises fundamental questions of ethical implication. Most ethical concepts deal exclusively with an individual framework; the family therapist needs a system concept to assess the interlocking ethical patterns in multiperson relationships. The individual model of reciprocal ethical attitudes tends to stress psychological dimensions, e.g., considerateness in understanding the other's personality. The system concept of a balance of justice focuses on the intertwining existential–relational dimensions of the family, as crossroads of genetic historic entities. One practical consequence of this attitude is that we encourage contact with rather than isolated emancipation from the extended family.

The issue of individual freedom of choice is one of the foundations of Western civilization. Whereas enforced treatment, based on incarceration, was for long the treatment of people designated as lunatics, the Age of Enlightenment introduced the value of appealing to the motivations of the free individual. Yet captive treatment of psychotics has prevailed, for what seem to be reasons of convenience and practicality. It is not easy to compel the uninclined individual to come to out-patient treatment and sustain the professional contract with the therapist. However, we are convinced that if a family is in therapy, even psychotic individuals should be hospitalized only if the rest of the family is unable to take responsibility for management of his problems.

Can the individual family member also be considered a captive of the therapist's notions of how a family should be changed? Who wants the change: Certain powerful family members who are legally in charge, or perhaps all family members, each within his own pursuit of happiness, or is it up to the therapist to supply the motivation to change the family according to his convictions and strategic designs? As therapists we should operate under the conviction that we cannot disregard either the individual or the family system as determinants of actions. We should not consider ourselves arbitrators who are called upon to dictate solutions, nor should we see our role as unrelated to a conflict between individual justices. We suggest that the therapist endorse every family member in seeking a just solution in the context of the relationships. His guiding role should be exerted toward finding what factors contribute to balances and imbalances in the justice of personal positions, attitudes, and action patterns within a family.

MAPPING OF LEDGERS

It is hoped that once the reader finds our notions about the dynamic significance of familial ledgers of justice compatible with his thinking, he will be able to apply it to the practical demands of his therapeutic work. The therapist's awareness of the principles of relational justice needs to be complemented through his acquiring clinical knowledge of both: configurations of justice issues and patterns of avoidance in families.

Any lastingly unjust relational position becomes explicit or implicit exploitation, depending also on the personal strength and background of the family member. A young woman who ventures into marriage as a hoped for restitution for her childhood deprivations, may find parenthood as an unexpectedly depleting and subjectively unfairly exploitative position to be in. Her unbalanced justice ledger can be further aggravated by the misfortune of early widowhood or by the birth of a brain damaged child.

In mapping out the ledger of justice in a family, the systemic distribution of responsibilities and carrying of burdens of obligations has to be learned in addition to observing what family members actually do to one another. In the case of the overburdened, immature, widowed mother of a brain damaged child the slate of a "well-sibling" is overloaded from his earliest age on. Despite denying to himself all the assertions of selfhood and unceasing devotion to unburden his mother, he may still be left with the feeling of not having done enough to alleviate his mother's burden. In addition, he may deplete himself in designing new ways to cover up for the social shortcomings of his retarded brother.

Furthermore, by watching for the manifestations of transference, i.e., emotionally determined repetitious relational attitudes toward himself, the family therapist wants to understand how these keep balance with member-to-member transferences. For instance, the overly devoted, willingly parentified "well" brother of the brain damaged child may have more need for but also more guilt over his transference toward the therapist. His excessive obligation to his family may make him more vulnerable to guilt of implicit disloyalty.

However, while mapping out the crucially important justice ledgers, the family-therapist should remember to connect them with each individual's movement toward his best potential for autonomous function. Under the pressure of invisible obligations one person may break into helpless bondage of pathology, another may grow under pressure into a responsible caretaker: nurse, physician, social worker or responsible worker in any field. By discharging obligations toward one's family of origin, one may win a new degree of freedom for justified self-assertion.

DEFINITIONS

The definition of being a family therapist rests more on the therapist's shared commitment for helping all members than on his "technical" insistence on seeing the family conjointly. In this sense, one could do family therapy by seeing one member of a family through whom one intervenes in the reciprocal systems of concern, obligation, and links of action–reaction. Although we value the family therapist's familiarity with individual dynamic concepts, we do not emphasize insight, consciousness, or confrontation. Unquestionably, these are all parts of the process of therapeutic change in family systems and individual members. All of these cognitively phrased therapeutic processes require courage and determination on the part of the individual. However, close relationships and therapeutic engagement with family relationships require an additional kind of courage: that of staying in the battlefield where the "shooting" never stops. Cognition and insight will never have as much direct relevance to action and change as commitment, obligations, devotion, and loyalty.

GOALS

The goals of family therapy are obviously broader than those of individual therapy although, in our opinion, the latter are inseparable from and should be included in the former. For example, the goal of the person's facing his ambivalently negative feelings toward his parents is to be complemented with the context of loyalty obligations among all members of the family. If one aim is to free the "patient" through actually doing something to exonerate his parents from blame, the possibilities of such an action program will depend on the balance of the justice ledger as well as the contributions of all other members.

The great issues of underlying binding multiperson system forces should not overshadow the therapist's concern with the matters that constitute each family member's conscious aspirations for autonomy and legitimate use of relationships. Whereas we suggest that denial of the existence of the often invisible relational system forces and refusal to repay basic existential obligations lead to false freedom, a mere submission to these forces and obligations would leave out the creative mandate of every human life as a legitimate system level of its own. One of the most important requirements for balancing requires an active commitment to a personal struggle for our psychological existence.

Therapeutic goals can be differentiated also according to their level of depth in reaching the motivational core of multiperson systems. For instance, in helping an adolescent or a young adult member individuate in the context of his family, therapeutic strategy can be designed in terms of a power-competitive model or the more deeply relevant loyalty obligation model. The first strategy may want to help the son against or at the expense of the restraining, possessive, etc. family members. The second one, seemingly, in contradiction, may want to devise ways in which the young individual can obtain inner freedom of growth through helping his parents, etc.

In considering justice ledgers as orienting goal concepts in family therapy, we do not want to reduce all therapeutic rationale to a model of systemic relational determinants. We do not propose to the reader to ignore all other, including individual-based and interactional, communicational, behavioral or game models. What we suggest is an integrated holistic approach in which the significance of these other dimensions of determinants is put into a theoretical framework compatible with their mutual balance with the deepest ledgers of obligations or justice. A brief listing of attempts to formulate systematic reviews of different, but ultimately integratable theoretical components include: Fenichel[36], psychoanalytical, individual; Watzlawick[88], communicational; Berne[7], game-transactional; and Zuk[95] triadic interactional. The beginner should be cautioned not to attempt to formulate therapeutic goals solely on the basis of any one theoretical model to the complete exclusion of the others.

The techniques of each family therapist will favor one or the other functional models of theory, often emphasizing the antithetical juxtaposition of one model against the other. Our relational theories of loyalty and justice balances, should help the therapist to define his value commitments to viewing himself and every family member as whole human beings in the live context of relational systems. Such view recognizes both the imbalance resulting from competitive individual assertions and everyone's need for periodic rebalancing of mutual commitments.

ACTIVITY OF THE THERAPIST

The therapist's role must be an active one; he is only as effective as he is active. However, the concept of *therapeutic activity* is one of the least clearly defined in the literature. Many authors imply that activity is related to those characterological and stylistic properties of the therapist which make him act like the "conductor" of an orchestra. Others conceive of activity as related to the therapist's suggestive, aggressive, personal style or manner of communication, as shown in his readiness for disregarding the habitual styles and values of the family's behavior.

Rather than any stylistic criteria, the process of therapeutic intervention must be based on the therapist's active programming of an ordered set of his expectations for the members of the family. Moreover, it is the *degree of relevance* of the therapeutic expectations that ultimately determines the degree of the therapist's activity. Specifically, while offering his expert and concerned assistance, the therapist must also demand commitment to exploration. He should respond with his concerned interest in return for the family's commitment to the painful, tiring, and often shameful process inevitable in relational confrontations.

While expecting commitment first, the experienced therapist can convey his capacity for sensitive empathy and courageous alliance in the anticipated difficult struggle. This alliance, however, should not promise soft compromise on controversial issues. Ultimately, the most concentrated impact of his effort will be directed at the *most resisted aspect* of family dynamics. The test of the therapist's activity, therefore, lies in his courageous entry into areas of implied murder, suicide, despair, desertion, exploitation, incest, child abuse, etc. His task is significantly easier if the family members have made these aspects explicit before his intervention.

One of the most crucial inner conflicts arises in the therapist when his sympathy and willingness to help the desperately suffering family members clashes with his determination to exact responsible and self-motivated "work" attitudes, even from those who appear to be victimized. In addition, as he becomes the target of the family members' needs and attitudes in transference, he must find the appropriate balance between human responsiveness and sufficient distance for working in a heated atmosphere of deep emotions.

A further demand on the therapist's capacity for activity lies in what one of the authors has described as "multidirectional partiality."[15] The therapist must be able to side with one member and then in turn with other members, instead of refusing to commit himself to anyone's claim for merit or justice. In entering the heated arena of member-to-member jealousies and alliances, the therapist begins to face the essence of relational dynamics—the bookkeeping of the reciprocity of merits and obligations.

It is as difficult to measure the degree of the therapist's activity through behavioral criteria as it is for outsiders to judge the subjective meaning of a relationship, e.g., marriage. For example, the therapist's capacity for staging or "directing" his display of feelings and his aggressive enforcement of responsiveness from the patient may not indicate as much activity in intervention as his capacity for consistence, which forces "sinking in" of points of leverage or personal impact. At times persistence may outwardly appear as silence, but outward "activity" may serve the family in denying and evading the obligation ledger.

An intrinsic capacity for courageously facing his own family relationships is one of the most crucial factors in enabling the family therapist to sustain his function. We believe that such capacity is more directly proportional to essential therapeutic activity than any behavioral characteristics.

We include among the criteria of therapeutic activity the degree of:

1. spontaneity of emotional expression in the proper context of relationships,

2. integrity or integration of deeper trust and loyalty commitment both between family members and between them and the therapist,

3. ability for facing the ethical and justice implications of human existence, especially when viewed in the context of intergenerational gratitude, pride, shame, and contempt,

4. genuineness of confrontation with the patient's total personality and his significant relationships from birth to death, and

5. inclusion of bodily functions of health and sexuality into the exploration.

Finally, we suggest that the same dimension which elicits the strongest resistance to intervention will point to the direction of progress and goal of therapeutic activity: *prevention*. The core of any family member's pathology is anchored in the balance of relationships. Pathogenesis, change, and prevention are based on the same "mechanisms."

TAKING SIDES

As for the family members' invitation to the therapist to become a *judge* of who is right or wrong, we tend neither to discourage nor accept this attempted role assignment, but rather expect the family members to face and elaborate their thoughts, feelings, and expectations about having been treated justly or exploited. What we feel comes closest to a "methodical" basic rule is that the motivational programming in shared relational dynamics derives from a process of *reciprocal obligation accounting*. "Technical" competence will depend on the therapist's capacity for vigorous thinking through of all interactions from the point of view of such accounting. "Working through" in this sense includes the rebalancing of two or more sides of relationships. This programming is quite different from that which is based on individual motivations. Individual motivations such as need for love, security, sexual fulfillment, aggressive expressions, etc., must be examined with regard to their degree of conflict or mutual fit. These individual needs must be understood also in terms of their *degree of autonomy* from invisible obligation structures.

THE THERAPIST IN HIS OWN FAMILY

It is through his commitment to the value of being open to issues of justice in the family ledger that the family therapist must face denial in the ledger of his own relationships. If the therapist strives to approach his own family relationships from the vantage point of multidirectional partiality, he is bound to confront his commitment as a family member to a particular set of personal positions. The family therapist's everyday struggle with families for openness and directness makes him tend to expect the same in his own family, in contrast to the psychoanalytic individual therapist who is likely to isolate his own internal elaboration of conflicts from interactions with the members of his family.

Inevitably, the therapist must encounter his own unworked-through loyalty commitments to his family of origin. As he devotes himself to clarification and rebalancing of the indebtedness, he is liable to engender new conflict with his nuclear family. At times a therapist becomes noticeably hypersensitive in those areas in the treatment of a family's relationship system which are identifiably connected with areas of struggle within his own family. The more genuinely the family therapist adopts a system outlook on the struggle for balancing needs and rights according to fairness, the more he runs the risk of conflict in his own family relationships. Whereas many individual therapists try to isolate their "conflicts" from those of their mate or children, the family therapist is less likely to rely on the efficacy of separate, individually achieved insight and working through.

LOYALTY AND TRUSTABILITY

Family therapy as a process impinges on important aspects of *invisible family loyalties*. Just as that which is symptom or psychopathology in the individual can mean implicit loyalty, therapeutic change or improvement, while consciously welcome, on a deeper level often implies invisible disloyalty to the family of origin (see Chapter 3). Thus, while the therapist feels called upon to build the necessary trust and therapeutic alliance with the family, the resulting threat to their invisible family loyalties may discourage family members from genuine cooperation. The therapist is in a bind: By actively opposing the family's unconscious, collusive sanctioning of the symptom, he becomes untrustable because of the family members' commitment to the "ethics" of unalterable loyalty. Technically, the therapist's best moves at such juncture are: (a) not to get caught in a one-to-one exploration of, e.g., the role of the exploited scapegoat, but to expand discussion to involve all members' points of view, and (b) to invite family members to openly examine their feelings and possible resentments towards the therapist.

Through emphasis on evaluating loyalties and obligations in all family relationships, the value of directness and open stock-taking is injected and endorsed. The therapeutic goal is facing and rebalancing rather than denying the loyalty ties. For example, an adolescent's passive loyalty through the protective pretense of not knowing that her mother had a postpartum psychosis can be transformed into an active loyalty, through a more honest communication about important past events and a concern for her mother's current needs.

In our experience, whenever the family comes close to considering abrupt termination, the family therapist should think through the potential impingement of any further change upon the expectations of family loyalty. He may have sided too soon with the processes of growth, liberation, success, and sexual capability, and overlooked the family's implicit loyalty requirements. For example, selective emphasis on an improved marital relationship can increase a couple's sense of implicit disloyalty to their families of origin, especially if simultaneously the couple's primary obligations are ignored. Termination can result out of their guilt over further abandonment of primary family ties under the guise of a "right to a life of their own."

Once the therapy process has survived the test of basic loyalty versus disloyalty, both to the families of origin and to the nuclear family, other connotations of *trust* become significant. Without trust in the therapist, of course, the family sees no reason to share painful and shameful information. The therapist may earn trust through his concern, experience, and sincerity, but he can still be defeated because his intervention is perceived by family members as lacking sensitivity to the stress of guilt generated by intrinsic disloyalty. Another issue of trust pertains to subgroups within the family. When the therapist is trusted by one, he then seems untrustable to another member or subgroup. The family members test the therapist's capacity for "multidirectional partiality." "If he can side with her against me, how can I trust him?" The therapist should in these instances uncover the obligations through which the balance of loyalties and subgroup struggles is maintained. Then, it should be possible to initiate a new negotiation about reciprocal benefits and exchanges among the members. A final level of trust pertains to *cotherapy*. If there are two or more therapists involved, their trust of each other and their comparative trustability for the family are likely to be subjected to a strenuous test. They should watch for any sign of their team being split as if they were a good and a bad parent.

TRANSFERENCE, PROJECTION, AND EXTRUSION OF THE THERAPIST

Transference in family therapy must be examined from a relational theoretical viewpoint. For instance, the repetitious, apparently senselessly retaliative interactions among family members should be considered as transference manifestations. These interactions are based on "inappropriate," attributive attitudes which derive from unresolved childhood relational issues of the "distorting" family members.

From the system point of view, the family as a whole constitutes a living account of the shifting balance of merit and exploitation. As imbalances in the account reach a critical level, the system makes compensations, often in personally inappropriate, unjust, "projective" ways (see our concept of "revolving slate" in Chapter 4, too). The whole system may suddenly need to scapegoat a member or an outsider. The amazing insensitivity during the initial phases of scapegoating, regarding damage done to the scapegoat, can be explained by the imbalance of merit–reward accounts which accumulated previously in the system.

The therapist can be caught in the rising tide of another kind of rebalancing move—for example, when he has successfully helped the family members exonerate an aged parent. After the initial relaxation of the family's guilt and resentment towards the parent, the therapist may become the needed culprit and target of collective inculpation. The economy of suddenly improved filial loyalty combined with scapegoating of a stranger in transference may prove irresistible.

TREATMENT OF BOTH SYSTEMS AND PERSONS

The concept of ledgers of justice or reciprocity underlines our thesis that such manifest phenomena as lack of communication, scapegoating, secretiveness, symbiotic closeness, depressive mood, hostile manipulativeness, etc., are in themselves epiphenomena rather than essentials of the pathogenic family system. Without understanding the *underlying balances and imbalances* of accounts, we cannot know, for instance, where more openness or expressiveness will lead the systemic process. A great portion of the family therapist's skill lies in his capacity to translate symptomatic behaviors into their corresponding merit balance equivalents (see Chapter 5).

In his effort to perform this translation, the family therapist can find a conceptual aid in what is called the *object–relations theory* of personality (see Guntrip[49]). Just as the accounting model helps him construct the multigenerational flow of give-and-take, object–relations theory enables the therapist to connect current interaction with the long-term "developmental" relational patterning of individual motivations. The individual who finds himself on the disadvantageous or exploited side of the merit imbalance will tend to unconsciously overvalue the relational impact of "bad objects," i.e., malicious persons of the past and present. The internal *configuration* of such bad objects will take the shape of a repertory of his "bad" past experiences with his parents and other members of the family of origin. Whoever then becomes the target for reexternalization will be treated accordingly. On the other hand, the *motivating pressure* for this attributive (projective or transference) effort comes from the *here-and-now accumulation of systemic imbalances* of family reciprocity, depending on the individual's current position within such unbalanced ledger.

It is probable that one's comparative lack of guilt about the unjustness of such projective exploitation of others is due to an internal sense of relief from guilt over disloyalty to the projector's parent. As he attributes the "badness" again and again to current partners in his relationships, the person in effect temporarily exonerates his parents from the responsibility of having caused his long-pent-up resentment over injustice. When the therapist becomes the captive "victim" of such attributions, he may gain a new perspective in understanding how strong the pressure is for rebalancing injustices in the system. Placed in the role of a "bad parent object," he may also gain an unexpectedly strong leverage for "activity" through expecting that family members both face and rebalance fundamental issues.

The question of *personality strength* required for successful therapeutic work must be redefined in order to be useful to the family therapist. Whereas in individual therapy the patient is expected to be sufficiently strong to examine the deeper motivations of his convictions and actions, family therapy requires of family members that they be able to face the present condition and future criteria of reciprocal, multipersonal merit balances in their relationships. Keeping this goal in mind, the family therapist should be interested not so much in a *causal* reconstruction or "fixing blame" as in finding resources of courage for exploring and endurance for changing long-established patterns. The family therapist must become a specialist in finding and utilizing the strengths of the most resourceful family members. Just as the individual therapist tries to form an alliance with the healthy parts of the patient's personality, the family therapist must ally himself with the unused resources in the "healthy" members for the benefit of all. It is for this reason that family therapy should be viewed as primarily a *preventive* intervention, aside from its being the most effective remedy for the symptoms of most designated patient members.

REBALANCING THROUGH REVERSAL INSTEAD OF REVIEWING PAST RELATIONSHIPS

The concepts of rebalancing and reversal parallel somewhat the concept of the defensive use of turning to the opposite (Fenichel) in individual theory. The similarity, however, is only a formal one: in both cases progress toward improved function should follow from the therapist's challenging the reversal, provided his patient or the family are ready to explore the possibility of change.

Turning an impulse or desire into its opposite serves the individual's defensive needs for avoiding confrontation with his own motivations and their consequences. Relational imbalance, on the other hand, may be caused and maintained by a collusively shared need of all family members for not facing the family's invisible ledger of obligations. Whereas the therapeutic goal of individual analysis or psychotherapy is oriented toward insight and psychological reintegration of the patient's denied or otherwise avoided strivings, the goal of reversing relational positions points toward an eventual rebalancing of mutual commitments and actions on the part of all family members.

Reversal has to start in the therapist's own mind. He has to adopt a dialectical outlook on evaluating the meaning of any apparently rigid role assignment or relational attitude. By reversing the signs, so to speak, he should try to understand, for example, in what way the allegedly disapproved sick and disturbed role position may also carry a particularly important invisibly responsible function for the rest of the family. If the antithetical, reversed outlook begins to make "operational" sense, the most important therapeutic clues should flow from it with surprising richness.

One important consideration is the reversed meaning of the position of the seemingly selfish, demanding, domineering member. By exploring the reverse possibility, the therapist may find the seeming exploiter to be the one most exploited and tied to his role by guilt-provoking invisible obligations. It is important to add that a family member can be exploited by the structural arrangement of relationships itself, without anyone's intention or active personal initiative.

The seemingly irresponsible drug-addicted youth may, on the other hand, be hopelessly caught in an overly concerned loyal attitude towards the family. Addiction to stealing may be related to an internalized obligation ledger according to which the kleptomaniac has been cheated by his environment in more ways than his visible stealing can rebalance. The parents' loving concern for their child's insufficient extent of peer relatedness may cover their unconscious wishes and maneuvers to prevent the same type of social contacts.

On a deeper and more encompassing level death, loss and grief can be made into resources for significant relational gains. Even anticipated death of a grandmother can accelerate the remedial effects of family therapy as illustrated in chapter 12. The anticipation of her mother's death from cancer was able to cause a person to invest new energies into a seemingly hopeless mother-daughter relationship.

It is never advisable to encourage devaluation of *the parent's position* within the family. Furthermore, it is axiomatic that no one wins where the outcome leads to shame or hate of the parent. However, it is highly desirable for the person to be able to recognize and face these feelings in himself. It is therefore crucial for the family therapist to support the exploration of such feelings in the context of the give-and-take of a parent–child dialogue, rather than in the privacy of any individual's self-reflections.

This is especially important when the aging parent is not expected to live much longer. Intergenerational confrontation of feelings should never lead to condemnation of the aged parent as an endpoint of the therapeutic endeavor. The therapist's skill and tactful attitude can avert such outcome. The confrontation is valuable if it leads to subsequent improvement of the relationship between the adult and his parent, rather than being primarily an exercise in openness or expressiveness.

An invisible confrontation is less likely to occur but is still possible after the death of an aged parent. The postponed resolution of mourning leads to a continuous need to be parented and freezes the person's relational availability. However, the mourning child can evoke memories of his relationship with the deceased—often through contacts with people who knew the parent—which may eventually reintegrate his understanding and feelings about the dead parent. In the process of reassessing and partially *exonerating* the resented parent, the mourner gains new freedom to further complete mourning, to free himself from projective resentment, and to become more available to new relationships. The true gainer is the next generation.

Whereas all emphasis on *one member's being sick* addresses the family through its weakness, supporting a multidirectional dialogue of action and concern capitalizes on the family's resources and strength. The family therapist must be unimpressed with the family designation of one member as the sick one. Or, for that matter, the allegedly best functioning, "well" member role. Nor should he subscribe to the idea that families are more fragile and vulnerable to work with than individuals. Contrary to notions of the value of privacy and exclusive commitment, it is responsible and courageous facing of challenges within the relationships that characterizes family therapy. Through such openness and courage, the ledgers of basic family commitments can gradually be explored and rebalanced.

Rebalancing of relationships is crucial to our thesis. We are not impressed by mere demonstrations of family dynamic or pathogenic forces. In exploring an incestuous situation, for instance, open admission of facts is not the final goal. Undoing of secretiveness should not only be followed by an evaluation of the exploitation and mutual victimization of incest, but also by tactful exploration of mutual concern, affection, and wishes for finding safer foundations for closeness.

The therapeutic phase which is characterized by a family member's readiness to face hitherto inaccessible memories of his childhood attitudes toward his parents tends to coincide with his growing capacity for improved, e.g., less projective interpersonal (marital, parental) relational attitudes. Readiness for reexamination of defensively avoided relationships can introduce such a striking, unpredictable attitudinal change. It may follow therapeutic emphasis on the person's actual rela-

tionship with his aging parents, or it may interlock with phasic intensifi-
cations and shifts in the transference significance of the therapist.

THE CHILD'S SYMPTOM AS A SIGNAL

Any desperate, dramatic *acting out* on the part of a child can always
be considered a signal that the family as a whole system is asking for
help. The need for help is shared by all, but the responsibility for change
should rest primarily with the adults. Paradoxically, the more extreme
the child's symptomatology, the more one should consider working
with the rest of the family.

The *adolescent* is often thought to be best treated on an individual
basis, because of his specific sensitivities about privacy at that age. In
our judgment, this opinion is valid only as long as therapy is thought of
as limited to verbal revelations and to search for insight-based change
of function. While we recognize the adolescent's right and need for
privacy in acquiring age-appropriate new relationships, we do not believe that genuine emotional growth can be achieved by ignoring the
context of the essential relationship systems. Family therapy can provide the necessary forum for a true liberation from obligations by facing
their live context. In treating families we have been just as available for
private sessions with the adolescent as for marital discussions with the
parents. Both parents and adolescents must commit themselves, however, to making such separate sessions at least as productive an exploration as a conjoint meeting with the family could be.

The therapist should not expect either self-effacing revelations about
the sexual, etc., privacies of the adolescent or complete, unreserved
readiness by the parents to let go of the adolescent. In most families it
is taboo to recognize the fact of filial indebtedness; however, it is wise
for the therapist to assume that such denial, if permitted, can lead to
unresolved resentment in the parents and unmanageable guilt in the
adolescent or young adult.

We have not been impressed by efforts to categorize family patterns
according to individual diagnostic or nosological entities. All psychological or behavioral symptom manifestations fit into and are largely determined by relational configurations. *Drug addiction* or *delinquent*
behavior of young people are examples of symptomatic manifestations
of conflict between individuals and multiperson systems. Without assigning any specific relational configuration to families harboring these
or related problems, we suggest that the therapist try to reinterpret the
apparently irresponsible or immoral behavior of the delinquent and

drug addict. By searching for a devoted, loyal, and redeemable or even valued familial contribution of this seeming culprit, the therapist may find the shortest way to an understanding of the deeper dynamic configuration of the system. Paradoxically, there seems to be a parallel between the symptomatic child's implicit role and the most accessible avenues for interventions on the part of the therapist. In learning how to help the child avoid the binds of his ambiguous familial obligations, the therapist can lay the foundation of his strategy in helping all the family members to reevaluate their positions.

TREATING THE SYSTEMIC ROOTS OF PARANOIA

The therapy of persons who use *projective blaming* or suspicious, paranoid, persecutory ideation has occupied the interests of psychotherapists for many years. Without claiming an exclusive or complete explanation of this tendency, we suggest that the solution to the problem must be based both on individual *and* relational strategies. Specifically, we suggest that repetitious, seemingly unalterable blaming or suspicion of innocent others is dynamically connected with the blamer's invisible loyalty to the ambivalently invested parent. The underlying loyalty sustained to one's questionably deserving parent, in turn, liberates one from part of the guilt over unjust blaming of others. Insight into the inappropriateness of the blaming, on the other hand, may be blocked by the person's deep conviction of the justness of his resentment over suffered injuries and by his desire for exonerating his parent at other people's expense. Without a chance for improving one's image or relationship with one's parent, no gains can be expected from facing the causes of resentment.

DURATION

Not all therapy is *long-term*. The length of therapy depends in part on the therapist's preferences and on the setting. We have seen therapeutic results from family interviews when one or no more than three sessions were planned. Last, but not least, the nature of the problem and the family members' capacity for achievement of change also determine the goals of therapy.

The family's goal may be limited to removal of the initial referral problem in the designated patient member. In our years of experience as both individual and family therapists, this usually occurs sooner in family than in individual therapy. Although there is no assurance that such individual symptomatic change is proof of a systemic rebalancing and reorientation in family relationships, this goal is a legitimate one and the therapist should be ready to accept termination of therapy at such a point.

The family members' motivation may be mobilized if the therapist tells them that he considers his work with them as short-term unless they demonstrate that they can face and explore important relationship problems and strive for change over a prolonged time. Thus, a simple, long-term dependence on the therapist would not qualify as a basis for prolonged therapy. At the point when motivation seems to have reached a plateau, it is to everyone's benefit if the therapist raises the question of termination. He can ask at the same time for the family members' feelings toward the therapist and about the question of accomplishments, limitations of progress, and remaining goals.

PROGRESS AND CHANGE

The criteria in *evaluation of progress* in family therapy are very different from those in individual therapy. Traditionally, evidence of improvement or change can be based on a person's functions: improved mood, more appropriate behavior, better physical health, improved sexual potency, etc. *Change* or lack of it can also be defined in familial functional dimensions: It depends on the quality and degree of openness, meaningful involvement, individuated rather than amorphously fused interactions, more meaningful communications, and more tolerance of growth or separation, etc. On a more fundamental level we are interested in knowing whether the hidden accounts of exploitations and obligations have been or can be confronted. If there is a capacity for facing these intra- and intergenerational balances of give-and-take, the question remains, how much are the family members capable of rebalancing the ledgers of obligation, merit, and exploitation?

INDICATION AND JUSTIFICATION: IN WHOSE BEHALF?

The question of *indications* and *contraindications* is an easily misleading one. Just as there is no specific indication for reasonable thinking or considerate, loving family relationships, there is no specific indication to justify the exploration of their absence or disturbance. If family therapy is defined as an avenue for constructive examination and utilization of hidden resources of relationships, it cannot be considered a specific technical measure and it can never be contraindicated in a general sense. It is true that lack of a capable family therapist may make the undertaking pointless or seemingly disruptive. It is unlikely, however, that families will subsequently function worse than their natural tendency requires or permits. In order to prevent needless loss of time and expenditure, the family's capacity for achieving the earlier-described goals should be evaluated by the therapist prior to committing himself to therapy.

Aside from these general cautions, we do not agree that divorce, severe psychopathology in a parent, tendency for intense initial defensiveness, prejudice against family therapy, or organic disease in family members constitute valid contraindications to family explorations. Rather, these conditions require a careful strategic thinking about whom to involve in therapy and how to develop leverages; what is required is that family members show motivation for meaningful— even if negatively colored—therapeutic involvement.

An even more crucial issue to consider is, in whose behalf is family therapy indicated or contraindicated? For example, is indication based on whether the school-phobic child improves in family treatment? Does it cease to exist when improvement has occurred? If the mother concurrently develops depression, does it represent a new basis for indication? Can the appearance of such new manifest symptomatology in another member constitute a contraindication? If a mother's manifest depressive phase helps her work through her entire outlook on life and relationships, is continued family therapy indicated for the child with the presenting problem, the mother, or the rest of the children who are likely to benefit from such rearrangement? We believe that the ultimate value of family therapy lies in prevention. By rearranging the criteria of justifiable expectations, therapy can prevent the formation of paralyzing binds which could otherwise produce symptoms and unhappiness in any apparently well member.

Epilogue

Having finished writing an essentially nontechnical book about family psychotherapy, we cannot ignore the broader social implications of our field. We believe that the relational dynamic or systems orientation has great relevance for our society's future. In so doing we do not consider ourselves as spokesmen of contemporary social sciences but as investigators whose expertise lies in an inside view of families and the way they present model systems for all social relationships.

David Cooper has entitled one of his books *The Death of the Family.*[29] Like many other political activists, he equates society's oppressive forces with those of the family. Moreover, most revolutionary political activists discredit psychotherapy as a conservator of a bourgeois social order. Many advocate overthrowing the order first and finding whether there will be any need left for psychotherapy thereafter. Historically, much of enlightened liberalism emerged in answer to exploitative and oppressive forces of the traditional family and conservative social establishment. Rather than monothetically advocating destruction of social structure, we believe that a more mature dialectical view suggests a systematic search for a fair balance between the individual's autonomous rights and his investments in the social system he is part of.

Any penetrating questioning of values of family and social order tends to overwhelm society's theorists; this is the age of oversaturation with overlapping and mutually extinguishing messages. All leaders and traditional establishments are liable to blame, but not because better alternatives are known. People seem to parentify an imaginary, nonexisting authority and then challenge it to become a better leader and, symbolically, a more concerned and loving parent.

Being a leader in our day is becoming less and less rewarding. The leader must recognize that his subordinates are likely to be more sophisticated and autonomous than at any previous time. The elected leader or even a dictator become servants of large political machines. The youth of any country are inclined to question slogans which gave leaders their mandates, and they are becoming distrustful of anyone who presents himself as an educational authority. Moreover, this is the age when a single hijacker can make a multibillion dollar company produce a huge ransom within hours. A handful of guerrillas can kidnap the ambassador of a great power or humiliate a proud government.

Permissive liberalism appears to have run its course in American society. It has reached its limits in a rising crime rate; there are signs of an anarchic disorganization. A variety of freedoms are more rapidly being utilized for subversion than for strengthening the justice and dignity of each man and his family. As a "backlash" effect we see people retreat to the timeworn moral sanctions of traditional society: fear of abortion or sexual expression, deification of the rights of the self-centered individual, and glorification of material progress and prudent acquisition as the ultimate goals of human life. Will mankind have time to develop a new hierarchy of values before overpopulation, pollution, and destructive weapon technology impose all-encompassing and devouring everyday emergencies? Where is the new teacher likely to come from? How will he be heard if people live without trust? How can a depleting pool of trust be replenished? If we feel abandoned and deserted in a free society, where do we turn to after freedom?

We suggest that the answer may lie in a thorough rethinking of the definitions of merit in every human relationship. Human needs are virtually limitless as motivational factors, whereas rights are commensurate with merit. Any consideration of need will never by itself lead to definable boundaries of interaction. Human rights must be redefined from a viewpoint of merit in relationships, rather than in terms of individual or group needs. The natural starting point for such a redefinition is between the parent and child or between the adult and his aging parent. The fact that my life originated from them creates an ineradicable bond of loyalty and obligation toward them.

The measurability of the balance of merit depends on an adequate definition of the criteria of reciprocity in human relationships. It is reasonably easy to define equivalent reciprocity in some interactions among equals. We can both play it by the rules or cheat. As long as the rules are clearly defined, there must be a way of measuring the extent of cheating. Equivalency of reciprocity among unequal partners, e.g., parent and infant, is more difficult to define. The manifestly self-sacrificing, devoted caretaker may at the same time obtain more gratification from this devotion than from any other life activity. Furthermore, while seemingly giving, the parent may exploit the infant in a thousand invisible and even unconscious ways.

There are many circumstances in which reciprocity is affected by nonreciprocal factors. Birth order of siblings, being born a female versus a male, early bereavements, birth defects, hereditary illnesses which hit one of several children, severe accidents, or unfortunate timing of birth can all affect the existence of a child in a nonreciprocal way. The afflicted child seems to obtain additional rights in view of his bad fate. In short, life produces inequality of opportunity or distributive justice. At whose expense should this be rebalanced?

In society as well, the fact of being born poor or a member of a certain nation, class, religious group, or geographic locality may create a built-in imbalance of the rights of entire groups of people. While it is true that the ideally strong individual can overcome the particular disadvantages of his fate, social justice should not be built on denial of the essential nonreciprocity among people. An imbalance of retributive justice can be added through unfair acts of one's fellows. The most effective method of help in any problem lies in *prevention.* No prevention can be designed without facing the criteria of relational reciprocity. The rebalancing of injustices is hampered by the Herculean task of undoing the denial, avoidance, and fear of retributive justice built into every social system.

The applications of the foregoing are numerous, and the rate of increase of social deterioration by default is appalling. It is small wonder that the youth of our times will not listen to what they deem to be irrelevant teaching, when the basis of trust and security of social structure is being pulled from under their feet.

FUTURE AREAS OF REDEFINITION OF RECIPROCITY, MERIT, AND JUSTICE

A thorough reorientation toward reciprocal justice as a value of highest societal priority would demand a corresponding examination of areas of unbalanced, intrinsic exploitation.

Material or success-oriented acquisitive society places a low value on the *educational* function as a whole. Financial and status rewards of teachers have been traditionally low in America, when compared with the prestige of business administration. Production of things has enjoyed a higher priority than "production" of well-educated human beings.

Schools are a main access route to what constitutes mental health and lack of health. Society expects from the child that he learn. Yet it is painfully clear that he can "give" attention only if he has been given a sense of trust in the fairness of the human world. Furthermore, he represents his family, to whom he owes first loyalty and who despite their overt approval are jealously watching his engagement in the school and peer worlds as signs of implicit disloyalty. Unless we can recognize the built-in unfairness of these expectations towards both the child and the teacher who is also forced into an overloaded defensive position, we may fail to achieve an adequate educational system, despite our best efforts.

The criteria of *success and failure* themselves are bound to change if we consider that through the phenomenon of "family homeostasis" the successful-appearing member tends invisibly to depend on the failing or less successful ones. Balance between successful external and supportive family roles is maintained through multiperson system arrangements of hidden loyalty expectations.

The contemporary *welfare system* is an important example of a major social activity in which reciprocity of fairness is inadequately considered. A system seemingly built on the rights of children and women can cause deprivation through its destructive effect on male roles and consequently on the family as a whole. Such a system must inevitably gravitate towards control of people through their unearned income, a principle detrimental to human dignity and to the fairness between recipient and taxpaying public.

Our entire *legal system* suffers from the lack of a definition of reciprocity when covert expectations and unconscious motivations in parents are involved. Judges find it inevitable, despite their better intuitive understanding, that they must apply the law to children to make them account for weaknesses within their family system. The court may have no solution but to place a child in another home or in an institution, even in cases where it can be demonstrated that the delinquency is unconsciously reinforced by the family situation. We feel the solution in these cases could lie in court commitment to mandatory family evaluation and treatment.

The issue of *criminal justice* as a necessary social safeguard should be considered separate from the issue of a humane outlook on the rights of jailed prisoners. Looking at the unilaterally disadvantaged positions of the prisoner as he faces the organized might of the law, it is natural to empathize with the underdog's role. The prisoner should be protected against the sadistic impulses of people to whom he is helplessly exposed. On the other hand, the weak and helpless situation of the prisoner should not be used to becloud his responsibility to pay for his unfair transgression, provided his guilt has been validly established.

Labor union versus management debates have come increasingly under scrutiny by society. It is obvious that while labor and management are busy spelling out their partisan needs and rights, the silent and absent third party is the public whose reciprocal contributions are usually denied and ignored by giving exclusive concern to reciprocity between these two parties. This nonreciprocal exploitation of the tax-paying public as a whole places an enormous burden on the democratic process of free society; it would require nonpolitical statesmanship to remedy the situation according to multilateral requirements of justice.

Consumers' rights movements and organizations are being discovered as essential for the survival of a fair democratic order. The individual in our age is no longer capable of detecting how he is being exploited by, for instance, a chemical additive to canned juice which may save the producer a penny on each can. When 10 years later the consumer and his family members develop a fatal illness as a result of the "mistake," they have no legal proof or even awareness of whom to retaliate against for the damage suffered, unless society develops consumer protection as one of its powerful arms.

Most *international relations* have been traditionally conducted in disregard for reciprocity. The foreign group is regarded with prejudice. There is a widespread approval of cheating, mistrust, and exploiting the out-group. Naturally, they in turn will treat the former group unfairly and vice versa *ad infinitum*. The lack of reciprocity in fair competition is then expected to be rebalanced through an attempt at crushing the opponent through superior armaments. Ultimately, everyone becomes a victim of alternating overretaliation. Indifference by the great powers to the real issues of justice in the industrially "backward" countries is potentially as violent and destructive as outright military intervention.

Somewhat paradoxically, *pacifistic*, guilt-ridden Western intellectuals seem to find it difficult to give high priority to definitions of justice. Yet nothing makes a soldier or guerilla more ready to kill than his conviction about injustice. The concept of peace as a human right is incomplete, as those who have been brutally conquered, humiliated, exploited, or imprisoned already know. Peace at all costs can seal prejudices and covertly executed genocide.

Sexual mores of our times are sadly confused as to the ethical priorities involved. Aspects of sexuality such as the morality of containment of any excessive pleasure and trustability of relationship based on the exclusiveness of sexual fidelity are not adequately separated from the far greater ethical issue of the responsibility of parenthood. Jealous chaperonage of the presumed rampant pleasure of others seems to remain man's principal preoccupation about sexual morality, in blatant disregard for the need for redefining the ethics of parenthood in an era of effective contraception.

As one important example, we regard the seeming progressive trend of no-fault divorce legislation as partly retrogressive, although we fully agree that it would be unfair to simply force a man and a woman to continue to live together because of the ethics of sexual fidelity. Yet to be judged fairly, divorce can only be considered in its three-generational ethical perspective. The burden of each spouse's invisible past loyalties and their obligations to the future of the subsequent generations are a crucially important area.

Divorce is being debated mainly on the basis of the needs and rights of the parents. The parents' rights are being defined chiefly in terms of right for exclusive sexual possession, instead of a right for reciprocal multigenerational consideration in the totality of life's functions. The main issue of responsibility toward one's own and the spouse's family and toward the emotional growth of one's children is underrated. For these reasons a mandatory family dynamic exploration period should precede any serious judicial consideration of divorce by parents.

A sizeable number of *women* are joining in efforts at assertiveness and "liberation." For thousands of years, women have deserved and been accorded societal protection and privileges to compensate for their biologically determined vulnerabilities. From the dawn of civilization it has concerned society that young women can be exploited by involuntary sexual participation through rape or seduction. If the male cannot be made responsible for fatherhood, the woman will be left with the unbalanced captive responsibility for pregnancy and parenthood. The physiological processes of menstruation, pregnancy, childbirth, lactation, etc., all tend to make women unilaterally vulnerable. They are entitled to receive compensatory measures from society so that reciprocal fairness can prevail. Otherwise the mothering capacity of many women will be undermined by their feeling of unilateral, sex-limited exploitation.

Furthermore, *old-age sexual needs* are discouraged by traditional societal attitudes. Not only are the old considered less attractive and a potential economical burden, but their right to romance is denied. Expressions like "dirty old man" are indicative of this bias against the validity of sexual needs as separate from reproductive ability. One of the last expressions of hypocritical finger-pointing occurs when residents of old-age homes express harmless romantic or sexual needs. Moreover, right to romance is but one area in which unfair segregation and scapegoating seem to be practiced on a large scale by society, with little regard for the deserved merits of the aged.

Masturbation, pornography, and other nonreproductive manifestations of sexuality are only somewhat less censured by current societal standards than by those of previous ages. Aesthetic condemnation of these manifestations should be balanced with a fair consideration of the probability of their essentially nonharmful, or even socially advantageous, "outlet" function. However, confusion of genuine ethical considerations with puritanic tradition is still striking when one realizes that most caretakers of old or mentally retarded people are determined to suppress all substitutive sexual manifestations in those under their custody. Puritanic values are not only condemnatory regarding pleasure, but they tend to subordinate the personal aspects of relationships to values of disciplined, acquisitive attitudes. However, promiscuously rebellious sexual "enlightenment" may be just as indifferent to the total human aspects of relationships as its seeming counterpart, puritanism.

The *mentally retarded* child is usually the focus of both overattention and frustration in the family, and of unadmitted resentment over the parents' guilt-laden frustration. The child's rights are stressed at the expense of his siblings, and the parents are at a loss when it comes to applying the same disciplinary measure to the retarded as to their other children. Much strain thus results both in family and society from a lack of definition of what constitutes fair reciprocity in the asymmetrical relationship between normals and retarded individuals.

Psychosomatic components in medical illnesses of all kinds will have to be reexamined from the point of view of their possible balancing function regarding unfair, nonreciprocal exploitation of or by someone closely related. We find that sexual dysfunction, for instance, is typically related to one's sensed disloyalty to the expectations of one's family of origin. It is conceivable that other bodily dysfunctions can also represent compensatory self-punitive measures.

The broad applications of the principles of family dynamics and therapy described here are going to meet harsh resistance by all societal forces who have a vested interest in maintaining avoidance and denial of the issues of reciprocity. Other implications may simply be radically new and require readjustment of thought and procedure. Our radical reorientation as to nosology, symptom, change, and evaluation criteria must affect deeply the entire *cost-accounting, insurance,* and *record-keeping* systems of mental health services. As yet there is no workable nomenclature for multiperson-based categories of nosology, change, and evaluation.

The principles that underlie our reasoning perhaps lack the sensationalism of the "new," and they cannot be simply learned without a fundamental rethinking and reorientation of our traditional acquisitive attitudes. Some people may still convince themselves that machinegunning of polar bears from helicopters and defoliating entire forests through the pushing of a button by a pilot are comparable to the heroic struggle with nature which characterized man from the cave to civilization. We wonder what would be the price of even a minimal reorientation regarding traditional biases.

However, a new attitude to man's relationship with man and with nature is developing at the dawn of the nuclear age. As modern technology enables man to destroy nature, without exposing himself to a fair fight with dangerous animals and the elements, the necessity of a renewed concern with reciprocity will be forced upon us if mankind is to survive without the checks and balances of nature. It is with the young generation where our hopes must lie, not only in their concerns with peace and ecology, but eventually in their recognition of the crucial significance of justice in all areas of human relationships. Yet we cannot exonerate the parent generation from their leadership and participatory obligations, even though change will primarily benefit the young generation. We believe that the implications of this book will be ultimately most productive in designing preventive programs aimed at improvement of family and social relationships in general.

References

1. Ackerman NW: Treating the Troubled Family. New York, Basic Books, 1966.
2. Aeschylus: The Complete Greek Tragedies, Vol. I. Edited by D Greene, R Lattimore. New York, Washington Square Press Pocket Books, 1967.
3. Alexander F: Psychoanalysis and Psychotherapy. New York, Norton, 1956.
4. Bateson G, Jackson DD, Haley J, Weakland JH: Toward a theory of schizophrenia. Behav Sci 1:251–264, 1956.
5. Bay C: The Structure of Freedom. New York, Atheneum, 1958.
6. Beach WB Jr: Psychosis in childhood. Northwest Med 56:438–442, 1957.
7. Berne E: Games People Play; The Psychology of Human Relationships. New York, Grove Press, 1964.
8. Blenkner M: Social work and family relationships in later life with some thoughts on filial maturity. Social Structure and the Family: Generational Relations. Edited by E Shanas and GF Streib. Englewood Cliffs, NJ, Prentice-Hall, 1965, pp 46–59.
9. Blitsten D: The World of the Family; A Comparative Study of Family Organizations in their Social and Cultural Settings. New York, Random House, 1963.
10. Boardman HE: A project to rescue children from inflicted injuries. Social Work 7: 43–51, 1962.
11. Boszormenyi-Nagy I: The concept of schizophrenia from the perspective of family treatment. Fam Process 1:103–113, 1962.
12. Boszormenyi-Nagy I: A theory of relationships: Experience and transaction. Intensive Family Therapy. Edited by I Boszormenyi-Nagy, JL Framo. New York, Harper & Row, 1965a, pp 33–86.
13. Boszormenyi-Nagy I: Intensive family therapy as process. Intensive Family Therapy. Edited by I Boszormenyi-Nagy, JL Framo. New York, Harper & Row, 1965b, pp 87–142.
14. Boszormenyi-Nagy I: The concept of change in conjoint family therapy. Psychotherapy for the Whole Family. Edited by AS Friedman, I Boszormenyi-Nagy, JE Jun-

greis, G Lincoln, HE Mitchell, JC Sonne, RV Speck, G Spivak. New York, Springer, 1965c, pp 305–319.

15. Boszormenyi-Nagy I: From family therapy to a psychology of relationships: Fictions of the individual and fictions of the family. Compr Psychiatry 7:408–423, 1966.

16. Boszormenyi-Nagy I: Relational modes and meaning. Family Therapy and Disturbed Families. Edited by GH Zuk, I Boszormenyi-Nagy, Palo Alto, Science and Behavior Books, 1967, pp 58–73.

17. Boszormenyi-Nagy I: Preface to: Family Interaction: A Dialogue Between Family Researchers and Family Therapists, 1st ed. Edited by JL Framo. New York, Springer, 1972, pp ix–xi.

18. Boszormenyi-Nagy I: Loyalty implications of the transference model in psychotherapy. Arch Gen Psychiatry, 27: 374–380, 1972.

19. Boszormenyi-Nagy I, Framo JL: Intensive Family Therapy. New York, Harper & Row, 1965.

20. Bowen M: The family as a unit of study and treatment. Am J Orthopsychiatry 31: 40–60, 1961.

21. Bowen M: Family psychotherapy with schizophrenia in the hospital and in private practice. Intensive Family Therapy. Edited by I Boszormenyi-Nagy and JL Framo. New York, Harper & Row, 1965, pp 213–244.

22. Bowen M: The use of family theory in clinical practice. Compr Psychiatry 7:345–374, 1966.

23. Brodey WM: Some family operations and schizophrenia; A study of 5 hospitalized families each with a schizophrenic member. Arch Gen Psychiatry 1:379–402, 1959.

24. Brody EM, Spark GM: Institutionalization of the aged: A family crisis. Fam Process 5: 76–90, 1966.

25. Buber M: Guilt and guilt feelings. Psychiatry 20:114–129, 1957.

26. Buber M: The Knowledge of Man: A Philosophy of the Interhuman. Edited by M Friedman. New York, Harper & Row, 1965.

27. Caffey J: Significance of the history in the diagnosis of traumatic injury to children. J Pediatr 67(suppl):1008–1014, 1965.

28. Chapman AH: Obsessions of infanticide. Arch Gen Psychiatry 1: 12–16, 1959.

29. Cooper D: The Death of the Family. New York, Pantheon, 1970.

30. Dickens C: Great Expectations. New York, Washington Square Press, 1956.

31. Dicks HV: Marital Tensions: Clinical Studies Toward a Psychological Theory of Interaction. New York, Basic Books, 1967.

32. Durkheim E(1897): Suicide. Translated by JA Spaulding, G Simpson. Edited by G Simpson. London, Routledge and Kegan Paul, 1952.

33. Erikson EH: Childhood and Society. New York, Norton, 1950.

34. Erikson EH: Identity and the life cycle. Psychol Issues 1(1):18–171, 1959.

35. Erikson EH: Identity, Youth and Crisis. New York, Norton, 1968.

36. Fenichel O: The Psychoanalytic Theory of Neurosis. New York, Norton, 1945.

37. Framo JL: Symptoms from a family transactional viewpoint. International Psychiatry Clinics. Vol. 7, No. 4. Edited by NW Ackerman. Boston, Little, Brown, & Co., 1970, pp 125–171.

38. Freud A: Normality and Pathology in Childhood. New York, International University Press, 1965.

39. Freud S(1924): The economic problem of masochism. Standard Edition 19:155–170. London, Hogarth, 1961.

40. Freud S(1923): The ego and the id. Standard Edition 19:1–66. London, Hogarth, 1961.

41. Freud S(1921): Group psychology and the analysis of the ego. Standard Edition 18:65–144, London, Hogarth, 1955.

42. Freud S(1916): Some character-types met within psychoanalytic work. Standard Edition 14:309–336, London, Hogarth, 1957.

43. Freud S(1913): Totem and taboo. Standard Edition 13:1–162, London, Hogarth, 1955.

44. Friedman AS, Boszormenyi-Nagy I, Jungreis JE, Lincoln G, Mitchell HE, Sonne JC, Speck RV, Spivak G: Psychotherapy for the Whole Family. New York, Springer, 1965.

45. Friedman AS: The "well" sibling in the 'sick' family: A Contradiction. International Jr., Social Psychiatry, Special Edition 2:47–53, 1964.

46. Ginsberg L: Legends of the Bible. New York, Jewish Publication Society of America, 1956.

47. Gouldner AW: The norm of reciprocity: A preliminary statement. Am Sociol Rev 25:161–178, 1960.

48. Greenson RR: The working alliance and the transference neuroses. Psychoanal Q 34:155–181, 1965.

49. Guntrip HJ: Personality Structure and Human Interaction: The Developing Synthesis of Psychodynamic Theory. New York, International University Press, 1961.

50. Harlow HF: The affectional systems. Behavior of Nonhuman Primates, Vol 2. Edited by AM Schrier, HF Harlow, F Stollnitz. New York, Academic Press, 1965.

51. Hastings J (ed): Encyclopedia of Religion and Ethics, Vol 8. New York, Scribner's, 1951.

52. Hastings J(ed): Encyclopedia of Religion and Ethics, Vol 4. New York, Scribner's, 1955.

53. Helfer RE, Pollock CB: The battered child syndrome. Adv Pediatr 15:9–27, 1968.

54. Hollender MH: The Practice of Psychoanalytic Psychotherapy. New York, Grune & Stratton, 1965.

55. Holmberg AR: Nomads of the Long Bow: The Siriono of Eastern Bolivia. Washington, D.C., Smithsonian Institute, 1950.

56. Johnson AM, Szurek SA: The genesis of antisocial acting out in children and adults. Psychoanal Q 21:323–343, 1952.

57. Kelsen H: What is Justice? Justice, Law and Politics in the Mirror of Science. Berkeley, University of California Press, 1957.

58. Kempe CH: The battered child and the hospital. Hosp Practice 4:44–57, October, 1969.

59. Laing RD: Family and individual structure. The Predicament of the Family; A Psychoanalytic Symposium. Edited by P Lomas. New York, International University Press, 1967.

60. Lederer WJ, Jackson DD: The Mirages of Marriage. New York, Norton, 1968.

61. Lennard HL, Bernstein A: Patterns of Human Interaction: An Introduction to Clinical Sociology. San Francisco, Jossey Bass, 1969.

62. Lennard HL, Epstein LJ, Bernstein A, Ransom DC: Hazards implicit in prescribing psychoactive drugs. Science 169: 438–441, 1970.

63. Luijpen WA: Existential Phenomenology. Pittsburgh, Duquesne University Press, 1965.

64. Marcuse H: One-Dimensional Man: Studies in the Ideology of Advanced Industrial Society. Boston, Beacon, 1966.

65. Meyerson AT: Amnesia for homicide ("pedicide"). Its treatment with hypnosis. Arch Gen Psychiatry 14:509–515, 1966.

66. Morris MG, Gould RW: Role reversal: A concept in dealing with the neglected/battered-child syndrome in The Neglected Battered Child Syndrome: Role Reversal in Parents. Child Welfare League of America Inc, 1963, pp 29–49.

67. Parsons T, Shils EA: Toward a General Theory of Action. Cambridge, Mass, Harvard University Press, 1951.

68. Pavenstedt E: A comparison of the child-rearing environment of upper-lower and very low-lower class families. Am J Orthopsychiatry 35:89–95, 1965.

69. Philbrick EB: Treating Parental Pathology Through Protective Services. Denver, The Children's Division, The American Humane Society, 1960.

70. Piaget J: The Moral Judgment of the Child. Glencoe, Ill, Free Press, 1932.

71. Rainwater L, Yancey WL: The Moynihan Report and the Politics of Controversy; A Transaction Social Science and Public Policy Report. Cambridge, Mass, MIT Press, 1967.

72. Reiner BS: Casework treatment of sexual confusion in character disorders. Social Casework 43:538–545, 1962.

73. Resnick PJ: Child murder by parents. A psychiatric review of filicide. Am J Psychiatry 126:325–334, 1969.

74. Ricoeur P: Freud and Philosophy: An Essay on Interpretation. New York, Yale University Press, 1969.

75. Riesman D: The Lonely Crowd. New York, Yale University Press, 1950.

76. Sandler J, Joffe WG: Towards a basic psychoanalytic model. Int J Psychoanal 50:79–90, 1969.

77. Sandler J, Rosenblatt B: The concepts of the representational world. Psychoanal Study Child 17:128–145, 1962.

78. Searles HF: The effort to drive the other person crazy—an element in the aetiology and psychotherapy of schizophrenia. Br J Med Psychol 32:1–18, 1959.

79. Silverman F: Radiological aspects of the battered child syndrome. The Battered Child. Edited by RE Helfer, CH Kempe. Chicago, University of Chicago Press, 1968, p 59–76.

80. Spark GM, Brody EM: The aged are family members. Fam Process 9:195–210, 1970.

81. Spitz RA: Anaclitic depression. Psychoanal Study Child 2:313–342, 1946.

82. Spitz RA: Hospitalism: A follow-up report. Psychoanal Study Child 2:113–117, 1946a.

83. Stierlin H: Aspects of relatedness in the psychotherapy of schizophrenia. Psychoanal Rev 51:355–364, 1964.

84. Stierlin H: Conflict and Reconciliation: A Study in Human Relations and Schizophrenia. New York, Doubleday-Anchor, 1969.

85. Szasz TS: Psychiatric Justice. New York, Macmillan, 1965.

86. Waelder R: Basic Theory of Psychoanalysis. New York, International Universities Press, 1960.

87. Waelder R, Morris J: The concept of justice and the quest for an absolutely just society: A dialogue. University of Pennsylvania Law Review, Vol 115, No 1, 1966.

88. Watzlawick P, Beavin JH, Jackson DD: Pragmatics of Human Communication: A Study of Interactional Patterns, Pathologies and Paradoxes. New York, Norton, 1967.

89. Webster's Third International Dictionary. Springfield, Mass, GS Merriam, 1961.

90. Weiss P, Weiss J: Right and Wrong: A Philosophical Dialogue between Father and Son. New York, Basic Books, 1967.

91. Whitaker CA: The Growing Edge in Techniques of Family Therapy. Edited by J Haley, L Hoffman. New York, Basic Books, 1967, pp 265–360.

92. Wynne LC: The study of intrafamilial alignments and splits in exploratory family therapy. Exploring the Base for Family Therapy. Edited by NW Ackerman, F Beatman, and SN Sherman. New York, Family Service Association of America, 1961, pp 95–115.

93. Wynne LC, Ryckoff IM, Day J, Hirsch SI: Pseudomutuality in the family relations of schizophrenics. Psychiatry 21: 205–220, 1958.

94. Young L: Wednesday's Children: A Study of Child Neglect and Abuse. New York, McGraw-Hill, 1964.

95. Zuk GH: Family Therapy: A Triadic Based Approach. New York, Behavioral Publications, Inc., 1971.

Indexes

AUTHOR INDEX

Ackerman NW, 260
Alexander F, 64
Anaximander, 70

Bateson, G, 11, 28, 83
Bay C, 68
Berne E, 11, 100, 366
Bernstein A, 145, 172
Blenkner M, 224
Blitsten D, 26
Boardman HE, 278
Boszormenyi-Nagy I, 4, 14, 27, 66, 100,
    112, 120, 132, 154, 199, 200, 226,
    252, 279, 282
Bowen M, 114, 130, 196, 201, 262
Brodey WM, 257, 260, 282
Brody EM, 222, 224, 260, 276
Buber M, 6, 7, 8, 37, 43, 45, 56, 65, 148,
    174, 184

Caffey J, 276
Cooper D, 17, 380

Day J, 4, 84
Dickens C, 65

Dicks HV, 26
Durkheim E, 39, 114

Einstein A, 73
Epstein LJ, 145
Erikson EH, 24, 39, 44, 45, 76, 106, 128,
    129, 249, 259, 275

Fairbairn WR, 153, 168
Fenichel O, 80, 278, 366, 373
Ferenczi S, 168
Framo JL, 185
Freud A, 180, 182, 199
Freud S, 37, 43, 67, 71, 128, 132, 160,
    167, 169, 170, 173, 174, 175, 177,
    179, 183, 186
Friedman AS, 262

Ginsberg L, 156
Gould RW, 277, 278
Gouldner AW, 56, 58, 59
Greenson RR, 192, 200
Guntrip HJ, 153, 168, 372

SUBJECT INDEX

Account(s)
  balance of, 372
  ethical, 160
  hidden, 378
  of reciprocity, 223, 369
  rebalancing of, 96
  unsettled, 173
Accountability
  individual vs collective, 77–80
  individual and multigenerational, 80
Accounting, 25
  debit-credit, 133
  double, 173
  existential formula, 66
  model, 372
  of obligations and merits, transgenerational, 46–48
  parent-child, 87
Achievement, as relational stagnation, 123–125
Acting-out, dramatic, as signal for family system, 376
Action
  corrective, 79
  dialogue, 359, 360
Addiction, 374
Adolescence, 22
Adolescent(s), 376
  defiant, 305
  individuation of, 107
Adoption, 71, 112

Adoption *(continued)*
  substitutive, 166
Age of Enlightenment, 72
Alienation, 114, 145
Alliance, 190, 205, 367
  working, 192, 194, 196, 198–214
    co-therapy system, family system and, 192–215
    initial steps in, 196–197
    therapeutic, with individual patients, 192
Altruism, 174
Ambivalence, 175, 193, 202, 209, 220
  guilt over, 176
Ambivalent attitudes, 202
Anomie, 26, 39, 111, 114
Antiauthoritarianism, 92
Autonomous function, 364
Autonomy, 32, 76, 97, 107, 365
  child's, 106–108
  individual, 126
  relational, 105
Availability, parental, 85

Balance(s), 177, 217, 222, 225
  between receiving and being used, 57
  invisible dynamic, 81
  of accounts, 372

397